CATCHER

CATCHER

How the Man Behind the Plate
Became an American Folk Hero

PETER MORRIS

Ivan R. Dee
CHICAGO 2009

www.ivanrdee.com

Library of Congress Cataloging-in-Publication Data:
Morris, Peter, 1962–
    Catcher : how the man behind the plate became an American folk hero / Peter Morris.
        p. cm.
    Includes bibliographical references and index.
    ISBN-13: 978-1-56663-822-7 (cloth : alk. paper)
    ISBN-10: 1-56663-822-4 (cloth : alk. paper)
    1. Catchers (Baseball)—United States—History. I. Title.
    GV872.M67 2009
    796.357'2309—dc22   2008046501

To Jim Lannen

Contents

Acknowledgments

WHILE WRITING THIS BOOK, I have relied heavily on the generosity of many wonderful people. Tom Shieber of the National Baseball Hall of Fame has once again been extraordinarily helpful in directing me to photographs and in suggesting research sources and angles. I am also indebted to Tim Wiles and his staff in the Hall of Fame's research department and to Pat Kelly of the Hall's photograph archive for their invaluable help. I am deeply grateful to David MacGregor, Ron Haas, David Ball, Jan Finkel, Ben Dettmar, Paul Sorrentino, and Pete Schram for reading all or part of the manuscript as it evolved and for offering insightful comments. Reed Howard, Charles Weatherby, Bill Anderson, Richard Malatzky, Bill Carle, Bruce Allardice, Peter Mancuso, Bobby Plapinger, Cappy Gagnon, Darryl Brock, Dennis Pajot, Marty Payne, Jim Lannen, Frank Ceresi, John Thorn, and Tom and Delecia Carey have also made valuable contributions to my research or to my thinking on key topics. I also wish to thank the many dear friends and family members, too numerous to name, who have provided a listening ear, friendship, and support throughout this project. Finally, I have again been blessed to have the help of Ivan R. Dee and his staff in turning my vision of a book that captured the heroic age of catching into a reality. While all of these people have contributed to making this book better, the shortcomings that remain are my responsibility alone.

P. M.

Haslett, Michigan
January 2009

"You have to have a catcher or you'll have a lot of passed balls."—Casey Stengel

CATCHER

Introduction:
A Generation in Search of a Hero

■ SOON AFTER the birth of a boy named Stephen in Newark, New Jersey, in 1871, ominous signs began to appear that he would struggle to find his place in the world. As the last of fourteen children of a devout fifty-two-year-old Methodist clergyman and his forty-four-year-old wife, Stephen's early years were shaped by his parents' puritanical views. Two years before his birth, his father had published a book entitled *Popular Amusements*, in which he took a dim view of dancing, tobacco, opium, alcohol, billiards, chess, and novel-reading. The book also predicted the demise of the then-new game of baseball, because "everyone connected with it seems to be regarded with a degree of suspicion." Some who knew Stephen during his early years believed they had already detected signs of rebellion against his father's views.

Then the sudden death of his father in 1880 turned the eight-year-old boy's world upside down. Forced to leave the parsonage, his mother temporarily sent the lad to live with an older brother. Even after reuniting with him in a new home in Asbury Park, she immersed herself in temperance work, which often kept her away from home for lengthy periods. As a result, a neighbor recalled that when Stephen was scarcely out of knee pants he often arrived "home from school or play, maybe skating on the lake, to find no supper. He would then range the neighborhood for food and companionship." The boy was finally sent off to school for good when he was thirteen. Thus during some of his most impressionable years he had been thrust out of a strict household and into a state of virtual orphanhood.

Stephen expressed his inner tumult by exploring many of the same worldly temptations that his father had condemned. Yet he did so in a strangely diffident way that suggested he felt haunted by the disapproval of his dead father and of his absent mother. Stephen cultivated a disaffected air and developed odd eating and sleeping habits that, along with his short stature and thin frame, made him appear disturbingly undernourished. Although cigarettes were still an uncommon vice, he habitually held a lit one in his fingers—but rarely was he seen to puff on it. It was as though he was deliberately striving to convince observers that he was unhealthy, when in fact he was blessed with both physical stamina and agility.

The young man attended four schools during the next five and a half years, and the frequent switches reinforced the persona he had already begun to develop. In the process, his sense of alienation hardened into a mask that hid his emotions. "It was his pose," recollected one classmate, "to take little interest in anything save poker and baseball, and even in speaking of these great matters there was in his manner a suggestion of *noblesse oblige.* Undoubtedly he felt himself peculiar, an oyster beneath whose lips there was already an irritating grain of some foreign substance." Outsiders saw in the youngster only a "contradiction, self-depreciation coupled with arrogance, which has puzzled so many."

Since Stephen was gifted with a rich and inventive imagination, he might have been expected to channel his pent-up energies into one of the fine arts. Instead he concentrated them on baseball, one of the many activities that had troubled his father. More particularly, Stephen became obsessed with the position that had become central to the now professional sport—the catcher. In contrast to his usual hesitancy, he reportedly boasted that no pitcher could throw a ball he couldn't catch bare-handed. The specific source of this statement is dubious, but such displays of courage were so fundamental to the catchers of this era that it seems likely Stephen said something along those lines. There is even reason to suspect that he dreamed of a career as a professional baseball player.

His mother had different plans for her son. In 1885, hoping that Stephen would find a religious calling, she enrolled him in the seminary where her late husband had once been principal. After two years she abandoned that hope and sent him to a military school, no doubt wishing either to make a soldier of her son or at least to instill some discipline in him. Once again reality would prove very different as schoolwork continued to have little interest to the youngster while baseball, more than ever, functioned as a substitute. He took great pride in being the catcher of the school baseball nine and continued to catch bare-handed, treating his increasingly sore hands with iodine and witch hazel. Eventually, however, he gave in and donned a buckskin glove.

He was off to Lafayette College in the fall of 1890, where his most frequent companions were the school's "motley crowd of baseball enthusiasts." He hoped to make the varsity team in the spring but was foiled by his chronic neglect of schoolwork, and he withdrew at the end of the semester. In January 1891, Stephen enrolled at Syracuse University, where he was entitled to a scholarship as the grandnephew of one of the founders. He moved into the Delta Upsilon fraternity house, and his attitude remained as lackadaisical as ever.

According to a classmate, Stephen "never seemed to be particularly interested in anything that transpired in college except baseball. He was somewhat careless in his dress and negligent of his lectures; was always cool, never worried about anything, smoked infinite tobacco and took life just as it came." One of Stephen's professors confirmed that he "would not be cramped by following a course of study he did not care for" and instead "devoted himself to athletics." Stephen's own summary of his college career was similar: "I went to Lafayette College but did not graduate. I found mining-engineering not at all to my taste. I preferred base-ball. Later I attended Syracuse University where I attempted to study literature but found base ball again more to my taste."

Baseball continued to bring out a side of him not otherwise evident. At Syracuse he immediately began to prepare for making the varsity baseball nine. Within four weeks of his arrival on campus, the student newspaper was predicting a bright future for the new arrival. One of his teammates later recalled that upon the call for tryouts, Stephen "must have been among the first to arrive as he obtained a fairly respectable and well-matched uniform. The uniforms in those days consisted of a miscellaneous lot of clothes purchased at second hand from the Syracuse Stars, the local professional ball team, and it was a case of 'first come, first served' in the assignment of garments."

Even so, the eager newcomer presented an odd appearance. "He should have worn white stockings of the heavy ribbed kind but of necessity he wore black of a fine knit that made his slender legs look like pipe stems," remembered that same teammate. "He was of a sallow complexion, his skin, hair and eyes appeared to be all of one dull and lifeless hue. That is, his eye balls were of the same deep cream tint but the iris was of a cold, bluish gray color. His hair never would stay combed and parted; even after a 'washup' following a game there were bound to be stray locks hanging down at the forehead and a bristly bunch at the end of the part in the back. [He] was very quick and active on his feet, his body was slender, his shoulders somewhat drooping, his chest not robust and his knees inclined somewhat to knock together. He was about five feet six inches in height and did not weigh over one hundred and twenty-five pounds."

It seemed inevitable that this frail, odd-looking lad would prove unable to stand the rigors of catching and would have to be used at a less taxing position, especially when spring practice began and he was paired with a pitcher who threw so hard that Stephen "seemed to bound back with every catch." Instead the slightly built catcher compensated with a gritty determination. A classmate recalled with admiration that he "always 'froze on to the ball,' as baseballese hath it, even though it came with such force as to make his slight figure seem to rebound with the impact." Typically Stephen declined to wear one of the new catcher's mitts that were now being used by professionals. He wore only a simple padded glove on his left hand.

His weak throwing arm raised another concern, as he initially had a difficult time making the all-important throw to second base. But Stephen adopted a novel technique to compensate for the deficiency: "He would not stand on his two feet and snap the ball down to the base. It was necessary for him to throw off his mask, cap and protector, give a hop and skip and throw with a complete body swing. The strain upon the ligaments of his shoulder would, at times, cause him to double up with pain."

His hard work and resourcefulness paid off when Stephen was named the starting catcher of the Syracuse University nine. As had been the case at previous schools, this honor brought out a new side of him and caused much of his reserve to disappear. As his pitcher, Mansfield French, later recalled: "He played ball with a fiendish glee. Usually of a quiet and taciturn mien, on the ball field he was constantly in motion, was free of speech, wantonly profane at times and indulged in biting sarcasms when a teammate made a poor play, but generous in praise of a good play." French added that one of Stephen's most notable idiosyncrasies was his "habit of striking his bare, clenched fist three or four times into the palm of his gloved hand to express his approval of a 'strike' when missed by the batter." When a strikeout resulted, "an expression of diabolical glee would light up his face, and he always expressed to me his appreciation when our

The Syracuse University varsity baseball team, 1891. The man in the middle of the first row was destined to become one of the greatest of American writers, but he would later write of these years, "I attended Syracuse University where I attempted to study literature but found base ball again more to my taste." *(Stephen Crane Collection, Special Collections Research Center, Syracuse University Library)*

opponents were retired at the end of their inning." The local press also took notice of the new catcher, commending the agility and headiness he showed behind the plate.

His success on the baseball diamond eased his struggles to communicate, as he "loved to talk baseball and took great delight in telling of his experiences of the ballfield and of his acquaintance, at least by newspaper reputation, with the leading professional players of those days. When on trips to play with other college teams he proved to be sociable and companionable." And his ability to "talk baseball" was accompanied by a new interest in other modes of communication. Stephen covered his disorderly room at the Delta Upsilon fraternity house with "baseball masks and bats, running trunks, chest-protectors and other athletic and literary sundries. . . . Certainly the occupant was nothing unless athletic and literary."

Stephen was becoming a voracious reader and was writing furiously. He began to haunt the city's Central Railroad Station and the local police court, which he came to regard as the most interesting place in Syracuse. There he found subjects for whom he felt a deep affinity: they needed to be studied and written about in order to be understood. Sometimes the results were published by a newspaper, but that wasn't his primary concern. It was the art of writing itself that consumed Stephen, and he churned out fresh material with a passion. According to some of his classmates, he wrote the first draft of a novel and left it lying around the fraternity house.

Yet the classroom still did not hold a similar fascination. Stephen withdrew from Syracuse after a single semester, ending both his ballplaying and his education. As he later explained, "I did little work at school, but confined my abilities, such as they were, to the diamond. Not that I disliked books, but the cut-and-dried curriculum of the college did not appeal to me. Humanity was a more interesting study . . . so, you see, I had first of all to recover from college; I had to build up." In order to "build up," he turned to writing full time, working as a journalist by day and grinding out his first novel at night.

Around this time Stephen was introduced to the noted writer Hamlin Garland, and the two men found they had a common interest. According to Garland, "We met occasionally thereafter to 'pass ball,' and to discuss the various theories which accounted for 'inshoots' and 'outdrops,' for he, like myself, was an ex-pitcher [sic] and gloried in being able to confound the laws of astronomy by making a sphere alter its course in mid-air." Garland agreed to read the younger man's novel and was so impressed by its grittily realistic portrayal of a prostitute's life that he encouraged Stephen to have it published. While sales of the privately printed novel were minimal, Garland helped bring it to the attention of other prominent men of letters, and it received favorable notices.

Before long the young author showed up in Garland's office with another manuscript in hand—or, to be precise, with half a manuscript, since the other half was "in hock" to the typist for the unpaid balance of fifteen dollars. The older writer began to read the first half and quickly realized that it would be well worth fifteen dollars to retrieve the remainder. By the time he finished reading, Garland was convinced he had stumbled upon a masterpiece. Yet he was mystified as to how the author, who was still in his early twenties and lacked even a whiff of battlefield experience, had managed to write a stunningly realistic and unsentimental account of life during the Civil War. The young man's cryptic response was that "all his knowledge of battle had been gained on the football field."

The novel was published in 1895 under the title *The Red Badge of Courage* and became an immediate success. Its twenty-three-year-old author, Stephen Crane, the young man whose life had revolved around becoming a catcher only a few years earlier, was thrust into the international limelight. In the five years between the publication of his classic novel and his premature death in 1900, Crane became as renowned for his raffish persona as for his writing, and all his doings were widely chronicled. Even his boyhood love of the national pastime was mentioned from time to time, prompting Crane to write to a friend in 1896: "I see that they are beginning to charge me with having played base ball. I am rather more proud of my base ball ability than of some other things."

In more than a century since Crane's death, *The Red Badge of Courage* has become a classic, and its author's writings and life have been examined from almost every conceivable angle. Yet little significance has been attached to his obsession with the catcher's position. It is of course mentioned in biographical studies, but it is given little weight in those sources and rarely figures at all in works of literary criticism. Even Crane's claim that he gained his knowledge of battle from the football field scarcely receives consideration.

This is a mistake. Stephen Crane's life and work both involved a theme that is universal in nature but that applied with particular force to the young men of his generation. For their fathers, the Civil War had been an event of supreme importance, not merely saving the Union and transforming the country but also testing and confirming their manhood. The sons of these men grew up hearing tales of the war and facing the reality that they had no similar benchmark in measuring their own courage. This was especially true of boys like Stephen Crane who spent many of their formative years in cities, far from the traditional rite-of-passage rituals afforded by the wilderness. Crane himself told a fellow writer that *The Red Badge of Courage* had been easy for him to write because he had been "unconsciously working the detail of the story out through most of his boyhood." That boyhood in turn had been shaped and defined by a dream of glory as a baseball catcher.

In some obvious ways, Stephen Crane's life was not typical. The image of a dead father who had written disapprovingly of the very things that fascinated his son undoubtedly set Stephen apart from his peers. And of course the ability to capture the essence of the Civil War experience in a novel was the result of a unique genius.

Yet in more important ways, Crane's obsession with being a baseball catcher was representative. Mastery of the intricacies of the position was seen by American boys who came of age in the 1870s and 1880s as the ultimate embodiment of courage, leadership, resolve, and daring—in short, it was their initiation into manhood. It was the closest they could come to the rigorous testing their fathers had experienced during the Civil War. Crane pursued it with a passion he never showed for other activities, only to abandon it abruptly in 1891. As we shall see, the timing was no coincidence, for 1891 marked a watershed year in the transformation of the catcher from a hero into a very different type of figure.

Crane's masterpiece also shows unmistakable indications of being informed by his time on the baseball field. The novel's central figure, the youthful Henry Fleming, has been raised by his widowed mother and has "dreamed of battles all his life." The distance between the battlefield and his experience only enhances the allure: "he had regarded battles as crimson blotches on the pages of the past. He had put them as things of the bygone with his thought-images of heavy crowns and high castles. There was a portion of the world's history which he had regarded as the time of wars, but it, he thought, had been long gone over the horizon and had disappeared forever." At the outbreak of the war, his mother "gives him hundreds of reasons why he was more valuable on the farm than on the field of battle." Yet the youthful protagonist cannot resist the tug of this opportunity to use the battlefield to prove his courage and be initiated into manhood. Instead when he first encounters battle, he flees, forcing a reexamination of the meaning of courage.

My intent is not to offer a close reading of Stephen Crane's work but rather to explore why the catcher's position captivated him and so many boys of his generation, and to suggest that this experience was a key reason why he so perfectly captured the essence of battlefield life in *The Red Badge of Courage*. In particular, the catcher acquired a special mystique for the men who came of age in the years immediately following the Civil War. Like Henry Fleming, the members of this generation came to think of battles as "things of the bygone" and to wonder if they would ever have the chance to earn their own badges of courage. Many of them joined Crane in seeing the catcher's position as the means of doing so.

While the life of Stephen Crane presents an especially dramatic illustration of this fixation with catching, he shared that ambition with countless other lads of his era. Some of them, like Crane, were men with special talents in other fields. A boy named Byron, for example, was born in 1863 and grew up in Cincinnati. Like Crane's, his devoutly religious parents wanted him to become a minister and disapproved of the game of baseball. Nonetheless Byron developed a passion for the game. Whenever possible he would sneak away "to see a game at the old Cincinnati grounds, and then walk three miles to his home with the secret stowed away in his breast."

In particular it was the position of catcher that fired his imagination, and Byron played that position for his high school and college teams. He would later remember being paired with a hard-throwing African-American pitcher named Davis, who "surely had a wicked inshoot and after the game I soaked my catching hand in hot salt water for hours." In one game Byron split his hand but insisted on staying in the game, a decision that left him with a permanent scar. The cumulative damage was still worse—he would recall that "By the finish of the season I was always black and blue from head to foot, and oftentimes unable to wear a hat by reason of the bumps and lumps."

Yet the hardships of the position only made him all the more proud that he did not rely upon protective equipment. "The only thing I wore to protect myself," he would later boast, "was a chunk of crude rubber gripped firmly between the teeth." He did allow himself a pair of fingerless gloves and added as much padding as he could, but these did little to protect his hands. And he remained unwilling to consider other forms of protection, explaining, "I viewed the mask with dark suspicion, feeling that it would make me appear less than game."

Just like Crane, this youngster dismayed his parents by showing a keen intelligence but little inclination to apply himself to schoolwork. Instead Byron's constrained energy seemed to emerge only when he was stationed behind the plate, where he energetically offered advice to his teammates and appeared to be transformed into an entirely different person.

Like Crane, Byron looked awkward and out of place behind the plate until tested, at which point he revealed a reserve of inner strength. One classmate recalled that he first saw Byron while watching a "scrub" game: "The first person who caught my eye was a big, husky kid with a shock of tan hair, squatted close up behind the player at bat. He wore a dirty white uniform and a pair of baby blue and white striped stockings. The way he was handling the pitcher's speed made the spectators open their eyes, and he was whizzing the ball around the bases at a rate calculated to keep the flies off the base runner." The dirty uniform became one of his signatures, in large part because, as Byron later confessed, he was afraid to take his uniform home for washing and let his mother know he was playing baseball.

In yet another parallel to the life of Stephen Crane, after an unpromising college career the aspiring catcher from Cincinnati became a successful journalist, finding the rigors of writing daily dispatches far more congenial than the abstract setting of the classroom. Eventually, however, Byron Bancroft "Ban" Johnson got back into baseball as president of a minor league named the Western League, which he then renamed the American League and reinvented as a major league. Johnson served as president of the "junior circuit" for nearly three decades and is now enshrined in the National Baseball Hall of Fame.

Another youngster known as Wallie became obsessed with catching while growing up in Ionia, Michigan. Like Stephen Crane, he lost his father at a young age and his widowed mother sent him to college to study for the priesthood. Instead his love for baseball remained while he graduated with a literary degree. A major league tryout ensued, but a single disastrous National League appearance prompted Wallie to study for the law. Yet even after beginning a legal practice in Mt. Pleasant, Michigan, the lure of catching remained so powerful that he leaped at the chance to return to catching in the minor leagues.

His partner was less pleased, however, and when Wallie returned to Mt. Pleasant that winter the two squared off as candidates for prosecuting attorney of the county. It was a heated campaign, with the former partner doing his best to imply that Wallie might leave the county without a prosecuting attorney if baseball were to beckon. Voters rejected that argument, however, and Wallie served the county with distinction. He then returned to baseball and, like Ban Johnson, served as president of a minor league. But at thirty-two, mental illness cut short Walter Walker's promising career and prevented him from enjoying the fame that Crane and Johnson experienced.

We know about these three men and their dreams of becoming catchers because of their outsized talents in other realms. Yet there was nothing unusual about their obsession. Countless of their forgotten peers who came of age in the years immediately following the Civil War also saw the man behind the plate as an iconic hero who embodied unbounded courage, extraordinary skill, and unmatched value. In turn, their generation's fascination would prove crucial because it led to a reexamination of the whole idea of heroism and helped pave the way for the athlete to become a widely accepted role model for America's youth.

Stephen Crane, Byron Johnson, and Wallie Walker shared far more in common than just their boyhood dreams of catching. Each was raised by deeply religious parents who did their best to encourage their sons to become clergymen. When those hopes had to be abandoned, each of the three turned to a profession that required mastery of the written word. Each of them possessed the talent, initiative, and determination to succeed at their chosen profession, and indeed at anything they chose. All three also achieved diverse and impressive accomplishments—Walker as a prosecuting attorney, Johnson as founder of the American League, and Crane as one of the greatest of American writers.

Yet at the same time each would struggle to achieve conventional measures of success. Crane, even after achieving worldwide fame, remained perpetually in debt and was dead before his thirtieth birthday. Walker was confined to an asylum at the age of thirty-two and spent the rest of his life there. Even Johnson's long tenure as American League president was a stormy one, culminating when he lost a power struggle and was forced to relinquish control of the league he had founded.

It was not just that all three showed a propensity to get sidetracked, but that they seemed to make conscious decisions to follow different paths. Each man, as we have seen, had no sooner proven himself in one field than he restlessly moved on to another—often one that offered less security and reduced financial rewards and that was generally viewed as less prestigious. In short, these boys who had dreamed of achieving success as catchers grew into men who showed little inclination for gauging themselves in traditional ways. The paths that they did choose tell us as much about the changing nature of the dreams of their generation as it does about the men themselves.

By the time Stephen Crane, Ban Johnson, and Wallie Walker began dreaming of becoming catchers, the American Dream was a long-established part of their culture. For their fathers, grandfathers, and great-grandfathers, it had represented an implicit promise: if you work hard and plan wisely, prosperity and success will follow. The model of these earlier generations had been Ben Franklin, whose *Poor Richard's Almanac* preached the homely virtues of early rising and honest toil, and whose *Autobiography* offered the prospect of a rags-to-riches ascent. The underlying message of these works was that a virtuous life would be rewarded with financial success.

Yet during the second half of the nineteenth century, faith in this message dwindled. As industrial capitalism took hold and brought with it torrents of change, there were more rags-to-riches stories than ever. At the same time, however, it became much more difficult to see a correspondence between wealth and virtues like hard work. Instead, wealth seemed increasingly to be the result of complex backroom financial transactions made by "robber barons" who held monopolistic control over entire industries. The intricacies of these dealings were incomprehensible to most Americans, but they understood the consequences.

An entire generation of young men grew up with the frustrated feeling that the rules for achieving success had changed in ways that didn't make sense to them. The depths of the problem are shown with special clarity in the lives of capable, energetic, and charismatic men like Crane, Johnson, and Walker, since these were the very young men whose gifts made it possible for them to succeed in this new environment. Instead they showed more interest in striving to achieve heroism by becoming catchers than in pursuing any recognizable form of the American Dream.

What had gone wrong?

*

To answer this question it is necessary to understand why the American hero has always been defined in terms of the wilderness. The roots of that relationship go back to America's earliest European settlers, who were predominantly refugees from religious oppression in Great Britain. They initially clustered in a few coastal colonies and sustained themselves by a shared faith in God and the security of their communities. When they did venture beyond the safety of their borders, they found the wilderness filled with danger from wild animals, an imposing landscape, a forbidding climate, and, most unsettling of all, Native Americans with very different ways of life.

At first many of the new settlers viewed the people they called Indians as childlike innocents who needed only to be converted to Christianity, but this changed after a disastrous war with the natives. Polar opposites increasingly dominated the Puritans' worldview, as they came to define every aspect of their environment as belonging to either civilization or savagery. "Beyond the rim of settlement," explains the historian Richard Slotkin, "the Englishman was the victim of forces beyond his understanding; within the fold, he could be a hero, conquering the forces of sin within the body politic or in his own mind."

Since the Puritans saw themselves as members of a closed circle of believers, they viewed any interaction with the wilderness and its inhabitants as a sinful act of giving in to temptation. They worried that subsequent generations would yield to temptation and adopt the Native Americans' practice of living for the day. So the Puritans emphasized the virtues of permanence, stability, and contentment with one's lot. Community leaders like Increase Mather denounced men who "coveted after the earth" and fell away from the faith, "all for land and elbow-room."

These warnings against active forms of heroism and against the pursuit of "elbow room" continued to carry considerable weight in the ensuing centuries, which helps us understand why Jonathan Crane was opposed to seemingly innocuous pleasure-seeking activities and would have been distressed that his son "took life just as it came." But with each new generation the precepts of the Puritans carried less force as venturing into new territory became a practical necessity in order to sustain a growing community.

It therefore became essential to reexamine the Puritans' reservations about the wilderness and individual heroism. For some, the perfect solution was to cast the farmer in the role of hero. The farmer, after all, was a man who ventured far enough into the wilderness to extend the community, but then concentrated his efforts on bringing order to chaos. The advantages of such a compromise were spelled out in J. Hector St. John de Crevecoeur's *Letters from an American Farmer*, in which the farm was idyllically depicted as a "utopian district, freed at once of the Indian menace and the corruptions of the city." Another prominent advocate of such a compromise was Ben Franklin, who suggested that it might "be the design of Providence to extirpate these Savages [the Native Americans] in order to make room for cultivators of the earth." As Slotkin observes, "The conquest of the New World, in Franklin's imagery, is a natural or an economic process, not the result of a willful march into the wilderness. . . . Thus the farmer, like the Puritan captive, is a mediating figure between the American wilderness and the civilized world." Underlying Franklin's formulation is the assumption that financial success serves as proof of inner worth—the skilled cultivator of the land will reap the rewards in the form of a bumper crop and a fat bankroll.

Yet ultimately all such efforts at compromise were doomed to fail. It was simply too difficult to reconcile the Puritans' worldview, in which God disapproved of man's efforts at heroism, with the new one that began to emerge. Crevecoeur's isolated farm was eventually encroached upon by society and its discontents, and he was forced to turn to the frontier in hopes of finding "a state approaching nearer to that of nature, unencumbered either with voluminous laws, or contradictory codes, often galling the very necks of those whom they protect."

With middle ground untenable, it became inevitable that the American hero would instead take a more threatening form, and by the end of the eighteenth century this figure had taken shape. There was of course no single model of heroism, and all versions of the model included borrowings from the Puritans, especially the notion that heroism should be accepted only reluctantly, never pursued. For many, the quintessential American hero was the distinctly unthreatening figure of George Washington, the gentleman farmer who becomes a soldier and statesman only when the need arises. But despite such inconsistencies, there was enough of a consensus to coalesce into a composite image that began to emerge.

This hero could go forth and do—well, again there wasn't always unanimity about specifically what he could do, but it was understood that he could do whatever needed doing. And despite disagreements over particulars, this hero was a sufficiently coherent model to inspire the generations of Americans who by the mid-eighteenth century had cleared the wildernesses and extended the once-clustered settlements from coast to coast.

More than any other man, Daniel Boone came to exemplify this new heroic ideal. Boone was a complex man, and portrayals of him differed widely depending on the region and the narrator. His love of the wilderness was proverbial, but in some accounts he is rendered as a natural philosopher in buckskin while in other versions he was just a man who craved adventure. Other accounts abounded in exaggeration and sheer fiction. Despite such complications, there is no dispute about the key traits that made Boone a hero to many yet a suspect figure to those who subscribed to the beliefs of the Puritans.

Boone possessed many attributes that the Puritans admired, including a love of his family, a strong work ethic, and a sense of purpose. Nevertheless his hardiness and self-reliance were at odds with the Puritans' beliefs because he seemed to trespass on the dividing line they had drawn between God's laws and man's duty. In particular, Boone represented a challenge to the Puritans' conviction that the Bible was the word of God and that it was man's duty to obey its laws. For a hunter and warrior like Boone, actions mattered more than words, so instead of relying on book learning, Boone was celebrated for his unerring ability to glean "a code of natural laws from the wilderness."

Boone's actions were just as subversive as his beliefs. In stark contrast with the Puritans' dread of the evils that lurked in the wilderness, he unapologetically relished the adventures that lay hidden there. He spent his early years on a farm, where—in a stinging rebuke to the Crevecoeurs and the Franklins—he was so bored that he constantly prayed for rain so that he could go hunting.

When he finally moved to the wilderness to stay, Boone discovered that special place where he belonged, and he became the preeminent hunter. This sense that he had found a long lost home was nicely conveyed by one of the many marvelous sayings attributed to him: "I can't say as ever I was lost, but I was bewildered once for three days." Portrayals of Boone emphasized that he had done what so many disillusioned city dwellers dreamed of doing by turning his back on success in the city to embrace a harder but more rewarding life in the wild. As one reporter put it, Boone "might have accumulated riches as readily as any man in Kentucky, but he *prefers the woods*, where you see him in the dress of the roughest, poorest hunter." Such depictions had understandable appeal to the growing number of American men who longed to escape from mundane jobs in the country's impersonal and increasingly crowded cities, and who wanted to believe that financial success was still the reward for a job well done.

This image of Boone was sustained by one of the best-known of the numerous legends that surrounded him—the exaggerated notion that Boone was constantly relocating to keep his distance from human settlements. "As civilization advanced," claimed a typical account, "so he, from time to time, retreated."

In a famous story, Boone is hunting in the woods and suddenly senses a nearby creature. Just when he is about to shoot, his keen understanding of his surroundings alerts him that something is wrong, and he lowers the rifle. The creature flees, and it turns out to be not an animal but a young woman. After Boone follows her back to her home, she ultimately becomes his wife.

Although almost certainly apocryphal, the tale exemplifies why Boone came to be viewed as a new model of American heroism. His ability to go out and get sustenance for himself meant that he did not depend upon the community to supply him with the necessities of life. Nor did he rely on the community for an education, since the lessons taught by his own senses were more valuable than book learning. He also displayed a perfect harmony with his surroundings that enabled him to make decisions instantaneously and flawlessly. And of course, in the end, he got the girl!

While it is easy to see why boys were thrilled and inspired by Boone, he was far more difficult to reconcile with the teachings passed down from the

Puritans. At first Boone was looked upon as a forerunner for the expansion of their culture—a man who would tame the wilderness so as to make it habitable for new settlers. But it gradually became clear that Boone's philosophy was closer to that of the Native Americans, especially their reverence for the hunter as a man who had attained oneness with nature.

This unsettling kinship with Native Americans meant that the Boone hero was, if you will, not the boy the typical middle-class girl could bring home to meet her parents. American ideals of womanhood had not kept pace with the new ideal for men, so finding an appropriate wife for such a figure proved a large problem. And that in turn raised concerns about the whole model of heroism.

An even more pressing issue was the torrent of change that was transforming and encroaching upon the frontier. As Americans rushed westward, waves of new settlers adopted the glamorous parts of the Boone persona but paid less attention to its more substantive qualities. The result was that, just as the Puritans had predicted, the quest for "land and elbow-room" descended into unprincipled speculation. Even on the frontier, paper transactions began to replace brave deeds as the basis of success. Daniel Boone was forced to become a land speculator, and he proved a failure in this very different world. Instead of representing a vista of new opportunity, the frontier was descending into a morass of greed, lawlessness, and vice.

In particular, the hero's use of violence became a crucial issue. As Martin Green notes in a cultural history, "Defining courage exclusively as a virtue . . . makes it something that shows itself negatively, a way of responding to other people's initiatives. We are shown our hero not being afraid, not backing down from a threat, not crying out under torture—always reacting to an enemy's initiative. Such a figure is a paradox—the nonviolent person who is better at violence than his enemies." Boone had at first been able to surmount this dilemma for two key reasons.

First, as illustrated by the story about his future wife, he possessed the discernment and good sense to make such decisions about the use of violence flawlessly. Second, the frontiersman's isolation meant that there was no one to take issue with his choices. But as soon as they were brought into question, as inevitably happened in a larger settlement, there was nothing to prevent a cycle of retaliation that made the whole basis of heroism seem suspect. Boone's instinctive ability to know when violence was necessary gave way to frontier justice—vigilante justice and lynch law—which set off waves of retribution.

Problems such as these became even more evident in America's cities, which were already bursting at the seams and now had to accommodate a steady stream of disenchanted frontiersmen who were returning from the West and bringing its new code of behavior with them. Whether partial to the traits embodied by Daniel Boone or suspicious of them, everyone agreed that they were out of place in the industrial city. Conflicts naturally arose, and these conflicts made it clear that all the traits that made a man like Boone a hero in the wilderness were rendered useless—or worse than useless—in the city. In the wilderness the ability to excel at violence without ever initiating it had been a crucial talent, but in the city it no longer applied. Boone's penchant for seeking out danger now seemed like recklessness while his selflessness could appear to be self-aggrandizement. So Americans began to wonder if the Boone type of hero was still relevant in the industrial city. Or was he just a transitional figure who had now outlived his usefulness?

Since Boone was lost without his wilderness, the first effort to update his model of heroism was to replace hunting with one of the new occupations spawned by western expansion. Many of the traits that distinguished Boone began to reemerge in mountain men, fur trappers, cowboys, and other distinctively Western occupations. Each of these groups of men enjoyed a brief vogue as American icons, and their influence endures to this day. Yet even more so than had been the case with Boone, they represented a model of heroism that could not be translated into different surroundings.

This is best illustrated by the character of the cowboy. Although the idyllic portrayal of the cowboy in the popular press ignored many of the realities of his life, there was still much about the cowboy that suited him to carry on Daniel Boone's legacy. The cowboy was a man who lived his life by a rigorous but unwritten code of behavior, who had to acquire a set of difficult skills and then demonstrate his mastery of those skills in tangible ways, who spent his life in the open, free of artifice, who possessed a "horse sense" that corresponded to Boone's self-taught astuteness, who had the ability to adapt himself to his oft-changing surroundings, and who had forged a special partnership with his horse.

It was this last relationship that best defined the cowboy, and there was no sentimentality involved. The cowboy needed first of all to break the horse, an ordeal that involved roping and throwing the creature, putting a hackamore or halter on its head, and tying it up. The horse naturally fought against the restraint for a prolonged period of time, sometimes as long as two days, but when it was over, "the harder [the horse had] fought the more complete was his final submission." The horse thereafter accepted "the idea of human supremacy"—or more properly the supremacy of the skilled cowboy, for he might try to pitch his rider if he sensed "incompetent horsemanship upon his back." The cowboy ensured the horse's continued submission by keeping lariats and ropes close at hand so that "the recollection of the lariat's spilling ability" and "fear of leather" would remain fresh in the creature's mind.

Now that they were a team, the cowboy and his horse could work in perfect harmony to achieve such complex tasks as roping cattle, hunting bears, and fighting battles. When separated from his horse, the cowboy appeared nonchalant and even lazy, treating his horse with neglectful disdain. This appearance was yet another way of demonstrating that it was only on horseback that the cowboy was truly at home. Part of the lore of the cowboy was that he never walked if he could ride, and he regarded tasks that could not be performed on horseback as too menial for him.

Once mounted, however, he was transformed into the picture of industry, willing to take on the most dangerous and difficult assignments without hesitation. As one observer marveled, "On horseback, the cowboy is a picturesque figure; afoot he is a waddling swan." Just as the wilderness had brought out Boone's special talents, so too the horse's back was where the cowboy belonged. "A cowboy," according to one famous definition, "is a man with guts and a horse." This is the stuff of myth. As we shall see, many of these attributes were passed on to the catcher.

The irony, however, is that the cowboy became an American folk hero only when his way of life was coming to an end. As the historian David Dary explains, "the occupation of the cowboy in this hemisphere was already more than three centuries old when eastern writers discovered the man on horseback during the years following the Civil War." Yet it was at this precise moment that it became clear that the cowboy's traditional way of living was doomed by westward expansion. As a result, many Eastern boys read tales about cowboys and traveled west to live that dream, only to quickly grow disillusioned and return home.

These exaggerated and fictional renderings of the cowboy and his fellow Western heroes created many related problems. The daily activities of these men lacked dramatic tension or a tidy moral lesson, so it became necessary to send them on a long series of improbable adventures. When the subject was a real person, the depiction of his behavior became even trickier since the actions of men who lived in a violent and lawless country rarely conformed to the expectations that they used violence only in retaliation or refrained from using profanity.

Before long, dime novelists took over and began to create Western heroes who were only loosely based on real people. Their supposed occupations also became vague; eventually, just transferring a man to the West was enough to bring out heroic qualities. The switch to fictional heroes had the advantage of reducing the likelihood that the originals would show up and give the lie to depictions of them. Yet even when crafted by ingenious writers of fiction, the expectations that mid- and late-nineteenth-century Americans had of their heroes remained too contradictory to be satisfactorily resolved.

An equally daunting paradox was that Americans retained the Puritans' suspicion of those who appeared actively to seek heroism. As Dixon Wecter observed, "the major idols of America have been men of good will. The strong man without scruple—from Barbarossa to Lenin—does not belong in our halls of fame. The man who would be king, like the legendary Aaron Burr, becomes a villain rather than a hero. . . . The boast of a Napoleon, echoed by Mussolini, 'I am not a man, but an event,' does not chime with the spirit of a democracy. No hero must announce that he is infallible. He must be greater than the average, but in ways agreeable to the average. . . . The hero is an instrument . . . the servant of his age." In the tradition of George Washington, the American hero could never pursue heroism, yet he needed to be prepared, forceful, and resolute when his moment arrived. It was, to put it mildly, a delicate balance.

The nature of his quest was just as tricky. In *The Hero with a Thousand Faces*, Joseph Campbell explains that "Typically the hero of the fairy tale achieves a domestic microcosmic triumph, and the hero of myth a world-historical, macrocosmic triumph." These are such polar opposites that it is only possible to accomplish one or the other. A similar choice must be made about the nature of the action, since "Popular tales represent the heroic action as physical; the higher religions show the deed to be moral." These two courses, Campbell notes, are not opposites and can be resolved. Yet in the case of the American hero, this was difficult to do because of the need either to accept or reject the constraints of the Puritans. This helps explain why some portrayals of Daniel Boone insisted that he was a natural philosopher while others depicted him as just a man of action.

In this context, everything about the Western hero was fraught with artificiality, contradictions, and paradoxes. Naturally this new type of hero couldn't make a living by means of obscure paper transactions, but it was much harder to find an appropriate activity for him. He had to wait patiently for a quest or mission, then pursue it relentlessly; yet he could never realize his goal since then his heroism would have to be referred to in the past tense. He needed a strong work ethic, yet he couldn't become trapped in the prosaic ambitions of the workaday world. He needed achievements that were impressive and tangible, yet he couldn't strive to accumulate worldly riches. It was vital that his courage and skill be demonstrable and measurable, yet the hero couldn't be a braggart or a show-off. In short, the Western hero had somehow to be a success without accomplishing anything specific or telling anyone about what he had done.

The impossibility of resolving all these paradoxes became ludicrously obvious when these heroes tried to find a wife. The murky social standing of the Western hero made it tricky for him to pursue a woman of high social status—and if he married her, it put an end to his questing days. As a result, dime novels served up an abundance of highly implausible plot twists in which a Western hero or his would-be wife emerged from disguise just in time to make the match acceptable. When the hero was finally married off, the next challenge was to ensure that he didn't abandon his mission by settling into comfortable domesticity. This led to even more blatant plot contrivances.

These contradictory expectations did not mean that the Western hero lost his ability to inspire Americans. Indeed, they showed just the opposite—that Americans longed for heroes more than ever and that the Boone model of heroism retained its ability to inspire the many Americans who felt trapped in the mercenary and unheroic life of the city. Teddy Roosevelt captured this feeling well when he wrote that ranching was "an occupation like those of vigorous, primitive pastoral peoples, having little in common with the humdrum, workaday business world of the nineteenth century; and the free ranchman in his manner of life shows more kinship to an Arab sheik than to a sleek city merchant or tradesman."

Yet while Americans still admired the self-reliant Western hero, few continued to believe that these men could embody all the contradictory things they supposedly represented. For most people these figures became a form of escapism—a nice story but one that was understood to include a large measure of fantasy. Only a highly gullible boy would seek to emulate or model his life after so implausible a figure. Like Crane's Henry Fleming, Americans came to think of these men as belonging to "a portion of the world's history which . . . had been long gone over the horizon and had disappeared forever." As a result, many Americans continued to long for a flesh-and-blood hero who really existed and whom they might actually meet.

By the 1870s the heroics of the Civil War were beginning to seem as "things of the bygone" to the younger generation. Civil War heroes often felt just as lost, since they returned home to find no outlet for their wartime skills. The need for suitable heroes became more urgent when an 1873 financial panic plunged the United States into a prolonged depression. The rapidly changing nature of the economy brought renewed scrutiny to the acquisition of wealth, and most Americans didn't like what they saw. The artisan tradition, which had long provided workers with a sense of accomplishment, continued to erode and now seemed unable to promise even financial security. In contrast, the wealthy might acquire phenomenal sums by means of obscure paper transactions. More than ever, Americans desired a hero who could reestablish the link between financial success and heroic conduct.

No more poignant example of this reality could be found than the man who lived in the White House from 1869 to 1877. Ulysses S. Grant had been one of the greatest Civil War heroes, acclaimed for both his tactical brilliance and his extraordinary calm under pressure. On the battlefield, Grant amazed contemporaries by seeming to be impervious to bullets flying around him. He had found the place where he belonged, and as long as he was there he showed courage and decisiveness. Yet once he was removed from the battlefield, all his heroic traits seemed to vanish. Between his service in the Mexican War and the Civil War, he had failed so miserably at business that people began avoiding him for fear he would ask for a loan. Riding the crest of his wartime heroism, he was elected president in 1868 only to see his two terms marred by a long series of scandals and gaffes, and by the country's descent into depression. No sooner did Grant leave office than he allowed himself to be swindled, placing him on the verge of bankruptcy. It was one more disheartening reminder that heroism could not be transplanted into the industrial city, particularly in the backrooms where wealth was acquired.

Yet the difficulty of adapting this model of heroism to the city made Americans more stubborn in the conviction that the traits they admired *ought* to be rewarded. An increasing number of men felt trapped in what Thoreau called "lives of quiet desperation," but at least they still wished to be able to point out successful role models to their sons. Meanwhile those boys, having heard countless tales of heroism in war and on the frontier, longed for someone who could demonstrate that heroism was still possible in the industrial city.

What was needed was, as Richard Slotkin puts it, a hero who "achieves and accumulates wealth not through drudgery and self-denial; but by seeking gratification in adventure." As a result, by the 1870s Americans were growing more adamant in rejecting those who mundanely tried to equate heroism with financial success. Daniel Boone and Ulysses S. Grant were both notoriously poor businessmen, but this shortcoming did nothing to diminish them in the eyes of their admirers. Meanwhile Ben Franklin took a pummeling from those who associated him primarily with the notion of equating wealth with virtue. Mark Twain wrote with biting irony in 1870 that Franklin was a man "of a vicious disposition, and early prostituted his talents to the invention of maxims and aphorisms calculated to inflict suffering upon the rising generation of all subsequent ages. His simplest acts, also, were contrived with a view to their being held up for the emulation of boys forever—boys who might otherwise have been happy. It was in this spirit that he became the son of a soap-boiler; and probably for no other reason than that the efforts of all future boys who tried to be anything might be looked upon with suspicion unless they were the sons of soap-boilers. With a malevolence which is without parallel in history, he would work all day and then sit up nights and let on to be studying algebra by the light of a smouldering fire, so that all other boys might have to do that also or else have Benjamin Franklin thrown up to them."

But while it was clear that Franklin and his simple success formulas could no longer serve as an inspiration to most young Americans, it was far less certain what would take their place. Old World models were of no help, as the hero was becoming a vanishing breed in Great Britain. In the early nineteenth century, Sir Walter Scott had had to reach into the distant recesses of history to discover heroes such as Ivanhoe and Rob Roy for his enormously popular romances. By the Victorian Era, novelists like Dickens and Thackeray were treating the hero as an outdated concept or even as an impossibility. It began to look like a dilemma that could not be resolved, since it seemed as though no hero could feel a sense of belonging in the city. Was it possible that the city itself was so out of harmony with nature that no one belonged there?

Into this void stepped the unlikeliest of hero figures—a man playing a scarcely disguised boy's game, and playing a position that often seemed like an afterthought, a position that became important despite specific efforts to keep it as unimportant as possible. After many ups and downs, the late-nineteenth- and early-twentieth-century catcher succeeded where other figures had failed by creating a model that translated the earlier American myths into a form that suited the new setting. The catcher would embody many of the traits of the archetypal American hero, including courage, resourcefulness, and a unique fitness to a specific task. He would bring those attributes to the industrial city and demonstrate that they still had value in the quintessentially American game of baseball. Finally, while he belonged *in* his new environment, he never belonged *to* it. He managed to retain a strong hint of the frontier.

The catcher, moreover, managed to fill that long-standing void without the help of inventive writers of fiction. His rise to prominence occurred simply because he was so able to resolve the long list of contradictory requirements that had thwarted earlier prospective heroes. He was, first of all, able to demonstrate his abilities in plain sight, where anyone could watch and verify them, instead of on a faraway frontier or battlefield where his exploits might be exaggerated in the retelling. In addition, he transcended the country's paradoxical attitude toward violence by fearlessly standing calm in the face of tremendous risk of injury, without ever himself initiating violence. He was a man on a mission, but the ongoing nature of sport meant that that mission was perpetually renewed and never had to be described in the past tense. His success was tangible, but it was measured by his victories for his club and his city rather than by the accumulation of individual wealth. Furthermore, the demands of his position drew attention to his abilities, so he could win recognition without the taint of being a show-off.

Finally, he managed to be a model of self-dependence even while being part of a team. As the Hall of Famer John Montgomery Ward put it, the other players relied on one another, "but the catcher has almost complete control of his own play, he is dependent upon no one but himself, and, in spite of everything and everybody, the nature of his work remains the same." The catcher, in short, became the ultimate example of the American ideal of the rugged individualist.

The extent to which any specific catcher consciously viewed himself as continuing the tradition of the Western hero cannot be determined. Nor was it the habit of sportswriters of the period to note it explicitly. Yet as we shall see, the language used to describe catchers during this period leaves no doubt that this connection was recognized, and it helps explain the role the position played in the lives of men like Stephen Crane, Ban Johnson, and Wallie Walker. Even the name of the position suggests this special status, since of course all the players on a baseball team regularly catch the ball. As late as 1856, any player who caught a ball might be referred to as a "catcher." But over the next few years the man behind the plate emerged as a player with a singular role, and after the Civil War he alone was granted the distinction of bearing this title.

The period when the catcher embodied all these paradoxical ideals was fairly brief and soon gave way to a backlash as the catcher began to don protective equipment. But even then it proved a resilient model and would reemerge in a revamped form that continues to exert influence. The catcher would become a key transitional figure who enabled the great American athletes of the twentieth century to become American folk heroes in the tradition of frontiersmen, mountain men, and cowboys. He would also do something even more remarkable by helping pave the way for one of the twentieth century's most extraordinary developments, the emergence of the athlete as hero and role model.

1

In the Beginning

"He who would occupy the post of honor as 'catcher,' must be able to catch expertly a swiftly delivered ball, or he will be admonished of his inexpertness by a request from some player to 'butter his fingers.'"—"Bob Lively," "Base Ball: How They Play the Game in New England" (1856)

■ IN THE mid-1870s the catcher seemed to emerge as a fully formed hero figure who was able to bring the ideals of the Western hero to the industrial city and show that they still mattered. While many frontiersmen, mountain men, and cowboys had been carefully airbrushed for heroism by clever storytellers, no conscious effort was made to transform the catcher into an American hero. The nature of the game in fact made this transformation highly unlikely.

The game we now know as baseball began to emerge from a variety of bat-and-ball games during the 1840s as men took up what had been a child's activity. Its adoption by men was accompanied by new degrees of structure and organization, as new rules were created and limits were placed on the number of players and the game's length. This in turn made it possible for clubs to compete against one another, which made it essential to make the rules as uniform as possible.

By the end of the 1850s there were only two versions of baseball with enough structure to stand a realistic chance of becoming a national standard. In a preview of the later rivalry between the Yankees and Red Sox, the two games would become known as the "New York Game" and the "Massachusetts Game" (though other names were more commonly used at the time).

The New York Game was based on a set of rules devised by the Knick-erbocker Club of New York City in the mid-1840s. This version took time to spread, but by the middle of the next decade it had come to be the game of choice in New York City and its environs. The rules created by the Knickerbockers stamped baseball as a game played by men. The hap-hazard, more-the-merrier features that had characterized the boys' game were replaced with structure and uniformity in the form of such rules as three outs per inning, two contesting sides, and, eventually, nine innings per game.

Other changes were also designed to show that baseball was now a man's activity. Running had been the biggest feature of most of the earlier versions, but this suggested a child's game, so the Knickerbockers intro-duced a harder ball that a strong man could wallop out of sight. They also eventually denounced as childish the rule allowing fielders to record outs by catching batted balls on the first bounce.

Yet while the framers of the New York Game went to considerable lengths to make the game appear manly, they drew a distinction between toughness and brutality. While their choice of a harder ball brought new excitement to the game, the ball remained rubbery enough to pose little danger of injury. They also eliminated the long-standing rule by which fielders threw the ball at base runners, recording an out when they hit one. As one observer explained, this feature of play proved incompatible with the new ball: "As the excitement of the game intensified the ball began to be made harder and heavier to aid the throwing. This led to an unusual number of accidents, resulting from the players being hit by a too solid ball. It was this dangerous outgrowth of town-ball playing which first sug-gested to some Yankee mind (whom nobody knows) to put basemen on the bases and let the ball be thrown to them instead of at the runner." This change was unpopular with many who "could not break themselves of the habit or resist the temptation to throw the ball at the base runner, which, while amusing to the spectators, was rather annoying to the party who was hit." For the Knickerbockers, however, safety came first.

The catcher's proximity to the plate put him in the greatest danger, so his safety was protected by several rules of the New York Game. To begin with, the pitcher was limited to an underhand delivery—a pitch was literally supposed to resemble the motion used to pitch a horseshoe. The inevitable result was that the ball did not arrive at home plate at a great rate of speed, which made the sharp foul tip unknown. The rules moreover gave the catcher no reason to stand close to the batter. Since strikeouts were exceedingly rare and fouls likely to be hit high in the air, it was good strategy as well as self-preservation for the catcher to stand twenty feet or so behind home plate.

The Knickerbockers also decreed a foul ball to be a nonevent. This represented a dramatic change from all previous bat-and-ball games, which either had no foul territory (as in cricket) or designated a foul to be an out. We don't know for sure why they did this, and the most likely explanation is that the shortage of available land in New York necessitated this revolutionary change. But whatever their intention, the rule afforded additional protection to the game's most vulnerable player since it gave batters every incentive to hit the ball in the direction of the fielders stationed at a safe distance. Thus while trying very hard to make their game appear manly, the Knickerbockers made just as much of an effort to preserve the health and safety of the players.

In stark contrast, the catcher was in constant danger in the Massachusetts Game. The "throwers" or "givers" used overhand motions when delivering the ball, and there was no foul territory, so batters learned to deflect swiftly pitched balls behind them, which would allow them to run to first base. This approach proved so difficult to defend that clubs often stationed two or three catchers, or "behind men," back of home plate. One early player reported that his club's catcher was always backed up by a "back scoot" and that, on playing fields bounded by a fence, these two men had the additional support of a "fence scoot." The fence scoot's job was important but not prestigious: he sat atop the fence and pursued any balls that went over it, which meant that he frequently "found himself crawling among those thorny bushes after the ball . . . oftentimes intensified by the hastening footsteps of the gardener and his dog."

Even with these extra defenders stationed behind home plate, there remained far more open space in that direction and Massachusetts Game batters tried to take advantage. "Some of the players," the pioneer James D'Wolf Lovett would later recall, "had a knack of shortening up their bat,—that is, grasping it near the middle,—and by a quick turn of the wrist striking the ball, as it passed them, in the same direction in which it was thrown, thus avoiding the fielders and giving the striker a good start on his bases. . . . This mode of back striking was carried so far that bats not more than 12 or 15 inches long and with a flat surface were used, and instead of making any attempt to strike with it, this bat was merely held at a sharp angle and the ball allowed to glance off it, over the catcher's head."

The regularity with which balls were deflected over his head created a ticklish dilemma for the catcher in the Massachusetts Game. The closer he stood to home plate, the better his chance of snagging such balls while they were still within reach. But the dangers to an unprotected man standing directly behind the batter were daunting—and they only grew worse when some brave New England catchers began inching forward.

The swift overhand deliveries of the "throwers" meant that batters in the Massachusetts Game were often overpowered and barely ticked the ball on their swings. Regardless of the number of strikes, the rules at this time were that the catcher could record an out by catching such a ball—"A tick and a ketch / Will always fetch" was a popular saying among early ballplayers. But a catcher who stood directly behind home plate had only a split second to react when a ticked ball changed directions, and grievous injuries could result.

Some Massachusetts Game batters even learned to take full swings and send the ball behind them with terrifying speed. One of them, for example, took advantage of his "right to knock the ball with his bat in any direction he chose" by grasping the bat "with both hands, pointing it towards the ground, the handle just touching his chest; the thrower would deliver the ball the usual way, to the right, when the striker would bring up the bat with great force, catch the ball with a smart blow, and send it over the head of the catcher and far behind him; he seldom missed the ball either, notwithstanding his novel mode of striking."

Despite the risks, catchers in the Massachusetts Game typically stood closer to the batter than did their New York counterparts. A few daring men began standing directly behind the batter. Lyman Johnson of the Massapoags of Sharon became known as the "pride of the club" for his stellar work behind the plate. Johnson didn't always wait for the pitch to pass the batsman, learning instead to dexterously "reach forward and take the ball from before the bat." Sam Bradstreet of the Haveracks of Boston likewise "could about pick a ball off a striker's bat."

But these men soon discovered that increased vulnerability to foul tips was not the only new danger that resulted from standing so close to the batter. Lyman Johnson paid the price for his courage when he "received a broken arm by a striker who saw through his little game and thought to teach him a lesson." James D'Wolf Lovett confirmed that Massachusetts Game catchers "sometimes got a bad blow from the bat as it was swung back . . . there is no doubt that catchers were sometimes intentionally disabled in this way."

As a result of these formidable hazards, Massachusetts Game catchers developed a special toughness and a devil-may-care attitude. Men brave enough to play the position typically held their hands in front of their face as the pitch whistled through the air and "stop[ped] with a solid *smack* in the catcher's hands." And rather than trying to take precautions, according to one player: "I have frequently heard the catcher tell the thrower, and have made the same request myself when catching, to throw as swift as he wished and aim for my face."

With the roles of the catcher and thrower being so crucial in the Massachusetts Game, a special mystique came to be associated with these two positions. As an early New England player explained, "The two best players upon each side—first and second mates, as they were called, by common consent—were catcher and thrower." This privilege was a double-edged sword, however: the "first and second mates" would earn great admiration if they performed well together but could expect criticism if they didn't live up to expectations. "The finest exhibition of skill in Base Ball playing is, I think, to witness the ball passed swiftly from 'thrower' to 'catcher' who being experts, seldom allow it to fall to the ground, and scarcely move their feet from the position they occupy," continued that same player, quickly adding, "he who would occupy the post of honor as 'catcher,' must be able to catch expertly a swiftly delivered ball, or he will be admonished of his inexpertness by a request from some player to 'butter his fingers.'"

While two fielders did the lion's share of the work in the Massachusetts Game, by contrast, players in the New York Game of the late 1850s took pride that, as one player put it, "a good pitcher and catcher alone are not sufficient to win a match." Mention was regularly made of the fact that the contributions of all nine players mattered. "The day has gone by," boasted one journalist, "when first-class clubs can be beaten by two or three good players among their opponents." And this feature was no accident. William R. Wheaton, one of the founders of the Knickerbocker Club, explained that its members sought an alternative to cricket, which they found "too slow and lazy a game. We didn't get enough exercise out of it. Only the bowler and the batter had anything to do, and the rest of the players might stand around all the afternoon without getting a chance to stretch their legs."

Just as important, the duties of the nine players were much more similar in the New York version. Since the underhand delivery made it difficult to overpower a batter, pitchers were judged primarily on their fielding. Although the catcher alone was stationed in foul territory, in other respects his duties were much like those of his teammates. He stood a safe distance behind the plate, not only for safety's sake but also because it made sense for him to do so. Batters in the New York Game had no incentive to try to foul pitches off, since they could not reach base on a foul. In addition, foul tips were rare occurrences in this version, since the underhand pitches meant that the batter supplied almost all the force—if he hit the ball squarely, it would go into fair territory. Thus most of the batted balls that came the catcher's way were the result of mistimed swings that propelled the ball high in the air. By standing farther back of the plate, the catcher had a better chance to record outs, especially since any batted ball caught on the first bounce counted as an out.

Catchers had a few additional duties, such as completing strikeouts, preventing passed balls, and throwing to bases, but once again the rules of the New York Game tended to downplay their importance. As one observer recalled, if an early player "could stop a ball with his shins, and hit a man between the bases, he was pronounced a prodigy in base-ball, and immediately installed as catcher." Even in the New York version, pitcher and catcher were generally viewed as the key players. But this was a matter of degree only, rather as the center fielder today is regarded as playing the most important outfield position, but only by a slim margin.

Thus, as the rest of the country chose between the versions of baseball played in New York and Boston, the stark contrast in the roles played by the pitcher and catcher figured as one of the major differences between the two games. The reason for preferring the less prominent role assigned to these two players in the New York Game seems equally clear.

Having the catcher and batter in such close proximity often marred games played under the Massachusetts rules. According to Lovett, arguments over whether a catcher had been deliberately struck by the batter's swing were the direct cause of "bad blood between rival teams." The possibility of serious injury to the catcher also made it difficult to depict the game as a healthful outdoor exercise. The Knickerbockers, as we have seen, were attentive to safety concerns when they crafted the New York rules, and undoubtedly they recognized that baseball could never gain acceptance as a gentlemanly pastime if players were regularly writhing around in the dirt in agony. They also recognized the importance of keeping all nine players involved in the action. Thus the tendency of Massachusetts Game catchers to stand directly behind the batter jeopardized both the camaraderie and the health benefits that baseball supposedly fostered.

Another important reason to avoid giving any one player too great a role was demonstrated in 1859, when the *New York Atlas* published a game account claiming that the Knickerbockers had lost because of "the foolishness, fancy airs and smart capers of [catcher Charles Schuyler DeBost]. Like a clown in a circus, he evidently plays for the applause of the audience at his 'monkey shines,' instead of trying to win the game. This is reprehensible, especially when playing against a Brooklyn club, where the reputation of the New Yorkers as players is at stake. But so long as the spectators applaud his tom-foolery, just so long will he exert the part of a clown." These harsh words hint at a sinister possibility—that allowing a single player to become so important would give him the power to determine, and even to fix, the outcome of a game.

The implication was not lost on readers of the article, for some of DeBost's friends took offense. In response, the *Atlas* published a lengthy follow-up article explaining that it had not intended to question DeBost's integrity. Nonetheless it offered a spirited defense of its original criticisms, explaining that "Mr. DeBost's fondness for display sometimes, in our opinion, leads him to neglect the true interests of the game . . . his 'peculiarities' were most loudly complained of by his warmest admirers on the occasion of the match between the Excelsior and Knickerbocker Clubs. We still fail to discover the extreme grace and refinement displayed, when a player in a match attempts to catch a ball with that portion of his body that is usually covered by his coat tail."

It was a revealing exchange in more ways than one, and offered a preview of a problem that was soon to bedevil the game. Even though baseball's gentlemanly associations still offered some protection against game-fixing, it shows that there was something inherently unsporting if most of the players in a team sport were hopelessly dependent on the performance of one teammate. Thus there were many good reasons to aim for a relatively even division of responsibilities among the nine players.

When the Civil War began in 1861, it was not yet clear whether the New York or the Massachusetts version would become the national standard. By the war's end, however, America had an undisputed national game, as the New York Game had swept the country, leaving the Massachusetts Game on the verge of extinction. The decisive triumph of the New York Game was the result of a combination of factors, including the prosaic reality that it was much more adaptable to a variety of field conditions. But it does seem clear that the outsized role and risk of injury of the catcher in the Massachusetts Game contributed to this version's sudden demise.

Then, just when it seemed that an irrevocable decision had been made about the catcher's role, a strange thing happened. In spite of intentions to the contrary, within ten years of the end of the Civil War the catcher's position under the New York rules became more dangerous and more important than it had been even in the Massachusetts Game. What had happened?

2

The Catcher as Tough Guy

"There is a ground sparrow's nest on the base-ball grounds, and a ball came within an inch of it twice yesterday. The motherbird sat on the fence, at a distance, and watched the game with a good deal of interest, and the birdlings did not seem to be at all frightened. Is it possible that any of those wee sparrows aspire to be a professional catcher or the captain of a nine?"
—*Milwaukee Daily Sentinel* (1877)

■ ONCE THE Knickerbockers' version of baseball became the national standard, its loose customs and rules came under more pressure than they could bear. A game that had been played for fun and exercise by amateurs in front of a few close friends was slowly transformed into a sport contested in front of paying spectators by two teams made up of professionals who did everything possible to win. Baseball clubs, which had consisted of nine local men, gradually gave way to teams of hired imports who were eventually supplemented by substitutes, managers, coaches, and so on.

These off-field developments forced equally dramatic changes on the field. New rules had to be constantly devised to address the new tactics and situations that emerged over the next three decades. At the outset it was less a case of adapting the rules than of creating rules where the Knickerbockers had provided only vague guidelines. But all too often, as soon as uniform rules were devised, the game's increasingly contentious and inventive players found loopholes in them and forced modifications and refinements.

This ongoing process put tremendous strain on the fabric of the game, as the rules-makers often clung to concepts long after they had been shown to be impractical. The umpire's position became especially arduous, as he had the unenviable task of applying abstract principles about how the game ought to be played on the basis of an often confusingly worded rulebook. Worse, while working alone from behind home plate, he was somehow supposed to be able to see and make accurate decisions about everything that took place on the field. The one certainty in his life was that on any close play he would be yelled at by one side or the other. As a result, many of the rules that had been devised in the boardroom had to be scrapped, revised, or disregarded because they proved unenforceable. The most dramatic and far-reaching example was the pitcher's transition from underhand pitcher to overhand thrower.

As we have seen, the Knickerbockers envisioned the function of delivering the ball to the plate as a relatively minor one. Rather like the referee tossing the ball up to begin a basketball match, the pitcher's role was to initiate the action and then become one of the nine fielders. This created a nice balance among the nine defensive players, with each fielder contributing and none being of inordinate importance. Alas, the Knickerbockers' rules provided no effective way to enforce the underhand delivery requirement. Once ballplayers became more concerned with winning than with conducting themselves like gentlemen, pitchers began to test the limitations of these delivery restrictions and found that they were very difficult to enforce.

Soon, instead of getting things started, pitchers were trying to *prevent* the action by throwing unreachable pitches. In desperation the rules-makers gave the umpires all sorts of new authority, yet every new idea they tried failed to prevent pitchers from dominating the game. By the mid-1870s pitchers' release points had reached their waists and were moving steadily higher. The 1880s saw the rules-makers admit defeat, as it became clear that the only pitching restriction that could be enforced was the distance between the pitcher and home plate. They continued to tinker with that distance until 1893, when they settled upon sixty feet six inches.

By getting his way, the pitcher ensured that he would never again be just another fielder, and by the 1870s he had assumed the pivotal role he still occupies. This in turn affected the role of every other man on the diamond. With fat pitches a rarity, infielders assumed greater importance than outfielders. Batters had to rethink their approaches at the plate and overhaul their swings. As umpires were forced to make more and more judgment calls, they completed the transition from revered figures to objects of abuse.

But no man was affected more dramatically than the pitcher's battery mate. As a direct result of the pitcher's new importance, catchers of the 1870s were forced to endure extraordinary amounts of pain. They also assumed an outsized role in the success or failure of a team, comparable to and sometimes even overshadowing the pitcher. At the same time the fact that pitchers had seized this authority led many to think of them as usurpers while catchers, who had merely responded to their new surroundings, fit the classic model of American heroism. As a result, catchers became the idols of thousands of boys like Stephen Crane, Byron Johnson, and Walter Walker.

*

The loose rule of the Knickerbockers that set everything in motion was the one providing that "The ball must be pitched, not thrown for the bat," and specifying no penalty for failing to do so. Pitchers soon began intentionally delivering wild offerings in hopes of tempting impatient batters to swing at them, and some even seemed to be aiming *at* the batters in hopes of intimidating them. Batters retaliated by waiting for a good pitch, often to the point of letting perfectly good pitches go past. Games ground to a halt with as many as seventy-five pitches being made in an at bat. At first this merely meant a lot more work for the man behind the plate. But before long the tediousness of these lengthy at bats forced new rules that changed the game forever and had an even more dramatic effect on the life of the catcher.

During the late 1850s and early 1860s the concepts of called balls and strikes were introduced by a series of rule changes. The aim was to prevent pitchers and batters from stalling, but there were unanticipated consequences. Pitchers in the New York Game discovered that they had a far more realistic chance to strike batters out and began concentrating on doing so, which transformed the game's most basic dynamic.

Strikeouts had always been included in the rules of this version of baseball, but until 1858 only a swing and a miss constituted a strike. With strictly underhand pitching, only a weak batter was likely to get anywhere close to exhausting his quota of strikes. On the rare occasions when a strikeout did occur, the catcher could complete the out by catching the pitch on the fly or the first hop, or even by blocking it and throwing the ball to first base before the batter could get there. Since it was not difficult to stop these slow pitches, there was no reason for the catcher to put himself in harm's way. Indeed, since he didn't typically catch the ball, he was occasionally referred to as the "behind" or "behind man."

Once pitchers began trying to strike batters out, the speedier pitches made for many fewer lazy foul pop-ups, giving the catcher less reason to stand far back near the backstop. Although they wore no protective equipment, some catchers began inching a bit closer to the plate, thereby giving themselves a better chance against would-be base-stealers. Doing so, however, made it clear that the skill level needed to play behind the plate had been greatly elevated by the emergence of swift pitching. The catcher's ability to handle speedy deliveries became crucial, since a strikeout pitch that got beyond him negated the pitcher's skill and instead gave the batter his base. It had also become essential for the catcher to be able to handle fast pitches cleanly, rather than just blocking them and picking them up, because only then was there a realistic chance of throwing out a base-stealer.

The new emphasis on strikeouts also changed the approach of batters, who could no longer swing with all their might because they now had to worry about protecting the plate. More defensive swings, combined with the much greater speed of the pitches, led to a dramatic increase in the number of balls that were tipped off the bat and subtly changed directions at the last instant. This posed a great hazard to the catchers who had moved closer to the batsman, causing the influential sportswriter Henry Chadwick to predict that if the trend continued, "both the strikers and catchers will have to pad themselves up like cricketers do." Thus only a few years after the Knickerbockers' game gained nationwide acceptance and seemed to make things safe for the catcher, the position was now on its way to becoming far more important and far more dangerous.

These new developments also created an enduring role for the catcher by assigning him a pivotal spot in the battle between the pitcher and the batter. If he caught a sharp foul tip, the batter was out (no matter how many previous strikes had occurred) and the catcher received hearty applause for the great skill and courage that such a catch required. If he failed to catch the foul tip, the pitch didn't count at all—not even as a strike—and the at bat continued as though nothing had happened. In addition, the requirement that a strikeout had to be completed by a catch (or equivalent play) by the man behind the plate now took on crucial significance, since pitches that were too speedy or too deceptive for batters to hit would all too often prove uncatchable.

In the years since, pitchers have developed new offerings and tactics, batters have responded with innovations of their own, and the game's rules-makers have sometimes stepped in when it seemed that one side or the other had too much of an advantage. Yet the one constant has been that it is ultimately the man behind the plate who ensures that a pleasing balance is maintained. His ability to catch a pitch makes it legitimate; if he can't do so, the ball will roll to the backstop and be worse than useless, since the batter will run safely to first base. It was thus no coincidence that at this time the catcher came to be known not by his station on the field but by his suddenly crucial role.

New York Mets manager Casey Stengel found a memorable way to express this principle when he commented on his club's decision to use their first pick in the 1961 expansion draft for a journeyman receiver, Hobie Landrith. Asked about the choice, Stengel reportedly explained, "You have to have a catcher or you'll have a lot of passed balls." The remark has become one of Stengel's most memorable observations and is often quoted. As silly as it sounds, it is a concise summary of why the catcher became so pivotal in the early years of baseball and what, despite many ups and downs, has remained the essence of the position ever since. As we shall see, every time a seemingly unhittable new pitch like the curveball, the spitball, or the knuckleball has come along, it has sent shock waves through baseball by reminding everyone of that old principle: you have to have a good catcher, or the pitcher's best offerings will roll to the backstop and nothing else the fielding side tries to do will matter.

The vitally important role now played by the catcher was demonstrated in 1860 by the emergence of baseball's first outstanding pitcher, Jim Creighton of the Excelsiors of Brooklyn. Creighton had developed a swift, rising pitch that he was able to deliver while still adhering to the letter of the pitching laws. But while the pitch gave batters fits, it was worse than useless without a catcher who could handle it. Fortunately Creighton had an outstanding catcher in Joe Leggett. Leggett's role in Creighton's development was considerable, as he became the first catcher to play the dual role as a pitcher's tutor and partner. After the 1859 season he advised the teenaged Creighton to spend the winter throwing an iron ball to develop his arm strength. Then, when Creighton returned for the 1860 season with "blinding" speed, it was Leggett's skill and fearlessness that made the delivery effective.

Creighton's dependence upon his catcher became obvious when Leggett was not available. In a three-game all-star series between the best players of Brooklyn and Philadelphia in 1862, the star outfielder Jack Chapman filled in catching Creighton's wicked deliveries. In the third inning, however, Chapman injured his hand, and with no other volunteers to handle Creighton's offerings, a new pitcher had to be substituted.

The emphasis on catching foul tips and completing strikeouts forced a rethinking of where the catcher should stand. Before the introduction of the called strike in 1858, New York catchers typically stood in an upright position twenty to twenty-five feet behind the plate. Many of them moved nearer to the plate with runners on bases in order to discourage base-stealing. They would also move noticeably closer if a batter were within one strike of striking out, but this was not a common occurrence. Yet even then they stayed quite a distance back of the plate so they would still be able to catch high pop fouls. Thus before 1858 no catcher playing by the Knickerbocker rules regularly positioned himself so near the plate as to be in great peril from foul balls.

According to the sportswriter William Rankin, the first man to do so was Folkert Rappelje Boerum of the Atlantics of Brooklyn in the summer of 1859. Rankin maintained that Boerum's new positioning "proved so great a success that it was adopted by all the leading clubs in the vicinity of New York." It is hard not to be a bit suspicious of Rankin's certainty in singling out one man as the originator—after all, terms such as "close" and "near" are imprecise, and many catchers tended to move forward under certain circumstances. Yet it makes perfect sense for this trend to have occurred in 1859, so it seems likely that Boerum played a significant role.

We can be more certain that Joe Leggett was the man who did the most to popularize this tactic. To begin with, standing in such a hazardous location when the hard-throwing Creighton was pitching created an unforgettable visual image. Leggett, marveled one sportswriter who had obviously never seen anything like it before, stood "so close to the batter, as to hardly give him any room to swing the bat and Creighton would pitch to *him* instead of the batter." Henry Chadwick confirmed, "It was not until Creighton introduced the swift underhand delivery that catching began to be anything of an arduous undertaking, and then Joe Leggett was found equal to the task of pluckily facing and holding the hot balls sent him, his plan of standing up close behind the bat being then regarded as quite a feat." More important, the Excelsiors acted as ambassadors for the game, going on regular tours at their own expense to demonstrate baseball's finer points in cities where the New York version was still a novelty. As they did so, Leggett's courageous positioning attracted praise and even awe.

Before long, Leggett and Boerum began to have imitators. A number of Brooklyn catchers, including Joe Howard, Frank Norton, Herbert Jewell, and Bob Ferguson, became known for their bold use of the up-close tactic during the 1860s. Philadelphia was emerging as baseball's other great hotbed, and its catchers strove to keep up with their New York counterparts. Irish-born Civil War veteran Fergy Malone became one of Philadelphia's first star catchers, and he too approached the plate at least occasionally. Meanwhile a young stonecutter named Doug Allison was catching for another local club when "I began to believe it possible to get close up to the bat so as to catch the ball and thereby prevent so many runners from stealing second and third base. . . . I first tried it going up on the side in order to allow the pitcher to throw them wide but gradually worked over behind the batter so as to fool him as well as the base runner. My success in this style of play was remarkable and naturally the talk of the place until our games began to draw crowds simply because 'Allison was behind the bat.'" The young catcher was soon signed to play professional baseball for the legendary Red Stockings of Cincinnati. As the game spread far and wide, catchers in towns like Rochester, New York, and Detroit also ventured close to the plate.

Still, most of the catchers of the 1860s were not as reckless. While there were spectacular benefits to standing close to the plate, there were also significant disadvantages, most notably the risk of losing a key player to injury. Those risks increased when some batters began "stepping back, so as to intimidate the catcher, and prevent him from playing close behind when there is a man on first." The Putnam club of Brooklyn had a catcher named Myron Masten who was considered "one of the finest catchers in the community; in fact, as a catcher, he ranked as high as Creighton does in his position. Cool and deliberate in his movements, and graceful withal, he was the great attraction whenever the Putnam club played. But the game was too arduous in its duties for him; and he had to retire, at his physician's request." Even Leggett was unable to handle the punishment for more than a few years. His hands became "puffed up and exceedingly painful, and a lame arm prevented his throwing to bases." After 1862 he played rarely. Leggett's peers gradually joined him on the sidelines, and most of their successors concluded that the risks of standing directly behind the batter were too great. Then, just when it seemed that safety would prevail, a number of new developments conspired to lure more catchers into close proximity with home plate, in the process making catchers even more crucial in the New York Game than they had been in the now-defunct Massachusetts Game.

No one exemplified these developments better than Nat Hicks. Born in 1845 and raised in New York City, Hicks served briefly in the New York Infantry's Fifteenth Regiment at the close of the Civil War. He took up baseball after the war, but his play attracted little attention until 1869, when he severed his longtime connection with the amateur Eagles and joined a semiprofessional club known as the Stars of Brooklyn. For the Eagles, the loss of their best player was devastating. "Since the secession of Hicks from the ranks of the veteran Eagles," noted one reporter, "they have met with defeat in every game they have played." For the Stars, however, the move was a windfall because it allowed the club's pitcher, a young man named Arthur "Candy" Cummings, to unleash a new pitch that would revolutionize baseball.

Cummings had been born in Massachusetts in 1848, so the baseball games he had watched as a boy had featured overhand "throwing." Even after moving to Brooklyn and learning the strictly underhand deliveries of the Knickerbockers' game, he never forgot the version played in Massachusetts. At some point he began experimenting to see whether an underhand pitcher could achieve the deceptive movement generated by the fast overhand throwers of his childhood.

In later years Cummings would give many different accounts of his experiments, some of which sound suspiciously as though he was providing his listeners with the kind of story they wanted to hear. The most colorful version had him throwing seashells at the beach, and the picturesque nature of this image has led it to become the best-known account. The evidence, however, points to a less dramatic sequence of events in which Cummings had to overcome two technical problems in order to bring back the ability of the old Massachusetts overhand throwers to make a pitched ball move away from the batter.

The first was finding a way to snap his wrist so sharply that he could curve a baseball while keeping both feet on the ground and swinging his arm alongside his body, as required by the rules of the New York Game. By no means was this the "Eureka!" type of moment suggested by the story of throwing seashells; instead, as Cummings himself explained, it involved a lengthy process of trial and error. "Every day I would be at it," he later recalled, "holding the ball in many different ways and throwing with a variety of motions. Of course, many of the ways in which I held or threw the ball were useless."

The second, equally important requirement was finding a catcher who could handle pitches that were too tricky for the batter. The curve was proving so elusive that some frustrated batters complained they should be allowed to leave the batter's box in pursuit of it. Others simply despaired of ever being able to hit the unhittable pitch. But catchers were just as befuddled, and the ensuing years produced regular claims about pitchers with "puzzling curves" followed by the obligatory disclaimer, "If a catcher can be found to hold him, it is claimed that he will prove . . . a mystery to batsmen." Thus the curveball came to exemplify the paradox that Stengel would humorously articulate—that the most lethal pitch had no value without a skilled catcher.

In Cummings's case, his first partner was a friend named Edward Chapelle. All the other boys in his neighborhood made fun of these efforts and referred to the pitch as "Cummings' crazy curve." But according to Cummings, Chapelle "believed in the possibility of pitching a curve ball and was anxious to see the idea worked out. From this date on I put in all my spare time practicing, Chapelle doing the catching."

Eventually Cummings mastered the pitch, but in order to use it against professional clubs he once more needed to find a catcher who could prevent it from rolling to the backstop. That was what made the Stars' acquisition of Nat Hicks such a historic event. While Hicks's role in the development of the curve has been forgotten, Cummings gave specific credit to Hicks in two accounts of the origins of the pitch. Still more telling is the fact that Cummings and Hicks were reunited on two more teams after their stint with the Stars. Thus Arthur Daley would claim in 1946: "The Hicks technique behind the plate not only had a revolutionary effect on the catching department but also caused a radical change in the pitching as well. Arthur Cummings 'invented' the curve ball while pitching to the close-up Hicks in 1870. . . . Later with the Phillies of 1874 the battery of Cummings and Hicks had no superior. Cummings has been formally installed in the Hall of Fame at Cooperstown, while Hicks has been generally overlooked. Any man who took the risks he recklessly took in his bare-hand catching style deserves some measure of glory."

Hicks's contemporaries also understood that it took a special talent to catch the curveball. Following the 1872 season, Henry Chadwick proclaimed Hicks to be one of the game's leading catchers because of his ability to handle "the side bias imparted to the ball . . . by Cummings, making the rebound from his delivery so eccentric as to require the most active movements on the part of the catcher to prevent passed balls." Hicks gained such a reputation for this skill that, when he wasn't catching for Cummings, he was usually paired with Bobby Mathews, the only other professional pitcher who mastered the underhand curveball.

Nat Hicks's ability to catch the curveball first brought him to prominence, but it was another quality that became his greatest legacy. Like many notable catching pioneers, he wasn't much of a hitter, and his other skills do not appear to have been extraordinary. But he made up for these deficiencies with a courage that bordered on recklessness, and by coincidence he came along just when baseball was offering a glorious opportunity to catchers with toughness and determination.

Pitchers, having already changed the game by carving out a greater role for themselves, continued to refine their techniques during the 1860s. Some unveiled elaborate motions that involved hops, skips, and jumps, while others settled for simply testing whether the umpire could enforce the requirement of an underhand delivery. The rules-makers eventually were able to eliminate the quirky motion, but they found the problem of delivery more difficult to combat. Revealingly, many were coming to believe that instead of creating rules for the manner of delivery, it made more sense to rely upon the principle that the catcher's ability to handle a pitch established its legitimacy. "No matter how swift a [pitcher] can deliver the ball to the bat by this or that method," reasoned Henry Chadwick, "the speed must always be governed by the ability of the catcher to stop and hold the ball. If, therefore, a player is found who can either pitch or throw the ball to the bat with more than ordinary speed, no rule is required to prohibit the delivery which admits of it, as the speed itself is prohibiting in its effect, from the lack of any player able to stop or hold the ball from such a delivery." While this approach was logical, the lure of speed proved irresistible and release points slowly rose, with a corresponding increase in strikeouts and lower scores.

At about the same time, the difficulty of recording outs prompted many prominent baseball clubs to switch to a less rubbery ball. Harry Wright's legendary Red Stockings of 1869, in particular, became associated with what became known as the "dead ball." As this new ball caught on, the typical score of a baseball game plummeted. Throughout the 1860s, scoring fifty or sixty runs in a game had been commonplace, and hard-hitting clubs occasionally topped the century mark. But scores began to drop in 1869, and the following season proved to be a watershed.

It was no coincidence that Harry Wright tried to persuade Nat Hicks to play with the Red Stockings in 1870. Wright already had a star catcher in Doug Allison, but he anticipated two new realities that were about to change baseball forever. The first was a brand-new recipe for winning baseball games: by preventing the other team from scoring instead of just trying to pile up more runs. The second was the most important ingredient in that recipe: a great catcher, or, better still, a couple of great catchers, so as to give your team a capable replacement in case of injury while at the same time preventing the other team from having one.

Although the idea of winning a ball game by shutting out the opponents seems obvious to us today, at the end of the 1860s it was far from that. Despite the thousands of games played in that decade as "base ball fever" swept the country, there were, according to the historian John H. Gruber, "exactly five shutouts prior to 1870." So a man who prepared for the 1870 season with the aim of trying to prevent the other team from scoring would have understandably been regarded as crazy. Harry Wright, however, had gained familiarity with shutouts the hard way—in 1860 he had been the catcher on the club that suffered baseball's first recorded shutout at the hands of Jim Creighton. Even though the ensuing decade had witnessed only a handful of other whitewashings, Wright was among the first to realize that the new "dead balls" and the reemergence of speedy pitching could make such games possible on a regular basis.

The 1870 season did indeed see that seemingly remote possibility become a reality. During that spring's games, scores plummeted, and an increasing number of clubs responded by opting for the "dead ball." Then on July 23, 1870, the unthinkable happened when the hard-hitting and highly paid White Stockings of Chicago went through an entire game without scoring. The baseball world reacted with astonishment and disbelief. In addition, since there had never been a need for a word to describe going an entire game without scoring, "being Chicagoed" became the standard term for being shut out. During the remainder of the decade, shutouts increased in frequency so dramatically that by its end even Harry Wright would advocate livelier baseballs. There was a price to be paid for this new development, however, and it was the catcher who paid it.

With the new emphasis on preventing runs, pitchers began gradually elevating their release points, and umpires found the old pitching rules unenforceable. As release points moved steadily upward, the "dead ball" began to be pitched with greater speed, and more pitchers learned how to make it veer unexpectedly. Under the circumstances, the prudent thing would have been for catchers to retreat out of the range of danger. Most did so, but Nat Hicks understood a crucial paradox: every change that made it more hazardous to stand near the batter was simultaneously increasing the benefits of doing so.

Most obviously, the increase in strikeouts meant far more opportunities for the catcher to complete these outs. Also crucial was a new emphasis on base-stealing. Along with efforts to prevent it, base-stealing had always been part of baseball, but the tactic took on far greater significance in lower-scoring games. After all, when teams were routinely scoring fifty or sixty runs per game, a batter who reached first base safely could be expected to cross the plate. Moreover, the prevalence of passed balls led many runners to wait for one to advance on, rather than risk being thrown out trying to steal.

This situation changed when baseball suddenly was transformed into a low-scoring game. With runs now scarce, taking a chance to try to move up a base seemed like a worthwhile risk to many base runners. Stealing bases was also becoming easier as a result of the more elaborate deliveries now being used by pitchers, which allowed base runners to get a better jump toward the next base. So it fell to catchers to try to prevent base-stealing, and, as Nat Hicks recognized, the best way to do so was by standing directly behind the batter to cut down the throwing distance. (Even catchers like Hicks who played close to the plate still did not crouch, though many did stoop slightly.)

Some of Hicks's contemporaries believed he was the first catcher to stand directly behind the batter. In fact, as we have seen, he did not originate the practice, nor was he alone in restoring it to prominence. Yet Hicks was without doubt the standard-bearer in the movement that led the positioning to become routine, as it has remained ever since.

What inspired Nat Hicks to move so close to the batter? Had his brief stint in the Civil War created the need to prove his own courage? Did he see it as the only way to continue his baseball career? Naturally we don't know for certain, and it may not matter. With the pitcher's role in the New York Game beginning to resemble that of the Massachusetts Game, it was probably inevitable that the catcher's role would follow suit. What we can be certain of is that the decision made by Hicks would inspire youngsters like Stephen Crane, Byron Johnson, and Wallie Walker to grow up dreaming of becoming catchers. It is just as indisputable that Hicks himself paid a terrible price for blazing that trail.

According to an obituary apparently written by Henry Chadwick, Hicks "created a sensation by catching behind the bat with his naked hands and body unprotected. His endurance was phenomenal in the face of the awful punishment he sustained. It was in the early seventies when Hicks first made his appearance on the diamond as a prominent figure. He was the catcher of the Eckfords, and participated in all the games which they played. He caught behind the bat close under the batsman and forced the other old line catchers to follow his example. [Bill] Craver of the Haymakers [of Troy, New York] was the only one to carry this catching feat to the same extent that Hicks did, and these two by their accurate throwing to bases were the first to put a stop to the big scores that were a feature of the earlier games."

It was an Independence Day game in 1873 that sealed Nat Hicks's reputation. For several weeks before this game he had been nursing a "very badly hurt forefinger." Then, on July 3, Hicks was "struck in the face with a sharp foul tip" and was compelled to leave the game. He arrived at the ballpark the next day with such a large bruise around his eye that "it was not thought by any that he could play at all, or if he attempted to play he would make a bungle of it, and thus lose the game for the New-York boys." Instead Hicks amazed everyone and, "so far from losing the game, he actually won it, by the most brilliant play that has been shown for years, and probably, under the circumstances, the finest play ever shown. He went into the game with his right eye almost knocked out of his head, and his nose and the whole right side of his face swollen to three times their normal size; and yet, notwithstanding this, nothing seemed too difficult for him to take. Player after player sank before his unfaltering nerve; and although struck four times during the game—once squarely on the mouth with the ball, once on the chest, and twice with the bat—he could not be driven away from his post. Indeed, taken all in all, no man ever exhibited more nerve and pluck, combined with cool judgment, than did this man, and he certainly deserved all the applause and commendation that he received." In leading his team to victory, Hicks recorded eleven putouts, five of them on "sharp fly tip catches."

And that was just one game! Over the course of his career, "The punishment the stout-hearted and thick-skinned Hicks absorbed was amazing. He lasted only eleven years in the big time, but during that period he had every finger in his hand broken at least once, his wrist broken, his eyebrow shattered, his nose smashed and, in a career-ending climax, his kneecap broken while trying to block off famed Pop Anson at the plate." Amazingly, the only injury that kept Hicks out of action for a prolonged period of time occurred when he became embroiled in a heated argument with umpire Bob Ferguson, who responded by hitting Hicks with a bat and breaking his arm. It is small wonder that Arthur Daley declared him to be "baseball's original tough guy."

Bill Craver, who was cited in Hicks's obituary as the other man to take "this catching feat to the same extent that Hicks did," was another Civil War veteran, having served for eighteen months in Company K of

New York's Thirteenth Heavy Artillery Regiment. Many years later Craver would file for an invalid pension, claiming he was "almost wholly unable to earn a support by manual labor by reason of left hand crippled—deafness proceeding from yellow fever." (The former malady sounds suspiciously like a baseball injury being passed off as a war wound, but deafness as a result of yellow fever was a common malady among soldiers.)

After the war Craver returned to his native Troy and became noted as a "disciple of Joe Leggett," someone who could stand right behind the plate and snatch the sharpest of foul tips without flinching. In particular, he showed an astonishing proficiency at handling the deliveries of his battery partner William "Cherokee" Fisher, who pitched with "cyclonic speed" but little control. Tales of the synchronicity between Fisher and Craver continued to be told for years afterward, with an account of a game written two decades later claiming that the way the pair "worked together that day will ever remain a part of the base ball history of the country."

So it seems fair to credit Nat Hicks and William Craver with being the leaders of a revolution that changed baseball. They didn't start the practice of standing close to the plate, and it is possible that Doug Allison or some now-forgotten catchers deserve a greater share of the credit. But Hicks and Craver unquestionably played crucial roles in forcing other catchers to follow their example or play another position. By doing so, they started what was a revolution in every sense of the word—one that would dramatically change how baseball would thereafter be played, who would participate in it, and what it would mean to American society.

The Knickerbockers and other early baseball clubs had been extensions of social clubs, and as a result the primary requirement for a position on their ball-playing clubs had been traits commonly shared with other members. By the 1860s, clubs had begun to admit members because of their baseball skills, a development that threatened the traditional notion of club membership. It also threatened something deeper: mid-nineteenth-century Americans' understanding of their relationship to God and their fellow men.

Americans had long since rejected the feudalistic Old World notion that a person's place in the social hierarchy was determined by God and that to try to advance one's station was to quarrel with the deity. They embraced the heady concept of progress and encouraged self-improvement. Yet at the same time they remained deeply attached to the idea of a divinely approved social order, which meant that advancement was an unsettling concept. By and large, Americans of the era approved of allowing people to climb the social ladder as long as their ascent occurred within strict limits. Specifically, the ability of less fortunate Americans to improve their lots had to be perceived as not coming either at the expense of the more fortunate or in a context that could upset the hierarchy.

This was a delicate balance to maintain, with the result that baseball made many people uncomfortable. In particular, there was staunch resistance to any suggestion that innate physical ability was the primary determinant of success in playing baseball. While we now accept this concept without much thought, it was troubling to nineteenth-century Americans because of the implication that the social hierarchy might not have divine approval. Perhaps this was one of the reasons why Stephen Crane's clergyman father was so opposed to baseball—and why Stephen himself became so passionate about the game.

Because of this issue, defenders of baseball went to extraordinary lengths to present the game as a test of character rather than just of physical prowess. The rhetoric that was used to do this was revealing. Baseball was constantly depicted as an activity that rewarded teamwork, discipline, patience, calm under pressure, practice, and good judgment. The game's most prominent sportswriter, Henry Chadwick, maintained: "The captain of a nine should be a good general player: and if he excels as a catcher, all the better, for that is his place in the field. . . . His moral qualifications should certainly include self-control, quickness of observation, good judgment, determination of character, a manly love of fair play, and gentlemanly deportment, to the extent, at least of keeping silent when accidental errors are committed by the fielders, and also in regard to the manner in which he issues his orders to his nine. His physical requisites should include the ability to occupy any position in the field creditably in case of emergency. But especially it is necessary that the captain of a nine should be well up in all the points of the game, and on the watch to take advantage of the errors of the opposing nine; and he should also be well posted in strategy, and especially be proof against despondency when the odds are against him in a match, and fortune frowns on him."

This was a message that Chadwick never missed an opportunity to hammer home. In his worldview, baseball was a test of character, and in the long run the team that showed superior "moral qualifications" would beat one with better raw talent. And, as the passage suggests, the leadership shown by the catcher was the key to developing the all-important teamwork and discipline.

In this context, the repositioning of the catcher led by Hicks and Craver raised another complication. The bravery that this decision required was undeniable and, with the Civil War still a recent memory, no one was about to raise questions of the value of courage. Yet were these catchers demonstrating courage or mere recklessness? Bravery during war was deemed heroic because it was done in the name of a great cause, but taking such risks during a baseball game seemed far less noble. Chadwick had special reason to be disturbed by this development since his half-brother, Sir Edwin Chadwick, had become one of the first great public health crusaders in England, and he too was constantly defending baseball as a healthful form of recreation. The sight of severely injured catchers undercut such messages.

The crucial role played by injuries also made it more difficult to depict baseball as a test of character in which teamwork made the difference between winning and losing. This became particularly evident in 1872 when two of the game's premier catchers, Doug Allison and Jim White, both experienced subpar seasons. Both were known for their integrity, and Chadwick couldn't even bring himself to consider the possibility that injuries had been a factor. But this left him in the awkward position of trying to argue that character could go into a slump.

Chadwick was forced to attribute Allison's struggles to "obstinate fits [that] come on him at times when things don't work as satisfactory to him as he thinks they should," and to blame White's off-year on "a lack of harmony in the nine he played with. The fact is, no catcher can play with the ability his skill and experience warrant unless he works with a superior team in the field, willing and able to back up his own strenuous exertions to win. A catcher may work like a beaver behind the bat, and yet by the careless play of the pitcher or the batsman his efforts may be rendered useless." These were not very convincing explanations, and as injuries to catchers became more frequent and more severe, their implausibility became increasingly evident.

The outsized role being assumed by the catcher and pitcher raised yet another troubling issue. As the 1870s progressed, it became more obvious that these two men could succeed *without* the backing of a good team. This development further undercut the cherished notion that teamwork was the key to baseball success, and, still more disturbingly, it again raised the specter that a single player could fix the outcome of a match.

William Craver, in particular, did much to heighten this concern. The renown he earned for his skill at handling "Cherokee" Fisher's fastballs while standing directly behind home plate was often overshadowed by his reputation for associating with gamblers. His Troy club was plagued by rumors of shady dealings during the 1860s, and following the 1870 season

Craver was formally expelled from baseball. He may well have been one of the players who prompted the Reverend Jonathan Crane to write in 1869 that "everyone connected with [baseball] seems to be regarded with a degree of suspicion." The 1870 banishment didn't stick, and Craver continued to have no trouble finding work in baseball, even after being publicly assaulted by a gambler in 1876, suggesting a double-cross. Finally Craver was banned for life after the 1877 season for his role in the National League's first game-fixing scandal. He returned to Troy and . . . became a policeman.

Hicks was a far less notorious character than Craver, but he too was the subject of occasional rumors and innuendos. Most of these concerned his sometimes thorny personality; there was never any solid evidence against him, and it is likely that he never fixed a game. Yet in a sense it didn't really matter. The outsized role that catchers had assumed meant that all eyes would be constantly upon them and that the finger of suspicion would be pointed whenever one of them had a poor game.

The catcher's new proximity to the batsman raised another concern. After the 1871 season, Henry Chadwick advocated a rule that would keep the catcher at least six feet from home plate. He explained: "The necessity for a rule of the kind has been apparent by the play of the last season. In fact, the position taken by some catchers who are apparently reckless of injuries in their strenuous efforts to take sharp fly tips close to the bat, has been such as to really amount to an obstruction to the batsman in striking at the ball."

Yet battles like this one could not be won by such voices of caution. While Chadwick had tried to link baseball to the Civil War by stressing the need for military concepts like teamwork and discipline, and by borrowing terms like "battery," war veterans like Hicks and Craver saw a very different parallel—the one between the catcher and the soldier who bravely places himself in the line of fire. This image resonated in the imaginations of countless younger men who had grown up hearing tales of Civil War heroism from their fathers and uncles and who were beginning to see catching as the way to earn their own badges of courage. In an 1875 game, for example, Dave Pierson "played so close to the bat that the White Stocking batters were annoyed, and in taking position [Scott] Hastings and [Mike] Golden objected to his position, putting their bats playfully on the back of his head as a gentle reminder of what might take place." But a "gentle reminder" would not accomplish much with someone trying to prove his manhood. As this suggests, the ability to bear up under excruciating pain often seemed to be the whole point of being a catcher in the early 1870s.

From every town in the country came tales of the toughness of a local hero. Tim Murnane described Billy Barnie as "one of the pluckiest catchers the game ever produced," adding that when Barnie caught hard-throwing Mike Golden in 1875, he "usually looked like a boy who had passed his hands under a trip-hammer after a game." An 1880 game ended in spectacular fashion "with a singular 'assist' credited to Barnie. He was catching, when a foul ball hit him squarely in the forehead and rebounded to the pitcher, who captured it squarely on the fly. Barnie, although stunned at first, was all right in a few minutes." In another game Barnie, "with vast thoughtlessness, attempted to stop one of ["The Only"] Nolan's balls with the index finger of his right hand. The finger had already been benumbed into blue frigidity and so snapped off short at the root of the finger nail." That hideous injury at least caused Barnie to leave the game "to have his hand dressed," but many catchers earned the admiration of onlookers by shaking off horrifying injuries and insisting on playing. An early Buffalo ballplayer maintained that "our catcher worked through a game with the blood dripping from his bruised hands. Only for the most serious injuries did a player ever quit the game." Terre Haute catcher "Brockie" Anderson "was struck on the end of his little finger on the right hand by a foul ball breaking the finger at the second joint and otherwise mutilating it. As a convincing proof of his pluck he wanted to continue in the game, but was prevented by his friends." A catcher from Salisbury, Maryland, named "Gid" Jordan "with bursted hands and blood trickling down his arms, caught like a fiend" until a game played in the early 1880s was well in hand and it was deemed safe to put in a substitute. Cornell University catcher John Humphries was ordered not to play because of an injury to his hand, "but would not give in and caught through the game, suffering all the time. When he got through his hand looked as though encased in a boxing-glove."

Particularly striking was how matter-of-factly catchers referred to their injuries. In 1879, John Clapp and Cal McVey were playing in California when a naive reporter made the mistake of telling them about a few minor injuries he had received while playing baseball. By way of response, "The veterans of the diamond field smiled at his words, and Mr. Clapp quietly remarked that he, too, had been slightly hurt on one or two occasions. Pointing to a scarcely noticeable hollow in his left cheek bone, he said that one side of his face had once been knocked in by a hot ball. His left eye had been closed once, his right eye three times, and his nose broken. 'From 1873 to 1877,' continued he, 'I was very fortunate, and not the slightest

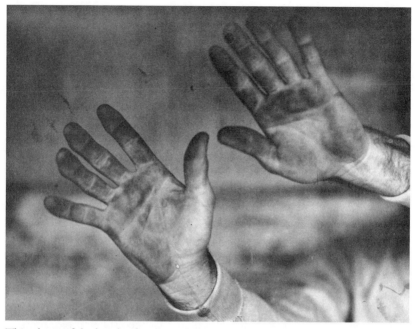

This photo of the hands of early-twentieth-century catcher George Gibson graph-ically illustrates the abuse that catchers took. Both of Gibson's sons became doc-tors, and when one decided to x-ray Gibson's right hand he "couldn't believe the number of times each finger had been broken." *(Courtesy of Frank Ceresi)*

accident occurred to me. I have been lucky this season also, and the only accident has been the knocking off of a finger nail.' McVey also told of a broken eyebrow and a few other unpleasant occurrences of like nature."

Likewise, Doug Allison's hands were turned into masses of "knotted and twisted joints" by the constant pounding of his calling. But in the tradition of the man for whom actions spoke louder than words, Allison nonchalantly referred to these injuries as "monuments for work well done" and found it amusing to recount stories about "how often he had been 'put to sleep' by catching foul tips in the face by mistake or winded by [pitcher] Asa Brainard's inshoots landing in his solar plexus."

Clearly Allison and his fellow catchers subscribed to the notion of heroism best summed up in Ralph Waldo Emerson's observation that the "false prudence which dotes on health and wealth is the butt and merri-ment of heroism." Perhaps they also recognized their battered hands as another sign of kinship with the cowboy, who was similarly known for having disfigured hands. These accounts of catchers' otherworldly stoicism in the face of unbearable pain frequently depicted the ordeal as a way of proving one's manhood. Charley Snyder of Louisville, for example, was described as "plucky, facing the hottest delivery and taking his knocks and bruises like a man."

The most legendary hands of the era were those of longtime Chicago catcher "Silver" Flint, who gave a reporter a guided tour of his disfigured paws in 1888. Indicating the gnarled forefinger on his left hand, he explained, "[Chicago pitcher] Larry Corcoran gave me this. It happened in Cleveland several years ago. Corcoran had pitched one of his straight drops. When I saw that the ball was going to strike the ground close to the batsman I placed my hands on the ground to block the drop, but I got them perhaps two inches too far away and the ball, which fell like a chunk of lead, struck this finger and crushed it to the bone. It did not pain me much at the time, but the next day the finger looked like the letter 'S,' and it has not straightened out much since. The finger is about the worst one I have in the collection." He also credited Corcoran with five other misshapen fingers: "He was the worst pitcher I ever caught. I mean by that, that he was the hardest on my fingers. I did not wear a glove in those days, and this accounts for a great many of the nasty knocks I received."

Two more of Flint's fingers had been "knocked out" when he was still an amateur, which meant that by the mid-1880s only his two middle fingers appeared normal. By then Corcoran was no longer a teammate and Flint had begun wearing gloves, so it seemed that those two digits would remain intact. Alas, that was not the case, as Flint explained while ruefully pointing to the middle finger of his right hand: "The battered finger I got in Pittsburg last season. It was in that famous fourteen inning game, when [Chicago pitcher John] Clarkson and [Pittsburgh pitcher Pud] Galvin were pitching like 'a house on fire.' The Pittsburgs had a man on third, with one man out. A desperate play had to be made. [Pittsburgh catcher Fred] Carroll who was at the bat, knocked a stiff ground ball to [Chicago infielder Tommy] Burns, and the man on third made a dash for home. With one of his terrific wrist throws Burns sent the ball toward the plate in a straight line. I thought I could eat it up, it came so straight and pretty. By some inadvertence I thrust my fingers instead of my palms toward the ball, which struck squarely on the end of this big finger. Of course I dropped the ball, and Pittsburg won the game by one run. That crook laid me up for two weeks. It shattered the bone and crushed the flesh so that blood flowed freely. [Now] I have but one straight finger—the great finger on my left hand."

Flint's onetime Chicago teammate, ballplayer-turned-evangelist Billy Sunday, added this testimonial: "I saw Flint get a hard one on his left hand, that split the poor fellow's fingers down a clean inch. Quick as a flash he reached for his shirt pocket, grabbed a rubber band, snapped it around his bleeding fingers, and gave a signal for another ball. Every finger on both of poor old Flint's hands had been broken at some time or another, and there was never a man who had as many marks to show for the game." Chicago semipro catcher Byron Clarke similarly recalled that Flint's "hands were so broken up that he could hardly hold a knife and fork. His hands were all thumbs, best expressed it, and we could hardly stand to sit at the table and see him eat."

As remarkable as Flint's hands appeared, people still couldn't resist the urge to indulge in blatant fabrications. In one popular story Flint and his Chicago teammates called on President Grover Cleveland at the White House, and "each member, of course, shook hands with the President. When the President's hand was released by 'Old Silver' the President was seen to quickly thrust it into the pocket of his coat. Then he felt about in his pocket a bit, took his hand out and looked at it with some surprise, remarking:—'Oh, I beg pardon; I thought you had given me a handful of walnuts.'" In another tale Flint was involved in a severe railroad accident and regained consciousness to find a surgeon examining him: "The gnarled fingers of the old catcher attracted attention and he started to place the fingers in splints. He had succeeded in getting one finger bound securely between splints when Silver asked: 'What the devil are you doing?' 'Mending your broken fingers,' replied the surgeon. Flint laughed and said, 'Doc, you are wasting your time. I am the catcher of the Chicago Base Ball Club.'"

The "mangled hands" of Jim "Deacon" McGuire also became "frequent subjects of sport photography and next to 'Silver' Flint . . . he was the most battered and bruised player that ever had a career in major ball." By the end of his lengthy career, many of the fingers on his gnarled hands had been broken several times, and nearly every one of his finger joints was "inlayed." An especially gruesome incident occurred when Detroit pitcher "Wild Bill" Donovan lived up to his nickname. As McGuire told it, "It was one of the wildest pitches Bill ever made and you know he made a lot of 'em. There was a man on first and I called for a pitch-out. Bill caught the signal and it was a pitch-out all right. I put out my hand and the ball caught the tip of my finger and bent it back stripping the flesh from the bone. Bob Emslie was umpiring back of the plate and took a look at it and fainted dead away." Yet like so many catchers, McGuire bore such injuries "without a murmur." And when someone suggested that the injury from the Donovan pitch must have kept him out of action for a long time, Mc-Guire replied matter-of-factly, "No, I was back in play before a week had ended—we were short of catchers."

In some instances it seemed as if this toughness was a trait shared by the entire ball club. Dan Loderick, for instance, was the star catcher for the Coal Heavers of Wilkes-Barre, Pennsylvania, in the early 1870s. In a game against the neighboring town of New Haven, "Things were going along swimmingly for the Coal Heavers, they having a good lead, when a foul tip caught Loderick on the middle finger of his right hand—no gloves or masks were used for protection in those days—and when the rooters saw 'Dan' dancing in agony about the plate their hopes for a big victory were dashed to earth. The plucky Loderick soon resumed his place behind the bat amid tumultuous cheers which were heard away over 'Deadhead' Hill and clear to the Empire. A short time thereafter a corking red hot foul took Dan squarely in the nose and the blood flew in every direction. A physician said Loderick's smelling apparatus was broken, and he should not play. That announcement made the New Haven boys dance in glee, for they felt confident that with Loderick out of the way they would have a cinch in bagging a victory."

Instead Loderick changed places with the team's second baseman, who proved just as adept behind the plate. Amazed, the visiting captain asked the Wilkes-Barre pitcher, "How much of that kind of timber have you in this star aggregation?" "This timber," replied the pitcher proudly, "is all alike. Some days we knock out half a dozen catchers, but we have no men on this team who can't go behind the bat and do the same kind of work."

Likewise, one early sportswriter recalled that when Troy Haymakers catcher Bill Craver's "hand had lost so many finger nails that he could no longer hang on to the ball," he was replaced by "Mart" King. King was not as skilled as Craver, but he was every bit as tough: "'Mart' was a hero in purpose if not a star in performance. No hurt could drive him out of the game. He, too, spurned all protection contrivances. Once a foul tip landed squarely between his eyes. It didn't even knock him down. He winced a little, shook his head, and went on with the game."

The assertion that King "spurned all protection contrivances" was quite literally true. Built on the "massive lines of a battleship," King shared his generation's characteristic "sneer for the cautious, so that there wasn't on or about him a sign of a glove, a mask or a liver pad." But he took this disdain to still greater extremes, as he proved when he joined the Haymakers and contemptuously referred to his new teammates as "dudes." When his outraged teammates demanded an explanation, King merely pointed to the caps on their heads and the shoes on their feet.

"Why the cap?" he asked indignantly. "It'll make you bald if you keep on wearing it—it will, sure's you're a foot high. Whaffor the shoes? Don't you know they'll send you to the chirop's? Sure they will. Can all that soft stuff." His new teammates could not resist this dare, and the Haymakers soon became noted for wearing neither caps nor shoes. King, meanwhile, came to be regarded as "a popular idol because of his strength and willingness and achievement."

Mart King further enhanced his reputation for toughness by insisting on treating his own injuries. "A finger nail torn from its roots meant nothing to him," recalled one sportswriter. "He would wrap a rag around it and go on with the game." Many other catchers expressed a similar disdain for medical advice. Bob Ferguson reported that catchers experienced their greatest trouble "with the knuckles, which become bruised, and the slightest touch causes the most intense pain. . . . I have known catchers' hands to become numb by constant pounding. Catchers have a hard time of it. They have to take good care of a staved finger, or the joint water will gather into one spot and become a callous substance, leaving a big lump. The only way to get rid of this is to rub the bruised spot frequently. I have removed several lumps from my finger in that way."

As Ferguson's comments suggest, the catcher's long experience with hand injuries made him uniquely qualified to tend to them. After every game, for example, Silver Flint rubbed "into his palms a mixture of alcohol, lemon juice, and rock salt, the effect of which is to render the skin tough and at the same time pliable, and thus to avoid cracks and splits. In the case of stone bruises or sprains he uses Pond's Extract, often working upon the injured part into midnight and after. In the Chicago-Cincinnati game of four innings and a half, which was played in the rain, Flint got a severe stone bruise on one of his joints, and he sat up till 3 o'clock the next morning rubbing that bruise with the Extract until every particle of inflammation had been overcome, and instead of being laid off for a week, as would have been the case had he neglected his hands, he caught in the next as though nothing had happened."

A California sportswriter portrayed this self-sufficiency as a tradition passed down from the first generation of catchers to venture close to the plate. He explained that if a West Coast catcher's "hand became split or a finger broken players followed the old trick of 'Poss' Miller of the Eckford team of Brooklyn, who came to California in 1863. For a break they just tied it up in a cat gut, and for a split they used a little hot paraffin or a little rosin."

As implied by these descriptions, the position's constant pounding often did more damage than any specific injury. "On a hot day," Jim O'Rourke would recall, "when the blood circulated freely, the catcher's hands would swell about the third inning. When swelling started the pain caused by impact with the ball decreased, because the swollen flesh made sort of a cushion. But on a cold day, when the blood did not course freely, and the hands would not swell, the pain was intense. I have seen catchers hold a piece of soft rubber in their mouths, and whenever the ball was pitched they would screw up their faces and bite on the rubber as hard as they could to offset the pain. On a warm day I have heard a catcher say proudly, along about the middle of the game, 'Oh, I am getting along fine—my hands are swelling up in great shape.'"

And of course the hands were not alone in enduring this abuse. Remember Ban Johnson's comment that "By the finish of the season I was always black and blue from head to foot," even to the extent of being "oftentimes unable to wear a hat by reason of the bumps and lumps"? O'Rourke confirmed, "My head has been so sore from being hit that I could not think and my hands so sore from catching that I could not hold an orange tossed from a distance of six feet."

Catchers were tough, tough guys.

3

The Catcher as Indispensable

"The backstop in a team was everything then, for wild curves, rising and drop balls, and gattling [sic] gun speed were new factors in the game."
—*Elmira Telegram* (1904)

WHILE TOUGHNESS was the most conspicuous attribute of catchers of the early 1870s, it was becoming clear that they also needed tremendous skill. The difficulty of finding someone who could satisfy both requirements meant that a good catcher was indispensable.

Although clubs liked to boast that they could replace their catcher if needed, it was becoming obvious that that wasn't true. When the pitcher from Wilkes-Barre bragged that any member of his team could go behind the bat and do exceptional work, everyone understood that this was just a boast. Similarly, the description of Mart King filling in for Bill Craver stressed that King "was a hero in purpose if not a star in performance"—in other words, King could match Craver's toughness but not his skill. Most clubs were simply lost if their catcher couldn't continue.

Moreover each passing year brought new changes that increased the catcher's stature and the uniqueness of his role. In 1865 the rules had at last been changed so that fielders could no longer record an out by catching a batted ball on the first bounce. An exception, however, was made for foul balls, and this underscored the reality that the catcher was now distinguished from his teammates in both the nature and the importance of his duties. Of course the role of the pitcher was also on the rise, but there was a crucial difference between the two players. The pitcher had acquired his added importance by bending the delivery rules and, worse, by doing so while standing in the middle of the diamond in plain view of everyone. He thus appeared more than ever to be a usurper. In stark contrast, the catcher fit the classic mold of the American hero because he was merely responding to his changed surroundings. He boldly strode closer to the plate, at great personal peril, not because he sought glory but because his teammates needed him.

The distinction between the two men continued to widen in the 1870s. The shutout, so recently an almost unheard-of phenomenon, became commonplace as batters were puzzled by curveballs and, when they did connect, were thwarted by the dead ball. So teams began to try to steal bases and gain a precious run, which brought another of the catcher's skills to prominence and made him seem still more indispensable.

Predictably, the sudden and dramatic nature of these trends provoked a backlash, but when it came it took a somewhat surprising and revealing form. Games in which the pitcher dominated were greeted with disdain—no-hitters were ignored by the press while games that featured a great many strikeouts evoked impatience and anger among spectators. Shutouts, by contrast, were treated with respect and even reverence, suggesting that they were considered to be the result of the pitcher receiving excellent support from his teammates.

It was as though everyone else in baseball had ganged up on the pitcher and, since they couldn't stop him from taking the scoring out of the game, were trying to deprive him of the credit for it. Baseballs began to feature still less rubber: the debut of the National League in 1876 coincided with the announcement that "The regulation ball to be used by the professional clubs this season is the 'all-yarn ball,' without the customary ounce of rubber in it." Meanwhile pitchers' release points continued to rise, creating more speed and more curveballs. This tended to make the pitcher less indispensable, since more pitchers were able to generate the great speed and master the deceptive curveballs that had once been the preserve of a select few.

For catchers, these developments accentuated the paradox that Nat Hicks had acknowledged when he moved closer to the plate. Ever speedier pitching and often rocklike balls made it still more dangerous to stand close to the batter. But at least the reward had increased, with a growing appreciation for the scarcity of catchers who were ready to place themselves in the line of fire.

No one appreciated or described this reality better than Frank L. Smith of Janesville, Wisconsin. Smith had firsthand understanding of the subject because he pitched for that town's first notable club, the Mutuals, in the early seventies. When he sat down in 1905 to write a history of baseball in Janesville, his recollections abounded with references to the catcher's crucial role.

He noted, for example, that in 1871 the team consisted of eight players who "proved to be the best that had represented Janesville up to that date, but unfortunately we were minus a catcher." And it soon became evident that this one deficiency undermined the entire team: "'Carley' Moon volunteered to catch, but he was unable to handle the balls delivered by 'Duck' Sutherland who then made his debute [sic] as a pitcher, being much the best that had worn a Mutual uniform up to that time. With a fair catcher we would have held our opponents down to a very few runs." Instead the Mutuals barely eked out a 20-19 win.

Baseball kept a low profile in Janesville until 1875, and then a renewed push to assemble a topflight nine was thwarted by a familiar problem: "The catcher wore no mask, gloves or pad and it was no real picnic to stand up behind the bat for nine innings. Those of our men who could at all play the position were liable to be laid up with sore hands or would have a feeling of timidity on account of being hit by a foul tip, so the result of some games depended altogether on how we were fixed behind the bat."

Smith thought a solution might be at hand when he discovered a young player named Abe Allen from nearby Milton. Allen had all the requisite skills to become a great catcher, except courage. As Smith tactfully put it, "it looked to me as though he would make a good catcher if his one great weakness of watching the bat instead of the ball could be overcome." So the two put in long hours in a local park, "striking at balls, which I just missed, in order to give him confidence and divert his mind from the bat."

Smith's confidence in the young catcher was rewarded when Allen led the Mutuals to an 18-4 upset of the mighty Forest Citys of Rockford. "Allen's catching and throwing to bases," recalled his proud mentor, "were simply perfection, inspiring the balance of the nine with a confidence that resulted in the finest exhibition of base ball playing ever exhibited by a Janesville nine, and which would have easily defeated any non-professional nine in the west." Yet in the club's next game, Allen was hit between the eyes with a foul tip. He tried to return in the following game but "had not recovered from the blow received at Elgin and try as he would, could not overcome the fear of a repetition, thereby weakening us to a great extent behind the bat, which exerting its natural influence upon the balance of the nine resulted in our defeat by a score of 18 to 10."

The 1876 season again began with high hopes, as the Mutuals now were backed by a stock company that allowed them to hire paid professionals and tour extensively. But far too much of the budget was spent on an often absurd search for a reliable catcher. Future major leaguer John Morissey began the season as the team's catcher and "possessed the ability all right but his hands would not stand the work." Another local named Joseph Doe was tried next, "but his pardonable fear of foul tips off the bat rendered his efforts very uncertain." And while the stockholders were willing to pay top dollar to bring in a replacement, "no catcher seemed available so we had to jog along in the best way possible."

The futility of this course became evident when the Mutuals' big summer tour reached St. Paul, Minnesota. An embarrassing 34-11 loss prompted Smith to write with disgust, "having no catcher the game was a farce and the gate money should have been refunded." The loss forced the club to resort to desperate measures: "something had to be done in a business way as we were fast losing our reputation and consequent drawing power. So we finally decided to fix up a pair of gloves for [John] Morissey, padding the palms and cutting off the fingers." The result was more proof of how essential a catcher was, as the Mutuals won the rematch 15 to 8. As Smith wryly commented, "These two games showed our nine without a catcher and with a catcher as 34 to 11 is to 8 to 15—no prizes for a correct answer."

Even with the gloves, Morissey's hands were so sore after the game that he "refused to catch" in the next contest. One of the team's infielders pluckily volunteered to catch one game and did so very well, but afterward his "hands were a sight to behold." A professional from Chicago was brought in for the next game, but he too was unable to bear up under the tremendous punishment.

As a result, Smith's accounts of the games of the ensuing month sounded a familiar refrain. Of a loss in Milwaukee he wrote sadly, "if we could have traded our three catchers for [Milwaukee catcher Frank] Bliss, the result of the game would have been reversed. Three different catchers in one game with nine passed balls—as far as they were concerned, I might as well have been pitching to the wide, wide world." Smith's account of another game noted wearily that while pitching, "he had his usual compliment [sic] of catchers before the game ended."

These setbacks prompted the directors to continue bringing in Chicago professionals until "our nine was becoming very much Chicago." After one especially bad loss, the Mutuals turned to a new catcher named

Leslie with extraordinary results: "It seems almost incredible that the same nine could on consecutive days play such entirely dissimilar games . . . but most of the discrepancy is accounted for by the fact of our having a catcher whose work behind the bat steadied the balance of the nine. The writer was sent in to pitch with Leslie at the receiving end of the battery, where they remained during the entire nine innings and I think all the real pleasure derived from playing the pitcher's position during the summer was concentrated in that one game—Leslie catching in almost faultless style—and the balance of the nine entering into the spirit of the occasion with a zest that was certainly encouraging."

But Leslie soon departed, without making enough of an impression for his given name to be recorded, and the team again began to struggle. Accordingly, Smith ended his summary of the season by concluding: "A first class battery would have helped us physically and financially, but this we were unable to secure in spite of our efforts. Players came here highly recommended and the mistake we made was in not dropping them at once instead of assigning them to other positions that could have been better taken care of by home talent."

This was an astute yet sobering reflection of the state of baseball in 1876. Rubberless baseballs and new pitching tactics had all but eliminated batting and in turn rendered fielding of comparatively little value—as long as the defensive team had a catcher who was skilled and healthy enough to handle the pitcher's best deliveries. If no such catcher was available, as Smith bluntly put it, the game became a farce.

Just as apparent in Smith's comments is that the formula for baseball success had become rather simple: spend all your money and efforts on procuring a good catcher and pitcher, and fill in the other seven positions with local men. That was precisely what Janesville did in 1877, signing two up-and-coming youngsters from Pennsylvania, pitcher John Montgomery Ward and catcher Albert "Doc" Bushong. The selections proved brilliant. Ward went on to a Hall of Fame career while Bushong, destined to become one of the game's best defensive catchers, "played in every game during the season, without mask or gloves, and was never hit in the face or troubled with sore hands—a remarkable record." Thus the Mutuals' 1877 season was marked by the consistency that had been so absent in the two preceding years.

Although Frank Smith articulated this state of affairs with special poignancy, there was nothing remotely unique about the situation in Janesville. The organizers of baseball clubs in towns all over the country were discovering that a good battery was of such importance that the other seven players were rendered all but irrelevant. The good news was that this prompted a flurry of activity, as even small towns figured it was worth trying to sign a professional battery and perhaps get lucky by suddenly having a ball club capable of competing with the country's largest cities. But this enthusiasm was typically short-lived, as the vast majority of these hired hands failed to live up to expectations.

The other seven members of the team naturally resented seeing so much attention lavished on two players. In some cases it seemed as though the catcher was the only player who mattered. A dramatic illustration of this attitude took place in 1878 when a club from Chicago arrived in Muskegon, Michigan, for a much-anticipated game. Controversy arose before the game could begin when the Chicago club found that its own catcher had been hired to play for the home side. The catcher admitted that he had agreed to play for the Muskegon team on this date, but explained that he had not been told that his own club would be the opponents. Meanwhile the host team maintained that they had no choice but to use the visiting team's catcher because their own catcher was "lame" and unable to play. When the Chicago team protested that this arrangement would leave them without a catcher, they were offered the use of the same Muskegon catcher who was purportedly too badly injured to play. What other players thought about this wrangle was not recorded.

Even for pitchers and catchers, this attention was a mixed blessing. The members of a new battery found themselves hailed as saviors upon their arrival in town—for instance, in 1877 when a club in Evansville believed it had signed left-handed curveball pitcher Robert Mitchell and his catching partner, team management took out a large advertisement in the local paper proclaiming: "IMMENSE ATTRACTION! ROBERT MITCHELL, THE GREAT LEFT-HAND PITCHER . . . [and] GEORGE MILLER, who has caught Mitchell successfully for several years." But inevitably many of these batteries didn't live up to sky-high expectations, and bitterness ensued. In the case of the Evansville club, the announcement of the signing of Mitchell and Miller proved premature, and both players were roundly denounced for the false hopes that had been raised. The expectations of other towns were dashed when the imported pitcher's curveball proved less mystifying than suggested by the advance notices, or when the catching half of the duo succumbed to injury.

At first excuses could be made, and newspapers were filled with apologetic notes explaining that a defeat would not have occurred "if catcher

'Joe' had not had his hands battered to the consistency of a puff ball."
Eventually, however, such alibis began to ring hollow, and the truth had to
be admitted. An 1879 game in St. Johns, Michigan, for example, was billed
as an important event because the visitors from the nearby town of Riley
"would bring a curve pitcher and professional catcher." But the spectators
went home disappointed when the catcher was injured in the first inning
and "the curve in the pitching seemed to result from the attraction of
gravitation more than anything else."

Even in the rare instances when a new pitcher and catcher were as
good as advertised, the situation could turn unpleasant if rival clubs began waving money at the rising stars. When a Detroit club hired pitcher
James A. Sullivan and catcher Edward Brown from Pittsburgh in 1876,
the team's play improved dramatically. Hopes were high as an upcoming
road trip approached, but neither Sullivan nor Brown showed up for the
train. Annoyance gradually turned to suspicion, and then to anger when
Sullivan was tracked down and he calmly explained that the two men were
jilting Detroit because they had been promised more money by a team in
Guelph, Ontario.

The anguish over losing the heart and soul of the club extended to the
entire community. One of the team's supporters was moved to capture the
traumatic loss in verse:

Now Mr. Sullivan! come back!
That run was hardly fair,
Though we have loved to see you "curve"
We'd like to see you square

Your "strike" is certainly too base!
Ah if you only knew
The while you pitch in Canada
How we pitch into you!

Oh, Hearken! For the proverb says
That pitchers do have ears—
"Come home!" "come home!" and dissipate
Our Cass begotten fears

And Mr. Brown, perhaps you think
You're quite a catch at Guelph!
But did it e'er occur to you
You're sure to catch yourself?

What was it, pray, that "forced you off!"
Maybe the need of "rocks"
Ah, well, a man who gobbles "fouls"
Is sly as any fox

You might have seen with half an eye—
But what's the use of that?
In your ability to see
You're quite "behind the bat"

But do not think to stop the ball—
We're not to be coerced,
We only grieve we didn't think
To "put you out at first"

Even major league clubs were unduly dependent on their battery. Boston had the best duo of the early to mid-seventies, pitcher A. G. Spalding and catcher Jim "Deacon" White, and dominated the first professional league, the National Association. By 1875 the Red Stockings had become so invincible that they started the season with twenty-three straight victories, the streak ending only when White had to sit out a game with a hand injury. Midway through that season Chicago signed Spalding, White, and two other key Boston players to contracts for the 1876 campaign. The signing played a major role in the National Association being replaced by the National League and in Chicago winning the new league's first championship.

After only a single year in Chicago, White decided to return to Boston, and so did the 1877 pennant, while the White Stockings nosedived to fifth in a six-team league. Although injuries and Spalding's decision to give up pitching contributed to Chicago's precipitous decline, neither was the main reason. To fill Spalding's place, Chicago had signed George Bradley, who was regarded by many as the game's best pitcher after doing scintillating work for St. Louis in 1876. Before the season, Chicago star Cal McVey predicted, "if anybody hits Brad clean for a base hit this year it will be a scratch."

Unfortunately for Chicago and McVey, the team management did not sign Bradley's battery mate John Clapp, believing instead that one of their returning players could catch him. Initially there was talk of letting Cap Anson catch, but in the end it was McVey who handled most of the catching. McVey was one of the game's best hitters and had the dexterity and versatility to handle almost any defensive position. In the 1860s that had

In 1872 a director of the Boston club was sent to the hometown of Jim "Deacon" White to try to talk White out of retirement. The director soon encountered "a clerical-looking man, with a tall hat," and realized that it was the great catcher when he noticed that the man possessed a "pair of the hardest-looking hands I ever saw, and one finger [that] was badly smashed." White eventually agreed to come out of retirement and led Boston to four pennants in a career that lasted eighteen more seasons. *(National Baseball Hall of Fame Library)*

been all that was required of a catcher, but things had changed, especially in the case of a hard-throwing pitcher like Bradley, of whom one reporter noted, "to catch Bradley requires a man who can stop a cannon-ball, and very few are equal to the task."

By midseason it was apparent that the Chicago management had made a disastrous mistake. The error was not in signing Bradley, whose pitching prompted Henry Chadwick to write that "his superior has not been seen on the Union Grounds this season." The problem was that, as the veteran sportswriter noted, "[Bradley] requires a catcher *par excellence* to enable him to pitch with his best effort."

Others were less tactful about pointing the finger at McVey. A Chicago sportswriter bemoaned: "half the strength of a pitcher's play lies in his having not only a catcher fully competent to support him, but especially a catcher who is familiar with the pitcher's peculiar style of delivery. In taking Bradley from the St. Louis Club they only withdrew one half the strength of that club's battery. They should also have engaged Clapp, or should have made sure of being able to supply his place. They did neither, and the result is their present weakness in having no man behind the bat able to give Bradley the same efficient support he had in 1876." The writer concluded, "McVey is simply a change catcher. . . . he is not capable of filling the position of Bradley's assistant, as the experience of the past month's play has shown. His hands get puffed up too soon, for one thing." This assessment was confirmed by a game account in a St. Louis paper that noted, "McVey's hands were . . . beaten almost to a pulp. This no doubt had an injurious effect upon the game. He caught pluckily, of course, but Bradley sacrificed considerably of his own effectiveness to a desire to ease up on McVey as much as possible." In the words of the *Chicago Tribune*, McVey "was not, is not, and never can be a catcher, especially for such a man as Bradley . . . he is not a catcher, because of his aptitude to get sore hands and to weaken his pitcher by making him pitch over the plate too much. . . . In 1876 [Bradley] was given by Clapp's efforts a great leeway in his work, and no man used strategy more; but in 1877 he claims that he felt himself confined to a narrower circle by the necessity of always thinking about his catcher, and pitching to him."

Making the situation especially striking was that Chicago continued to feature a star-studded lineup. As the *New York Times* observed, "The Chicago players are very unfortunate in having no regular catcher able to give adequate support to their pitchers. In all other respects they are exceptionably [sic] strong, being possessed of two excellent pitchers and a very strong field of players to guard the bases and the out-field." Yet it scarcely mattered—the lack of a dependable catcher offset the prowess of eight of the game's best players. As we shall see, many other clubs of the 1870s were reduced to helplessness when a catcher left or was injured. A good catcher was truly indispensable.

4

The Catcher as One in a Million

"To be, or not to be: that is the question. . . . For who would bear the whips and scorns of time . . . who would fardels bear,/ To grunt and sweat under a weary life,/ But that the dread of something after death,/ The undiscover'd country from whose bourn/ No traveller returns, puzzles the will/ And makes us rather bear those ills we have/ Than fly to others that we know not of?"—*Hamlet*

"Who would be a candidate for the governorship and fardels bear (whatever fardels are) when a base-ball catcher is the hero of men and darling of the ladies, with $7,000 a year?"—*Boston Transcript* (1878)

AS IT BECAME CLEAR that the catcher was indispensable, the belief arose that the man who played the position must possess certain intangible characteristics. As early as 1872—five years before Chicago's unwise decision to make Cal McVey its everyday catcher—Henry Chadwick observed that "McVey is a catcher who is not *at home* in the position. He plays finely there as he would any where in the field, but he does not excel in that special position as others do." By the mid-1870s that sense had coalesced into a mystique in which the catcher was a man with a unique gift and a special calling.

Of course the pitcher was arguably just as essential, yet he continued to be haunted by the perception that he had sought his central role, grabbing some of the glory that by right should be shared by all nine players. This rendered the pitcher somewhat suspect, and his increased reliance on the evasive curveball made him seem even more of a trickster. The catcher, however, was perfectly suited for the model of the American hero, demonstrating courage, resourcefulness, skill, and leadership just when many Americans were looking for someone who embodied these traits.

"I used to travel with the Nationals and Olympics to all of their out-of-town games," one Washington, D.C., youngster later recalled. "[Harry] Berthrong was my beau-ideal of a catcher and a base runner of class A." Jim "Deacon" White "used to fill the small boys with awe and admiration—and the adults all shared the latter feeling—as he stood behind the bat and scooped the ball with cat-like quickness." Harvard catcher Archie Bush was looked up to as "one of the greatest catchers whom the game has ever seen. As he stood erect, close behind the batter, in an easy, graceful pose, glove-less, maskless, fearless, to those of us who remember him, he made a picture of what the ideal ballplayer should be." As a later commentator would recall, "In the old days the boys on the lot thought the greatest honor was behind the bat." It was this adulation that stirred the hearts of Stephen Crane, Byron Johnson, Wallie Walker, and countless other boys.

Paternal disapproval undoubtedly dimmed the ardor of some, but as is always the case, a parent's prohibitions can make things look all the more appealing. Like Crane and Johnson, Charley Bennett became a catcher "against his father's wishes," and no doubt he and many of his peers took secret pleasure in the opportunity to rebel. In Bennett's case he had the further satisfaction of being viewed by the next generation as "a perfect model . . . for years afterwards, to cultivate a position behind the bat, a la Bennett was considered the proper caper for young and aspiring catches [sic] to assume."

It didn't hurt that young women were also beginning to pay attention to baseball stars. Ball games had begun to function as mating rituals, with prime portions of the grandstand reserved so that the fair young belles of the community could watch some of its most eligible bachelors. Naturally the catcher's pivotal role often made him the object of the attention of these young women. One game account noted of Nat Hicks's catching that "quite a bevy of girls were looking at him, and when this is the case he catches in the highest style of the art." Another young lady reportedly confided to one of her friends that the local catcher was "just too brave for anything. We girls think he is the nicest one in every club. I think the catcher is very cute and heroic." Some catchers were suspected of going out of their way to attract this kind of notice, such as Frank Norton, who was chided for having "one bad fault, and that is endeavoring to make fancy catches when the ladies are on the ground. Those look pretty but are not safe."

Catchers could also realistically dream of becoming the pride and joy of their hometown. This was true even in some major league cities, where the boast of having a nonpareil catcher could give the locals pride in a very bad team. The city of Worcester, Massachusetts, for example, had a National League team for three seasons and finished in the cellar in two of those years. Local fans nonetheless took considerable consolation from the knowledge that they had "the star backstop of the country at the time," and they proudly boasted "that no catcher in the country was able even to unbuckle the latchet of 'Doc' Bushong's shoes." Detroit succeeded Worcester as the league's doormat—the team "was considered more or less of a joke up until 1885. However, it was the pride and boast of the Detroit fans to claim [that] in [Charley] Bennett they had the star catcher in the whole country."

This fierce hometown pride was especially apparent in smaller villages, where the local ball club often became a surrogate for the entire community. The famed attorney Clarence Darrow conveyed this nicely when writing about his youthful days on the baseball diamonds of Kinsman, Ohio: "When we heard of the professional game in which men cared nothing whatever for patriotism but only for money—games in which rival towns would hire the best players from a natural enemy—we could scarcely believe the tale was true. No Kinsman boy would any more give aid and comfort to a rival town than would a loyal soldier open a gate in the wall to let an enemy march in."

A talented catcher, in particular, could become the local standard-bearer. Long after leaving his native Ithaca for major league stardom, John Clapp returned to represent the town in key matches. On one occasion he left his major league team in the lurch in order to play for Ithaca in a big showdown with archrival Binghamton. When his major league team fined him for doing so, Clapp responded by switching teams at season's end. Needless to add, he was regarded as a hero in Ithaca.

The mystique of the catcher was further enhanced by the sense that his most important skills were internal ones, which became apparent only when tested. Most evidently, good catchers came in a wide variety of shapes and sizes during the 1870s. There were small men like Tommy Barlow, Little Joe Roche, Shorty Ewell, and Mike McGeary, whose agility and quickness allowed them to range far and wide to snatch balls. Nat Hicks was a large, powerfully built man who could use his body to absorb blows, and by the end of the decade he was being joined by others, such as "Silver" Flint and Lew Brown. Meanwhile Jim White and Charley Mills were both tall, slender men whose exceptional reach helped them corral errant pitches. Only fat men were not seen behind the plate in the 1870s; quickness was so vital that even talented catchers who put on weight were liable to find themselves out of a job.

Another essential qualification was great hands, but this too was difficult to quantify. Catching with bare hands demanded an entirely different technique from the method that became customary after fielding gloves came into use. As a 1910 article explained, "One thing that must be remembered is this: The method of taking a ball was absolutely different in the old time from the way we catch it now. The fielder of today does his best to receive the shock upon the thickly padded palm, and even burrows a pocket in the glove to insure the ball's coming against the palm at every whack. Not so in the long ago. In those days, when there were no gloves, or only these leather-tipped things for the catcher and first bagger, the palm was kept out of the way, if possible, for there was a swell chance for a stone bruise. Ever get one? Lordy! Lordy! How they hurt! and how they stick by you! The writer had one that lasted three years, but that is a digression. Anyway, the oldtimers aimed to catch the ball in a trap or spring box made of the fingers. They showed wonderful deftness in taking every pitch and every throw upon the fingers, and seldom letting it strike the palm. Once in a while, however, there was a miscue, and either a stone bruise or a split hand resulted. The fingers, too, gave way before the shock, and most of the oldtime players had their digits twisted, gnarled and horribly distorted."

But using the fingers to catch a hard ball meant that the technique had to be perfect in order to avoid injury. As Johnny Ward explained, "Some players catch with the fingers pointing toward the ball, but such men are continually being hurt. A slight foul-tip diverts the course of the ball just enough to carry it against the end of the fingers, and on account of their position the necessary result is a break or dislocation. But with the hands held [properly] there is a 'give' to the fingers and the chances of injury are much reduced. For a low ball the hands should be held so that the fingers point downward, and for a waist ball, by crouching slightly it may be taken in the same manner as a high ball."

This is a subtle skill, hard to notice from a distance and even harder to describe. When a catcher had the special knack for receiving the deliveries of a particular pitcher, his work looked almost effortless. Jim White was known as "a model for catchers in his style of handling the ball—that is, in his method of making his hands a sort of spring-box, by which he destroys half the force of the blow." A Syracuse reporter marveled that White

Catching great Charley Bennett demonstrates the proper catching technique of the early catcher—slightly stooped, with both hands together to catch the ball, and legs far apart to allow him to lunge in either direction after a foul tip or an errant pitch. *(Library of Congress)*

"seemed to be endowed with the ability to take whatever the pitcher sent no matter how 'hot' they came. He snatched them almost before they had time to pass the bat, and almost invariably in time to make them count 'one out' when there was a shadow of opportunity in that direction." Another put it more concisely: "White behind the bat is just simply perfection." Catching, when done by a great like White, seemed to entail nothing more than putting out your hands—note the plural, for catching was exclusively a two-handed activity—and choosing the perfect moment at which to pluck the ball out of the air.

Of course nothing could be farther from the truth. "Doc" Bushong maintained that one of the special gifts a catcher had to possess was "the skill or 'knack' required to catch a pitched ball after it has been struck at." He explained, "The fact of the bat going between the sight and the ball makes a sensation upon the mind. That makes a man invariably jump, throwing his hands and body away from the ball instead of standing perfectly still and reaching for it. To the million it is an impossibility to get rid of this feeling." Thus the natural catcher was a one-in-a-million occurrence.

In addition, only the natural catcher could resist the urge to reach out and try to grab a pitch prematurely. The specific term for this mistake was "fighting the ball." This phrase is still used today, but rather loosely, and few are aware that it once had a very specific and uncomplimentary meaning, being used when a player attempted to "get the ball before it reaches him." As John McGraw explained, the most basic precept for a catcher was that he "should not 'fight the ball,' that is, trying to catch it before it reaches his hands. Let the hands give with the ball, and at the same time bring the body in a position to throw, and to stop base running you must be able to get the ball away very quickly." It sounds easy, but most aspiring catchers found this to be another knack that either came naturally or not at all.

Since this technique sounded (and sometimes looked) so much easier than it actually was, descriptions began to depict it as a test of character. During an 1869 game in which Jim White was wowing the crowd, his opposite number "muffed four foul tips in the sixth innings, one after another, in the most chicken-hearted style, and disappointed the audience quite as badly as himself." Jack Doyle was just as blunt, observing that "ambitious but youthful back-stops" are often guilty of the fault that "is called among ball players 'fighting the ball.' By this I mean the man who is in too great a hurry to catch the ball. This overeagerness seems to be due to excessive nervous energy. The man who allows himself to become so excited will frequently try to catch the ball before it really gets to him. I once knew a catcher whose blood boiled so feverishly in a tight game that I have seen him grasp a ball even before the batsman had a chance to hit at it."

The greatest test of a catcher's courage came after he suffered an injury, because, as had happened to Frank L. Smith's protégé Abe Allen, such a player often developed a fatal fear of the ball. George Wright, who went on to a Hall of Fame career as the game's first great shortstop, began his career as a catcher. But, as he later admitted, "one day a foul tip struck me in the throat and it hurt me so much that I never afterward was able to muster up sufficient courage to catch."

This emphasis on catchers learning to be impervious to danger was another skill that suggested parallels to early American heroes. Most obvi-

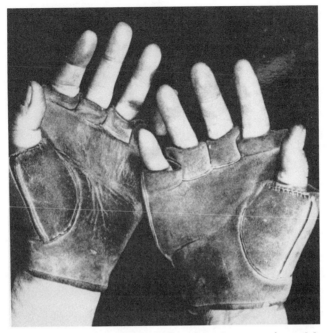

Catching was a two-handed activity before the mitt came along. Most of the catchers who wore gloves before 1888 cut the fingers off, which made it easier to throw. Since catchers grabbed the ball with their fingers, the gloves offered limited protection. As one former catcher explained after the adoption of the mitt, "The oldtimers aimed to catch the ball in a trap or spring box made of the fingers. They showed wonderful deftness in taking every pitch and every throw upon the fingers, and seldom letting it strike the palm. Once in a while, however, there was a miscue, and either a stone bruise or a split hand resulted." By contrast, "The fielder of today does his best to receive the shock upon the thickly padded palm, and even burrows a pocket in the glove to insure the ball's coming against the palm at every whack." *(National Baseball Hall of Fame Library)*

ously, their courage and resiliency recalls soldiers like Ulysses S. Grant, who could remain calm while bullets flew around them. It also suggests a compelling parallel to the skills of the Western gunslinger. The first requirement in a gunfight was being lightning-quick on the draw, but a quick trigger was of no value if the shooter rushed and missed his shot. "The most important lesson I ever learned," claimed Wyatt Earp, "was that the winner of a gunplay usually was the one who took his time." In the same way, the catcher needed the seemingly contradictory abilities of being cat-quick and yet also patient. So it is easy to see why overcoming a tendency to fight the ball came to be seen as the ultimate test of courage.

In catching, as in gunfighting, this skill affected the all-important ability to stay healthy. No catcher could avoid banged-up fingers, and even Jim White's hands eventually became "gnarled and his fingers crooked and distorted, widened at the tips." Yet White always managed to avoid incapacitating injuries. Some assumed that this was just a by-product of his long partnership with the soft-throwing Spalding, but White showed the same knack when paired with flamethrowers like Al Pratt. As an astute observer explained, "Part of a catcher's effectiveness lies in his ability to avoid punishing his hands and caring for his gloves. Men who fight the ball, as ['Doc'] Kennedy always did, are invariably unreliable, because of being hurt. The other extreme is Bushong, and the luck—as it is termed—of the two men is proverbial. One is always out and the other always in condition. Careful treatment of the hands—skillful, instead of rough and ready handling of the ball, and suitable gloves instead of using anything that may be available, is the difference in the men. Care pays." Long after his playing career ended, Fleetwood Walker was sharing tips on the art of catching barehanded without breaking fingers.

As these descriptions suggest, a knack for receiving a baseball instead of "fighting" it was also directly linked to the final essential requirement of the catcher: reflexes keen enough to dodge foul tips and thereby stay healthy. There was a strong hint of Darwinian natural selection in the frequent references to the catcher having to possess catlike quickness in order to survive. "As for the catcher, working behind the bat without a mask, glove or chest protector," explained reporter Will Irwin, "he had to be as graceful and quick as a cat, even to live." Irwin went on to describe how his uncle, John O'Neil, "retired in 1870 because a foul tip caught him in the hollow of a shoulder, just where the modern catcher is heavily protected, and spoiled his throwing forever." Another aspiring catcher named Jim Mutrie signed his first professional contract in 1875 with a club in Lewiston, Maine, but in his very first game he suffered a broken collarbone that ended his season; Mutrie instead went on to fame as a manager. By contrast, a man like early Atlanta star George Cassin was said to have "showed himself a born catcher. He was quick as lightning and active as a cat."

Consummate catchers like Jim White and Doc Bushong made staying out of danger look easy because of the "cool, quiet manner" in which they waited until the very last moment and then seemed to pluck the pitched ball out of the air. "When foul tips were 'out,'" recalled fellow catcher Byron Clarke, "there was no catcher like Jim White. He was called 'the cat' behind the bat, for he was the quickest man on earth back in the '70's." And this ability naturally was increased when a catcher was working with a familiar pitching partner. White's longtime battery partner, A. G. Spalding, credited White with being the "greatest natural catcher that I ever saw. . . . He was as quick as a cat."

The rare catcher who possessed these catlike reflexes also needed the courage to maintain his technique as the ball approached. "A catcher should not stand directly back of the plate," explained Johnny Ward, "but rather in line with its outside corner." Thus stationed, the catcher cut down the angles by which foul tips could hit him and gave himself a vital extra split second of reaction time. This stance also gave catchers what Will Irwin called "a system of protecting their heads and breasts with their arms." As Tim Murnane later recalled, in the mid-1870s it was considered "quite an art for a catcher to judge the angle of the ball as it sped over the plate. The catcher would turn his head to the right or left a trifle so that if the ball passed his hands it would not land full in the face. Not every catcher, however, was able to do this with ease and grace." On another occasion Murnane explained that a natural catcher's "head would always go in the opposite direction to the hand when taking the ball from the pitcher. This was to avoid foul tips, and the catcher that could not avoid getting foul tips in the face was considered as unnatural a man for the position as a player of the present time trying to work with both hands covered with big mits [sic]."

Once the curveball began to come into vogue in 1872, it became clear that no amount of toughness could overcome poor technique. Bill Craver epitomized pluck and perseverance, causing Chadwick to write in 1872, "We have never seen his superior in courage and endurance as displayed in the plucky facing of the hottest balls sent to the bat, and that patient bearing of the punishment incident to such work." Yet by then Craver's body was beginning to break down from the relentless abuse, and his technique was blamed. Chadwick explained, "With him it is simply bull dog perseverance in stopping swift balls pitched to him. . . . He never relieves himself by the skillful fielding, which, at the same time that it lessens the force of the blow to the hands, ensures more certainty of holding the balls, but he simply stops it suddenly while in the full power of its swiftest progress." And indeed, Craver, for all his courage, would struggle to remain a regular catcher after the advent of the curveball and higher release points. As Chadwick wrote of Craver's approach on another occasion, "It is, of course, plucky to do this, but it is a lamentable waste of pluck." For the catcher of the 1870s, staying healthy was the result of skill, not luck, and it was the most important skill he could have.

A catcher also needed to be expert at throwing to bases, but this too was a skill that looked easy only because the natural catcher could make it appear effortless. A strong throwing arm was a requirement for both members of the battery, but the similarities ended there. While the pitcher could take his time before releasing the ball, the catcher's success in throwing out base-stealers depended on his ability to make a fluid transition from catching to throwing. As he shifted from his stooped position to a throwing motion, he resembled nothing so much as a gunslinger (and indeed runners who are caught stealing are still often referred to as having been "gunned down" by the catcher). Buck Ewing, for instance, was said to be able to uncork a hard, accurate throw "from any position that he might be placed in. . . . He was right-handed and got the ball away from him with remarkable quickness and accuracy. Frequently he took no step when throwing and never threw from over his shoulder or head, but snapped the ball with a side arm swing that made the balls he threw strike a baseman's hand like a lump of lead." The comparison to a gunslinger was more explicit in a description of early Atlanta catching star George Cassin, who "could throw to second like a shot out of a shovel, often getting the ball to [second baseman Willis] Biggers before the runner measured half the ground from first."

The transition to throwing was made more difficult by the lack of padding on the catcher's hands. As a sportswriter later explained, before the introduction of the mitt the catcher's "fingers gave way" when the pitch arrived, "forming a sort of spring box to receive the shock. So heavy was the impact that the hand naturally, unconsciously recoiled, and the ball was delayed a fraction of a second before the catcher would gather it up and shoot it down to second. Short was that delay—only a passing instant—but that fleeting margin of time meant all in all to the hustling runner."

The proximity of the batter added another complication to the catcher's effort to throw out a base-stealer. "The catcher not only has to make a quick and accurate throw," explained "Doc" Bushong, "but he has to take into consideration the man at the bat. The latter is frequently in the way, or, if he is not, he tries to be. By either a motion of the body or bat, it is his aim to balk the catcher." Once again, whether a catcher displayed a strong throwing arm during practice sessions didn't really matter. It was only un-

As explained in this advertisement for catcher's gloves, the fact that they did not "interfere with throwing" was their most important feature. They were not expected to help catch the ball, since proper catching technique meant using the fingers. (*National Baseball Hall of Fame Library*)

der the pressure of a game situation that he could demonstrate whether he had the right stuff to be a successful catcher. As Bushong put it, "throwing to second base especially is the test by which most catchers are tried and found wanting."

Because so many of a catcher's most important skills revealed themselves only when tested, it became an article of faith that the defining attribute of a great catcher was character. A man who couldn't handle the pressure would inevitably lunge for pitches—at best he would be ill-prepared to throw out base-stealers or would muff the ball, while a more likely scenario would see him debilitated by injury. Meanwhile the right man would patiently wait until the perfect moment to receive the ball and thereby be ready for all events while also keeping out of harm's way.

The special gifts of the natural catcher gave him and his entire team confidence. Since he had faith in his ability to catch the ball cleanly, he felt no pressure to rush into his throwing motion when a runner tried to steal. Meanwhile, knowing that he would make a strong and accurate throw meant that he had no need to try to reach out early and "fight" the pitch. His confidence was in turn passed along to his teammates and even to fans. At the same time a catcher's lack of faith in his ability could be just as contagious. "No other position poorly played can cause so much distraction among spectators and one's own team," declared Bushong. "There is nothing like poor catching to make the opposing team strong and jubilant."

The sense that internal skills and the ability to handle pressure were the catcher's most crucial virtues naturally encouraged every young boy to dream of playing the position. So too did the fact that a catcher's defensive prowess was so critical to the team that he might succeed in spite of a total absence of key baseball skills. Many early catchers were extraordinarily feeble hitters. Of the twelve catchers who caught one hundred major league games in the 1870s, seven compiled slugging averages of less than .325 during the decade, and eight had on-base percentages below .300. Tommy Barlow was such a weak hitter that he began using a bat only two feet long and is often credited with inventing the bunt. Amateur catcher Dan Loderick also became renowned for the "bunt and run act."

Other catchers were so slow that they struggled with the most basic baserunning tasks. Wilbert Robinson was a legendary lead-foot, and reports that journeyman catcher Rudolph Kemmler had stolen a base prompted someone to quip that the base "must have been left out over night." Yet the humor was also a backhanded compliment: such shortcomings showed that there was no mold for catchers. Each catcher created his own. Once he proved under pressure that he could handle a great pitcher, nothing else really mattered. The catcher was *sui generis*.

The result was a near mystical sense that a catcher might prove to be the perfect complement for a specific pitcher. The aura of a supernatural bond was especially evident in a description of Chicago's efforts in 1874 to find a partner for hard-throwing pitcher Jim Devlin. Devlin had "acquired such speed [that] doubts were expressed about any one being able to catch for him," and those fears mounted when "a large number of Chicago amateur ball-tossers" became "sufficiently enthusiastic" to "brave a trial of catching for Devlin," only to be "compelled to retire in short order."

Finally Scott Hastings of Bloomington, Illinois, was summoned to see "if he could catch Devlin's red-hot underhand throw." When the newcomer arrived at the ballpark, "Devlin was just beginning to pitch. Scott watched him for a while, and saw him shiver the board fence he was pitching at, and then calmly took off his coat and went to work and showed such a creditable exhibition of catching that he was loudly applauded by the large audience who witnessed the work. The following day positions were taken on the field, with Chicago's best amateurs at the bat, and out of 125 balls struck at, but ten went beyond the base, and Hastings having but two passed balls, which is said to be the finest exhibition of pitching and catching ever witnessed in Chicago."

As this account clearly implies, the indispensability of the catcher, combined with the sense that a special bond enabled a catcher to handle a specific pitcher, created the aura of myth or even fairy tale. If the catcher's heroism was an internal attribute that revealed itself only under extraordinary circumstances, he was like King Arthur pulling the sword from the stone, or like Alexander cutting the Gordian knot. At the same time he was clearly in the tradition of frontiersmen like Daniel Boone who were truly at home only in the wilderness, soldiers like Ulysses S. Grant who were transformed by the chaos of the battlefield, and the cowboys whose gifts became apparent only when they were on horseback. Like these American heroes, the catcher was a man who might look unprepossessing, but he and he alone had the ability to catch a particular pitcher. As a diehard fan would later recall, when Devlin was in his prime, "Hastings was the only man who could catch him."

A similar story was told in Michigan, where a brilliant young left-handed pitcher named Charles Baldwin from the small town of Hastings could "throw a fast one packed with dynamite" and "a puzzling curve which on account of its weaving in and out had been dubbed the 'snake ball.'"

But for a while it appeared that Baldwin's career would be aborted by an inability to find a catcher who could work with him. Then came word of someone named Jim McGuire, who lived fifty miles away in Albion and was reputed to be "hardier than a pine knot," have "a pair of hands like those of a giant," and be able to "catch anything and anybody."

When this catcher was sent for, miraculously he proved as good as advertised. The Hastings club became highly successful but could play only on weekends because McGuire was serving an apprenticeship as an iron molder in Albion. Word of the standout duo soon spread, and both went on to National League stardom (where, in tribute to their clean-living ways, they became known by the nicknames of "Lady" Baldwin and "Deacon" McGuire).

This image of the catcher as a man with a special affinity for a great pitcher would prove every bit as powerful as perceptions of him as a tough guy and an indispensable part of his team's success. The belief in these partnerships became so strong, in fact, that questions were raised about whether the game's preeminent catchers could handle different styles of pitching. Henry Chadwick wrote of the illustrious Doug Allison: "This past season Allison caught finely from [George] Zettlein's pitching, but he was not active enough for ["Phonnie"] Martin's delivery."

It was not uncommon for accounts to suggest that a catcher might look average when paired with mediocre pitching, only to reveal his true mettle when paired with a star pitcher. Charley Bennett, for instance, caught for two years for a local semipro club without attracting attention. But when given "the honor of catching for Cal. Hawk, the first real professional hurler the game ever had . . . 'Charlie' says that he found no more difficulty in handling the great Hawk's delivery than he did in holding the hurler that threw his arm off for beans." Buck Ewing played for one of the best amateur clubs in Cincinnati in 1880, but the idea of that city's National League team signing Ewing and two of his teammates was laughed off with the remark, "Nobody will pay to see a lot of Mill Creek Bottom amateurs play ball." Later that season, Ewing received a tryout from the National League club in Troy, New York, but even astute manager Bob Ferguson was unsure of Ewing's potential until he gave him the chance to catch star pitcher Tim Keefe. Then Ewing's true worth manifested itself, and Keefe urged Ferguson, "You get this boy, Ewing, at once. Don't let him escape. He will be a wonder."

The idea that a catcher might shine with one pitcher but not with another gave youngsters yet another reason to nurture dreams of becoming professional catchers. These hopefuls already knew that size was not a requirement for becoming a great catcher, nor was speed or batting skill. A lad who didn't excel at catching the local pitcher could still hope to be the perfect complement for some great pitcher.

Another new development gave youngsters like Stephen Crane one more reason to believe they might hook their fortunes to a rising star pitcher. In 1872 the Cleveland entry in the National Association (the first major league) took the novel course of signing two well-known pitchers, Rynie Wolters and Al Pratt, and two highly regarded catchers, Jim White and Scott Hastings. Since it was then standard for professional clubs to sign only nine players, this seemed a peculiar decision. With catchers being prone to injuries and pitchers to inconsistency, clubs always signed a "change pitcher" and a "change catcher," but these were players who also manned other positions and would switch with the regular members of the battery when needed. Thus Cleveland's decision to hire two specialists at each position struck most observers as overkill.

Not so, insisted Henry Chadwick. The influential sportswriter commended the club's directors for "securing the services of two regular pitchers and catchers. It has been well known for several seasons past that no nine in the professional arena can be considered complete without a change pitcher. But the past season's experience has pretty conclusively shown that it is also equally important that every first-class professional nine should possess two regular pitchers and catchers, and for this reason, that in the season's campaign it will be found that the regular pitcher of the club, no matter how skillful he may be, will be punished by the batsmen of one nine, or perhaps two or three, with more effect than by the remainder of the opposing nines, and in such cases it becomes necessary to have another 'regular' pitcher at command to place in position when he can accomplish that which the other one fails to do."

Thus instead of having one regular pitcher and a backup for emergencies, Chadwick advocated engaging two skilled pitchers and using them in turn, according to the opponent. Making the pitcher more of a specialist would allow a similar opportunity for the catcher: "Another important adjunct to two regular pitchers is two catchers, each familiar with the play of his own pitcher. This want you have also met in having two such splendid catchers as White and Hastings, two men who have no superiors in their position, for though others may catch with equal effect, the thorough control of temper, the coolness, nerve and pluck, and the perfect reliability of both these men gives them superiority over others who may equal them in fielding skill."

As it turned out, Cleveland suffered through a disastrous campaign in 1872. The Chicago Fire had caused most of the clubs in the Great Lakes region to disband, so it proved all but impossible to persuade other clubs to travel to Cleveland. On the field the club's bold new scheme was undermined when both pitchers struggled. By August the club had disbanded, and Jim White was so disheartened that he chose to retire. (A Boston director was sent to his hometown to talk White out of retirement, and he became the cornerstone of the next five pennant winners and played eighteen more seasons in the major leagues.)

But while Cleveland did not benefit from their innovation, the next few seasons demonstrated the advantages of having more than one regular battery. With release points continuing to rise, pitchers' arms began to feel the strain of hard throwing and the torque that was created in unleashing a curveball. Pitchers were rarely given time off to recover—there was limited understanding of the biomechanics of pitching and still some resentment of pitchers for claiming so large a role for themselves—but even those who doubted the legitimacy of sore arms recognized that hard throwers were prone to losing their effectiveness. And no one could deny that the new pitching techniques were much harder on the bodies of catchers.

So more and more teams began to feature a couple of talented pitchers and two experienced catchers. The curveball, in particular, spurred this trend, since many veteran catchers found the new pitch difficult to handle. In an 1872 game, Nat Hicks had to be brought in from right field to replace a catcher who was struggling with the curved offerings of Bobby Mathews, a switch that prompted Henry Chadwick to observe, "The wisdom of having two regular catchers as well as pitchers in a nine was now made clearly manifest." In his season-ending wrap-up, Chadwick observed that the catcher's importance had increased significantly, "it being next to impossible to employ strategic tactics in pitching with any effect unless the pitcher be supported by a plucky, active, skillful and intelligent catcher."

A key component of this new philosophy was that pitchers and catchers began to be thought of as a partnership that should not be broken up if at all possible. Both members of the battery came to believe that finding the right comrade would yield a whole that was greater than its individual parts. Some had already found their mate—remember the Evansville paper that billed the "immense attraction" of the "great left-hand pitcher" and the catcher who had caught him "successfully for several years"? Others, such as the Troy pitcher who threatened to leave his team in 1878 after complaining that "he cannot pitch with justice to himself with a poor catcher behind the bat," were still searching. Either way, baseball was energized by this faith that the ideal partner was out there somewhere.

Clubs that tried to get by with just one pitcher and catcher nonetheless embraced the notion of a special bond between the two men. The most notable instance occurred in Indianapolis in 1878, when team president W. B. Pettit plastered the town with large photos of team pitcher Ed Nolan and team catcher "Silver" Flint, with the inscriptions "The Only Nolan" and "The Champion Catcher of America." This caused considerable discussion about "the good or bad taste of hanging up such pictures in the windows about town. The jokes cracked at the expense of the unfortunate Nolan are innumerable, and in last Thursday's game, when he began to be hit pretty freely, the crowd sang out with one accord, 'The Only Nolan— shoot him.'. . . Putting aside any question of taste, it may be questioned whether Mr. Pettit has not put more of a load on Nolan than he can carry. To be 'The Only Nolan,' he must win right away, and it isn't yet sure that he can do that."

As faith in these mystical partnerships grew, some observers tried to explain why they developed. One popular theory held that certain catchers should be paired with hard-throwing pitchers and others with curveballers. Another common belief was that a left-handed catcher was better suited to work with a fellow southpaw. Others suggested that a catcher's size helped explain why he might work well with one pitcher but poorly with another. Predictably, Henry Chadwick saw these partnerships as proof that teamwork was the essence of baseball, commenting that "no catcher can play with the ability his skill and experience warrant unless he works with a superior team in the field, willing and able to back up his own strenuous exertions to win. A catcher may work like a beaver behind the bat, and yet by the careless play of the pitcher or the baseman his efforts may be rendered useless."

To many, however, there was no way to predict whether a particular pitcher and catcher would achieve harmony. It was a bond as strong and as intangible as the one that leads to a happy marriage—and sometimes there were suggestive parallels that recalled the days when they were known as the "first and second mate." According to an 1879 account, "[Pitcher Morrie] Critchley and [catcher Jim] Keenan are apparently inseparable. They refuse to part, and when one makes a contract it is for both. There are probably no two men in the profession who play better together as pitcher and catcher." Major league battery mates Charles Getzein and Ed Gastfield grew up playing marbles together and acted as best men at each other's weddings. Connie Mack was one of several ballplayers to marry the sister of his battery mate. Pitcher George Bradley and catcher Tom Miller worked together in Philadelphia and then moved as a pair to St. Louis in 1875. Miller died the following spring and, according to a widely circulated account, "In his last moments he was delirious, and fancied he was at his place in the ball-field, facing his old pitcher, Bradley. His last words were: 'Two outs, Brad—steady, now—he wants a high ball—steady, Brad—there, I knew it; that settles it.'"

This belief that battery mates shared a mystical link had an important practical consequence. "Catchers and pitchers," remarked the *Chicago Tribune* in 1879, "are beginning to make a point of practicing and hiring in teams. This is a good idea, and, if followed up, would produce much more effective catching and pitching." By the 1880s the value of this idea was apparent enough that most catchers became "specialists. Pitcher Smith would pitch only to Catcher Jones. Pitcher Kelly would pitch only to Catcher O'Reilly."

Obviously this provided more jobs for catchers and therefore more reason for youngsters to dream of stepping into that role. Just as important, this new myth seemed fresher and more attainable to the growing numbers of city lads than did the idea of proving themselves on a remote frontier or on battlefields that seemed like "things of the bygone." And so the Stephen Cranes and Ban Johnsons and Wallie Walkers continued to believe in a new version of the American Dream that replaced Ben Franklin's prosaic homilies with one that put a uniquely American spin on enchanting myths like the Sword in the Stone. They dreamed that one day they might become the star catcher whose prowess was envied by every boy and admired by every girl.

5

The Catcher as the Man in Disguise

"Catching is the most elusive position on the field, its skills, its demands, even its view of the world—looking out from rather than in to home plate—at odds with the other positions. As catchers are hidden from us by mask and armor, so their skills are hidden. The best-caught game is the one least noticed."—David Falkner

■ WHEN THE scouting profession developed in the twentieth century, one of its most enduring myths was the one summed up in the phrase "the arm behind the barn." Every baseball scout dreamed of finding that ultimate hidden gem—a pitcher with a magical arm who had never before ventured off the family farm. Talent hunters were inspired to leave no stone unturned, and men who specialized in searching for such raw prospects came to be known as "backwood scouts."

As we have seen, a no less powerful mystique developed around the nineteenth-century catcher: he had to be incredibly brave, his key talents were internal rather than external, he was able to form a special bond with a comrade, and once found he became indispensable. In short, he was one in a million. Catchers were thus the nineteenth-century equivalent of "the arm behind the barn" in that every team manager dreamed of discovering one. The difference was that with formal scouting still in the future, most managers could only hope that the right man would show up on their doorstep.

After the 1871 season, for instance, up-and-coming catcher John Clapp wrote to Boston manager Harry Wright from his home in Ithaca, New York, to see if a job was available. Wright responded with a long list of questions:

"What caliber and speed of pitching had [Clapp] caught the previous year? Was [Clapp] sure he could 'catch a swift pitcher' like Al Spalding 'up to or close behind' the batter? Could he substitute at any infield position in the event of injury? Could he successfully bat against swift pitching, and was he prepared to go to Boston at his own expense and display the level of his baseball skills?" We do not know Clapp's response, but he did sign with a different team and developed into one of the game's best catchers.

Wright undoubtedly regretted letting Clapp slip away, yet there was no way for a manager to determine whether a catcher was the man he desperately needed without going to the expense of auditioning every aspirant. So many baseball managers lost sleep wondering whether that great catcher was out there somewhere, perhaps playing catch behind a barn with his brother. So if an aspiring catcher showed up, he was likely to get a long audition.

The dire need for catchers and the lack of an effective way of finding them produced a peculiarly American version of an old myth. The predictable part was that the successful applicants came out of nowhere and were frequently cloaked in disguise. Yet, equally important, many of the tales concerned impostors who also tried their hand and were found not merely wanting but laughably short of the standard. It was part Sword in the Stone and part *Gong Show* or *American Idol*, since each applicant would either be deemed worthy to "occupy the post of honor as 'catcher' . . . or he will be admonished of his inexpertness by a request from some player to 'butter his fingers.'"

Because this was an American saga, it was permeated by a sense that the chosen one would come from obscurity, and indeed from so remote a region that he could breathe fresh life into his city brethren. "Nearly all of our great catchers," wrote one sportswriter, "came from humble homes in some quiet hamlet, where the curfew jolts the juvenile population off the village green at 9:00 p. m., and the principal pastime is guessing on the age of the nearest pullet [a young hen]. It is the duty of the catcher to tame brush league pitchers who are long on saliva and short on about everything else." Just as the undiscovered twentieth-century pitcher was "the arm behind the barn," so too the nineteenth-century catcher might be lurking on any farm in the American heartland.

A few catchers did indeed embody this rustic ideal. Most notably, Jim "Deacon" White grew up on a farm playing catch with his cousin and nearest neighbor (who became a major leaguer) and his brothers (one of whom became a major leaguer). He did not even learn of the New York

Walter Walker caught only a single major league game—with disastrous results—and then was released while he was at home attending his brother's funeral. Yet the experience didn't sour him on baseball at all, and even after becoming a lawyer he abandoned his practice when given the chance to catch for a minor league team. When Walker later ran for county prosecuting attorney, his opponent (his former law partner) unsuccessfully tried to convince voters that Walker might similarly leave the county in the lurch if baseball beckoned. *(Collection of Peter Morris)*

Game until after the Civil War, but within a few years he had become one of its greatest players. He kept a farm every off-season, and rumors regularly circulated that he would retire from baseball and stick to minding "the cows, watermelons, turnips and such." One sportswriter suggested that this background contributed to White's fabled calm under pressure. "It made no difference how anxious the other players and the crowd were to win the game, or how close it stood," this writer maintained, "the Deacon was just as slow and measured in his actions as if he were hoeing corn." He appeared so fluid that, as Henry Chadwick put it, "The fact is, White is what [Jim] Creighton was—a natural ball player."

But farmer's sons like Jim White were the exceptions among the great early catchers. By and large, city boys like Leggett, Hicks, and Craver established the position as one for the toughest of the tough. But you'd never know that from reading contemporary accounts.

Consider, for instance, the clear echoes of the Sword in the Stone myth in this 1879 account of how catcher Doug Allison was discovered by Cincinnati Red Stockings director Colonel John P. Joyce: "When it came to securing a catcher, Mr. Joyce went to Philadelphia. The City of Brotherly Love was at this time wild over the national pastime, and hundreds of clubs were playing wherever suitable space could be found. Joyce with his pocket full of cigars would start out every morning and spend the day in watching the players wherever games were in progress. Thus day after day was passed among a mob of unknown players, many of whom have since achieved notoriety, but none of them exhibiting evidences of sufficient ability to warrant their being engaged. After patient waiting, he one day found himself in a dispirited mood in a Manayunk brick-yard watching a game, and his attention was arrested by a tall, ungainly, verdant-looking, poorly-clad young man, who, out of his position, was all awkwardness, and, in his position, the embodiment of grace and perfection. Five minutes' observation convinced him that the long-sought was before him. The young man was named Allison, a marble-cutter by trade. A conditional engagement was at once made with him at a salary of $20 per week, his railroad-fare to Cincinnati to be paid, as well as his expenses while there on trial. The Colonel had grave doubts as to whether or not the awkward youth would meet with favor among the members, who were imperative in their demand that the players should be men of social standing, having ability to grace the parlor as well as the field. He took the safe side, and did some telegraphing on the subject before starting, that if published would be ludicrous in the extreme. With misgivings, he attired the new acquisition in a faultless suit, and started West with him. Arriving in Cincinnati he buried him for one night in the St. James Hotel, and the next afternoon produced the goods on a field where a game had been made up for test purposes. A jury of critical members sat on the Club-house porch. As Allison, now in uniform, stepped upon the field with an old cotton handkerchief about his neck, the noses of the jury individually and collectively were elevated about three pegs. The aforesaid handkerchief was wrested from his neck by Joyce, whose face was scarlet when he saw it. Play was called, and in a moment behind the bat the ungainly boy was transformed into the skillful catcher. [Pitcher Asa] Brainard was dumbfounded, and could scarcely believe the evidence of his senses. He pitched with all his speed, and made use of every trick to confuse him, but his efforts were fruitless. The first striker went out on a foul tip, beautifully taken. The next man was put out by a magnificent line throw that went to second like a shot. The jury took him to its bosom and wept, and from that day forward Allison was known as the great catcher, whose excellencies have never since been equaled."

The story of the discovery of Doug Allison was retold frequently, and some accounts included picturesque new details. In one version the young catcher was described as "a tanned and freckled country boy whose boots and clothes were covered with brickyard clay. On his head was a 25-cent straw hat with half the rim gone." Allison's status as country bumpkin was revealed when he "sat in his hotel room all morning, expecting breakfast to be served him there, even though he hadn't ordered it." Another intriguing description focused on Allison's first games against outside competition, played in Columbus. According to this account, Allison "was a gawky looking sort of fellow, and created a poor impression." But once again, everything changed when the first pitch was thrown: "as soon as he began work behind the bat," the "young Philadelphia brick-yard player . . . captur[ed] everybody by the ease with which he handled the rapid delivery of both [Harry] Wright and [Asa] Brainard," and with throws to second base that seemed to have been "propelled from a catapult." In classic fairy tale tradition, Allison's catching helped the Red Stockings complete an undefeated season in 1869.

The themes of the Allison saga were echoed in Louisville president Charles E. Chase's description of how he discovered a catcher named Billy Holbert. "One day, when we were in Philadelphia," Chase recalled, "we ran out into one of the mining towns of Pennsylvania to play a game with the club there, it being an 'off day' with us. There was a rough crowd of spectators present, principally the men who worked in the mines. We had nobody with us to umpire the game and told the manager of the other club to select some one. He said he knew of a man who was somewhat of a ball player, and he would get him to act. He accordingly called a man out of the crowd and told us he would do. The man was one of the most remarkable specimens I ever saw. His clothes were ragged and dirty, his face covered with coal dust, and his shaggy, brown hair stuck out through the holes in his hat in several places. We agreed to take him, however, and the game commenced. Everything went all right until the fourth inning when [Charley] Snyder, our catcher, in attempting to run home from third base slipped and sprained his ankle."

This would have been a serious problem under any circumstances, but it was exacerbated by the fact that hard-throwing Jim Devlin was pitching for Louisville. As Chase explained, "We had no one to take his place, and I turned to Jack Chapman, who managed the nine, and said to him: 'Jack, you had better go in and catch the rest of the game.' He replied that he could not catch, and I told him it didn't make any difference, just so he stopped the balls, as the game was of no consequence. While we were discussing the matter the umpire sidled up to us and said: 'Let me catch the rest of the game.' I looked at him again and commenced to laugh, but Chapman remarked: 'Let him try then; it doesn't make any difference,' and I told him to go ahead. He borrowed Snyder's shoes, and Devlin commenced to pitch him a few balls for practice. He let them come easy for awhile and then sent them like a shot, but the miner clung on manfully. The game was commenced again, and I never was more surprised in my life. He finished the remaining five innings without an error or a passed ball, and not a single man stole second on him. When the game was finished I asked him his name and he said it was Holbert. I wanted to know how much he made, and he replied $1.50 a day. I found on further questioning that he would like to play [baseball] for a living, and I engaged him on the spot. I gave him money enough to pay his expenses to Philadelphia, and he joined us there the next day. He said he wanted to get a suit of clothes, and I gave him $25. He went out, and when he returned he had on the queerest looking suit I ever saw. The color was very gaudy, and the coat had stripes on it about as wide as my hand, while the pants were cut like a song and dance man's, and he had a tall plug hat. He was 'guyed' unmercifully, but took it good-humoredly, and caught for us against the Athletics the next day, and had not a single error and but one passed ball. That was the first championship game he ever took part in." Holbert too would go on to a long major league career that lasted for more than a decade. Even by the standard of the catchers of the era, he was an inept hitter, becoming the only player in baseball history to bat two thousand times without hitting a home run. It didn't matter in the least. His defensive prowess alone enabled him to become one of only twenty-five nineteenth-century catchers to catch more than five hundred major league games.

Longtime National League president Nick Young told a similar story about his playing days with the Olympic club of Washington in the late 1860s. The club was "looking for a catcher who could handle [Ed] Leech, their pitcher, [and] some one picked up [David] Force, who had been playing in various nines. Dave came to Washington with a pair of corduroy pantaloons, evidently at one time the property of a taller member of his family. Well, his shortness of stature rather tickled the large crowd who had come out to see him experimented with. Everybody thought it was a huge joke, and nobody expected that the little fellow was going to do anything. But to the astonishment of everybody he took his position and for an hour and a half he caught Leech with an ease that startled everybody. Leech tried his hardest, but the swiftest balls were handled without the least show of difficulty. The trial settled the matter, and Dave remained as catcher."

The similarities between these three accounts are striking. In each case the ballplayer's attire and other aspects of his appearance suggest such ungainly awkwardness as to provoke laughter. Yet when put to the test, the true ability of each man is revealed. No doubt these picturesque elements had been exaggerated as they were told and retold. Yet what really mattered was the underlying message—that a star catcher might be out there anywhere, often lurking behind the most implausible disguise.

Another remarkable element in these descriptions is the ability of these men in disguise to do immediately, with minimal effort and preparation, what others could not accomplish at all. No messy, prolonged wrestling is needed to remove the proverbial sword from the stone; the newcomer simply steps in and makes it look easy. The catcher's status as mythical hero was becoming apparent.

The catcher's mastery of his position allowed him to assume an air of deceptive nonchalance that recalled other heroic figures. The cowboy, for example, was noted for his "usual languor. With utmost nonchalance he will saddle and harness his horse in the morning, chatting and smoking, using more time than is necessary. But after he has mounted his steed . . . he is a different person." The description is particularly reminiscent of the ones given by Stephen Crane's classmates, who recalled that his "quiet and taciturn mien" disappeared when he played ball, which he did with "a fiendish glee." A similar transformation occurred with other catchers. When Chub Sullivan joined the Chicago White Stockings in 1877, he was described as "a plucky, cool sort of fellow. He stands carelessly up to the bat, but catches all that comes his way."

Another striking element in the accounts of new catchers is how often recruits from large industrial cities were portrayed as Daniel Boone–like figures, more at home in the wilderness than in civilization. Allison, despite the references to his "verdant-looking" appearance and his being a "tanned and freckled country boy," was from Philadelphia and had been a cricket wicket-keeper before taking up baseball; Holbert was born in Baltimore and grew up in the coal-mining town of Laurel, Maryland. In similar fashion, one reporter joked in 1884 that rookie catcher Henry Oxley must have arrived from the "Green Mountains" because he owned neither a mask (which had been introduced in 1877) nor a chest protector (which was new). He explained that Oxley noticed "the catcher of the other club strapping on a chest protector, so he asked him what he was doing that for." Even after the newcomer put the device on, he didn't understand that it needed to be inflated to offer protection, until another player took pity on him and showed him how to blow it up. Oxley in fact was one of only two major leaguers born in Prince Edward Island, but he had lived in Boston since infancy.

In some of these accounts the catcher does not recognize his own gift. Cal Broughton lived on a farm just outside of Janesville, Wisconsin, and was a longtime member of that city's semipro team, but when he signed a National League contract, press coverage stressed that the new player was "a farmer and a good one at that. He comes merely to try his ability against the best players." Jack Boyle was discovered only because he tagged along to catch a pitcher being given a tryout by Cincinnati in 1886. Team manager O. P. Caylor was instead struck by Boyle's skill behind the plate and asked him his profession. "When I work, I work in the rolling mill," was Boyle's reply, and Caylor promptly offered him a contract matching his pay at the mill.

Other early catchers from big cities were similarly depicted as naive innocents. Tom Sullivan was the nineteenth century's Yogi Berra—despite being raised in St. Louis, he remained blissfully unaware of much of modern life. Sullivan received the nickname "Sleeper" because of his unfamiliarity with the Pullman sleeper cars. According to one version of this oft-told tale, "Tom Sullivan, the catcher, made a remark once which, among ball players, makes his name as familiar as the name of Pullman. When Tom first signed he had never traveled much and had never used a Pullman sleeper. Upon taking his first trip he was told that they would occupy sleepers. Tom followed the balance of the club into the sleeper, the berths of which were, of course, not made up. After sitting there awhile Tom remarked: 'Well I'm blowed if I don't think it is money throwed away to pay extra just because the seats face each other. As far as I am concerned I had as lief ride in a common car and turn the seats myself.' From that day to this common day coaches are 'Sullivan Sleepers' among ball players." Another version had Sullivan entering the day coach, mistaking it for the sleeping car, and telling the team manager that "he should not have bought him a sleeping berth, that any of the other cars was good enough for him." Either way the message was the same.

A somewhat similar anecdote was told about George "Shorty" Ewell, a Philadelphia native who was hired in 1870 as catcher for the Olympics of

Washington—the same job that David Force had auditioned for in such memorable fashion a few years earlier. Team manager Nick Young left the clubhouse and gave Ewell strict instructions not to let anybody touch a small bottle of brandy. Pitcher Ed Leech then came in and asked if he could have a sip of brandy, but Ewell told him that he'd have to wait until Mr. Young came back. "Very well," Leech replied, "never mind, it's perfectly immaterial." It was the wrong thing to say: "then up came Shorty, his eyes sparkling with wrath and his fists doubled up as he made for Leech, saying: 'You call me that agin and I'll bust you wide open. I want you to understand that I don't allow any man to call me them words without a fight. You take that back, or off comes your ear.' Leech did what any wise man would have done—explained to Shorty that no insult was intended, and went away convinced that 'perfectly immaterial' wasn't as good an expression for Shorty's use as 'It don't matter a d--n.'"

St. Louis catcher Jimmy Adams was the subject of the same kinds of tales. His teammates took advantage of his lack of familiarity with the ways of the world to convince him that cuspidors were china vases, that finger bowls were goblets, and that he could light a cigar by unscrewing a light bulb and touching the wires. Stories like these seem clearly intended to suggest that these catchers shared Daniel Boone's fabled rejection of the social hierarchy and its conventions.

The disguises might also take other forms. An anecdote told about former Yale baseball star Bill Hutchison offered yet another take on the powerful idea of the star catcher whose talents are hidden. As the story went, Hutchison "once had a good laugh on an audience at a baseball game in Kansas City. The catcher of the Kansas City club was disabled in the early part of the game, and they were at their wits' end as to what they should do, when a stranger, dressed in the height of fashion, stepped out and said he would catch. Both players and audience laughed at the apparent dude, but their mirth soon changed to wonder and astonishment when he caught the balance of the game without an error of any kind. When asked his name, he quietly answered, 'Hutchinson [sic], of Yale.' That was quite enough." Hutchison had in fact been primarily a shortstop while at Yale, and upon graduation had turned down professional baseball offers, preferring to enter business. (He later changed his mind and became one of the National League's best pitchers.)

University of Michigan law student Frank Bliss also showed that the walls of academia could serve as a hiding place for the great catcher. Like Hutchison, Bliss declined to pursue baseball as a career, but he did spend several summers playing professionally. While doing so he displayed the requisite toughness; one account noted, "A foul tip crippled Bliss' hand, but that plucky catcher came up smiling and was warmly applauded." He also had the necessary ability. As a University of Michigan teammate recalled, "He was a wonder. Besides being a great catcher, he had the unusual distinction of always playing with his trousers tucked in long boots." Was Bliss's use of these long boots just another of the distinctive fashion statements that so many early catchers seem to have favored? Or had he craftily contrived one of the earliest shin protectors? Either way, he was yet another example that a catcher's internal merit could not be judged by outward appearance.

Hutchison and Bliss strengthened this message by showing it to be truly universal. Inner character and skill might be hidden behind the picturesque rusticity of a Bill Holbert, or behind the garb of an unsophisticated urbanite like "Sleeper" Sullivan, or even within the ivory tower of academia. It was never safe to judge a man solely on the basis of appearances.

Indeed it often seemed as though the one safe assumption about a catcher was that his appearance would confound people's expectations. Jim White, for instance, was "a very quiet man personally inclined to the serious side of life and scarcely one who would be taken for an athlete." In 1872 one of the directors of the Boston club was dispatched to try to talk White out of retirement but did not know what he looked like. Soon after arriving in White's hometown, he encountered "a clerical-looking man, with a tall hat," and correctly deduced that it was the great catcher because of the telltale "pair of the hardest-looking hands I ever saw, and one finger [that] was badly smashed."

An 1878 article noted that "Jim White is a steady kind of man in his likings. He has played ball in Boston, Chicago and Cincinnati for seven or eight years past, and where he has played the champion pennant has generally been found at the end of the season. . . . [He is] said to be studying for the ministry when his ball-playing days are over. The boys call him 'the Deacon,' because he reads his Bible and drinks water, and does not get mad and swear when a red-leg drops a ball or the umpire makes a doubtful decision. It has been the mission of 'Our Jim' to demonstrate that a boy with the right sort of sand in him may play ball for a salary and yet set a good example of plain, every-day manhood to some other men who captain railroads and banks and insurance companies." So the powerful image of the catcher as man in disguise could also be used to make it a suitable model for Christian youth.

The underlying message of all these tales about catchers in disguise is a powerful one: people must be judged on their hidden, inner qualities rather than on their outward appearance. Sports has always been especially well suited to conveying this message because the result of an athletic competition is so clear-cut. Bigots, for example, are likely to remain convinced that members of specific racial and ethnic groups are innately smarter or more industrious, despite all evidence to the contrary. But the outcome of a ball game cannot be fudged, and as baseball came to be seen as a test of character, it presented an opportunity to confront prejudice. In particular, as the catcher's position assumed transcendent importance, it helped open baseball's doors—at least temporarily—to members of oppressed racial and ethnic groups.

The Irish were the victims of terrible discrimination after the Great Potato Famine sent waves of refugees to America, and baseball became an important means for them to prove themselves. Prominent catchers like Fergy Malone and "Sleeper" Sullivan had been born in Ireland, and many others were the children of famine refugees.

Members of visible minority groups also came to see the catching position as a gateway to opportunity. The first Native American to reach the major leagues was Tommy Oran, who first made his name as a catcher for several St. Louis clubs. The first Hispanic to play in the National League was a catcher known as Vincent Nava, who was born and raised in San Francisco. Nava's dark skin attracted a great deal of comment when he came east, much of it ill-informed. He was often referred to as being either a Cuban or an African American but in fact, as Joel S. Franks has shown, Nava was born in California to a British father and a Mexican mother.

Intriguingly, Nava's real name was Vincent Irwin, and it was by that name that he was known while playing ball in his native San Francisco. When he first came east in 1882, he was initially referred to as Vincent Irwin, but he soon became known as Nava in baseball circles. Even so, Californians still clung to the earlier name, referring to him as "Vincent Nava, known on this coast as 'Sandy' Irwin." The reasons for his name change remain unclear. Franks speculated that Nava may have been motivated by pride in his heritage, but also noted that he could have been trying to make clear that he was not of African-American descent.

Catching proved an especially appealing entry point into baseball for African Americans. Societal acceptance of racial integration was in constant flux during the Reconstruction Era, and that, combined with the crucial importance of the catcher, enabled several pioneers to make their marks.

A club from Baraboo, Wisconsin, won a big Fourth of July tournament in the mid-1870s because of the support the team's pitcher received from "a colored Pullman porter named Johnson, who was surely an artist behind the bat. The catcher in those days had no protection in the way of mask, or chest protector, and to avoid being hit by foul tips, etc., they depended entirely on their ability to dodge." An African-American catcher named Will Smith anchored the Saginaw town team in the late 1870s. And in Port Henry, New York, "a stalwart negro named John Carsaw caught behind the bat" in the early 1880s, earning a reputation as "a good catcher, a strong thrower to bases and a heavy hitter." Carsaw was also remembered for wearing the first chest protector to be seen in the region, a white contraption that "contrasted strongly with the color of the man who wore it."

Far and away the most prominent African-American catcher of the era was Moses Fleetwood Walker. After attending Oberlin College and the University of Michigan, Walker became the only nineteenth-century African American to have a prolonged major league tenure when he spent the entire 1884 season catching for Toledo of the American Association. Like so many of the era's catchers, Walker wasn't much of a hitter, but his defensive skills and toughness helped him surmount prejudice and become invaluable.

Toledo pitcher Tony Mullane reported that Walker "was the best catcher I ever worked with, but I disliked a Negro and whenever I had to pitch to him I used to pitch anything I wanted without looking at his signals. One day he signaled me for a curve and I shot a fast ball at him. He caught it and walked down to me. He said, 'I'll catch you without signals, but I won't catch you if you are going to cross me when I give you signals.' And all the rest of that season he caught me and caught anything I pitched without knowing what was coming." Like all catchers, Walker exhibited great courage. One of Toledo's batboys recalled seeing "his fingers split open and bleeding, but he would go right on catching. He had more nerve and grit than anybody I have ever seen."

Although Walker played in the major leagues for only a year, he continued to catch for better minor league teams through 1889. Then the clandestine drawing of baseball's color line cost him his spot. By then, as we shall see, changes to the game and the emergence of catching equipment and mitts made a stalwart catcher no longer indispensable. There is every reason to believe that it was no coincidence that African-American catchers lost their spots on professional rosters at the moment the position lost its prestige.

Catcher Moses Fleetwood "Fleet" Walker was the first African American to become a major league regular, and his pioneer status testified to how essential it was to have a skilled man behind the plate. The catcher's position thus became an important beacon of opportunity. It was probably no coincidence that Walker was released, and baseball's unwritten color barrier erected, just when the introduction of the catcher's mitt made it far less important to have a great defensive catcher. *(National Baseball Hall of Fame Library)*

*

The strength of the belief that a catcher might lurk behind the most implausible of disguises ensured that for every Doug Allison or Bill Holbert, there would be many counterexamples. Streams of young men who aspired to become the next great catcher wrote to professional teams and begged for tryouts. Of course, similar young men imagined themselves to be star pitchers or infielders or batters, but they were usually laughed off if they had no credentials.

Athletics executive Charles Mason reported in 1883: "Our mail every day contains applications from players in country towns who are impressed with the idea that they possess some unusual ability, principally as pitchers; and to listen to some of the remarkable descriptions of 'curves' and 'shoots' that they claim as original, would make your head swim. Here is an application from a young man up in the country who says that he has discovered a new curve that is impossible to be hit, and that with it he can strike out the heaviest batsmen as fast as they come up to the plate. He would be a valuable man to secure if there was anything in his claim, but try him and he would be hit out of the 'box' in one inning." Mason explained that such applicants were typically invited to a tryout only if they were recommended by a credible source.

In the case of aspiring catchers, however, club managers were haunted by the nagging hope that this applicant might be that one-in-a-million hidden gem. Even if the player's resumé contained nothing but failures, there remained the possibility that he might have the knack for handling the team's pitcher. Thus the mystique surrounding the position, combined with the perpetual need for catchers, brought even the most unpromising-looking catching aspirants a tryout.

If they showed even a hint of promise, or if their timing was good, they might also get an opportunity in a major league game. Charles Mason concluded his comments by admitting that the Athletics had made one notable exception to their usual practice: "Last season, for instance, we heard of a catcher in Massachusetts, and being in need of such a player we sent for him, giving him $200 in advance. He caught two innings in an exhibition game and proved a monumental failure. The same evening he left for home and that was the last we ever heard of him."

Many other aspiring catchers received similar opportunities despite having little or no experience. Some spectacularly unsuccessful efforts became as legendary as the successes of the Holberts and Allisons. After all, the natural catcher made his job look so easy that it was possible to forget how hard it really was. So it took the efforts of men like Fred Gunkle to remind everyone that the natural catcher was truly rare.

Gunkle was an obscure Chicago amateur player in May 1879 when he heard that Cleveland's catchers had been plagued by injuries. He took a train to Cleveland, and the desperate team let him catch for pitcher Jim McCormick in that day's National League game. But Gunkle proved so incapable of catching McCormick that the local paper wrote in disgust, "all that was necessary for a man to score a run was to get to first base somehow, passed balls would do the rest." After being charged with seven passed balls and three errors, Gunkle switched places with one of the outfielders. He was last seen headed for the train station after the game, though one reporter speculated that he would "have to walk back to Chicago as it was doubted he could catch well enough to catch the train."

Not surprisingly, that was the end of Fred Gunkle's professional playing career, and he was soon forgotten. A player who had had an equally short stint in the National League the preceding year was not as fortunate. During a long road trip that began in late July 1878, Milwaukee had the misfortune of losing to injury all three of its players with catching experience—Billy Holbert, Charley Bennett, and Billy Foley. Manager Jack Chapman sent an urgent telegraph to Milwaukee ordering reserve Jake Knowdell to meet the club in Cincinnati, but Knowdell didn't arrive in time for the team's August 15 game. So Chapman enlisted a local amateur named Alfred Jennings to catch hard-throwing Mike Golden.

It was a disaster from the outset. "We were all mixed up in our signs," recalled Jennings later. "I signed for an outcurve and got an in-shoot which broke a couple of fingers. 'Go, ahead,' I said, 'I'll stay here all day even if I have to stop 'em with my elbows! You can't drive me away!' Well they didn't, but I had seventeen passed balls that afternoon."

His dismal performance would have soon been forgotten if not for *Cincinnati Enquirer* sportswriter O. P. Caylor. Caylor knew a good story when he saw one, and he embellished Jennings's helpless plight for effect. Knowdell, in his version, was on a fishing trip while the neophyte Jennings (who "has umpired an occasional game, and several times played with the boys down in Mill-creek") was hired on the basis of appearance. "He looked so large and handsome and so very like a catcher," wrote Caylor dryly, "that Manager Chapman was mashed, and straightway engaged him, and clinched the bargain with a dinner."

Judging a catcher on outward appearances was of course a cardinal mistake, and Caylor outdid himself in describing the predictable results: "When Al pulled on his sole-leather gloves and posed near the grand stand at three o'clock, the crowd scarcely breathed. Zip came the ball from Golden's hand; bang it went against the back-stop, because Al had stooped too late to pick it up. It took several minutes for him to gauge the speed of Golden's pitching, but he got it down fine at last, and stopped a ball, every once in a while. But the low comedy parts came in when the new catcher went up close behind the bat. A batter had but to get on first base and the run was scored. They went to second and third without danger, and tallied on a passed ball. Be it said to his credit, though, that Jennings never flinched, but stood up against Golden's hot pitching with great nerve and stood the punishment bravely. He was strong enough last night to whisper that if Knowdell doesn't get here by to-morrow he is willing to catch for

[Milwaukee's other pitcher, Sam] Weaver, but Weaver says he'll paralyze him if he attempts it."

To top it off, the unfortunate recruit was dubbed with an unforgettable nickname in the article's headline, which proclaimed: "The Coming Catcher; Alamazoo Jennings Makes His Debut; His Hands Gave Out, But His Gall Lasted." Caylor's account was widely quoted and reprinted. Even Jennings admitted, "I read a few lines and wanted to fight. I read a few lines more and had to laugh."

Jennings went on to a long career as a professional umpire but was never again referred to by his given names. The "Alamazoo" nickname stuck to him "like wax." He also had to endure countless retellings of his major league debut, which grew more exaggerated with the passage of time. In 1888 a Milwaukee sportswriter referred to Jennings's "famous record of twenty-six passed balls in one game." Caylor also couldn't resist getting in additional digs, reporting in 1887 that Jennings had made "the awful threat that he will go to catching again. His Golden (N.B.—Note the joke) opportunity in that capacity created a panic. But since that time, we have had several earthquakes, and are growing bolder."

Although no other catching fill-in could rival the notoriety of Alamazoo Jennings, there were a host of similar tales. In a four-day span in May 1884, the dreams of aspiring catchers Marcus Kragen, Alex Gardner, and Wallie Walker were all burst. Kragen traveled all the way from San Francisco to Washington, D.C., for a chance at glory as a major league catcher, only to commit fourteen passed balls in three games and soon find himself making the long journey home to California. Across town, Alex Gardner was charged with six errors and six passed balls in his lone major league game, even though pitcher Ed Trumbull soon let up in a game that was called after only seven innings.

Gardner's debut came only two days after that of Walter Walker, the young man described in the Introduction, who would give up several promising career opportunities to try to become a catcher. When Walker first reported to camp, he created a favorable impression by his ability to catch hard-throwing, deceptive left-handed pitcher Dupee Shaw. One account placed him in the tradition of naturals like Doug Allison and Billy Holbert by gushing, "Walker caught, and though he never saw Shaw previous to the first instant he caught him perfectly." But soon Walker's hands became very sore and his catching suffered. When finally given a chance to handle Shaw in a major league game, he committed two errors and a handful of passed balls, which led to his release.

A man identified only by the surname of Murphy was a major league catcher for "about thirty seconds" during the 1884 season. After the release of Walter Walker, Detroit could not find a catcher to handle Dupee Shaw's offerings. The frustrated southpaw finally jumped to Boston's entry in the Union Association, where the chance to again work with veteran catcher Lew Brown, the man who had originally discovered him, enabled Shaw to regain his effectiveness. But when Brown did not show up for the team's August 16 game, rookie Ed Crane had to fill in. A second-inning fastball from Shaw "nearly tore Crane's forefinger out by the roots . . . [and] left the Bostons without a catcher. After a long delay a young man by the name of Murphy was found in the grand stand who claimed to be a catcher." It was taken for granted that the new catcher would not be able to handle Shaw's deliveries, so the southpaw traded places with the team's other pitcher, James Burke, who had been playing the outfield. Yet even Burke's less demanding offerings proved overwhelming to Murphy: "three errors and two runs in about thirty seconds settled his business and he was sent to left field, [Tom] O'Brien coming to catch Burke and [Frank] Butler going to second." Amazingly, Boston won the game 6-4.

Indeed, many catching aspirants were literally men in disguise. In addition to Murphy, other catchers who didn't stick around long enough to have their given names recorded for posterity included a man named Jones who tried his hand at catching for Baltimore in 1874, a fellow named Bestick whose unsuccessful stint came in 1872, a man named Haley who committed seventeen passed balls in two games, and an elusive chap named Gilroy who actually played nine games for two different major league clubs without leaving a name or forwarding address. Finally there was a man named O'Donnell who caught just a single game for Philadelphia's Union Association club on July 16, 1884, and whose entire major league career was encapsulated in these words by *Sporting Life*: "A catcher from Littlestown, Pa., attempted to catch for [Sam] Weaver, but was not equal to the task."

It is anybody's guess whether these mystery men deliberately concealed their identities or whether it was just a case of nobody caring enough to record their given names. But others clearly did try to keep their identities a secret. Kragen, for instance, played under the name of Mike Creegan because of parental disapproval, and his true identity has only recently been established. The famed Yale catcher Al Hubbard used the alias "Al West" to catch one major league game, though he was too well known for his true identity to remain a secret. A man who caught a single game for Washington in 1884 under the name of "Rollinson" has now been tentatively identified as another famed collegiate catcher named William Winslow, but some doubt remains.

Many of these men may have chosen these disguises because, like Kragen's and Hubbard's, their families shared Reverend Jonathan Crane's "suspicion" of the men who played professional baseball. It also seems likely, however, that at least a few of them wanted to find out if they would be successful before revealing their true identities. After all, almost half of the approximately five hundred men who caught in the major leagues during the nineteenth century caught ten games or fewer, and well over a hundred of them caught only a single major league game. So it made sense for these men to hedge their bets.

Or perhaps some of them feared the fate that befell a man named Wright who signed to catch with a minor league club in London, Ontario, in 1887. This unfortunate man proved so woefully inept behind the plate that the club had him arrested for having received an advance under false pretenses.

While it certainly wasn't their intention, the failures of men like "Alamazoo" Jennings, Fred Gunkle, and the mysterious men known only by their surnames contributed to the mystique of the catcher. Like Henry Fleming in *The Red Badge of Courage*, they had grown up dreaming of achieving heroism under pressure, only to fail when the opportunity presented itself. But their misfortune nonetheless confirmed how extraordinary it was when a Doug Allison or a Billy Holbert could appear from nowhere and overcome the million-to-one odds against becoming a star major league catcher.

6

The Breaking Point

"The catcher occasionally gets a hot foul tip on his stomach, but it rarely disables him for a wonder. Most of the heroes who stand behind the bat hold a bit of rubber between their front teeth and lips to guard against having their teeth knocked out."—*Boston Globe* (1876)

■ BY THE mid-1870s the catcher had attained an extraordinary degree of prestige and importance, and a formidable mystique had begun to surround him. Yet by then, signs were emerging that this state of affairs could not last.

For the better part of a decade, pitchers' release points had been steadily rising, and baseballs had been growing more and more inert. As a result, scores continued to decline, with matters reaching their nadir on May 11, 1877, when a twenty-four-inning scoreless tie between Harvard University and the professional Manchester club was played with a baseball that was very hard to begin with and eventually became so "punky" that it was impossible to hit out of the infield. Yet instead of being derided as a farce, many viewed this game as a historic event and would later cite it as a landmark. What this game really symbolized was that baseball had reached a breaking point and that these trends could not continue.

Obviously scores couldn't go any lower, but it was just as apparent that the other trends couldn't continue. The catcher's role had become so outsized that the game was rendered boring and predictable, a development that hindered efforts to establish professional baseball on a sound financial footing. More than anything else, catchers were victims of their own success. The curveball began attracting notice in 1872, then swept the country in 1874 and 1875 with results that were initially invigorating. Clubs that had lacked the resources to compete with better-financed rivals now saw that everything had changed. Instead of the daunting task of assembling nine great players, all they had to do was find a skilled curveballer and his catching partner.

As for the other seven players, between strikeouts and foul tips a good pitcher and catcher could now account for so many outs that it no longer seemed to matter much whether they were any good or not. Overpowering pitching had always led to foul tips, and the frequency of such outs increased as pitchers baffled batters with repertoires of "the outward and inner curve, of the rising and of that most deceitful of all, the diving ball." Talented batteries seemed to be in such control that when they "got tired of a batter they would just let him tick the ball" and the catcher would record the out. Even when a ball was put in play, it was rarely struck solidly enough to test the fielders. An 1875 game account observed that the battery made up of George Bradley and Tom Miller "constitute the main strength of the club. They are not supported by a first-class field, but, if their work of to-day is a criterion, they do not need one. The field were called upon to do but the easiest kind of play, to stop weak 'bunts,' catch puny fly balls and fouls, and scarcely a ball was struck that would bother an ordinary player."

Dissatisfaction with this state of affairs mounted. George Wright, who had decided catching was too dangerous and became instead the game's best shortstop, lamented that pitchers and catchers were now so dominant that "if your pitcher gives out you might as well stop playing, and it is just the same with the catcher." He preferred the days when "the pitcher was of no more importance than any other man in the team." Meanwhile things kept getting worse for those players who did not pitch or catch. Cleveland's 1872 tactic of signing two top-flight pitchers and catchers soon spread, and before long many clubs were replacing incumbent outfielders and sometimes even infielders with spare pitchers and catchers. All too often, these extra pitchers and catchers were better paid than players with experience at other positions.

Soon it wasn't just fellow players who felt abused; spectators and journalists were tiring of the monotony of strikeout after strikeout, occasionally punctuated by a caught foul tip. A Louisville baseball fan complained that when professional clubs visited, "Four-fifths of the outs (by the local club) in these games were by strikes and fouls . . . giving no chance to display the chief beauty of the game, viz., the in and outfielders. Professional clubs or their managers seem to forget that the spectators paid for admission, and desired to see the whole nine performing and not merely two of their players." Even Harvard University president Charles Eliot eventually joined the chorus of disapproval, sniffing that baseball was a poor game because "nobody on the outside derives any healthful exercise from it except the catcher and the pitcher."

Adding to baseball's woes, the mid-1870s saw accusations of game-fixing reach epidemic proportions. Many factors lay behind this dispiriting development, but one of the biggest was the dominance and singular role of the catcher. When baseball had been a game in which the contributions of all nine men mattered, fixing a game was a monumental task; by contrast, in the mid-1870s bribing a catcher was all that it took for pitch after pitch to roll to the backstop, making the result a foregone conclusion. Many of the fix rumors were baseless, but since it was impossible to prove that a game was on the level, they were likely to fly whenever a catcher had a bad game. True or not, each new allegation contributed to a toxic atmosphere reminiscent of Jonathan Crane's comment that "everyone connected with [baseball] seems to be regarded with a degree of suspicion."

As fatigue with 1-0 pitchers' duels and suspicion of the outcomes grew, the "base ball fever" of the mid-seventies began to fade. Pressure mounted to reduce the importance of the pitcher and catcher and once more make all the players active participants. In particular, the combination of the catcher's great importance, his susceptibility to injury, and his vulnerability to bribes (or rumors of them) made it imperative that his role be curtailed.

Pitchers were typically just as well paid, but they at least could usually be counted on to pitch day after day. Catchers, on the other hand, were a constant injury risk, and when an injury came, it often meant hiring an expensive replacement and paying him as well. Just as important, the ever-higher release points resulted in pitches that were now taking a terrible toll on the catcher's body. His undeniable courage seemed more and more like folly. As one observer noted in 1877, "but few catchers in the country can stand up before the present cannon-ball throwing, and those few are being rapidly battered into oblivion." Sportswriters were kept busy writing reports such as this one: "The Lowells need a catcher just at present. [Dennis] Sullivan's finger will keep him from playing for several days, and [William] Hawes and [Ed] Stoughton are both lame and unfit to stand behind the bat." No matter how many catchers a team had, it could never rest secure.

When a team's starting catcher was disabled, the results became tediously predictable and fans stayed home. This was pointedly illustrated during the National League's inaugural season in 1876. One of the main complaints about the National Association had been its admission of weak cooperative teams, which divided the circuit into haves and have-nots. In particular, the new eight-club league aimed to end the monotony of Boston and its nonpareil battery of Spalding and White running away with every pennant.

Unfortunately the National League's maiden season showed that parity remained elusive. With Jim White having already signed with Chicago for a reported $2,500, John Clapp took advantage of being the best available catcher. He met with representatives of the Boston, Hartford, and St. Louis clubs at Earle's Hotel in New York and "stated to them that he was on the auction block; that he had a surety offered him of $2,500, and that the club paying the largest amount over that sum would secure his services. He then left them to make their 'sealed proposals,' and the result was that John opened the envelopes in their presence, and said, in a moment: 'Gentlemen, I will play in St. Louis.' The offer accepted was in the neighborhood of $3,000, but what the others were it is difficult to state."

Hartford responded by signing Doug Allison for the princely salary of $2,000 while Charley Snyder signed with Louisville for the same amount and New York scooped up catcher Nat Hicks (and his longtime battery mate Bobby Mathews). That exhausted the supply of catchers who could be relied upon to provide star play and to stay healthy, leaving the other three clubs to suffer.

Worse, the five teams that had signed a star catcher had also recruited at least one experienced backup, and Hartford, which was using hard-throwing Tommy Bond to pitch, had signed both Bill Harbridge and Dick Higham. Thus Chicago, Hartford, and Louisville entered the 1876 season with catchers who had combined to catch more than one hundred games during the 1875 season while the receivers signed by New York and St. Louis each had caught at least sixty games. In contrast, Philadelphia, Cincinnati, and Boston had failed to enlist a single experienced catcher. Philadelphia's management did sign Fergy Malone to a lucrative $250-a-month contract, only to have shareholders initially vote down the signing. Boston and Cincinnati also came up empty, with even Chicago amateur Patrick Quinn declining Cincinnati's offer. So each of these three teams handed the crucial job to rookies and ended up paying their primary receiver $1,000 or less.

When the 1876 season ended, the standings were nearly in lockstep with the amount spent on catching. Chicago won the pennant, with St. Louis and Hartford close behind. In mid-June, Boston turned to rookie Lew Brown, and his surprisingly good performance enabled the team to finish fourth, though this was quite a comedown after four straight pennants. Louisville and New York came in fifth and sixth respectively. Lagging hopelessly behind were Philadelphia, which used no fewer than ten different catchers, and Cincinnati, which split the workload between three unimpressive rookies, none of whom would ever again catch regularly in the major leagues.

The only thing that couldn't be predicted was injuries. When they sidelined a team's primary catcher, a slump inevitably followed. Hartford, for instance, stayed close on Chicago's heels until Tommy Bond's lightning pitching disabled Allison, Harbridge, and Higham. With all three "suffering from sore hands, the result of the great pace, Bond was unable to send in his swiftest balls or to get on the curve with full effect, the result being his comparatively easy punishment." Chicago seized the opportunity to forge an insurmountable lead in the pennant race.

Injuries to catchers also took their toll on other teams. Jim Devlin, now with Louisville, was throwing so hard that catcher Charley Snyder, "to face it at all, had to stand with his back almost against the lower part of the members' stand." Even with these precautions, Snyder's hands soon became very sore and Devlin, "having no one to hold him had to pitch easier than usual." Predictably, batters feasted on these deliveries. Philadelphia went through one catcher after another, prompting reporters to file dispiriting reports such as this one: "The Athletics again appeared in the field without a catcher to-day, and Burge [John Bergh], of Our Boys' Club, of this city [Boston], filled the position until the third inning, when they sent him into the field, and [Ed] Ritterson, with very sore hands, was called. He was struck by a ball in the throat in the sixth inning, and Burge was recalled."

So even after the creation of a new league and the breakup of professional baseball's first dynasty, the National League's historic first season ended with yet another pennant for the battery of Spalding and White. Moreover the pennant-winning Chicago White Stockings struck many as survivors more than vanquishers, with White having avoided injury yet again. Some attributed White's endurance to Spalding's less taxing deliveries: "The Chicago team has one advantage in possessing Spalding as their pitcher, and that is that, unlike [Tommy] Bond, [George] Bradley, [Jim]

Devlin and the other curved-line and swift-pace pitchers, he is not so hard on his catcher as they are, as his thorough command of the ball, his intimate knowledge of the batsmen, and his strategic skill, make his delivery the least costly in wear and tear of the catcher." Others noted that White was taking advantage of his extraordinary throwing arm to move farther from the plate: "We no longer see him come up close to the bat after two strikes have been called on a batsman, he preferring to stay back and take the chances on a foul, and, not getting one, throwing the man out at first base. And how he can throw! Most catchers are afraid to throw from the back stop . . . as the distance is so considerable, but not so with White. The moment the ball reaches him after three strikes have been called and he has failed to get it on the first bound, he lets it go to first base like a rifle shot. Twice while playing the Mutuals here he had occasion to make this kind of play, and the way he did it created more applause from the spectators than any single point of play I have ever witnessed."

Whatever the reason for White's durability, by the close of the 1876 season many were starting to believe that having a catcher with the skill and ability to stay healthy was the only thing that really mattered. That perspective was dramatically illustrated by an observer in Philadelphia, which won only fourteen games and skipped a late-season road trip because of financial woes, prompting the National League to revoke the franchise. Nonetheless one observer concluded late in the disastrous season that "Some of the best talent in the profession is in the nine this year, and had they had a catcher like Clapp, White or some other 'staying' players, a long list of victories would have resulted in lieu of defeats. Coons [Bill Coon], Ritterson and Malone did all they could; but neither [sic] was capable of withstanding the swift delivery of [Lon] Knight and [George] Zettlein, nor, indeed, could either of the latter 'let himself out' with crippled men behind the bat."

While this faith that the right catcher was all that it took to transform a cellar-dweller into a pennant contender was very optimistic, such claims were not impossible. When the New York version of baseball began to assume permanent shape in the late 1850s, one of its selling points was that the contributions of all the players mattered. Now, less than two decades later, baseball relied to an undue extent on just two of those nine players—and in particular on the ability of one of them to stay healthy. This new reality was crippling baseball's appeal. And what savvy businessman would want to become involved in an enterprise in which all the planning in the world could be undone by a single foul tip?

Subsequent years told a similar story. Boston manager Harry Wright learned his lesson from the 1876 season and lured Jim White back to Boston for the 1877 campaign while also signing Lew Brown to an unprecedented four-year contract. With Brown doing a fine job of catching Tommy Bond and White leading the league in batting, slugging, runs batted in, and a number of other offensive categories, the pennant returned to Boston. Meanwhile Cal McVey's inability to handle George Bradley's pitching caused Chicago to plummet to fifth in what was now a six-team league. The White Stockings were saved the indignity of finishing in the basement only by Cincinnati, which teetered on the brink of bankruptcy and spent a second consecutive year unsuccessfully experimenting with unproven catchers.

Cincinnati rebounded in 1878 by signing Jim White, who returned to catching full time by forming a battery with his brother Will. Although now a full seven years older than any other regular catcher in the league, White came close to playing on his sixth consecutive pennant winner. After two straight years in the league's cellar, Cincinnati finished a close second, only four games behind Boston. This dramatic improvement sent the heartening message that rapid turnabouts were possible, but it also once more demonstrated how closely a team's fate was tied to the health of its catcher.

The 1878 season did see greater parity among the league's catchers: five of the six teams had a veteran catcher who stayed relatively healthy. The exception was the new entry from Milwaukee—the club that became so desperate it used Alamazoo Jennings. What made Milwaukee's season so disheartening was that manager John Chapman had taken every possible precaution, signing Billy Holbert, the phenom who was covered in coal dust when discovered, and the up-and-coming youngster Charley Bennett. Both men, however, were plagued by injuries, and a desperate Chapman "telegraphed all over the country for a man who can catch," only to learn that "catchers are scarce." All too many game accounts reported sadly, "[Mike] Golden was not able to pitch with his usual force." Eventually Chapman bowed to reality and began using Sam Weaver as his primary pitcher, but Milwaukee ended a distant last and watching the club's games was almost as painful as trying to handle Golden's deliveries.

"There are a number of persons who are cursing the Milwaukees because they don't win games and suggest bad management, sell-outs, and all that sort of nonsense," observed one sportswriter. But he knew better, explaining, "The simple fact is that the Milwaukees are playing without a catcher." An even more succinct summary of this sad truth was conveyed in a headline that read, "It Is Heart-Breaking; A Good Club Demoralized for the Want of a Catcher." Milwaukee's baseball enthusiasts were just as demoralized, and the franchise was surrendered at season's end—the city did not reenter the National League until 1953. But the loss was not just Milwaukee's. In a six-team league, any given team was involved in one of every three games played, which meant that an injury to one team's catcher could give spectators a good reason to stay away from one-third of the games played in the league that season. That represented a lot of money. Something had to be done.

Semipro and amateur clubs stood to lose less revenue, but their games were just as prone to ruin by instability behind the bat. The comments of Janesville Mutuals pitcher Frank L. Smith illustrated just how dramatically the fortunes of semipro teams rose and fell based on the health of their catcher. A similar chorus of laments came from semipro clubs with injured catchers throughout the country.

Games between these clubs could also be disrupted if one of the teams surreptitiously imported a top-flight battery. A much-anticipated contest that was supposed to decide the "amateur" championship of Illinois was one of many casualties. The host Bloomington club protested vigorously when the Blue Sox of Jacksonville "brought a paid pitcher, named [Dean] Simpson, alias Dean, from St. Louis, and a paid catcher named Parker from Quincy. Captain Cheney, of the Bloomington Club, endeavored to conclude matters by offering to play the game by having Simpson play any other position except that of pitcher. After a short but good natured wrangle, [the] Blue Sox left the ground, the Bloomingtons afterward playing a picked nine and refunding gate fees."

Collegiate competition too was affected dramatically. After Northwestern University defeated a rival school in an 1875 game to win a coveted silver ball, the losing side refused to surrender the trophy until they were shown proof that Northwestern's catcher was in fact a student. When the New York College Association championship was won by Union College in 1880, accusations flew that the Schenectady school had won only by passing off William Ahearn, a semiprofessional catcher from Troy, as a "student." By 1884 the dire need for catchers had prompted one college to offer what was in effect the first athletic scholarship. "The Amherst College University nine," reported the *Cleveland Herald*, "has a young catcher, named Sullivan, whom they are sending through college and paying his expenses for his ball playing qualities. He was picked up in Keene, N.H."

Some amateur clubs found it so hard to find a catcher capable of handling a hard-throwing pitcher that they were inclined to give up. In a throwback to the rules once used in the Massachusetts Game, a few clubs began stationing a second man—known as a pigtail or hindcatcher—behind the catcher. One aspiring amateur pitcher wrote to Harry Wright for a tryout and informed him, "The batsman can not hit the ball, so it will not be necessary if you engage me to have any men in the field. You can put the other eight men back of the bat, as it will take them all to stop the ball." This letter-writer was presumably a bit deranged, but the problem he described was familiar and real. The game was broken and needed radical surgery.

7

Protecting the Catcher's Face
(But Bruising His Ego)

An old man sat in his easy-chair,
Smoking his pipe of clay,
Thinking of years when he was young,
Thus whiling his hours away.

Thinking when he was but a boy,
So full of mirth and glee,
And we hear him say "How things have changed;
They are not as they used to be.

"When I was young, and played baseball
With the Reds of Sixty-nine,
We then knew how to play the game;
We all were right in line.

"We used no mattress on our hands,
No cage upon our face;
We stood right up and caught the ball
With courage and with grace."
                                    —Harry Ellard

BY THE mid-seventies the need to do something about the catcher's dominant role had become urgent. Teams were paying enormous amounts for a good catcher, then living in constant fear that he would be injured.

The inordinate role of the pitcher and catcher also made a mockery of the efforts of sportswriters like Henry Chadwick to depict baseball as a game that rewarded teamwork. The other seven players were growing resentful about their diminished roles.

Perhaps most critically, far too many baseball games were boring to watch. All too often, one side had a battery that worked together effectively and could prevent its opponents from scoring at all by means of a long string of strikeouts and caught foul tips, while the other side lacked a skilled catcher and allowed runs with predictable regularity. Supporters of the losing side could only hope that the opposing catcher would get injured or accept a bribe, or that their team could lure another team's catcher into breaking his contract. None of these sentiments was exactly sporting, and the days when baseball could be seen as a test of character seemed very far away indeed.

And if both sides had great catchers, the resulting lack of runs was beginning to strike some as tedious. "In these days of scientific base ball, when 15 or 24 innings are played without either side scoring," one observer wrote after the celebrated twenty-four-inning scoreless tie of 1877, "it is refreshing to read of an old-fashioned muffin game where every player scores a home run on passed balls, etc." An Indianapolis sportswriter grumbled that local pitcher Ed "The Only" Nolan seemed to think "that he was not playing base ball unless about every other batter struck out on him. The consequence was that he wore out the catcher, himself, and the audiences. It may be more scientific playing, but it is not nearly so satisfactory to the crowd. Spectators enjoy the sport much more when hits and runs are made and a chance given for exhibitions of good fielding and base running. Strictly scientific games, where the scores are kept down, never were and never can be very popular because they become tiresome and exceedingly monotonous." These writers had pinpointed a basic truth that had been neglected by the advocates of low-scoring "model games" and "scientific base ball"—that a passed ball is inherently more exciting than a pitch the catcher snags.

After five years of steadily building, the calls for change became a crescendo. A poem published in the *New York Sunday Mercury* began, "Let up on the scientific/ Give us more of play terrific." A *Cincinnati Commercial* sportswriter tried in vain to find anyone who wasn't anxious to see more scoring. "There is no doubt at all," he wrote, "about the vast majority of patrons and admirers of baseball in this city being tired of the present style of the game. We believed that was the general feeling, and a few days ago made some energetic statements in favor of 'less science and more baseball playing,' and were not disappointed in the manner the suggestion was received by the public. But we were surprised to find how strongly the people feel upon the subject, and how emphatically they pronounce against the present fearfully and wonderfully scientific game, and how earnestly all the oldest and most experienced baseballists declare for a return to the old style of straight-arm pitching. Yesterday we talked, in the course of reportorial perambulations about the city, with at least fifteen gentlemen prominently interested in baseball, either pecuniarily, or from love of the game, or both. Without exception, they indorsed what had been said concerning the character of the game, and enthusiastically approved of any movement or agitation toward bringing about a reform in the game, and a return to the simple, cheaper and more exciting game of former days. In fact, public opinion, in this city at least, appears to be unanimous upon the subject. We know the president of the association and the directors to be in favor of the proposed change. We know the baseball reporters of the various city papers to be a unit in opinion on the subject, and we have yet to hear from the oldest patrons of the game a dissenting voice. Now there is a great deal to be said on the other side of the matter, and we tried in vain to find somebody to say it and advocate the present style of playing, but failed to do so. Everybody we met were on the other side. If there is anybody who has got a good word to say for the scientific game, we would be glad to hear from them."

Despite this overwhelming consensus that something needed to be done, balancing the workloads of the nine players proved difficult to accomplish. To begin with, everyone had his own ideas about how to increase scoring and excitement, with the most common proposal being to turn back the clock. In 1877 a sportswriter spoke for many when he suggested that a return to old-style pitching would be necessary, since "One of the great objections to [George] Bradley and all pitchers of this style is that he wears out a catcher so soon."

Yet there was a critical flaw in the idea of turning back the clock. The new delivery styles had emerged not because anyone believed they were good for the game, but because all the rules crafted to prevent these deliveries had proved unenforceable. None of those who called for a return to the old style of pitching had a solution to this vexing problem. Moreover the National League's reliance on local umpires made it impractical— visiting teams felt fortunate if they weren't out-and-out robbed by a partisan umpire, so no one wanted to give these men additional authority regarding release points. The futility of pitching restrictions was once again illustrated in 1878. Still unwilling to wave the white flag, the National League decreed that pitchers had to release the ball from below the waist. Pitchers simply responded by wearing their belts at deceptively high levels.

The latest failed efforts to enact delivery restrictions proved what Henry Chadwick had said back in 1872: the only effective way of preventing pitchers from throwing with all their might was the reality that the catcher could not handle such pitches. Thus a return to underhand pitching would occur only if catchers were to admit that they could no longer stand up to hard-throwing pitchers. But there were far too many determined and fearless young men for that to happen. Even when one went down with injuries, as we have seen, numerous volunteers were eager to replace him.

Discussion continued about other rules changes that might increase scoring, but most of the ideas had major shortcomings. Harry Wright, who had also come to believe that more scoring would be a good thing, proposed in 1876 that a foul ball caught on the first bounce should no longer constitute an out. This would undoubtedly have increased offense and reduced the ability of the catcher to dominate the game. Ironically, however, the proposal was defeated out of concern for the catcher's health. As an opponent explained, "the catcher who faces swift pitching is overworked now, and, since the effect of the new scheme would be to put additional labor on him, it seems an unwise change. If the catcher had no bound-catch to depend on, he would be obliged to be under the bat nearly all the game, and no living player could stand that for any length of time." Many other rules changes were suggested, including renewal of the sentiment that it would be only fair to allow the batter to leave his box in order to chase those elusive curveballs. Yet no consensus emerged, in part because so many continued naively to insist that it was possible to return to the days when the pitcher adhered to the underhand delivery restrictions.

At the close of the 1876 season one sportswriter predicted that "one of two things is probable—that there will be a return to the old style of pitching, or any style of throwing will be allowed. The tendency is towards the latter, but when that style becomes legal, if ever, it will be necessary to use a softer ball, as it would be impossible for any catcher to face swift and straight-hand throwing with the ball now in use." But neither of these courses was practicable. In particular, the days when baseball was looked upon as a child's game were a far too recent memory to consider a return to a soft ball.

Accordingly, at the National League meetings it was decided to modify the composition of the baseball but in a different direction. Boston sporting goods manufacturer Louis Mahn was hired to create the league's official baseball, with instructions to replace the "mush ball" with "a lively, hard, and uniform ball." In hopes of preventing clubs from ignoring the rules by introducing baseballs with little or no rubber, plans were also made for each ball to be inspected by the league secretary, sealed in foil, placed in a box, and delivered to the umpire.

This seemed a promising approach, but things didn't go as the league had hoped. When Mahn's official baseballs were unveiled, they proved "too soft, and, after a little use, grew flabby on the outside, so that one could be picked up by the slack like a kitten by the scruff of its neck or a small boy by the slack of his breeches." So Mahn was instructed to try again "to make a harder and livelier ball." This, however, was no easy matter, especially with little time left before the start of the season. In order to achieve the desired liveliness, Mahn had to use nearly pure rubber, but an ounce of this purer rubber took up nearly twice as much space as before. Finding it impossible to meet the requirements for both weight and circumference, a desperate Mahn tried using cotton yarn instead of the traditional woolen yarn and found that he could wind the new yarn tightly enough to meet all the specifications.

Unfortunately the change gave the ball "the same degree of pliability that would exist in a billiard-ball covered with thin and tightly-stretched horse-hide—not more." In addition, while the ball with woolen yarn became "mellowed" after a few innings and could "be handled without pain," the one with cotton could not "by any possible amount of use be softened at all." Fielders began to fear for their safety, and of course it was catchers who suffered the most. "Base balls these days," wrote one sportswriter, "are so hard and projected with a rifle movement of such force that a catcher, after two days' consecutive service behind the bat, has a pair of hands like the jaws of a crocodile." The league was flooded with complaints, making it necessary to bring the softer baseball back on an emergency basis.

After additional tinkering, Mahn eventually produced a ball that proved satisfactory, and the next few years saw scoring in the National League gradually rise. But the rival International Association had no procedure for checking its official baseballs and continued to be plagued by "mush balls" that could not be hit "out of the diamond" because their cores were made of "a lump of mud rubber, which bears no resemblance to the ounce of rubber which should have been there." So it was clear that modifying the baseball to increase offense was no simple matter, and when it went wrong the fielders suffered, with catchers inevitably bearing the greatest burden.

With the game's leaders unable to find a way out of this dilemma, players were forced to make their own adjustments. One welcome change saw batters slowly but surely become accustomed to the break of the curveball. In 1874 and 1875 most of them had flailed helplessly at the evasive pitch, returning to the bench in despair. But over the next few years they gradually learned to gauge its trajectory, which helped them hit it when it broke over the plate and lay off it when it didn't. The curve remained a very effective pitch, but it no longer seemed unhittable. This change, coupled with the new ball, led to a gradual increase in scoring by the end of the 1870s.

While the game could afford to take a gradual approach to addressing the scoring drought, there was more urgency to protecting the catcher from the dangers he faced. One approach was to continue firmly reminding pitchers who threw too hard of the need to let up. It is revealing that one of the most effective approaches was to compare uncooperative pitchers to wild horses that needed to be broken. Tommy Bond was let go by Hartford after his hard-throwing ways injured all the team's catchers in 1876. Harry Wright signed Bond to pitch for Boston, but it was made clear to him that he needed to change his ways. "Probably Bond has been taught a lesson from the experience of the past season," scolded Henry Chadwick, "and under Harry Wright's teaching will not be likely to put his catchers through such an ordeal as he frequently did Allison, Higham and Harbidge [sic]; but if he has not, he assuredly will not find White, standing in the catcher's position, willing to submit to any such unnecessary punishment."

Bond did indeed reform and led Boston to the National League pennant in 1877, but other pitchers refused to be "broken." Buffalo released budding pitching star Larry Corcoran at the end of that season because the hard-throwing young pitcher "showed no sympathy for his catcher." Releasing star pitchers was, however, an extreme reaction. The issue would continue to resurface until a permanent solution emerged.

Another modest effort in this direction came when clubs began to use larger men as catchers. The late 1870s saw the rise of powerfully built yet agile catchers such as Silver Flint and Lew Brown (who, according to Tim Murnane, "was as stiff as an oak tree and as supple as the willow, and yet he weighed over 200 pounds"). Clubs began eagerly recruiting sturdy young catchers such as Orlando Curtis of East Somerville, Massachusetts, who had been recommended by several noted players and reportedly could lift a 100-pound dumbbell with one hand. One reporter gushed that the 180-pound Curtis possessed hands that "are even larger than Brown's, much like peck baskets, and open like a chaise top to receive the ball, and he is expected to develop into a style of catching similar to Brown's."

Alas, just hiring bigger catchers didn't solve the problem either. While their strength and bulk may have prevented a few injuries, these traits did not help them avoid the foul tips that sidelined so many catchers. Agility remained the catcher's most crucial skill, and those who were as "stiff as an oak tree" typically lacked the suppleness of the willow tree. The much-ballyhooed Orlando Curtis, for instance, never played in the major leagues.

Some clubs became so desperate that they tried moving a star player from another position to behind the plate, but these moves invariably backfired and showed that the ability to play catcher either came naturally or not at all. In 1879, for example, with Silver Flint injured, Chicago asked infielder Ed Williamson, one of the best all-around athletes in the game, to fill in. After only two games he was hastily returned to third base with "his hands badly bothered by two days behind the bat so that he will do well to stop anything to-day."

With no permanent solution in sight, the 1877 season saw catchers finally don the game's first piece of highly visible protective equipment. At first, the mask seemed to be no more than a sensible response to the dangers of catching. But eventually this piece of protective equipment and the ones that followed changed the nature of the position and the lives of the men who played it.

The man most directly responsible for introducing the mask was a Harvard student named James Tyng. In 1876 he played center field for the school's baseball team and also switched positions with team catcher Harry Thatcher whenever Thatcher's "hands got sore, an occurrence which happened quite frequently, as the well padded catcher's gloves of the present day were almost unknown, and we had to get along the best we could with ordinary buckskin gloves with the fingers cut off. The only protection then in use from foul tips was a small piece of rubber held between the teeth, and which, if struck by the ball, it was popularly supposed would prevent the disagreeable contingency of being forced to swallow one's teeth." When Thatcher graduated, team captain Fred Thayer asked Tyng to succeed him as the school's regular catcher. "To this my family was strongly

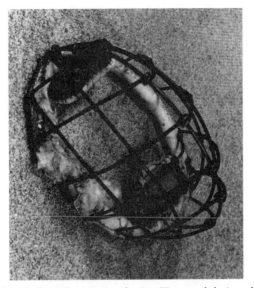

The pioneering baseball mask was worn by Jim Tyng and designed by fellow Harvard student Fred Thayer with the help of a wire maker. Spectators expressed their feelings about the mask by yelling "mad dog" and "muzzle 'em" whenever Tyng stepped on the field, while opposing players greeted him with "good natured though somewhat derisive pity." One sportswriter responded by predicting, "The near future may bring about many other improvements in the equipments of a base ball player, and we shall probably soon behold the spectacle of a player sculling around the bases with stove funnels on his legs, and boiler irons across his stomach." *(National Baseball Hall of Fame Library)*

opposed," recalled Tyng later, "and I told Thayer I would not be allowed to catch unless he could get up some protection for the face, and suggested that a mask somewhat in the nature of a fencing mask might answer the purpose."

With the help of a wire maker, Thayer devised such a mask, and it proved revolutionary. Tyng may not have been the first catcher to wear a mask—Thatcher later claimed to have experimented with one in the spring of 1876. But by his own account he had been "ridiculed the first time I wore the mask, partly because it was a new thing, and partly because the people considered that a catcher did not need any protection for his face. I threw the mask away." By contrast, Tyng's response to such jeers was to go right on wearing the mask. "When it made its first appearance on the field," he recollected, "it was a subject of ridicule to the 'bleaching board' element, and all such guys as 'mad dog' and 'muzzle 'em' were very frequent whenever I went up behind the bat; while on the part of the opposing players I was subjected to good natured though somewhat derisive pity."

As these responses suggest, Tyng's mask created a stirring visual impression. According to one account, it was "a cumbersome affair with broad strips of flattened iron that covered the face." Whereas the rubber mouthpiece had remained well hidden and elicited no response, the conspicuous nature of the mask forced people to voice an opinion, and they were quick to do so. A writer for the *Providence Dispatch* led the chorus of derision, predicting, "The near future may bring about many other improvements in the equipments of a base ball player, and we shall probably soon behold the spectacle of a player sculling around the bases with stove funnels on his legs, and boiler irons across his stomach." And the *Harvard Lampoon* was prompted to wonder whether a knight wearing full armor would become "the new safety uniform of the Harvard base ball nine." Little did the writers of these words imagine that catchers would soon be wearing additional equipment that in fact made them resemble these seemingly far-fetched images.

Another newspaper expressed indignation: "There is a great deal of beastly humbug in contrivances to protect men from things which do not happen. There is about as much sense in putting a lightning rod on a catcher as there is a mask." Yet this claim simply didn't jibe with reality. Like the new mask or not, everyone who knew anything about baseball recognized the peril of being a catcher. Far closer to the mark was the *Norristown Herald*, which dryly suggested "that the best protection in base-ball is to hire another fellow to take your place, while you sit on the fence and watch the player get crippled."

Meanwhile Henry Chadwick became the leading defender of Tyng's mask. The catcher's ascendance had been a great blow to Chadwick's vision of baseball because it placed a greater premium on individual performance than on team play while undermining his efforts to depict the game as a healthful recreation. His pleas to protect the catcher by forcing him to stand a safe distance behind the plate had fallen on deaf ears—but the mask gave him another chance to promote his favorite themes.

In column after column Chadwick extolled the virtues of the mask and urged its use. Yet with the image of the catcher as tough guy still in full force, most catchers joined Ban Johnson in regarding the new piece of equipment with "dark suspicion." The idea of wearing so conspicuous a piece of protective equipment on their faces seemed to be an attack on both their personal courage and the image of the catcher as a self-reliant do-it-yourselfer in the tradition of heroes like Daniel Boone.

When Pete Hotaling of Syracuse became the first catcher to wear a mask in Chicago, the crowd mocked him with catcalls about the "'rat-trap' and 'the bird-cage.'" When White Stockings team president William Hulbert saw Cal McVey practicing with one, he ordered him, "Don't you ever let me see you with that trap on in a game." Louisville catcher Charley Snyder bought a mask on a trip to Boston but seemed reluctant to wear it, prompting speculation that "he hasn't mustered up a sufficient amount of heart or cheek, whichever it may be, to introduce it to a Louisville audience yet."

The reservations of these catchers were compounded by the far-from-ideal design of the first masks. A hard foul might drive the brass wires into the catcher's face and cut him severely. When he tried to throw, the mask was "apt to jar the head, thereby upsetting the aim of the thrower." The catcher's vision was also obstructed by the mask, which could impede both his receiving and his ability to make accurate throws to the bases. Tyng's mask was "constructed of upright bars about an inch apart, and stands out from the face three or four inches," which naturally made it difficult for the catcher to see. Another early mask was described as being "almost as large as a water bucket and so heavy that many catchers discarded them on account of the weight and also that it took too long to throw them off." The mask was undermining not only the catcher's image but the extraordinary skill the position required.

As a result, the first professional catchers to experiment with the mask were quick to abandon it. After Phil Powers of London, Ontario, was struck in the eye by a foul tip, he agreed to "put on the cage" so as to "save himself from further injury." But the mask "militated against his catching," and he seems to have discarded it soon afterward. Mike Dorgan became the first catcher to wear one in a National League game on August 8, 1877, but he was recovering from an injury at the time and seems to have discontinued its use once his injury healed. Scott Hastings also tried one but found that it "bothers his playing" and went back to using just a rubber mouthpiece. Bill Harbridge, according to a later account, "made several attempts to catch with the mask on and each time threw it off in disgust. He claimed he could not see the ball through the wires of his mask."

Chadwick became just as frustrated, and in August he complained, "The amateur catchers have wisely adopted this valuable invention, and why the professional catchers do not use it, is a puzzle." Sensing that the mystique of the catcher as the ultimate tough guy was the biggest problem, he took the offensive, accusing professional catchers of lacking "as a class, the moral courage to face the music of the fire of chaff and raillery from the crowd, which the wearing of the mask frequently elicits. Plucky enough to face the dangerous fire of balls from the swift pitcher, they tremble before the remarks of the small boys of the crowd of spectators, and prefer to run the risk of broken cheek bones, dislocated jaws, a smashed nose or blackened eyes, than stand the chaff of the fools in the assemblage." A week later he lamented, "The idea seems to prevail among a prejudiced few that it is not plucky or manly to wear the mask."

Opposition to the mask began to dwindle soon after these harsh words were written, though Chadwick's comments may not have had a direct influence. Instead it appears that ballplayers overcame their initial reservations about the mask when they began to see its practical advantages. Thayer himself "visited the club room of the Boston nine, then at 39 Eliot street, and spoke to Harry and George Wright and others of the players present about the new invention. Most of them laughed at the idea of a man going around with a cage on his head. Harry, however, always ready and curious enough to look at anything new in base ball, asked Thayer to bring in the affair. The young man accordingly did so, and stood at one end of the room with it on, allowing the players to throw balls at it, which he easily butted off." According to Tyng, "For the first year, if I remember rightly, hardly anyone besides myself used the mask, but broken noses and damaged eyes soon brought conviction that catching behind steel bars was preferable to unnecessarily exposing one's features as a target for erratic foul tips, and the general adoption of the mask was the consequence."

The turning point seems to have come early in August 1877, when the Peck & Snyder sporting goods firm began advertising a mask that, it was claimed, could "be put on and off in a moment." The new mask also obstructed the catcher's vision less than Tyng's. At about the same time John Clapp was struck in the face by a foul ball, forcing him to try wearing a mask for protection. When he returned to action, Clapp continued to wear the mask. Before long a sportswriter remarked, "The catcher's mask is, it seems, destined to come in general use. It was much ridiculed when it was first adopted by a player in Boston, and afterwards when Hotaling of the Syracuse Stars put it on the crowds annoyed him greatly by their humorous remarks and shouts. Now, however, Clapp and Dorgan also use it, and others will certainly follow. It certainly does not add to the beauty

Catchers found the mask designed by Thayer to be "a cumbersome affair," so many new designs were tried, including this 1878 model. But many of the early masks obstructed the catcher's vision and were difficult to put on and take off. On some models the wires might cut the catcher's face when the mask was hit by a ball; others were so flimsy that they broke when hit by foul balls. *(National Baseball Hall of Fame Library)*

of the game to see noses broken, jaws demolished and foreheads laid open, and the mask is a 'needed innovation.'"

With the mask's benefits becoming apparent and its greatest drawbacks addressed, the mood shifted rapidly. Instead of worrying that they would appear cowardly if they donned a mask, catchers began to fear they would be behind the times if they *didn't* wear one. The sportswriter John Gruber later used an apt analogy to capture the plight of these catchers: "we can imagine other sturdy backstops of the ancient baseball days scornfully rejecting the artificial aid. Like the chivalrous knights of the twelfth century, when cannons were first employed in battle, they considered it a reflection on their bravery to use gunpowder, and so had holes shot through themselves while swinging their swords and wielding their battleaxes without coming face to face with the enemy." By 1878 almost all the professional catchers in the East appear to have tired of having "holes shot through themselves while swinging their swords" and had begun wearing masks.

The adoption of the catcher's mask did not in and of itself revolutionize baseball. Yet it set in motion a chain of events that would fundamen-
tally alter the catcher's position and the game itself. The acceptance of
masks paved the way for the chest protector and the mitt to be introduced
with much less resistance. In addition, the mask and the other new protective equipment that followed made it possible to make other changes
to the game's rules, apparatus, and strategies without constantly worrying
about the danger to the catcher. In the end, though the mask undoubtedly
prevented many injuries, it may have caused the catcher even more harm,
both physically and psychologically.

The emotional toll that wearing the mask took on catchers is of course
difficult to quantify, but it was not the less real. Even though the vast majority of professional catchers adopted the mask within a year of its introduction, the backlash continued. Long after there was any realistic chance of
reverting to a time without protective equipment, derisive comments were
still being directed at catchers who wore the mask. The fact that many of
the catching greats of the 1870s had left baseball (or switched positions) at
about the time of the mask's adoption made it easy to draw unflattering
comparisons between the old guard of catchers and the new breed.

An obvious reason for this prolonged backlash was that the mask was
so much more conspicuous than the limited protective equipment that
had been worn earlier. It also seems likely that this dislike of the mask
was intensified by its resemblance to another new invention made of wire.
After an Illinois farmer named Joseph Glidden received the first patent for
barbed wire in 1874, the new invention soon threatened the open-range
culture of Western ranchers. Quickly overcoming initial resistance, the use
of barbed wire to enclose Western ranches increased exponentially between
1874 and 1880. It was the cowboy who paid the price for this dramatic
transformation of the Western landscape. As David Dary notes, "in nearly
each instance where the fences were erected, it marked the beginning of
the end of the cowboy's open-range culture."

This upheaval stirred bitterness, and the sabotage of barbed-wire fences
led to violent conflicts in several Western states. With wealthy cattlemen
benefiting from the new fences, these uprisings were gradually suppressed,
and barbed wire began to crisscross the West. Nonetheless cowboys continued to loathe the barbed-wire fences, which struck them as being "*not
in harmony with the land.*" They expressed their disgust by describing the
new fences as "the curse of the country" and by referring to barbed wire as
the "devil's hatband."

Eventually sturdier, more functional masks were devised, such as this one from 1901. While the look is not that different, masks such as this one were much better suited to the demands of the catcher's position. *(National Baseball Hall of Fame Library)*

With both of these wire inventions entering the scene at the same moment and disrupting the lives of two iconic American figures, it seems logical to assume a connection. Notably, resistance to the mask continued far longer in the West. In 1883, five years after the mask had become a standard item in the East, a transplanted New Yorker named Rooney Sweeney tried to wear one in a game in California. Sweeney promptly "was 'booed' until he took it off in disgust."

Whatever the reasons, this passionate antipathy toward the mask continued, and it gathered momentum when additional pieces of protective equipment were added to the catcher's gear. All too often, this disdain was expressed in the form of unflattering comments about the men who wore the new equipment. Considering the adulation that had so recently been bestowed upon the catcher, such undeserved criticism must have been disheartening.

Meanwhile those who had not played the position failed to understand that, despite the tangible benefits of the mask in preventing injuries, catching remained a tremendously hazardous position. The false sense of security was especially well demonstrated in 1878 when a club in Easton,

Maryland, denied a report that its catcher had broken his nose, maintaining that he had suffered only a bruise. "Base ball is one of the healthiest games," stated one observer, "and gives more and better exercise than anything else. It is true there is some danger in it, but what is there no danger in?" Besides, he added, the club had "now procured a mask and there is no more danger in that quarter."

Unrealistic expectations of the mask's ability to prevent injuries led to a series of changes in the game, each of which eliminated safeguards that had protected the catcher and thereby put him in greater danger. One of the first occurred almost immediately, as catchers began to play closer to the plate far more often. At the close of the 1877 season Henry Chadwick noted this new trend, and even this staunch opponent of risk-taking endorsed the new positioning in certain situations.

The game's rules-makers followed suit in 1879 with several rules changes that showed they no longer considered the catcher's safety a priority. The strikeout rule was overhauled so that the catcher had to catch the ball on the fly to complete an out. At the same time the "foul bound" rule—which allowed a fielder to record an out by catching a foul ball on the first bounce—was eliminated. This latter rule change was reversed after one season, but within a few years the foul bound rule was permanently scrapped, thereby depriving the catcher of another of the distinctions that had set him apart. The game's strategies underwent a similar shift. If a pitcher was in danger of surrendering a base on balls, for example, it became customary for the catcher to stand directly behind the plate and provide "the pitcher a guide."

Each of these new developments can be traced to the conviction that the mask had made it safe for the catcher to stand in close proximity to the batter. But the new perils they created paled in comparison with the most important consequence of the introduction of the mask.

Although pitchers' release points had moved steadily upward during the 1870s, everyone understood that a return to the overhand motion used in the Massachusetts Game wouldn't be possible because catchers could not bear the resulting abuse. While many pitchers were testing the umpire's indulgence with deliveries from well above the waist, all-out overhand throwing remained out of the question. Moreover, as we have seen, hard-throwing pitchers like Tommy Bond, Jim Devlin, and Mike Golden had to ease up when working with an inexperienced or ailing battery mate. Pitchers who didn't do so knew they might be released for showing "no sympathy for his catcher," as had happened to Larry Corcoran.

Everything changed with the emergence of the mask. Pitchers ceased to feel any compunction about throwing the ball with all their might, and began to toy with delivery heights of shoulder level or higher. And in the aftermath of the belt-raising fiasco of 1878, the game's rules-makers finally recognized the futility of creating rules that umpires could not enforce.

In 1880 the National League took a bold new approach by moving the pitcher five feet farther from the plate. This offered tangible relief to catchers and prefigured the direction of future rules changes. The powers-that-be had at last begun to acknowledge that delivery restrictions were unenforceable; within a few years they entirely "gave up trying to fight the pitchers . . . and the pitching rules were so amended that the pitcher could throw or pitch the ball as suited his fancy." Thereafter rules-makers would instead try to limit the role of the pitcher and protect the catcher in ways that could be enforced—by lowering the number of balls required for a walk, by reducing the size of and eventually eliminating the pitcher's box, and by moving the pitcher still farther from the plate.

Any benefits that catchers might have realized from the 1880 decision to move the pitcher farther away were offset when pitchers found new ways to generate speed. In addition to throwing overhand, they put still more force behind their deliveries by means of increasingly complex wind-ups and running starts. "The twirler," recalled one observer, "was allowed to take a deliberate run of several feet or even yards before delivering the ball to the bat. Some of the big men, Jim Whitney of Boston, for instance, got the method down so fine that they managed to work up speed which not only puzzled the batsman to a ridiculous degree, but also frightened many of them out of their wits. A pitcher weighing 200 pounds had a tre-mendous advantage for the reason that he was enabled to put just so much more momentum into his delivery."

Whitney's "hop, step and jump" delivery proved downright scary to batters who had never seen anything like it before. At the same time it brought renewed attention to the old principle that there was no value to an unhittable pitch that was also uncatchable. In contrast to the offer-ings of Creighton and the early curveballers, Whitney's pitches were more likely to injure the catcher than to elude him. As one observer recollected: "Whitney, with his long legs and preliminary movements, was able to soak the ball to his catcher with frightful power. He used up both Mike Hines and Mertie Hackett, his backstops, [in a single] year, but he puzzled the best batters in the National League." But as Casey Stengel understood, this formulation was backward—it should have been reversed ("He puzzled the best batters . . . BUT he used up both . . . his backstops"), because Whitney's ability to overwhelm batters was all too often negated by the toll he took on catchers.

One of Whitney's catchers lasted fewer than twenty-four hours. Before the 1884 season, Boston signed "Burpee" Belyea, the "champion catcher of St. John, New Brunswick," to play on its reserve team. But when Belyea reported to the club, he was paired with Whitney, who "was in good form, and sent in several of his chain-lightning shots for the new man to capture. He succeeded in stopping them, and that is about all. It is reported he left the city the same night on a gravel train with his hand tied up in poultices and meal-sacks to take the swelling out of them."

Whitney was a native of New York State but had first come to prominence while pitching in California. Several descriptions of his novel delivery alluded to this background by explicitly reviving the comparison of such hard-throwing pitchers to wild horses that needed to be broken by an expert cowboy. "Boston's new pitcher," wrote one sportswriter, "uses six feet and one inch of body when he prepares to deliver the ball. He is said to throw such a swift ball that it will pass through a batsman's club without knocking it out of his hands. Harry Wright is now busy preparing plans for a patent catcher to gate in and retain the wild delivery of his untamed California 'bonanza.'" According to another imaginative scribe, "With the batsman in position, Whitney revolves the ball in his hands several times, then suddenly he curls himself up like a boy attacked with the grips or a dog retiring for the night, whirls his leg, his right arm shoots straight from the shoulder and the first thing the sorely perplexed striker knows, the sphere has been discharged and started on its errand. . . . Out of all this hysterical demonstration Whitney manages to put a great deal of speed in the ball and to practice considerable deception. But the batter is always in danger because he doesn't know, neither does Whitney, but what the sphere may land on his ear instead of in [catcher Charley] Snyder's hands. . . . Like the untamed steed of the Western wilds, he ought to be subdued, broken or driven with a curb-bit. . . . [Snyder was] kept as busy handling the rather wayward delivery of Whitney as a boy warding off the assaults of an angry bumble bee."

Instead of submitting to being broken in, Whitney became just as notorious as Larry Corcoran for his lack of compassion toward his catchers. During the seventh inning of an 1885 game in Philadelphia, "Whitney made several wild pitches, and because catcher Hackett was unable to stop the balls he kicked [argued], and Capt. [John] Morrill had to give both

This 1895 ad, while containing several factual misstatements, describes how the modifications to the catcher's mask improved the catcher's vision, comfort, and safety. (*National Baseball Hall of Fame Library*)

a lecture. When the Bostons took their seats and the Phillies went in the field Whitney again began abusing Hackett, and said he would not pitch any longer with Hackett behind the bat. Mr. Morrill again had to silence him. In the eighth and ninth [innings] the home team pounded him freely, and he blamed Hackett for it. For this he was hooted and jeered by all the spectators, and as Hackett went to the bat the crowd cheered him loudly. Everybody present sided with Hackett, who caught an excellent game, which angered Whitney still more. As Whitney stepped up to the bat he was again hooted. At the end of the game he was very mad and uttered some inaudible words, which a great many believed were threats at Hackett."

Each of these descriptions of Whitney is quite revealing. The hard-throwing pitcher clearly believed he was the dominant member of the battery—he saw himself as the cowboy while his catcher was the horse. But nobody else saw it that way. Even the spectators jeered Whitney for his presumption, and the sportswriter compared him to a horse in need of being broken. Whitney had not truly earned this authority but was just the latest in the long line of pitchers who had usurped power instead of earning it.

For pitchers of the early 1880s, speed came to be seen as the prime qualification. Diminutive but rifle-armed Larry Corcoran was signed by Chicago and, with the capable support of Silver Flint, became a star. But Corcoran continued to show little sympathy for his catchers, as illustrated by Flint's memorable description of how many of his mangled fingers were the result of Corcoran's deliveries.

The injuries to so many of the catchers paired with Whitney and Corcoran underscored the reality that the protection offered by the mask remained most imperfect. Even after the initial problem of wires that could be driven into the catcher's face had been addressed, masks continued to offer only limited shock absorption. An 1883 game account reported, "In the fifth inning [John Piggott] knocked a foul ball that tore [George Myers's] mask from in front of his face. [Fleet] Walker promptly loaned him the use of his, and the next ball, which was nearly a counterpart of the former, struck the catcher a terrible blow in the side that for a few moments threatened to disable him. Other players came to his assistance and in a short time, though weak, he was able to resume his position." Nor was it unheard of for early masks to break when struck hard enough.

More important, the mask offered no protection to the rest of the catcher's body, which was now taking more of a beating than ever. While countless examples of this carnage could be cited, perhaps the most extraordinary one occurred in yet another of Boston's games during the eventful 1884 season that saw Whitney "use up" most of the team's catchers. In this particular game, played in Detroit on September 26, the team's only remaining experienced catcher, Mertie Hackett, suffered a serious enough injury that he was allowed to leave the game. Rookie Tom Gunning took his place, and soon "a foul tip nearly knocked off his right leg, and he lay down for a minute. The next disaster came from a foul tip that tipped back a finger nail. Then another one sent a thumb back until it looked like the hammer of a gun at full cock." Since there was no other experienced catcher on hand to replace Gunning, teammates Charley Buffinton and Ezra Sutton "each tried to pull [the thumb] back into place, and after they had exhausted their surgical knowledge in vain, Joe Farrell took Gunning over to the back seats and a medical man straightened the thumb out in a jiffy. Still Gunning came up smiling. Next, a foul ball struck him in the groin, and he dropped once more. Odds of two to one were offered that he could not come up for another round and found no takers. When he stood up for the last time, he was ghastly pale." Fortunately it was Charley Buffinton rather than Whitney who was pitching, and Buffinton "reduced his pace," which enabled Gunning to complete the game.

As a consequence of all these changes to the game—more time spent close to the plate, overhand pitching, running starts, and the preeminence of speed pitching—the years following the introduction of the mask saw the catcher's position become more hazardous instead of safer. The extent to which the mask was directly responsible for these changes is debatable—the new piece of protective equipment did start the chain of events in motion, but many of them might have occurred anyway.

A couple of conclusions, however, are beyond question. The first is that, by the start of the 1880s, the fastball had assumed the role played by the curveball in the mid-1870s: it was a pitch that had the power to render major league batters helpless, but it could also be so hard on catchers as to be worse than useless. This new reality was starkly illustrated by the case of a pitcher named James O'Neill from Woodstock, Ontario. O'Neill inspired awe with a fastball that no batter in the region could hit, yet he experienced little success because no local catcher could handle his offerings. Then the great Lew Brown, suspended by Boston for drinking and in need of an income, headed for "the wilds of Canada." With Brown's capable support, young O'Neill was suddenly transformed into a world-beater. As fellow pitcher Curry Foley put it, "No man had ever been found to catch

O'Neil [sic] until 'The Horse' (Brown) made his appearance; and the ease with which Lew handled 'the cannon ball pitcher,' as O'Neil was called, fairly electrified the natives."

The next season O'Neill and Brown were signed to play for Detroit's new entry in the National League. But Brown hurt his arm, and "nobody else could hold O'Neil. [Detroit manager Frank] Bancroft reluctantly let him go." As he did so, Bancroft sadly explained, "He is the fastest pitcher I have ever seen, but if he gets pitching wild it will take four men and a truck horse to stop his cannon shoots." O'Neill bounced around for a couple of years, pitching well when he had a catcher who could handle his fastball, and struggling the rest of the time. Eventually he was converted to the outfield, where he became known as "Tip" O'Neill and blossomed into one of the era's most feared hitters.

The second point beyond question is that the catcher's role changed dramatically in the years immediately following the introduction of the mask. The mask created the illusion that the catcher was no longer a bold risk-taker. In reality, his position now posed more hazards than ever, but many of the new dangers were subtle ones that escaped the notice of most observers.

This was a most unhappy paradox, and things were about to get worse.

8

"A Lot of Fools in the Crowd Laugh at Him"

"With the pillows allowed at the present time the catchers above named would consider backstopping child's play."—Tim Murnane

■ THE INTRODUCTION of the mask finally provided much-needed protection for the catcher's face. But it also played a key role in the acceptance of overhand deliveries and a series of other new developments that increased the risk to the rest of the catcher's body. It soon became necessary to add more protection.

Just as the hidden rubber mouthpiece had preceded the mask, so too the first chest protectors were secretly worn under the uniform. A catcher named William Clare began to experiment with wearing extra padding under his uniform shirt in 1876, and no doubt other catchers made similar efforts to reduce the risk of injury. It was not, however, until 1883 that the first major step toward developing the chest protector was made by Detroit catcher Charley Bennett.

Like James Tyng, Bennett attributed his decision to wear the new piece of equipment to the concerns of a family member. His new wife Alice was worried about all the blows to his chest and created a "crude but very substantial shield . . . by sewing strips of cork of a good thickness in between heavy bedticking material." Charley tried it out and found that he could allow pitches to hit him square in the chest without experiencing "the slightest jar." While he wore the contraption underneath his jersey "for fear of fans roasting him for being chicken-hearted," its presence there was obvious enough that several newspapers reported on the new device.

Then a Hartford inventor named William Gray turned his attention to devising a better chest protector. Gray, who would later invent the pay telephone, used the same principle as the then-new pneumatic tire in designing an inflatable, padded protector that shielded the catcher's entire chest and groin area without obstructing his movement. After he sold the patent to Albert Spalding's sporting goods company, an ad for Gray's Patent Body Protector appeared in the 1884 *Reach Guide*.

As had happened with the mask, the availability of a professionally manufactured version proved crucial in the adoption of the chest protector. Skeptical ballplayers experimented with Gray's inflatable device and were amazed by its effectiveness. Jim White, now with Buffalo, and teammate Jim O'Rourke gave it an especially thorough workout before the 1884 season: "O'Rourke put the thing on and White amused himself by pounding it with fists and clubs, and jumping on it. As a final test, O'Rourke allowed White to stand ten feet away and throw a base ball at him as swiftly as he could and says he felt not the slightest inconvenience." Results like that were hard to ignore.

The chest protector met with some resistance. An 1890 article claimed, "This most useful piece of the base-ball paraphernalia had a hard time getting a foothold. The catchers were slow in adopting it, and the spectators at first guyed as baby-play. [Jack] Clements, the great catcher of the Philadelphia League team, was the first to wear a catcher's protector in a game before a Cincinnati crowd. . . . Considerable fun was made of the protector, and the writer distinctly remembers that it was made the subject of adverse newspaper comment by one of the best base-ball authorities in America."

Nonetheless the vast majority of comment in the newspapers was favorable. A writer for the *Brooklyn Eagle*—probably Henry Chadwick—offered this staunch defense of the chest protector: "the catcher who refuses to wear such a protector from severe injuries simply because 'it looks so queer,' or because a lot of fools in the crowd laugh at him, is no better than the idiots who quiz him."

In another parallel to the mask, once the initial doubts had been overcome, Gray's Body Protector caught on rapidly. "The chest protector is coming into general use," remarked *Sporting Life* matter-of-factly in July. "It is as necessary as the mask." Soon catchers were being mocked as behind the times if they did not wear one. Remember the account that suggested that Henry Oxley must be from the "Green Mountains" because he owned neither a mask nor one of the inflatable chest protectors? That

William Gray's invention of the inflatable chest protector prompted sporting
goods manufacturers to boast in their ads that the new device "renders it impossible for the catcher to be injured while playing close to the batter." The claim was
preposterous, but the reduced prestige of the catcher's position as a consequence of
his protection was very real. *(National Baseball Hall of Fame Library)*

account was written in August 1884, only a few months after the chest protector was being hailed as a novelty.

Blunt but effective ads by Spalding's company hastened the adoption of the chest protector by catchers at all levels. One of the ads showed a catcher writhing in pain and counseled, "If only the poor lad had purchased any one of a number of models of Gray's Patented Catcher Protector, now manufactured exclusively by A. G. Spalding and Company, such fate could be avoided." Despite a few stubborn holdouts, by 1892 Pittsburgh catcher "Doggie" Miller was reportedly "the only catcher in the country who does not use a chest protector when playing behind the bat. He has a clavicle which has several shades the better of it when matched against the resisting powers of a rubber bag inflated with air."

As with the mask, the chest protector by itself did not appear to have a revolutionary effect on the game of baseball. Yet it was another major step in the transformation of the catcher's position, in no small part because it too created a striking visual impression. Spalding's ads would eventually claim that use of the protector "renders it impossible for the catcher to be injured while playing close to the batter." Catchers obviously knew that this was untrue, and others presumably recognized this as well, at least intellectually. Nonetheless the catcher's image was greatly affected by the new protective gear, and his prestige was further diminished.

While the mask's introduction had prompted speculation that the catcher would one day resemble a knight in armor, the adoption of the chest protector struck many as the fulfillment of that prediction. "[Ed] McKenna, the catcher of the Nationals," remarked one 1884 account, "wore in yesterday's game the first body-protector ever used in a championship game in this city. It is made of rubber cloth and inflated with air. He looked like a knight of old equipped in armor for a battle when he donned his mask and other trappings."

A knight at least was an honorable comparison; other metaphors were less flattering. Another sportswriter quipped that sturdily built Rudolph Kemmler "looks like a back-stop when he wears the body protector." It was a simile that proved to have staying power. The term "backstop" had almost always been used to refer to the fence located behind the catcher, but immediately after the introduction of the chest protector it emerged as a synonym for the ballplayer himself. Eventually even the term "backstop" did not seem emphatic enough, and some began referring to the "mere backstop."

This might seem like a minor semantic issue, but in fact the term "backstop" epitomized the dramatic decline in the catcher's prestige. So too did other new terms such as "sheepskin," which was "contemptuously" used to designate the new piece of equipment. Others dubbed it the "wind-pad" and referred to its wearers as wind-paddists. One sportswriter described Harry Decker's new chest protector as "a contrivance that likened him to a muffin-maker." While the catcher of the 1870s had been noted for not wearing protection, the catcher of the 1880s was becoming synonymous with his equipment. The catcher of the 1870s had been spoken of in terms usually reserved for mythic heroes, or by means of comparison to the reflexes of a cat or the tenacity of a bulldog. It was the unhappy lot of the catcher of the 1880s to be compared instead to sheep and inanimate objects.

Once again this shift was emblematic of a broader change that described the work Americans did. In the artisan tradition, skilled workers had been referred to as smiths—blacksmiths, tinsmiths, locksmiths, coppersmiths. The word "smith" was an active term derived from "smite" ("to hit"), and it conveyed distinction since the smith possessed a special knack for a chosen object. But the Industrial Revolution replaced smiths with "machinists," who seemed to be passive extensions of the machines they tended. Likewise, references to catchers as "backstops" and "wind-paddists" spoke volumes about the status of the man behind the plate.

The diminished prestige of the catcher who wore the new equipment was neatly encapsulated in an anecdote told by Hall of Famer Dan Brouthers in 1917. Brouthers recalled that in 1903 Poughkeepsie's catcher was "a little fellow named [Joseph] Cox. He wasn't any bigger than a minute, but he could lick his weight in wildcats, and five times his weight in Poughkeepsie cops." Note how the description of Cox's size specifically places him in the tradition of the small, agile catcher of the 1870s while the reference to his ability to "lick his weight in wildcats" suggests his kinship with Daniel Boone.

The Boone parallel was reinforced when the batter began deliberately to swing his bat far behind him so as to strike Cox's hand. Finally the little catcher had had enough and, as the batter took off toward first base, "Cox galloped after him like a wolf." Five policemen then swarmed out of the stands and surrounded Cox near first base, and Brouthers's description of what happened next used metaphors that evoke both the soldier on the battlefield and the cowboy at the roundup. "For the next few minutes," Brouthers recounted, "the neighborhood of first base looked like a bayonet charge between trenches. All you could see was dust and flying helmets. Cox would make a charge, and then draw back, get his distance, lower his head and go back at the cops like a bull."

Then this stirring scene was brought to a ludicrous conclusion. As Brouthers told it, "At last one policeman got behind the catcher and caught him by the strap of the chest protector, and pulled on it. That brought the chest protector itself up under Cox's chin and nearly choked him. Even while he was in that position he managed to get the club away from one cop and threw it as far as second base. He almost made a clean put out too, because the club just missed the shortstop's sconce. But Cox's wind gave out at last and he collapsed and was gently led away to the hoose gow." The image of Cox being choked by his own chest protector embodied the plight of the catcher whose protective equipment interfered with his dreams of carrying on the tradition of the great Western frontiersman and the heroic Civil War soldier.

The new equipment also changed the job requirements of the position in ways that symbolized this reduced prestige. While the catcher was a man who used his dexterity to stop balls, the "backstop" could allow them merely to bounce off his chest. Catchers became bigger, less agile, and, no longer needing the skills that had defined them, all but interchangeable. Tim Murnane was struck by yet another unflattering analogy, writing, "With the advent of the pad and big gloves catchers grew up like mushrooms in a meadow. It was simply stand in front of the rifle shots and the ball would find some soft spot."

Understandably, interest in becoming a catcher dropped as the 1880s progressed. The position remained the most dangerous one on the baseball field, yet that risk was no longer perceived as glamorous or heroic. Adding insult to injury, it also became expensive to be a catcher since both masks and chest protectors carried a hefty price tag.

Meanwhile a third protective device was being developed that would complete the protection of the catcher's upper body while underscoring his transformation from nonpareil to nonentity. The catcher's hands had always been the subject of the most relentless abuse and, while other parts of the catcher's body were finally getting relief, the toll on his hands was becoming so bad that it became common wisdom that "No two fingers of a professional baseball catcher point in the same direction." Midway through the 1885 season, catcher Eddie Fusselback's hands had been "so pounded out of shape that he has been released at his own request, and will catch no more this season." A widely circulated 1883 anecdote maintained that a well-known catcher was "presented by a young lady with a manicure case, and became very angry on the strength of the belief that it was a joke, inasmuch as he hasn't had a finger-nail for six years."

Catchers had begun experimenting with gloves in the 1860s, and during the 1870s their use became common. But these were worn on both hands, so they had to be light kid gloves that did not impede the throwing motion. Jim McGuire, who wore a pair of these light gloves during the early part of his career, confirmed that they were "really no protection at all." Some catchers, such as Jim White, Silver Flint, and "Doc" Bushong, declined to wear them or eventually rejected them because they offered so little cushioning.

But the advent of pitchers' overhand releases and running starts made it essential to provide more relief for the catcher's hands in the 1880s. "Catching a swift pitcher, and all pitchers nowadays are more or less swift," wrote a perceptive observer in 1886, "tends to wear a man out in a season or two." In the 1870s a skilled catcher had been able to avoid serious injury if he used proper technique, but this too had changed. It was now considered impossible to "lay down rules whereby a catcher can save himself," and thus it had become "a difficult task to draw the line between the correct and incorrect methods of catching." In short, the skill that had once set the catcher apart no longer much mattered.

With no alternatives left but the inevitability of shortened careers, several well-known catchers, including Jim "Deacon" McGuire, Chief Zimmer, Wilbert Robinson, and Lou Criger, began using beefsteaks in their gloves. Others, including "Doc" Bushong, preferred padding their gloves with sponges. Still others resorted to stuffing grass or cotton batting into their gloves for extra protection. By 1886 many catchers were wearing "gloves more suited for a four-round knocker-out than to a baseball player."

A few catchers devised bizarre contraptions to protect their hands. A catcher in San Marcos, Texas, unveiled a homemade mitt "made of a piece of pine board. Excelsior was used for padding and this was enclosed with a piece of black oilcloth, which was tacked around the board, leaving ample space for the hand. How the San Marcos catcher held the ball as it struck the board of a mitt was a mystery, but he did." Two Baltimore catchers inserted a shock absorber described as "a three-pound lead plate" inside their gloves. All of these experiments showed how difficult it was to provide enough cushioning for the hands without making it impossible to snag the ball. The fingers were most vulnerable to injury, yet padding there interfered with the acts of catching and throwing. And so the search for a better solution continued.

In retrospect the emergence of the catcher's mitt may appear inevitable. Even so perceptive an eyewitness as Tim Murnane later maintained that "the big mit [sic] came by a natural evolution from the kid glove." Yet the process wasn't nearly that simple because creating such a glove entailed both design innovation and a fundamental reexamination of how to catch a ball. To begin with, there was no precedent for a glove larger than a man's hand, and developing an effective one was no easy matter. This was compounded by the reality that as long as the two-handed technique was used in catching, the mitt would be counterproductive. So the introduction of the catcher's mitt is partly a story of an invention that protected the man's hands, but also the tale of a revolution that challenged and ultimately swept away the accepted wisdom about the men who played the position.

By 1884 most catchers used two gloves of very different thickness. Of necessity they still used little padding on their throwing hand, and most of them removed the fingers entirely in order to make it easier to throw. The palms of their catching hands, however, were liable to be padded with as much protection as was possible without interfering with their ability to catch.

But that was the rub: padding didn't help a player secure a baseball. The best that could be hoped for was that the padding didn't make it more difficult to catch the ball. As described earlier, barehanded ballplayers caught with their fingers, so they were reluctant to change to a mitt that forced them to catch with their palms. For purposes of comparison, imagine being asked to catch a Frisbee while wearing a catcher's mitt or a fielder's glove, or for that matter to do any feat requiring manual dexterity while wearing gloves. The question isn't whether the glove will help, but *how much it will hinder*. Many catchers therefore continued to keep padding on both hands to a minimum and removed the fingers from the gloves on both hands.

A new padded glove was introduced in 1884 that featured fingers made of "stiff cowhide, jointed at the bottom with buckskin. The finger-ends are stout enough to withstand the severest blow, thus preventing the breaking of joints, from which men behind the bat have so long suffered." This was a promising approach for reducing the risk of injury, but it once again seemed doubtful that a baseball could be reliably caught while wearing such a contraption.

Not surprisingly, catchers were reluctant to use gloves that featured innovative designs. When George Myers became one of the first National League catchers to wear a left-hand glove that didn't have the fingers cut off, it "caused a general laugh. The fingers were so long and the surface of the glove so broad that Meyers [sic] found it difficult at first to hold

Catching great Albert "Doc" Bushong posed for this picture in 1888, the year professional catchers first began wearing mitts. By 1886, Bushong was moving away from the traditional two-handed catching method and was wearing a glove on his left hand that was considered unusually large for the era. It was described as "a conglomeration of ragged buckskin, string, sponges and cloth." But as this picture clearly shows, the glove remained very small and provided limited cushioning. *(National Baseball Hall of Fame Library)*

a pitched ball. He was catching the great Henry Boyle in those days and Boyle had blinding speed. Meyers had broken all of his fingers, also both thumbs in handling Boyle with the fingerless gloves, so that he readily tried the new one, and after much perseverance he proved that it had merit. After that all the catchers adopted a finger glove for the left hand. The glove was improved upon when the manufacturer put solid leather tips on the ends of the fingers to protect the nails."

Even this account oversimplifies what happened because, in order to make mitts effective, catchers first had to discard the traditional two-handed catching method and learn instead to "do most of the stopping with his left hand, protected by a thickly padded glove. Such a glove cannot be worn upon the right hand as it renders accurate throwing impossible." In addition, they had to begin catching pitches with the palms of their hands instead of the fingers. Between 1884 and 1886 that is precisely what occurred as most of the game's catchers began to modify their techniques and thereby pave the way for the mitt.

Some sources credit "Doc" Bushong with pioneering the new method of allowing the nonthrowing hand to absorb most of the shock, because he wanted to preserve his right hand for his postbaseball career in dentistry. Bushong does indeed appear to have been a contributor. By 1886 he was wearing a "left-hand glove" that attracted attention for its size and for being "a conglomeration of ragged buckskin, string, sponges and cloth." And soon Bushong had developed a new technique: "I have learned that in receiving a right handed pitcher I get all the balls on my left hand. With a left handed pitcher it is just the reverse, and I get all the balls on my right hand. As we catch more right handed pitchers than left handers, our catchers' left hands are generally battered out of shape. For throwing to bases a left handed pitcher is the best, and we are able to get the ball down to second much quicker than with a right handed pitcher. When a runner is on first and about to start to steal second, the pitcher should send a straight, speedy ball over the plate, so that the catcher can get it down ahead of the runner."

But a revolution of this sort is the work of more than just one man, and many others joined Bushong in making the transition. Another article credited Buck Ewing, Silver Flint, and Charley Bennett with being among the first "to show that one hand was sufficient to catch a pitched ball." One of the biggest steps occurred during the 1886 season when Bennett forcefully demonstrated how much things had changed by electing to wear "only one glove, as he can throw better with one bare hand."

Although there is no way to be sure which catchers led the way, it didn't matter much anyway. What mattered was that the profession as a whole began to experiment with the new method of catching. Once they did, they discovered something we now take for granted—that it is still possible to catch a baseball reliably while wearing a thick pad that has a rudimentary pocket, and that the pain from impact is reduced dramatically. As one sportswriter put it, between 1885 and 1888 "the most prominent catchers demonstrated that the left hand had to bear the brunt of the shock consequent on the pitcher's delivery, and that the glove for this hand, in order to be successful, would have to be a peculiar type, far different from any thus far presented." The new technique soon caught on and, as this observer recalled, "the catchers learned with marvelous speed to take the play upon the fat, safe palm."

Now it became possible for the oversize mitt to emerge, and in quick order there came the experimenting and tinkering necessary to perfect one. A couple of catchers later claimed to have been wearing mitts as early as 1885 or '86, but these appear to have just been large gloves with extra padding. In 1888, however, several minor league catchers began wearing true catcher's mitts.

There are an impressive number of claimants to have been the inventor. Kansas City catcher Joe Gunson unveiled a mitt for a Decoration Day (now Memorial Day) doubleheader in 1888. Gunson later explained that he was trying to protect an injured finger: "I took the glove I was then wearing—a glove which was something like the kid gloves they wear today—stitched all of the fingers together and made a mitt. Then I fixed up a padding and put it all around the finger ends, sewed a wire in it to help keep its shape, padded the center of the glove with sheepskin and wool and covered the entire mitt with buckskin. The next afternoon I kept my promise to [manager Jimmy] Manning and caught both games."

Others credited Toronto catcher Harry Decker. According to an eyewitness, the hands of the team's other catcher, Dave Oldfield, had become terribly "swelled and bunged" from trying to catch a hard-throwing pitcher. Decker joked that what Oldfield needed was "a mattress made in the style of a glove . . . suppose you get some leather like this and a lot of felt stuffing—like this (picking up a lot of rubbish from the ground) and make a big mitten this way." He used the odds and ends in the clubhouse to make one, but when it was finished he and his teammates realized it was no joke.

Meanwhile Jack McCloskey claimed to have created the first catcher's mitt by starting with a padded finger glove and improving it by "putting a circle of wire around it and filling it with padding. In addition I put a piece of leather on the pocket of the glove." In 1887, McCloskey shared the idea with pitcher Ted Kennedy, who made some additional modifications and let his catcher, Bill Traffley, wear it while playing for Des Moines in 1888. And several other credible sources believed that the mitt rigged up by Kennedy was "the first good one."

As these accounts suggest, the basic principles of the mitt were simple enough that its discovery was inevitable once the need for it emerged. So it is no surprise that there were dissenting views about who made "the first good one." In all likelihood it was one of those cases where a number of people independently got to about the same point at about the same time.

It was an idea whose time had come in more ways than one. In stark contrast to the reception accorded the mask a decade earlier, there was no substantial resistance to the mitt. A number of factors contributed to its surprisingly easy acceptance. For one thing, the mask and chest protector and the fact that many fielders were now wearing gloves reduced the possibility of opposition. Despite the ongoing resentment that many felt toward the intrusion of equipment, the prominence of these other implements made it difficult to argue that catchers shouldn't be able to protect their hands.

An even more pressing consideration was the sheer number of debilitating hand injuries resulting from overhand deliveries by pitchers who showed no "sympathy" for their battery mates. It was one thing to encourage a catcher to shake off a blow to the head or chest, but a catcher with an injured hand was liable to hurt his team by his inability to throw to the bases or fulfill the other duties of his position. The early 1880s thus saw catchers being sidelined by injuries with alarming frequency.

Not only were such injuries becoming more commonplace, but they were becoming more devastating to the clubs affected, since access to capable replacements had been curtailed. During the 1870s there were no true minor leagues, which gave major league clubs the luxury of carrying ten or at most eleven players and picking up a semipro if multiple injuries struck. But the 1880s saw the birth of several minor leagues, and their teams snatched up the players who would previously have been available when the need arose.

This forced clubs to make new contingency plans, usually entailing considerable expense. In 1883, Baltimore secretary and treasurer William S. Gittinger offered Yale catcher Allen Hubbard the lofty salary of $600 per month and a cash advance of $1,000, only to have Hubbard turn it down because of his family's opposition to professional ballplaying. A desperate Gittinger then let it be known that he would "give any manager in the country a bonus of $1,000 for a first-class catcher, and will pay the catcher himself an increase on present salary." Other teams sought to avoid ending up in such a predicament by signing entire fleets of catchers, regardless of cost. Cincinnati won a fierce bidding war for Bill Traffley in 1883, though the club already had two other catchers. The Northwestern League club in Bay City, Michigan, agreed to 1884 contracts with fourteen players, five of whom were catchers. Before the 1887 season, Harry Wright, now managing Philadelphia, signed no fewer than six catchers. Meanwhile catchers were often being forced into retirement from baseball within a year or two. Clearly it was now in everyone's best interests to reduce the likelihood of an injured catcher.

Resistance to the mitt was thus limited to a few initial gasps of astonishment. In 1888, for instance, National League star Buck Ewing "created a sensation by wearing an immense glove on his left hand while taking Tim Keefe's hot shot behind the bat at the old Polo grounds. His first appearance with the glove, which looked for all the world like a big boxing glove crushed out flat by a road roller, caused a shout of laughter from the assemblage." At the end of the game, however, Ewing "declared that his hand was not swollen a particle, and that thereafter nothing could tempt him to relinquish his new guard to his big left hand. All through that season Buck wore the glove, and soon it was recognized as indispensable in the paraphernalia of the big back stop." Rather than having any qualms about wearing the mitt, Ewing seemed to go out of his way to draw attention to it, adding "stuffing to the glove and covering it with patches of new leather. The growth of the glove was closely watched by the fans, who marveled at its expansion. Any rip in it was instantly mended by Buck himself with any kind of leather, so that it sure was one of the most conspicuous things on the ball field, with its patches of all sorts of hide. It really became one of the attractions of the game, and scores of fans, influenced by newspaper comments, went to the game merely to get a look at Buck's glove. Naturally, manufacturers took the hint and began making the big glove."

Ewing and other catchers soon followed Bennett's lead in discarding the second glove altogether. Then they took another step toward a true one-handed technique, allowing the nonthrowing hand to absorb almost all the shock by "perfect[ing] a movement of the left wrist that placed the mitt in the right position to receive the ball." Ewing in particular barely used his throwing hand at all when catching pitches, and the results were as spectacular as his mitt. He told one reporter, presumably with some exaggeration, that "during an entire season he didn't catch more than a dozen pitched balls with his bare hand. He used to enjoy catching the puzzling curves of [Tim] Keefe, [Mickey] Welch and [Ed "Cannonball"] Crane with the mitt, which made it almost impossible to have a passed ball."

As the techniques used by catchers changed, they no longer appeared heroic. "[Doc] Bushong's method," wrote a sportswriter in 1886, "is such a remarkable one as to have become the talk of all who have observed him. He squats, as it were, on his 'haunches,' bends his body down until it is almost parallel with the ground, places his hands about an inch from his kneecaps and thus leaves his elbows sticking out from the whole make-up in a ridiculous manner. The only thing to which he can be properly compared is the appearance of a large frog sitting on the traditional log and making ready to spring into the depths of his favorite pond. In this ridiculous posture 'the Doctor' waits patiently until the ball is within reach when he makes a sudden snap at it." Once again, the choice of metaphors is revealing. When the catcher was the beau ideal of American boys, he had evoked comparisons to the quickness of a cat and the tenacity of a bulldog, but now even a great catcher like Bushong reminded observers of a "ridiculous" frog.

All by itself, the mitt's effect on the catching position was revolutionary. Still greater was the cumulative effect of the three new pieces of equipment that had been added in just over a decade's time. Together they wrought an extraordinary transformation of the catcher's duties, safety, and technique—and they had just as great an impact on his psyche.

In 1894, Jack Doyle offered some surprising tips to aspiring catchers. "My advice to youngsters who are ambitious to become great catchers," wrote Doyle, "is 'to get in front of the ball.' By this I mean that every catcher should catch the ball directly in front of him, and not at either side of him. The idea of side catching is to escape the danger of having the ball hit one in front or anywhere, but it is well known by this time to all who have paid any attention to the subject that this style of catching will not do. You will find that the men who practice it in the league to-day are gradually but surely losing caste. A catcher cannot afford to flinch, no matter how speedy the delivery he is catching. He wants at all times to get right in front of the ball and to stay there. That is his only safety and salvation, for the man who dodges and squirms is much more apt to get injured than the man who boldly faces the enemy." These suggestions must have horrified a generation of catchers who had prided themselves on using their lightning-fast reflexes to dodge foul tips and thereby escape injury. It is small wonder that many of them came to believe that the new gear had removed the skill from playing the position.

Even more shocking, however, was what Doyle had to say about the hazards of being behind the plate: "I do not think catching is dangerous if a man is quick witted and has control of himself . . . boys, if you want to catch, go in and do it. If you have brains and can use them in all-around play, there is no need why you should be afraid to catch behind the bat." Imagine what Stephen Crane, now out of catching for four years and

This 1898 ad shows how the mitt had revolutionized catching—note the disclaimer that a "throwing glove" is no longer included. These mitts were available for the left or right hand, but this too soon changed as the catcher's position became the exclusive domain of right-handers. *(National Baseball Hall of Fame Library)*

putting the finishing touches on *The Red Badge of Courage*, would have thought had he happened to read these words.

Doyle's advice underscored a paradox that was growing evident. While the catcher's body was much better protected from bruises, his self-esteem had become vulnerable. Despite the grave hazards that still existed, the mask and chest protector had robbed the catcher of his image as the ultimate warrior. The introduction of the mitt now robbed him of most of the consolations that remained.

No longer were his hands the badges of courage that could be displayed with nonchalant pride to horrified onlookers. At the same time he also lost the aura of the gunslinger who shifted adroitly from catching to throwing out base-stealers. His basic duties hadn't really changed, but everything about the catcher's job appeared simple now that he was encased in protective equipment.

Even the success of catchers at throwing out base-stealers was attributed to the new equipment. According to catcher Dick Buckley, "The fat mitten stopped the runner. How? Well, get a glove of the type used by catchers up to 1889, get a modern padded mitten, have somebody throw you a ball, and it will all dawn upon you in a second. When the old pitchers, firing from a short distance and yet hurling them across with all their steam, sent them into the thin-palmed finger tipped glove of those days, the catcher always, and instinctively, drew back his hands as the bullet struck into the frail protection. Suppose a baserunner was under way, the catcher disengaged the ball from the glove and shot it down as fast as he knew how. Well, after the big mitt arrived, the whole method of taking the pitch changed immediately. The catcher soon found that he could take the full shock of the fastest delivery in that great paw, and that he did not have to draw back his hands. What did this mean to the baserunner, and to the catcher's chance of trapping him? Only this; that the catcher, able to get the ball out of his big glove and ready for the throw in speedier time than when he wore the little glove, had just that much margin on the runner. And bases are made or lost by fractions of a second."

As Buckley's comments suggest, the introduction of the mitt continued the dispiriting tendency of the catcher's new equipment to deprive him of his former mystique. Just as the mask and chest protector relieved the catcher of a need for agility and lightning reflexes to keep him safe, so too the mitt eliminated the value of other subtle skills. The art of receiving the ball no longer had the same importance now that the catcher had a virtual pillow on his hand, with the result that the phrase "fighting the

As shown in these photos of the front and back of a 1913 mitt, it continued to be refined and enlarged. By this time catchers could allow the ball to strike the palm of their catching hand, then use the throwing hand to secure the ball in the mitt. *(National Baseball Hall of Fame Library)*

ball" gradually lost its precise meaning. The technique used to throw to second base also was simplified by the mitt, since the catcher's hand no longer recoiled upon impact with the pitch. Two other insightful articles echoed Buckley's description of how the mitt inhibited base-stealing and reduced the skill needed to play the catcher's position. One of them went so far as to maintain: "in the latter part of 1888 came the big glove into use, and from that day began the decline in base running and the accompanying retrogression of heady, brainy catching."

The implication that the catcher's equipment did his job for him was especially apparent in a sarcastic 1890 article that claimed: "Louisville has a wonderful catcher. He is not a member of the Louisville Club. He is, perhaps, the only living backstop who can perform the difficult task of catching behind a bat without the assistance of those requisites—his hands. This phenomenon is Joe Netter, thirty years of age. He is compactly built, has black hair and eyes, and does not differ apparently from the ordinary run of men. He is jovial and good-natured, and was never known to refuse to take part in a game of ball. There is one part of Joe's body which he evidently has some grievance against, and that is his stomach. It has attained Aldermanic proportions, and when coming down the street it always appears somewhat in advance of its owner. Joe has two hands and five fingers on each hand, but in catching a game he seldom uses them. He allows the ball to hit his body, and then he 'blocks' it. [Gus] Weyhing, [Guy] Hecker and many of the speediest pitchers in the profession have tested Netter's staying qualities and they pronounce him marvelous. Several clubs have made him flattering offers, but he declined them all. 'The time is near at hand,' said he, 'when cannons will be substituted for pitchers, and then I can command an enormous salary.'" Imagine what the likes of Nat Hicks and Mart King must have thought of catching having come to involve little more than letting pitches bounce off your amply padded stomach.

One of the fundamental tenets of the catcher's position had been that some men lacked the courage to play there and would have to be moved somewhere safer. Yet by the turn of the century there were reports of players choosing to play behind the plate because it seemed a less hazardous position. "I can kill myself in one year pitching," Lou Criger claimed, "but I can catch all my life and not hurt myself."

In short, catchers were no longer seen as being men who possessed a unique, transcendent gift, and they never would be again. Their ability to catch a fast pitch bare-handed and nimbly shift into throwing mode had once been recognized as a special art, mastered by only a select few. The willingness of these men to perform such tasks in the face of grave danger had made them heroes to countless boys. But the equipment that now protected their bodies had removed these distinctions, with even catchers like Jack Doyle and Lou Criger claiming that the position was not dangerous.

All these changes left no place in the game for old-school catchers, and one by one they departed the scene. Mart King, the catcher so attached to the ideal of manly self-reliance that he refused even to wear shoes or a cap, sensed the change coming before most of his peers. He "retired from the game inveighing against an effete civilization which demanded protection where none was asked for." King was joined by two of the other tough-guy catchers in 1877, a year which, more than any other, marked the changing of the guard. The season began with conspicuous protective equipment unknown and ended with the mask firmly established, a development that paved the way for the rest of the catcher's garb. At the same time the two most prominent exemplars of catching toughness stepped aside. Nat Hicks abruptly retired in May, explaining only that he was through with baseball.

The end of Bill Craver's career was even more symbolic. At thirty-two, his days as a full-time catcher were over, and he signed with Louisville for the 1877 season with the understanding that he would be the team's regular shortstop and fill in for catcher Charley Snyder only when needed. Even in this role Craver was considered so indispensable that the club was willing to overlook the rumors of shady activity that had long swirled around him. Louisville director Charles Chase noted that "[Craver's] reputation is not first-class, but all I can say is that we have taken him with our eyes wide open, and we are willing to abide the result. Craver can play ball, as every one knows, and when he comes with us he will have to either play or quit, and he fully understands this."

Chase's statement spoke volumes about the extraordinary value of a good catcher in the mid-1870s. So too did the idea that Craver could no longer be an everyday catcher but could be relied upon to be the team's starting shortstop, a position he had never before played regularly. (No wonder George Wright, long regarded as the game's premier shortstop, expressed bitterness about the way pitchers and catchers overshadowed the other seven players.)

For much of the year Chase had every reason to be pleased with his club. Snyder stayed healthy while catching hard-throwing pitcher Jim Devlin, and Craver made a smooth transition to shortstop, enabling Louisville to lead the National League for much of the year. Then the club began to slump, first losing a series of games to nonleague teams and then dropping enough league games to be caught and passed by Boston. The losses to outside teams raised suspicions, and an investigation implicated Craver, Devlin, and two other players in a game-fixing scandal.

With evidence mounting, the other three players confessed to throwing the nonleague games, though whether the league games were fixed remains in doubt. Craver, however, steadfastly declined either to cooperate or confess. All four men were banned for life by the National League, but even this latest scandal didn't prevent Craver's hometown Troy team (which had joined the International Association) from trying to sign him for the 1878 season.

Thus the 1877 season saw both the appearance of the catcher's mask and the departure of the two most prominent tough-guy catchers. Also headed toward the exit that year was the redoubtable Doug Allison, who never again caught regularly in the major leagues after the 1877 season. The changing of the guard was so complete that in 1878 Deacon White was the only catcher over the age of twenty-three to catch as many as twenty National League games.

The same phenomenon occurred in 1889 when the rise to prominence of the mitt coincided with another mass exodus of catchers known for their defensive prowess. With all his skills rendered unimportant by the new equipment, Silver Flint "went behind the bat but fifteen times [in 1889].

This was too much for his sensitive nature, and he decided to step down and out." Ben Guiney, a top amateur catcher in Detroit and college classmate of Wallie Walker, reportedly announced in this same year, "If they're going to dress me up like a deep-sea diver it's time for me to quit." As his comments suggest, catchers took these changes personally, and they resented them.

Doc Bushong wrote a spirited defense of the catcher's value that same year, but even his optimism sometimes faltered. After a lengthy explanation of why the catcher was still of crucial importance, he concluded that these factors had "in times past, made catchers so scarce" and now afforded "the really good catcher one of the most solid situations in base ball." It was a stunning admission. Not long ago, catchers had been folk heroes who were idolized by countless American boys. Now they could boast only of having job security. Bushong himself was relegated to back-up status in 1889, and he retired the following season.

The reality that the catcher was no longer indispensable seems also to have played a role in the release of another highly regarded defensive catcher in 1889, and his departure represented a much more serious loss for baseball. The pioneer African-American catcher Fleetwood Walker was let go by Syracuse of the International League in August, and his release marked the final step in the drawing of the color line in the high-level minor leagues. Only a few years earlier the unique status of the catcher had made the position a beacon of opportunity. Owners could not afford to turn away a great catcher regardless of his background or skin color, which meant that men of diverse ethnic and racial origins recognized the catcher's position as a way to be judged solely on the basis of their ability. But with catchers now regarded as interchangeable, owners could tacitly agree to draw the color line.

More than two decades later, when Walker spoke at a convention of African-American Masons in Toledo, he emphasized that he had never worn a catcher's mitt. In all likelihood he was doing more than boasting about his own toughness. Probably he also recognized that the introduction of the mitt had played a large role in ending his career, since it led to the belief that any man wearing one could do a competent job of filling in behind the plate.

The catcher's status continued to decline over the next couple of years as the mitt was fine-tuned and the new and improved version seemed further to confirm that the catcher's equipment could now do his job for him. As with the mask, each new refinement was heralded by sporting goods firms in ads misleadingly implying that all the dangers of catching had been eliminated. By 1891 the A. J. Reach sporting goods company was claiming that its mitts now had a "leather back, thus preventing the back of the hand being hurt," while rival Keefe & Becannon was advertising the Buck Ewing mitt, which purportedly made it "impossible to break the fingers." Sportswriters sometimes foolishly repeated these claims. An 1890 article maintained that the thumb of the new mitt was "a sufficient bulwark to make it impossible for a foul tip, fly, or hand-thrown ball to put the human thumb out of joint," while the editor of *Sporting Life* raved that "with this glove such a thing as a broken finger is impossible and catching is made wonderfully easy."

The reality that the catcher was no longer indispensable was underscored by an 1889 rules change that literally made catchers interchangeable. With a few exceptions, substitutions had never been allowed in baseball. Players could switch positions at will, and courtesy runners for ailing base runners were sometimes permitted. During the 1870s, teams were allowed to insert a substitute in the first few innings, but this was intended only to prevent teams from stalling until a latecomer arrived. Even this loophole was eliminated by the start of the 1880s, and a player could be replaced only in the case of serious illness or injury.

The problem with this rule was that the opposing captain had to agree that the injury was serious enough to prevent the player from remaining in the game. This meant that a captain could gain an advantage by denying such claims, and arguments often ensued. Chicago player-manager "Cap" Anson became especially notorious for denying such substitutions, and naturally it was usually catchers who were involved. An especially contentious incident occurred on August 28, 1886, when Philadelphia's Jim McGuire made an unsuccessful attempt to catch a high pitch and came away nursing his finger.

When McGuire tried to withdraw from the game, Anson protested and asked umpire Phil Powers for a ruling. Powers, who had been a catcher during the position's glory years, sided with Anson. This infuriated Philadelphia captain Arthur Irwin, who argued at length and finally instructed McGuire to stand well back of the plate. The game quickly degenerated into a farce, prompting a forty-minute delay. Anson finally conceded the point and let the replacement enter the game, but after the lengthy interruption, "the interest had been destroyed, and when the umpire called the game at the end of the eighth inning everybody was glad to get away." A war of words continued in the press for weeks, and became so contentious that depositions were actually taken of the players involved.

A strikingly similar incident occurred two years later, with Anson and Powers again playing key roles. On September 12, 1888, with Chicago hosting New York, a fifth-inning wild pitch bounced up and struck New York captain and catcher "Buck" Ewing on the wrist. Ewing did not appear to be seriously injured, but after Chicago pushed across five runs to take a commanding lead, he asked to be relieved. Anson protested, and Powers ordered Ewing to remain in the game. Ewing refused, prompting a heated argument that ended with the game being forfeited to Chicago. Fans again left unhappy, and each side accused the other of unsporting behavior.

The rules change passed in the winter of 1889 allowed discretionary substitutions for the first time. Henry Chadwick's comments left no doubt that the impetus for the new rule had been the catcher's vulnerability in general and the Ewing incident in particular: "The most radical change made in the playing rules by the committee was that which allows the introduction of a new player in the nine as substitute for a player retired by the captain for causes other than the customary disabling of a player by 'illness or injury.' Under the new code if the captain of either team in a match game finds that the pitcher is giving out or that his catcher's hands are not in good condition, though neither player is disabled to the extent covered by the terms 'illness or injury,' he can at the end of any innings [retire] from service on the field and substitute a new player, and such retired player can not again take part in the game."

The initial rule allowed only one such substitution per game, but it was expanded in each of the next two off-seasons, and by 1891 unlimited substitutions were permitted. As with the emergence of the catcher's equipment, the new rule provided much-needed relief from the ardors of the position by allowing injured catchers to leave the game. Symbolically it completed a fifteen-year process that stripped the catcher of his special status. He had gone from being indispensable to being interchangeable.

Not all the changes that took place during these years tended in the same direction; with so much turmoil, there was inevitably a good deal of ebb and flow. As late as 1885 there were still frequent calls for "doing away with the style of play known as 'the pitcher's game,' in which the brunt of the work of the attack in a contest falls upon the pitcher and catcher, while the majority of the fielders stand idly by as mere lookers on." This in turn meant that the reduced importance and mystique of the catcher was a gradual process, and young men such as Stephen Crane who came of age during the 1880s continued to view the catcher as their beau ideal.

Nevertheless the cumulative effect of these changes to the catcher's position is difficult to overstate. It is no exaggeration to say that the catcher of the early 1890s played a different position from the one played by the catcher of the mid-1870s. Many of the basics remained the same, and catching was still the most dangerous position and one of the most crucial. But beneath the surface a profound and irrevocable transformation had occurred. In exchange for the protection afforded by their new equipment, catchers had lost their status as folk heroes. These men who had grown up dreaming of playing the most dangerous and essential position on the baseball field were faced with the challenge of trying to redefine their self-images and their identities.

9

The Thinking-Man Catcher

"Heroism feels and never reasons, and therefore is always right; and although a different breeding, different religion, and greater intellectual activity would have modified or even reversed the particular action, yet for the hero that thing he does is the highest deed, and is not open to the censure of philosophers or divines."—Ralph Waldo Emerson

THE CATCHERS of the 1880s and 1890s faced an unhappy predicament. They were young men who, like Stephen Crane, had grown up during the 1870s dreaming of attaining the catcher's mystique and indispensability. Now, having overcome great odds to achieve that dream, they found the prestige of the position in a nosedive that led them to be perceived increasingly as "mere backstops."

Their response to this situation was to reinvent the position in two new molds. Some, as we'll explore in this chapter, tried to restore the Chadwick model of the catcher who adapts to his new circumstances by means of what Chadwick called "headwork." Others, as we'll see in the next chapter, became desperadoes who struck all but their fellow catchers as being rebels without a cause.

The 1880s saw a new emphasis on the catcher as the embodiment of such attributes as teamwork, leadership, and resourcefulness. In one way this development was not new at all, since Henry Chadwick had long preached that baseball was a test of character. Yet the harsh reality had often belied Chadwick's idealistic pronouncements by showing that the most critical baseball skills are individual in nature. Teamwork and character have little to do with a fielder's ability to field a sharply hit ground ball or make a hard, accurate throw, while a batter's performance is even more isolated from those of his teammates.

There were of course facets of baseball as it was played before 1880 that did exhibit the importance of teamwork. Pitchers used considerable craft by varying their location and by mixing changes of pace with their fastballs. And, as we have seen, they depended upon a catcher who could handle their best offerings.

Even in the case of pitchers and catchers, however, true teamwork played a fairly limited role. Its most prominent example was the signals that fielders were using by the late 1860s to communicate information about defensive strategy and placement. Catchers played a key role, with an 1869 game account noting that Red Stockings catcher Doug Allison used signs to instruct the pitcher and basemen as to "the proper thing to do at the right moment." Henry Chadwick naturally seized on this trend, and by 1867 he was instructing pitchers to attempt pickoffs only when signaled to do so by the catcher. In the ensuing years he gradually built upon the idea and began recommending that the catcher do "the 'headwork' in strategic play by directing—through private signals—the pitcher how to deliver particular balls." By 1874 he was suggesting that "if the pitcher is familiar with a certain habit of the batsman before him of hitting at a favourite ball, he should give the catcher a sign informing him that he is going to send in a slower or swifter ball or a higher or lower one than ordinarily is pitched."

Yet a closer examination suggests that this was one of Chadwick's pet ideas, and that in fact professional catchers of the 1870s found the idea of exchanging information about the upcoming pitch unnecessary, if not insulting. These were, after all, men who prided themselves on their ability to adapt to whatever the pitcher unleashed—recall, for example, how Scott Hastings had needed only to watch Jim Devlin's "red-hot underhand throw" in 1875 in order to catch him masterfully. So most catchers ignored this part of Chadwick's advice. While they continued to signal the pitcher if they noticed a runner sneaking off base, they took little interest in learning anything about the pitch he was about to deliver. A. G. Spalding recalled, "Deacon Jim White was the greatest natural catcher that I ever saw. White came to Boston from Cleveland in '71 [sic] and had never worked with signs from his pitcher. The first time he went to catch for me I bothered him with my slow ball, but Jim soon mastered it, and never asked for a sign of any kind."

When the curveball was introduced, it became more useful for the catcher to know what was coming, but even then most catchers remained unwilling to admit the need for such help. As with protective equipment, catchers perceived signals as a threat—an outlook that reveals another parallel with the cowboy. The ultimate compliment that a cattleman could pay to a newly hired cowboy was to tell him nothing about the ranch's horses; this showed he had faith in the cowboy's ability to master and ride any horse. Likewise, catchers took pride in their ability to catch any pitch without being told what was coming. What's more, the surreptitious nature of signals seemed at odds with the ideal of manly forthrightness. With their self-image as rugged individualists seemingly being called into question, most catchers stubbornly resisted the change.

Thus almost no one but Chadwick referred to the catchers of the 1870s using such signals. The perception that this sort of signal was a sign of weakness is apparent on one of the few occasions when the subject was mentioned. According to an 1879 note in the *Boston Globe*, "It is said that [Silver] Flint, catcher of the Chicagos, by a system of sign-language, which no one has been able to fathom, wholly relieves [pitcher Terry] Larkin from the duty of watching either the first or second base. This is done by Flint, who, in the catcher's position, has a good view of all the bases. He signals Larkin to throw either to first or second, and by the same signal notifies [first baseman Cap] Anson, [second baseman Joe] Quest or [shortstop John] Peters to be on the lookout for the ball." This prompted the *Chicago Tribune* to retort, "There is nothing at all mysterious about the signal. It consists of Flint turning his cap around on his head. [Boston catcher Charley] Snyder's signal to [pitcher Tommy] Bond is made by putting his hands on his knees."

The *Globe*'s original note began with the vague "it is said" and then made clear that Flint's signals were intended only to convey defensive strategy. Nevertheless the *Tribune* felt it necessary to refute the implication that there was anything sneaky or secretive about the signals, going so far as to describe the ones used by two of the game's leading catchers. Clearly this was not just a question of strategy but one that touched on the catcher's self-image and identity.

Flint's very different view of his own role was dramatically illustrated by a description of his method of coaching a young pitcher. It drew an explicit parallel to a cowboy breaking in a horse. Whenever his manager, Cap Anson, asked him to try out an aspiring young pitcher, Flint would take off his catching glove, even though "in nine cases out of ten the pitchers that Anson assigned to Flint were lusty young fellows with more strength than accuracy." Flint would then take the pitcher "down to the corner of

Frank "Silver" Flint was paired with some of the game's best fastball pitchers for more than a decade, and the toll it took on his hands became legendary. One particularly fanciful story had the great catcher being knocked unconscious in a railroad accident. Upon coming to, he found that a doctor had assumed that Flint's hands were damaged in the crash, and he was preparing to operate on them. Flint laughed and said, "Doc, you are wasting your time. I am the catcher of the Chicago Base Ball Club." *(National Baseball Hall of Fame Library)*

the park, and with bare hands stop the balls as fast as they were thrown. It was his policy to make the 'young blood' think they were pitching very slow balls until they became tired. Then he would don gloves and begin to do coaching. However, he would never give any advice to a 'colt' until he was sure he was tired out and convinced that he was not a 'cyclone.'"

On one memorable occasion, Anson brought in a very hard-throwing young pitcher for a tryout. Flint's hands were soon "swelled to twice their normal size" but he "dared not squeal," especially after several of his teammates came over to watch and to chuckle at the catcher's expense. So this ritual continued for three more days, with the pitcher continuing to try to prove his merit and Flint unwilling to relent. (In the same way it might take days for a cowboy to break a horse, but at the end the "harder [the horse] fought, the more complete was his final submission.") Finally, on "the fourth day, when the youngster began to play out, Flint had nerve enough to tell him that his arm was not very strong and began giving him tips on how to pitch to the sluggers of the League."

Despite its apparent madness, there was a method to this procedure. Men like Flint distrusted signals and refused simply to claim authority, as the pitcher had once done, because that would undermine their self-image. They continued to believe that the authority to lead could only be earned by the demonstration of superior fortitude and endurance.

Even a Harvard catcher named Francis Mason seemed intent on downplaying the importance of signs. Mason reported in 1893 that he employed only two signs, even though his pitcher had four different pitches—one of the signs was for either a fastball or an "inshoot" (a pitch that broke toward the batter), while the other could mean either a slow curve or a drop ball. So how did he know which specific pitch was coming? He didn't, relying instead on his familiarity with his partner. "I try to learn my pitcher's delivery so thoroughly that I can instinctively tell what ball is coming, even if a different curve is pitched to the one signalled for," he said. "The ability to do this is most important. Every pitcher is liable to mistake a signal or become a bit rattled at some stage when a passed ball would lose a game."

Reluctance to employ signals was not restricted to catchers. When Baltimore began using signals to coach base runners in 1885, many spectators were upset by the innovation. They preferred the old method of hollering and thereby showing team spirit. When an 1887 game was delayed while the pitcher and catcher discussed their signals, fans became restless and one of them yelled, "Get a telephone." One can understand why catchers were especially hostile toward yet another new development that eroded their stature as heroes.

In the years to come, other catchers would protest against the use of signals in terms that made it clear they considered the tactic sneaky and unmanly. This was spectacularly demonstrated when Dallas manager Jack McCloskey unveiled an especially complex system. In the manner of today's coaches and managers, McCloskey used such actions as shifting his scorecard from one hand to the other, scratching his ear, kicking the grass, or taking a chew of tobacco to convey his wishes.

But the system baffled and exasperated the team's catcher, Tub Welch. Matters came to a head when Welch missed a crucial hit-and-run sign and was confronted after the game by McCloskey. According to a teammate, Welch angrily responded, "If you use your pipes so we can hear you and cut out de mitt stuff we can rap to exactly what you want. De reason I got twisted on dat hit-and-run gag is dat you put a chew of gum in your face instead of tobacco."

The exchange was probably exaggerated for effect, but there is little reason to doubt its essential truth. Catchers like Welch had chosen the position because it embodied a cherished, specific ideal of manliness, only to see it slowly stripped of the characteristics that had made it so appealing. To them, the idea of communicating by surreptitious acts instead of by spirited hollering was more proof that something had gone terribly wrong.

Of course their unhappiness did not slow the powerful forces that were changing their position forever. So most catchers adapted, though with great reluctance. Through the 1880s, signals about pitch selection became a bigger and bigger part of the catcher's role and began to transform the position. In conjunction with the now well-established idea of a special partnership between catcher and pitcher, these private communications created the belief that a catcher had to learn to think along with a specific pitcher. This in turn further strengthened the tendency for catchers to become specialists who worked solely with one pitcher.

As catchers began to use signals and adjust to the rigors of their position by donning equipment, Henry Chadwick's longtime pronouncements began to be realized. The mental demands of the position increased as the physical ones diminished. The symbolic associations of the catcher's position underwent a corresponding shift. In the 1870s it had been a place where a man proved his courage by standing firm in the face of terrible danger. During the 1880s it was transformed into a privileged vantage point from which the catcher could scan the entire field and gather information that he would then convey to his teammates.

This transition was captured in an 1883 article that began with the intriguing declaration, "The modern catcher is equally important in a baseball nine as is the pitcher." There was nothing new about this idea, but what had changed became clear when the writer spelled out the requirements of the "modern catcher." Those qualifications included many familiar ones, such as a strong arm, the agility to handle wild pitches, and a "cool, level head." Batting and baserunning skills were described as helpful, but not as obligatory. These requirements, however, were mentioned only briefly, and the grave dangers of the position were alluded to only in a passing reference to the need for "pluck and endurance."

Instead, most of the commentary described how the "modern catcher" and the pitcher had become so valuable to each other "that the strong points of either cannot be brought out, except by mutual support and excellence." The writer added that the "true catcher should almost direct the in-field work, coach the pitcher and especially watch bases and by signs instruct his pitcher when to throw and his basemen when to dodge the men on the base so as to receive his swift, sharp throw, to catch the player away from his base." Clearly the old ideal exemplified by catchers like Nat Hicks was giving way to the one that Henry Chadwick had championed for so long.

As the 1880s proceeded, the idea of the pitcher and catcher exchanging information about pitch selection became established. At first the prevailing belief was that the pitcher should initiate the signals. The author of the 1883 article about the "modern catcher," for example, wrote disapprovingly: "In these days, it has become almost a fashion for old catchers to give the pitcher signs to pitch. Such is not the catcher's office. A pitcher, to be effective, should deliver his ball as he chooses himself, sizing up his batsman and signing to his catcher what he pitches. Unless such tactics are followed[,] half the pitcher's effectiveness is destroyed."

Despite such comments, catchers began taking more and more responsibility during the 1880s. Johnny Ward offered this summary in 1888: "Until within a few years this sign was always given by the pitcher, but now it is almost the universal practice for the catcher to give it to the pitcher, and if the latter doesn't want to pitch the ball asked for he changes the sign by a shake of the head." Ward somewhat overstated the case. His claim that until the last few years the pitcher had "always" originated the signal is contradicted by the statement in the 1883 article that it had "become almost a fashion" for veteran catchers to do so. There are other indications of catchers beginning to assume this role earlier than Ward acknowledges while veteran pitchers like Charley Radbourn and Bill Hutchison were continuing to give signs into the 1890s.

In a few instances, battery partners struggled for control. When veteran catcher John Clapp was paired with Jim McCormick for Cleveland in 1881, the two could not "work together as a team. Both are capable of running the battery, and both want to boss the job, and as neither will yield to the other in occupying a subordinate position in directing the battery, they necessarily clash, and the result is divided opinions and ideas and a failure in team work together. Now, [the team's other catcher, 'Doc'] Kennedy and McCormick work together as a team splendidly, simply because McCormick runs the battery and has all the say in its direction; that is, he gets Kennedy to catch for his pitching, whereas Clapp wants McCormick to pitch for his catching, which is quite a different thing." More amusingly, pitcher Al Krumm grumbled in 1889 that while pitching for Dayton his "catchers would catch nothing but a straight ball and out-curve, and when a pitcher shook his head and delivered anything else, they jumped aside and let it pass as a wild pitch." The similarity of the pitcher and catcher to a horse and its rider prompted some differences of opinion as to which player was which.

Nevertheless the trend described by Ward unquestionably occurred. In the years immediately after the advent of the curveball, if the pitcher and catcher exchanged pitch information at all, it was the norm for the pitcher to let the catcher know what was coming. But during the mid-1880s this changed dramatically, and it became customary for catchers to give the signals.

The main reason for the catcher assuming this duty was pragmatic. The pitcher's exposed location in the middle of the infield made any signs he gave visible to all, while the catcher was at least partially concealed from prying eyes. Harvard catcher Francis Mason, for instance, explained that he gave signals "by shutting my eyes, while holding my hands to the sides of my mask so as to prevent it being seen." Even the few pitchers who continued to call their own pitches began to take elaborate precautions; Bill Hutchison, for instance, would give the signal that mattered but also shake his "head 'yes' or 'no' pretending the catcher is calling them."

To some extent the change was cosmetic. After all, pitchers delivered the ball and reserved the right to shake off the catcher's signal (or just ignore it, as Tony Mullane had done). Catcher Doc Bushong explained in 1888, "it has always been my practice to give the signs, and if satisfactory, the pitcher would deliver the ball as directed. If not, a shake of the head or a hesitation would lead to a change." Pitcher Ted Breitenstein confirmed in 1894, "The catcher calls for the kind of ball he thinks I should deliver, but if it is against my judgment, I reverse it by an agreed signal." So in essence the pitcher still had the final say.

Yet while catchers did not have complete authority over pitch selection, their assumption of signal-calling responsibilities was an important development. After all, many pitchers of the 1870s had delivered whatever pitch suited their fancy without consultation or communication. So the fact that the catcher now played a key role in the decision-making process was, in and of itself, a big step in transforming the tough-guy catcher of the 1870s into the thinking-man catcher of the 1880s.

An 1886 article, for instance, concluded that allowing the catcher to give the signs "is a better plan when the catcher is a cool and experienced man." The choice of words implies an important corollary: if the catcher is giving the signals, he must be a "cool and experienced man." As more and more catchers began to give signals to pitchers, a new perception of them emerged. In the 1870s a good catcher had been essential to the pitcher because his coolness under fire, adaptability, courage, and skill enabled the pitcher to use his full arsenal. The donning of protective equipment had greatly diminished that role, with many beginning to see the catcher as just a "backstop" who let pitches bounce off his amply protected body. Signal-calling offered the catcher the chance for a new image: a man whose resourcefulness, experience, and powers of observation enabled him to get the best out of a pitcher.

This idea was naturally championed by Henry Chadwick. "More than ever before," the veteran sportswriter announced in 1890, "was it plainly manifested last season that without team work together by the two battery players no pitcher, no matter what his individual ability in the position may be, can hope to be successful. 'How can I pitch to-day?' says the rattled star pitcher, 'when I have not got my regular catcher?' And that regular catcher is the player who knows every signal of his pitcher, and who is familiar with all his strategic points of play, and knows how to ably assist him in his work."

By this time Chadwick had been advancing similar notions for decades without any noticeable effect on how catchers regarded their role. But now some catchers were making comments that sounded remarkably similar. Doc Bushong commented in 1888, "The 'pairing' of pitchers and catchers so they can work steadily together, is always beneficial."

He was not alone in starting to sound a lot like Chadwick. In a revealing 1889 article, sportswriter Tim Murnane maintained that the "combination" plays that could be made by teammates working in unison were "as varied as the moves in a game of chess. A team of inferior players can accomplish more in the long run by what is termed team work, than a club composed entirely of star players can where there is no united action." Unlike Chadwick, who was usually vague about specifics, Murnane was able to use his experience as a former major league ballplayer to provide concrete illustrations. He explained, for example, why the strengths and weaknesses of particular infielders help determine which one should be chosen to field a ball in a given situation.

While catchers did not figure directly in most of these plays, Murnane stressed that "the catcher should have well-defined signals with every man in the infield." This again was a familiar Chadwick theme, but the ballplayer-turned-sportswriter was able to show that the idea now had tangible benefits. Until recently, catchers had taken little interest in learning what pitch was coming, so passing that information along must have struck them as a low priority at best. Just as important, the shortstop of the 1870s was essentially a rover who had little responsibility for plays at second base. This left limited opportunity for situational repositioning, since each of the three basemen had to be prepared to cover his base whenever the need arose. But as Murnane pointed out—and illustrated with a wealth of specific examples—things had changed by 1889. There were, he observed, "new wrinkles being introduced year after year by the leading professionals."

The shortstop's transformation into an infielder was one important factor in this new environment, but an even bigger one was the bunt. An 1885 rule change that legalized flat bats had the unanticipated result of popularizing bunts (which had enjoyed a brief vogue in the early 1870s thanks to Tommy Barlow, but had quickly fallen out of favor). Soon bunts became a common occurrence, and they changed the way teams played defense. As long as hitters took full swings, reaction was the crux of fielding. The bunt, in contrast, made it possible to anticipate where the ball would end up and placed a premium on preparation and execution. Just as important, bunts ensured that catchers would no longer work in isolation from the infielders. Now, for the first time, the game regularly featured batted balls that could be fielded by either the catcher or an infielder. So catchers assumed the important new responsibility of deciding whether to scramble out and field such balls themselves or allow a teammate do so, and then advising him what to do with the ball.

Other plays that involved interaction between the catcher and the infielders also received greater emphasis. During the 1870s teams at bat made regular and effective use of double steals with runners on first and third. Because shortstops rarely covered second base, the catcher's options when the trail runner took off for second base were severely limited. He could either allow the base to be stolen uncontested, or he could hazard a throw to second base, knowing that at best one runner would be retired and the other would advance, while there was a good chance that both runners would advance. Some catchers did try throwing the ball to the shortstop for a quick return home, but this was unlikely to fool an experienced base runner as long as the shortstop was stationed far from the base.

This changed at the end of the 1870s when shortstops began to stand much closer to second base. After the 1879 season, Henry Chadwick observed that catchers were taking advantage by "throwing to short-stop when a runner was on third, and another ran down from first to second to get the man on third home. This was not done in the old style of throwing to short-stop's position, but in throwing a little to the left of second base, the short-stop jumping forward and taking the ball and promptly returning it to the catcher in time. When the ball is swiftly thrown and accurately returned, the play invariably yields an out; but it must be understood by signal to be done effectively." During the 1880s, having two fielders close to second base enabled defenses to unveil many new variations. The new options showed how important it was for catchers to make the right decision and to use signals to work in concert with the infielders.

The increased perception of the catcher as a man who tried to outthink the opposition was further enhanced by other new developments. For one thing, there was a growing belief that doing the little things and playing well as a team made the difference between winning and losing. Once again, this was an idea that Chadwick had long championed, but his advocacy had been belied by practical realities. In the 1860s, with scores frequently reaching the fifties and sixties or higher, it was hard to see the little things as being that important. Scores had plummeted during the 1870s but had sent the message that only the pitcher's ability to fool batters and the catcher's ability to hold those offerings really mattered. But as the 1880s wore on, enough of a balance was struck that for the first time doing the little things and working as a team really did seem crucial.

The consequences of the greater parity among major league teams were nicely summed up by Charles Comiskey when he claimed in 1889, "There is little difference in the actual playing strength of teams nowadays. Nearly all professional ball players can catch a ball when it is thrown to them, and he is a poor one indeed who cannot get a safe hit once in a while. When I size up a team I do not look at the players' batting or fielding records. A winning team is made up of players who will 'turn tricks' when they see a chance—men who study points and work every advantage to win." That same year Doc Bushong contended that the catcher was the deciding factor in many of those tight games: "The great number of games the New York club won last year by such a close margin as one run, might easily have been turned into victories for the opposing teams but for the fact of superb catching and throwing, and thus preventing any more runs from being scored."

This new perception increased the emphasis on the catcher's thought processes in a number of specific ways. Led by Gus Schmelz of Columbus, managers began for the first time to sacrifice outs and the chance for a big inning in favor of one-run strategies. Regardless of the score, until the late 1880s "once a man got to first base the next batter walked to the plate and promptly attempted to knock the cover off the ball." But in the 1890s it became the norm to bunt in such situations: "The modern principle of baseball is to first make one run, if your opponents have none, and to continue always to try for one run as long as you are in the lead, or not more than a run or two behind." The change was so dramatic that Baltimore manager Ned Hanlon declared in 1897 that "we didn't play ball in 1889 as we play it now."

The more offenses tried to manufacture runs by investing in strategies like stolen bases, bunts, and hit-and-run plays, the more defenses were forced to coordinate their efforts to respond. The catcher took the lead role by signaling the strategic approach to his teammates. Before long, defenses began taking the initiative instead of simply reacting to what the batting team did. Comiskey's maxim that a winning team was one that could "turn tricks" began to apply every bit as much to the defensive side as to the offense, with catchers once again at the forefront of this battle of wits.

Of course, trying to outthink the opposing team was not unheard of among tough-guy catchers of the 1870s like Nat Hicks and Bill Craver. In an 1870 exhibition game in New Orleans, Craver "shrewdly" noted that passed balls were rebounding off the padded fence behind the plate in a predictable manner, and he devised a scheme. With a runner on third base, he informed pitcher Levi Meyerle that he planned to let the next pitch get past him. Sure enough, the runner "stepped into the trap" and took off for home while Craver retrieved the ball and threw it to Meyerle covering the plate in plenty of time to retire the surprised runner.

Another tricky tactic employed by early catchers was to deliberately drop third strikes with the bases loaded. Under the rules of the day, the batter and runners were forced to run, which made it easy for the catcher to step on home plate and then relay the ball around the bases for a double or even a triple play. This rule eventually had to be changed because it "looked like cold-blooded murder, as it gave the fielder an unfair advantage over the runners." But Craver was known for trying this tactic with only a couple of runners on base, thereby boldly passing up the certain out in the hope of starting a double play.

Nat Hicks also used deception on occasion. In an 1877 game he "turned about carelessly, and, without calling time, purposely walked toward the Grand Stand. [Base-runner Mike] Golden fell into the trap and started for home. [Pitcher Bobby] Mitchell, having the ball in his hand, easily ran in and caught him before he reached the home plate."

By and large, however, tricks struck Americans of the era as sporting only when they involved risk on both sides. The play designed by Craver in New Orleans involved both skill and risk, since it could easily have gone wrong and made Craver look foolish. Similarly, Craver's use of the intentional dropped third strike with fewer than three runners on base could easily have backfired—for that reason he seems to have been alone in using it in those circumstances. Both plays thus fit the heroic spirit of the tough-guy catcher of the 1870s.

By contrast, trick plays that sought to gain an advantage without any corresponding risk were viewed with suspicion, or worse. The dropped-third-strike play, for example, gave the appearance of being "cold-blooded murder" and thus seemed at odds with the ideal of the catcher as the embodiment of manly forthrightness. Deep reservations were also expressed about the hidden-ball trick, which was popularized by catcher Tommy Barlow in the early 1870s. At first the tactic struck some as clever, but the perception shifted when defensive players began trying it over and over again. The fact that they risked nothing by doing so brought back unpleasant reminders of the days when pitchers could endlessly delay the game by delivering a long series of wild pitches in hopes that the batter would eventually swing at one. Before long the hidden-ball trick started to be looked upon with contempt, sportswriters denouncing it as a tactic "unworthy of a fair and manly player" and many clubs refusing to use it.

Most catchers of the 1870s viewed such tricks as at best an unnecessary artifice and at worst as scarcely better than cheating. But things had changed by the late 1880s. With new emphasis on the notion that a single run could decide the game, the thinking-man catcher had fewer scruples about using tricks to outwit the opposition.

The most dramatic example involved the rule that a caught foul tip was an out, regardless of how many strikes were on the batter. Now that the mitt left one hand unoccupied, catchers learned to exploit the rule by using that hand to make noises that simulated a foul tip when none had occurred. Connie Mack became especially associated with this tactic, and he later admitted that when "a batter would swing at a ball and miss it cleanly I would frequently clip the tip of my big mitt with the finger tips of my right hand, making a sound exactly as though the batter had tipped the ball with his bat and, as I caught the ball, the umpire invariably called the batter out on a caught 'foul tip.'"

Tired of such tactics and the arguments they provoked, the rules-makers addressed the issue after the 1888 season and decreed that, except on the final strike, a foul ball would have to go at least ten feet in the air for a catch to count as an out. It was one more disheartening development for the catcher, who lost yet another of the key skills that had once made his position special.

It must be noted that back in the 1870s Bill Craver also "had a way of snapping his fingers, claiming the ball tipped the bat, and often making outs in this way." Other catchers who preceded Mack, including Charley Snyder and Mike DePangher, were also said to snap their fingers to convince umpires that the ball had been tipped. Mike Kelly tried snapping a rubber band to achieve this end, while an amateur catcher in Pittsburgh attached a gum band to his glove and released it to make a deceptive noise.

But there were two critical differences. First, in the days when the two-hand catch was still essential, this tactic involved risk and could easily backfire. By contrast, when Mack and his contemporaries did the exact same thing, it looked more like a cheap trick that proved yet again that the new equipment made the catcher's job easy. Second, the new generation looked at such tactics differently. Connie Mack, who would become known as a pillar of integrity, later boasted about having recorded outs in this way and expressed no remorse. While we cannot be certain, it seems likely that Craver, despite his shady reputation, felt more scruples about using it.

And that was the paradox of the transformation of the catcher's position. The ideal of manliness to which Craver and his peers subscribed taught them to view baseball as a game in which superior courage and skill led to victory. As a result, they considered it unmanly to resort to any sort of trick to attain that end. In contrast, thinking-man catchers like Mack and Doc Bushong felt this outlook had become obsolete when catchers had sensibly donned equipment. They came to believe that outthinking an adversary (even if it meant bending the rules) was a perfectly legitimate means of winning.

That paradox in turn reflects a deeper one that surrounded the emergence of the thinking-man catcher in the 1880s. With the tough-guy catcher image a casualty of the emergence of protective equipment, the new ideal was the only real hope for catchers to forge a new image. Yet for many it wasn't what they had grown up dreaming of becoming.

10

The Catcher as Desperado

"I often used to wonder what happened to the old-time players if they were hit on the head by such rock-like balls as those of my father's day."—Judge Fred E. Crane

AS WE HAVE SEEN, protective equipment became an unsettling development for catchers. Some of them were able to adapt by embracing a new standard of the catcher as a thinking man, whose signals showed his ingenuity and ability to lead his teammates. But others had little use for an ideal so different from the model of heroism to which they subscribed.

Worse, they found little sympathy. Catching was still a dangerous and demanding position, yet it was no longer perceived that way. Most sportswriters followed Henry Chadwick in depicting the thinking-man model as a step in the right direction, often equating it with "scientific baseball" and progress. Like many others before and since, catchers discovered that when a new development is viewed as progress, it becomes very difficult to stand in its way.

A catcher such as Henry Oxley, for instance, was mockingly described as coming from the "Green Mountains" because of his unfamiliarity with the latest equipment. In like manner it became evident that nothing catchers could say would stop the relentless march of any development that was equated with progress. Catchers like Tub Welch who protested the advent of signals were easy to dismiss by parodying their complaints ("If you use your pipes so we can hear you and cut out de mitt stuff we can rap to exactly what you want"). But most didn't bother to try. Catchers of the old school were, after all, deeply attached to the philosophy that actions spoke louder than words.

Even Stephen Crane, one of the most gifted of American writers, abruptly abandoned his boyhood dream of catching in 1891 and almost never wrote about the subject in the nine remaining years of his life. On the rare occasions when he did, it was in cryptic comments such as his 1896 remark about being "rather more proud of my base ball ability than of some other things." With a writer of Crane's ability unwilling or unable to discuss his onetime love, it is small wonder that other catchers made no effort to articulate their thoughts on the subject. Instead, as men of deeds they used actions to proclaim their frustration with the way their beloved position had changed. These acts were not understood as messages, so these men were perceived as rebels without a cause.

And indeed they had no cause that stood any chance of succeeding, since the days when the catcher had been the embodiment of manly courage were gone forever. To the extent they had a message, it was a simple lament about what they had lost, and even if they had been able to articulate it, nothing was about to bring back those old days. So all too often these men settled for engaging in boorish misdeeds and criminal activity. They cultivated odd appearances, took risks for risk's sake, broke rules just to see what would happen, and when caught made palpably ridiculous excuses. This does not, of course, justify the crimes and reprehensible actions that will be described in this chapter. But a confused message is a message nonetheless, and these acts, even when deplorable, need to be understood as part of a pattern. Denied the opportunity to fulfill the myth that had inspired them, they resorted to self-mythologizing.

The fact that these catchers had neither a cause nor a message that could be readily articulated placed them in the company of a growing number of Americans. The artisan had been a man distinguished by his mastery of a craft; the frontiersman a man distinguished by his kinship with nature; the soldier a man distinguished by his ability to recognize when violence was needed; the cowboy a man distinguished by his oneness with his horse; and the catcher a man distinguished by a set of skills that borrowed from all these comrades. As the end of the nineteenth century approached, all these men found that their special abilities no longer seemed to matter. They were being asked to step aside in the name of "progress" or "science" or some such abstraction. Baseball equipment provided one of the many poignant examples. "Large bat manufacturers," a sportswriter explained in 1879, "have deprived the carpenter, the turner and other hewers of wood of a considerable share of profitable business done on a small scale."

Many of these displaced men responded by leading what Thoreau called "lives of quiet desperation." But many chose instead to rebel and become desperadoes.

More than a few of these catchers made symbolic gestures that suggested either a desire to restore prestige to the position or, more troubling, stubborn denial that the loss had taken place. Some, for example, tried to follow the lead of the 1870s catchers who had stood out because they cultivated a distinctive appearance. Typical was Wesley Blogg, who had an undistinguished career but was remembered as the only player in the history of the American Association to wear a beard. While Stephen Crane's habit of constantly holding a cigarette that he rarely smoked suggested a self-conscious effort to make himself the center of attention, he had nothing on an African-American catcher named Johnson who amazed Wisconsin audiences by dodging fouls "with remarkable agility, often smoking a cigar at the same time." Other catchers were accused of deliberately making plays look harder than they were in order to impress onlookers. An 1883 game account remarked, "Little [Billy] Hunter of Saginaw worked the grand stand almost to death yesterday. . . . Every other ball pitched Hunter would execute a combined acrobatic song and dance, fall on his side (each move a picture), and the spectators would applaud."

More than any other single factor, it was frustration over the sudden lack of attention paid him that seems to have motivated the desperado catcher of the 1880s. Without having to try, the catcher of the 1870s had known that all eyes were upon him during a game because the hopes of the club, and often of an entire community, rested upon his performance and his ability to stay healthy. By contrast, the catcher of the 1880s knew that he was no longer the focus of attention. His mask and other new equipment not only robbed him of his mystique of toughness but also meant that he might not be recognized once he walked off the field. Thus even while many of the decade's catchers were trying to create a new model of the thinking-man catcher, just as many were seeking a way to restore heroism to the position.

Many manifested this disillusionment by engaging in activities that seemed solely aimed to demonstrate their willingness to take risks. A notable example occurred when the Washington Monument was completed in December 1884. Before the monument had even been dedicated, veteran catchers Charley Snyder and Phil Baker and two other local ballplayers decided to see if they could catch a ball thrown from near its top. Despite the great hazards of the endeavor—the difficulty of gauging the ball's trajectory and the wintry conditions—the players made repeated efforts, with Baker holding on to one ball momentarily before having it slip away. Word of their efforts prompted other displays, such as an attempt by a catcher in Erie, Pennsylvania, to snare a ball dropped from the top of a waterworks standpipe, a distance of 248 feet. After seven tries, "the deed was accomplished, but the catcher declared the sphere weighed a ton." Not to be outdone, the irrepressible Lew Brown reportedly once watched a circus performer catch a ball fired from a cannon and went to the management with an offer to catch the same ball fired at any speed that the "cannon would stand" for $2,500. The offer was politely declined.

More disturbing than the affinity for risk was the penchant of many catchers for criminal activity. Such acts were not, of course, restricted to catchers, as many ballplayers of the era had run-ins with the law. While a career in baseball did not yet produce great wealth, ballplayers did work relatively few hours per day, and their workday was always over by sundown. Nothing in the backgrounds of these men prepared them for using free evenings in strange towns constructively, and the results were predictable.

But while pitchers, infielders, and outfielders also encountered legal difficulties, catchers were arrested with disturbing regularity. Moreover an inordinate number of their crimes were ones that no sane, sober person could have expected to get away with. They were impulsive acts, frequently fueled by alcohol, which seemed designed more to attract attention than to gain anything tangible.

Almost as soon as it became common for catchers to be hired to work as "revolving" professionals, incidents of this sort began to occur. A particularly notable example was Patsy Dockney, who was born in Ireland around 1844 and grew up in Hoboken. Dockney served for nearly three years in New Jersey's Twenty-first Infantry during the Civil War, and then within months of being mustered out began to establish himself as a star catcher. Soon came an invitation to catch for the Athletics of Philadelphia, where Dockney proved so good at catching hard-throwing pitcher Dick McBride that he was offered a job as an inspector of fireplugs to keep him in town.

Dockney quickly earned renown for his skill and toughness. His reputation was cemented by an incident that occurred when the Athletics traveled to St. Louis to face the clubs of that city. According to a later account,

Dockney got into a knife fight on the night before the first game and ended up with a severely slashed chest: "The wound ran from one shoulder to the other and blood streamed in torrents. Dockney, unconscious, was picked up, placed into an ambulance and hurried to a hospital. There physicians took something like fifty stitches in his chest and also were compelled to place strips of plaster across to assist in holding the torn parts together. So critical was Dockney's condition, that a nurse was assigned to his bedside during the night."

When morning came, Dockney asked the nurse to fetch him a glass of water and then took advantage of her momentary absence to get dressed and report to the ballpark. The team's manager had been told by a doctor that it would be months before Dockney would be able to play again, so he demanded an explanation. The catcher, in the tradition of men of few words, merely replied: "Well, maybe he's changed his mind since then—anyway, I'm here to play. You haven't got any other catcher except me and I guess you can use me all right."

Of course Dockney was right, since nobody else could handle Mc-Bride's fastball, and he caught that day's game. The results were predictable: "Due to his weakened condition Dockney's judgment of the pitches was rather poor. Nearly a dozen of the swift heaves of McBride went through Dockney's outstretched hand—and each and every one struck him on the chest, on the very spot where the butcher knife had made the terrible gash. Every time a ball smashed against Dockney's chest spurts of blood would issue forth. Twice Dockney dropped from pain and weakness, but each time he got up and resumed catching. He endured until the last man was out—and then he collapsed utterly."

While the melodramatic elements in this description suggest some exaggeration, there is corroboration from a reliable enough source to regard it as authentic. There is also plenty of evidence that Dockney possessed a combination of skill and courage that could have enabled him to take a place alongside Joe Leggett, Nat Hicks, and Bill Craver as one of the game's first catching legends. He became the subject of colorful stories about his old Irish-style mustache and about a home run he once hit that traveled clear over the pagoda in center field at Brooklyn's Union Grounds. Instead, Patsy Dockney became best remembered for the frequency of his barroom brawls.

It seems unlikely that Dockney inspected many of Philadelphia's fire-plugs, since the only routine he followed was "to play ball every afternoon and fight and drink every night. He was a tough of the toughs." At first his talent caused onlookers to make excuses for his behavior. One article implausibly claimed that yet another stab wound had been the result not of a brawl but of being "stabbed by a drunken man with whom [Dockney] was not acquainted and with whom he had no words." But soon the pattern was too obvious to be ignored or to be compatible with an athletic career. After wearing out his welcome in Philadelphia, Dockney drifted to a professional club in Cincinnati, where his nocturnal activities continued. He was soon out of baseball altogether and by 1871 was facing charges of larceny. Sometime in the 1880s he died in obscurity, reportedly as the result of yet another barroom stabbing.

This willingness of baseball enthusiasts to overlook the disturbing behavior of a star catcher continued. The men who ran ball clubs made a habit of signing talented but troubled players "with our eyes wide open," with the result that isolated acts of misconduct frequently became recurring patterns.

The strange case of Tommy Barlow offered a particularly dramatic illustration of how a man's value as a catcher could incline others not to intervene. Barlow was a Brooklyn native who overcame several obstacles to rise to prominence as catcher for the Atlantics. A small man, he was such a weak hitter that he began using a miniature bat to bunt the ball when this tactic was still all but unknown. Yet his defensive skills were impressive enough to compensate for this deficiency. At the close of the 1872 season Henry Chadwick wrote a glowing tribute to Barlow's skill and character, describing him as "a regular, earnest and plucky worker, and one of the most active of catchers, Tommy watching the ball and handling it with the agility of a cat. He was also on the *qui vive* in playing points; in fact he played the position finely throughout the season. A feature of his play was his thorough good humor, and especially his avoidance of that error of catchers, bullying the umpire, one of the greatest mistakes a catcher or pitcher can make. In this respect Tommy Barlow was the model catcher of the season, and when we add that he was thoroughly reliable we give him credit for the best requisite of a professional player."

Shortly thereafter, however, Barlow's career hit the skids. He missed much of the 1874 season with an undisclosed injury, and in 1875 switched to shortstop. By 1877 he was in jail for stealing a pair of stockings and providing reporters with a lurid explanation of his rapid descent. Barlow explained that three or four years earlier he had been struck by a ball while catching and was then injected with morphine to relieve the pain. Hopeless addiction to morphine ensued, with the result that he now claimed to have no memory of his crime. "I was once catcher for the Mutuals, also the Atlantics," boasted Barlow, before adding plaintively, "but no one would think it to look at me now." He added that he had no hope of recovering and expected soon to die.

Questions about the veracity of this account remain. The baseball historian David Arcidiacono notes that no game took place on the date cited by Barlow in one of the accounts and that there is no contemporary description of such an injury. Despite these problems, Barlow's version of events remains plausible. Severe blows to the head were an all-too-common part of the lot of the catchers of his era and certainly could have led to an addiction to morphine (and to a confused recollection of some of the details).

Tommy Barlow was released from jail before long and made a short-lived effort to get back into baseball. He was last heard from in 1880, and by 1888 there were several references to his being dead. Yet his passing was never noted by the sporting papers that had so recently chronicled his exploits, and many baseball researchers have tried without success to determine when and where he died.

As a result, mystery still swirls around Barlow. Was a blow to the head—or perhaps a series of such blows—really responsible? Recent studies of National Football League players have shown that repeated concussions can produce both memory impairment and severe behavioral changes. Could Barlow, as he claimed, have been suffering from similar symptoms? Or was his precipitous decline the result of character flaws? Did the thrill of being a star catcher in an era when catchers were viewed as folk heroes create a bloated sense of entitlement? Did he thus believe that he could get away with anything and then cynically use the hardships of the catching position as an excuse for criminal behavior and morphine addiction?

Those questions become more pressing in considering the 1880s, when an alarming number of catchers exhibited similarly precipitous declines. John J. "Rooney" Sweeney's promising career ended prematurely after a series of arrests for such acts as kicking a woman and stealing from a teammate after a poker game. Sweeney obtained a position as a New York City firefighter but eventually had to resign in the face of department disciplinary charges.

Jimmy Adams, the St. Louis catcher whose teammates took advantage of his naiveté to convince him that cuspidors were china vases, was playing for a St. Louis semipro club in the 1894 season when he got himself in trouble. His team was playing in Edwardsville, Illinois, but Adams had to miss the game with an injury. Instead he spent the day at a local watering hole and ended up under arrest for, ironically, throwing a cuspidor at the saloon keeper. He spent the rest of the year in jail. Upon his release, Adams stuck to the straight and narrow for a couple of years and was able to revive his career. But then word came in 1897 that the once "promising amateur" catcher was now "an inmate of the Illinois penitentiary at Chester where he is serving a sentence for Grand Larceny."

The career of an up-and-coming young catcher named Arthur Twineham was boosted by detailed profiles of him that regularly appeared in the *Sporting News*. Twineham also showed signs of being a good family man, as a series of notes detailed the jobs he held in the off-season to support his wife and children. His career was almost derailed before it started, as he was released early in the 1891 season by Spokane and a few months later was cut by a team in Pendleton, Oregon, because of a drinking problem. But he recovered and was in the majors by 1893, even serving briefly as captain of St. Louis's struggling National League entry.

Eventually Twineham's drinking problems resurfaced and ruined his career. In 1901 he was committed to a Memphis insane asylum, leaving his wife and children in dire straits. Before long Twineham was released, and he seemed to have recovered so fully that he was hired to work in the dynamite department of the Repauno Chemical Company in New Jersey. But another relapse followed, and after one last unsuccessful attempt to return to baseball he was last heard from in 1904 when he was arrested for stealing whiskey bottles from a hotel.

Then there was Jake Knowdell, the catcher whose fishing trip reportedly paved the way for Alamazoo Jennings's memorable major league debut. Knowdell made his own big league debut for the Brooklyn Atlantics in 1874 and gained a reputation for being "cool and us[ing] good judgment." But he soon began to exhibit erratic behavior that eventually degenerated into madness. During an 1885 "spree" at Coney Island, he walked into a drugstore and requested morphine. Offered a dose, he explained that he instead wanted an entire "bottle in order that he might poison himself. He was sent home in charge of an officer." Fewer than two years later Knowdell stole his brother-in-law's wallet and again displayed such bizarre conduct that a newspaper account concluded, "He is believed by his friends to be insane."

Charley Hoover showed enough early promise at the outset of his career to be compared to the great Mike Kelly. "Hoover is a perfect ringer for Kelly. He is built like Mike, and does not make a move that is not a reminder of [Kelly]," raved one sportswriter. He added, "today's practice went far to confirm that opinion. After catching a while for [Charles] Brynan, he took a turn at the bat, and then caught for [Mark] Baldwin, who turned loose and pitched with apparently more speed than ever. Everywhere Hoover stood like Kelly, caught like Kelly, and received and threw like Kelly."

Thereafter Hoover reminded observers of Mike Kelly only in his appetite for alcohol, as his brief major league career was overshadowed by a lengthy list of minor league stops that usually ended with his being run out of town by the police. In 1887, Hoover was arrested in Lincoln, Missouri, for shooting at a hack driver who refused to stop a cab that the ballplayer hailed. A judge let him off with a fine and a promise to leave town. Within a few years he was also persona non grata in Lincoln, Nebraska, having been released from that city's jail "on the condition that he was to leave town at once which he did, and we hope he won't return for he is a disgrace to the city. Hoover has not any principle about him. All he thinks of is drinking whiskey and fighting."

Hoover drifted out to California and soon earned a reputation as "an out and out desperado [who] carries shooting irons at all times." Before long he was back in the Midwest, where, despite his well-known history, teams continued to sign him and later regret it. The next season saw a drunken Hoover jailed in Quincy, Illinois, for attempting to drive his horse into a saloon. And his 1895 release by a team in Jacksonville, Illinois, prompted that town's *Sporting News* correspondent to write that the incorrigible backstop should be banned from the league for good. Having already been banished from two different towns called Lincoln, he was now on the verge of wearing out his welcome in the entire Land of Lincoln. Hoover permanently disappeared from the baseball scene in 1898 when he was sentenced to five years in prison for check forgery. His prison record mentioned that his body bore two mementos of his ballplaying career—a tattoo of a baseball player and a set of "broken and gnarled fingers."

While the crimes and misdeeds of Barlow, Sweeney, Adams, Twineham, Knowdell, and Hoover are acts for which they must bear individual accountability, the pattern is too clear to overlook. Almost all these men were arrested for crimes within a few years of the outset of their major league careers, yet few if any of them sought to profit from their crimes. Their deeds were impulsive and spontaneous, committed with little or no effort to avoid detection. They stood little to gain from their acts while the risks were enormous.

Each of them was risking throwing away a promising career in baseball. Some had already made progress toward establishing successful postbaseball careers and were also jeopardizing those preparations. What would lead a man to risk so much in order to steal a few bottles of whiskey or a pair of stockings or for some momentary thrill? Obviously the influence of liquor and the temptations of the baseball lifestyle provide a partial explanation, but those factors do not satisfactorily explain why the lives of so many catchers followed the same unhappy course. It's hard not to suspect that risk-taking had become a narcotic that acted on these men as powerfully as alcohol.

Another telling parallel is that most of these men seemingly recovered from their initial brushes with trouble and were able to convince others they had reformed. Yet each man proved ultimately unable to conquer his demons and suffered relapses. Their lives spiraled precipitously downward, as they seemed so powerless to change their self-destructive patterns of behavior that observers concluded that mental health was a key issue.

A final parallel is especially striking: all six men were heroes for at least a short time. Their accomplishments were widely reported in the sporting presses, as were their arrests and related troubles. Yet the passings of these six men did not warrant even the briefest of mentions in the national sporting presses or in the local papers that had once covered their exploits so devotedly. Moreover they died in such obscurity that diligent research has still failed to uncover the dates or places of death for any of the six. To show how unusual this is, as of 2008 there are only twenty-five men who played at least fifty major league games and whose death information is unknown. And five of these catchers—all except Adams, whose major league career was brief—are on that very short list.

While the cause of any single ruined life cannot be ascribed with certainty, two possibilities must be mentioned because they offer potential explanations for why so many catchers followed similar paths of self-destruction. The first is that their behavior was a response to shattered dreams. All these men were born in the 1850s or 1860s and grew up hearing tales of the Civil War as the proving ground of manhood and about frontiersmen like Daniel Boone as the model of heroism. Their success as catchers seemed at first to be the ideal substitute for combat experience and gave their lives meaning and purpose. But disillusionment set in when the prestige of catching began to decline—Barlow's arrest occurred in the same year as the introduction of the catcher's mask, and the troubles of the others came in the ensuing years as the status of the position was in free fall. According to this theory, catchers such as these sought to recreate the aura of courage by taking increasingly outrageous risks.

The other explanation is that their behavior was the result of one of the most fearful hazards of their position—being struck in the head by foul balls. At first there is a natural inclination to see this as an excuse. No professional catcher is known to have died as an immediate result of a foul ball. And there are relatively few recorded instances of catchers taking a foul ball off the head and then being out of action for a long period of time.

Yet recent experience has shown the need to rethink this mind-set. Injuries to other parts of the body—such as the hand injuries described in an earlier chapter—often force a player out of action for a substantial length of time. But these injuries typically heal in time, allowing the player to return as good as new or very close to it. By contrast, brain concussions produce far more subtle and insidious results. The victim may often barely notice the initial trauma, and in most cases quickly feels well enough to return to action. Unfortunately the nature of such injuries is that they may never heal and will often grow progressively worse over a long period of time, especially if one endures additional blows to the head.

This sad reality has been brought home by the tragic decline of many former athletic heroes as a result of an irreversible form of brain damage known as chronic traumatic encephalopathy (CTE). The susceptibility of boxers to CTE is so well recognized that the condition is often referred to as boxer's dementia, punch-drunk syndrome, or *dementia pugilistica*. A rash of recent cases has shown that athletes in other sports are also vulnerable and that the symptoms begin to manifest themselves far earlier than previously thought.

This was brought home with particular force by the deaths of former NFL players Justin Strzelczyk, Andre Waters, Terry Long, and Mike Webster, all at disturbingly young ages. While none of the four men died as a direct result of brain damage, postmortems revealed each man to be suffering from an advanced case of chronic traumatic encephalopathy. That underlying condition appears to have been responsible for the cognitive impairment and erratic behavior displayed by all four men, which in turn contributed to their deaths.

The link between these tragedies and concussions sustained during competition was strengthened by a study published in the official journal of the American College of Sports Medicine. According to the article, the results of a survey of 595 former NFL players "call into question how effectively retired professional football players with a history of three or more concussions are able to meet the mental and physical demands of life after playing professional football." The study also suggested that multiple concussions may manifest themselves in unpredictable ways, including depression, forgetfulness, inappropriate behavior, and thoughts of suicide. So it seems plausible that at least some of the catchers whose declines are described in this chapter were experiencing the aftereffects of repeated brain trauma.

Football is far from alone in being touched by this disturbing new awareness of the lingering effects of concussions. The 2007 homicidal outburst by professional wrestler Chris Benoit has been linked to the numerous concussions he suffered. A disturbing number of National Hockey League players have been forced into retirement in recent years by repeated concussions. The international football (soccer) community is also coming to recognize concussions as a serious issue among its players. And in 2007 longtime catcher Mike Matheny became the first major league baseball player known to have retired as a direct result of postconcussion syndrome.

In addition, several tragedies have been attributed to being hit in the head by a foul tip during a professional ball game. One involved a catcher of the 1880s named Jeff Dolan, who "was struck by a ball on the temple while playing behind the bat, and from that moment was insane." Dolan had to be committed to an insane asylum at Napa, California, where it became "his custom to go into the yard and take up a position as if behind the bat." Dolan never recovered and died in 1890. A catcher named Samuel Lindsley from Catskill, New York, was struck on the forehead by a foul tip in an 1877 game and knocked unconscious. After two weeks he felt well enough to return to work, but he soon "manifested symptoms of insanity, and it became necessary to keep him manacled and strapped."

A much more recent incident occurred when home plate umpire Cal Drummond was struck in the mask by a foul tip during an American League game played in Baltimore on June 10, 1969. When it happened, the injury seemed so inconsequential that no one even recorded which batter had hit the foul. After the game, however, Drummond lapsed into unconsciousness and spent a week in a Baltimore hospital. By the following spring he seemed on his way to recovery and began a minor league rehabilitation stint in preparation for his return to the major leagues. But during his final minor league game in Des Moines, Drummond collapsed and died. An autopsy attributed his death to the lingering effects of the foul tip eleven months earlier.

Drummond's death is an especially vivid illustration of how subtle and stealthy the course of a brain injury can be. It also points to the disturbing reality that, even with today's far better medical technology, there remains a lack of understanding of the severity of invisible injuries. Too often head injuries are still euphemized as "having your bell rung," and apparent recovery suggests that no damage has been done. The National Football League has been so slow to respond to the dangers of multiple concussions that one critic has accused the league of a "tobacco-industry-like refusal to acknowledge the depths of the problem." Indeed, until very recently it was not uncommon for athletes who had suffered such injuries to be encouraged to show their toughness by continuing to play. Andre Waters, one of the NFL players whose death has been linked to CTE, once said for example that after suffering a concussion, "I'd sniff some smelling salts, then go back in there."

Such an attitude was taken for granted in the tough-guy culture of the nineteenth-century catcher, and it is disturbing to think about the consequences. An all-too-typical 1876 game account offered this description of a game in Pittsburgh: "[Catchers Packey] Dillon, of the Reds, and Clark, of the Braddocks, were both painfully hurt during the game. The first was struck in the jaw by a hot foul, and afterward had one of his fingers knocked out of joint. Clark received a similar hard hit on the temple, knocking him out of time." Both Dillon and Clark remained in this game, and while each man eventually swapped positions with a teammate, the switches were made as a result of hand injuries, not the blows to the head.

In some cases catchers who exhibited ominous warning signs were made the objects of feeble efforts at humor. In 1891 longtime catcher Tom Deasley began to display signs of dementia, reportedly coming under the delusion that he was the groundskeeper at Philadelphia's Athletic Park and showing up for work each day. But his former battery mate, Jack Lynch, responded by telling a series of Yogi Berra-esque tales at Deasley's expense.

The reminiscences of Luther Green, an early ballplayer from Thomson, Illinois, make for still more unsettling reading. "Waldo Ward was hit twice in one game and never played again as long as I was acquainted with him," wrote Green of his hometown's catcher. "The first was a foul tip that struck him squarely between the eyes and knocked him unconscious." Ward was out cold and "was still dazed," but since "no one had noticed it," he remained in the game. In his next at bat he was struck by a pitched ball "and he went down again. It was several hours before he recognized anyone and also months afterward before he recovered and his catching days were over."

It should be emphasized that Matheny and Drummond wore masks that offer far better protection than the ones available to nineteenth-century catchers. Recall, for example, Ban Johnson's matter-of-fact revelation that he was "oftentimes unable to wear a hat by reason of the bumps and lumps." Can there be any doubt that many nineteenth-century catchers suffered concussions during games, and that the vast majority of them showed their toughness by insisting on continuing to play, thereby greatly increasing the risk of catastrophic brain injuries?

Former football players and boxers who suffer memory loss are all too often allowed to fade into obscurity by the fans who applauded and even idolized them, the sportswriters who chronicled their exploits, and the sporting promoters and executives who profited from their talents. The hidden nature of the connection between their conditions and the sport they played makes it easy to ignore the painful truth. As Merril Hoge, a former NFL teammate of both Webster and Long, notes, "We understand, as players, the ramifications and dangers of paralysis for one reason—we see a person in a wheelchair and can identify with that visually. When somebody has had brain trauma to a level that they do not function normally, we don't see that. We don't witness a person walking around lost or drooling or confused, because they can't be out in society." So the absence of information about the deaths of so many of these pioneer catchers is sadly predictable and another reason to suspect that at least some of them were suffering from a form of brain damage that slowly robbed them of the ability to function in society.

One thing is certain: a nineteenth-century catcher suffering from brain damage would not have been accurately diagnosed, let alone treated. Even today the fact that CTE manifests itself in difficult-to-recognize forms such as mood swings and forgetfulness makes it very difficult to diagnose. In the nineteenth century, with no understanding of the condition, the symptoms of a man suffering from CTE would have been ignored for as long as possible, and then he would have been locked up.

The lives of a number of other nineteenth-century catchers exhibited disquieting parallels with those of Tommy Barlow, Rooney Sweeney, Jimmy Adams, Arthur Twineham, Jake Knowdell, and Charley Hoover. As noted earlier, the first thirty-two years of Wallie Walker's life saw him gain distinction as an industrious lawyer and minor league executive, but his last three decades were spent in an insane asylum. Other catchers such as Marshall Quinton, Ed Whiting, John Bancker, and Jack Brennan also had troubled lives after baseball, and their deaths also went unrecorded at the time, coming to light only recently as the result of research by the author and by the indefatigable researcher Richard Malatzky.

Even some catchers whose deaths were recorded exhibited some of the same symptoms. Frank Ringo's drinking problems ruined his promising career. He then seemed to reform, going eight months without liquor and getting married. But when he tried to return to baseball in March 1889, he made the mistake of going out with friends after a game and having a drink of alcoholic cider. A two-week binge ensued, which ended when he took a fatal dose of morphine. Clarence "Kid" Baldwin reached the major leagues while still a teenager and seemed destined to become one of the game's best catchers. But his career was sidetracked by drink and hard living, and by thirty he was being cited as a cautionary example of "whisky bringing a player absolutely to the gutter." A year and a half later Baldwin was sentenced to an asylum after a hearing during which he rambled incoherently and looked so shockingly downtrodden that the *Sporting News* published a grim set of before-and-after drawings. One week after being institutionalized, Baldwin was dead at the age of thirty-two. Billy Earle, who was known as the "little globe-trotter" for his involvement in a Spalding-organized 1889 world tour, was hit and nearly killed by a pitched ball in 1896. Within two years he had become a hopeless morphine addict and deserted his wife; only a two-month stay in a Baltimore hospital enabled him finally to kick the habit. Unlike so many of his colleagues, Earle lived to a ripe old age, but the addiction had ended his ball-playing career.

Another poignant example was Charles Bradley, who was born in 1864 in the oil regions of Pennsylvania and surrounded with luxury by his wealthy and adoring parents. At college he acquired a good education and a taste for the finer things in life, exhibiting a charming tenor voice, mastery of the piano, and a gift for foreign languages. Yet Bradley dreamed of a career in professional baseball, and "his great ability as a catcher won for him the soubriquet of 'The Stonewall Backstop.'"

Naturally his parents disapproved. This disagreement, coupled with the rejection of a young woman he loved, turned Bradley into an exile. Then an 1886 knee injury put major league stardom out of reach. In the classic model of the tragic hero, he continued to pursue the now-unattainable goal with any club that would give him a chance, and he became unwilling to mention his past. "He drifted carelessly from place to place," recalled one teammate, "his ambition gone, and his only care being to drown his 'aching void.' I well remember his favorite ballad: 'When other lips and other hearts their tales of love shall tell.' How soulfully poor 'Brad' used to drink in the melody of his own clear tenor voice when its ending, 'Then you'll remember me,' had come, and how sadly he would turn away to hide his tears!'"

Charles Bradley's downward cycle ended in predictably melodramatic fashion. He finished the 1888 season with Dallas and spent the winter there, consorting with a prostitute known as Dollie Love and getting into fights at local taverns. One of these confrontations, in November 1888, resulted in Bradley drawing a pistol and shooting a man in the arm. Two months later Bradley was on the receiving end: he was shot to death at the corner of Main and Austin streets by a rival for Dollie Love's affections. At his funeral his body lay beneath "a beautiful floral base ball mask."

Marty Bergen became Boston's regular catcher in 1896 and soon established a reputation for steady work behind the plate and for disturbing behavior off the field. In particular, Bergen was prone to "fits of melancholia" and to paranoid delusions that his teammates were out to get him. Outsiders assumed that his erratic behavior had to be a symptom of alcoholism, but those closer to the situation insisted that Bergen never touched a drop. As one sportswriter put it, "Marty Bergen, the great catcher of the Bostons, does not drink, chew or smoke, yet he is the hardest man in the league to manage. The hardest drinker in the league never gave a manager more trouble than this same Marty Bergen. In short, Bergen is a crank."

Things became much worse in 1899 when Bergen's son died and his wife was diagnosed with tuberculosis. Already obsessively protective of his family, the dual blows seemed to drive him over the edge. In July he complained of being sick in the middle of a road trip and deserted the team to return home. His teammates and manager were too alienated by the catcher's earlier behavior to sympathize; one account described Bergen as "the best catcher in America, as well as the most capricious. . . . None of the Boston players seem to take much stock in Bergen's sickness. Neither does manager [Frank] Selee. They think it is simply another one of Martie's sulking spells." The signs of a serious problem were ignored until January 19, 1900, when Bergen killed his wife and two remaining children, then took his own life.

Even Joe Leggett, the gentlemanly catcher who pioneered playing close to home plate so that Jim Creighton could make full use of his "underhand throws," shocked and disappointed his many admirers after his playing days ended. Entrusted with collecting liquor license payments for the city of Brooklyn, he pocketed several thousand dollars and fled when the crime was detected. He apparently moved to Texas and, like so many of his successors, died in obscurity.

There is no way to know whether Charles Bradley's melancholy saga, Joe Leggett's embezzlement, Marty Bergen's homicidal outburst, or any of these other examples of postbaseball misconduct can be attributed to the dangers and stress of the catching position. Yet there are far too many of them not to at least consider the possibility of such a link. One final example vividly illustrates both the possibility of such a connection and the impossibility of conclusively establishing a cause-and-effect relationship. There is no way to do justice to Harry Decker's bizarre life without letting him have a chapter of his own.

11

Harry Decker,
the "Don Juan of Shaven Head"

"Decker's hallucination is that he owns the City of Chicago. He was in the habit of entering saloons and ordering wine for everybody present and then walking out with the belief that the place belonged to him and he could give away his own wares if he saw fit."—*Chicago Tribune* (1893)

THERE ARE inherent difficulties in reconstructing the life of a man who, as one frustrated observer noted, "changes his name each time he boards a train." Even Harry Decker's exact name and the details of his birth remain a bit confusing. He most frequently claimed that his name was Earle Harry Decker and that he was born September 3, 1864, in Lockport, Illinois. It seems unlikely that someone would make up those details, but they haven't been corroborated, and with Harry Decker nothing can ever be taken for granted.

What we do know is that he was the younger of two children of Phillip Decker and Margaret Vosburgh, natives of Columbia County, New York, who moved to Illinois around 1862. They may indeed have lived briefly in Lockport, but by 1867 the family had settled in the booming city of Chicago, which proved an ideal location. Phillip Decker was a skilled carpenter, and he soon established a prosperous contracting business. He listed more than $10,000 in property by the time of the 1870 Census, and while the Great Fire of the following year may have been a temporary setback, it also provided a rush of new building work. Harry Decker never wanted for anything while growing up.

Harry inherited his father's manual dexterity, but he appears to have shown little inclination to get into the family business. Instead he was gripped by the same fascination with catching that had consumed Stephen Crane, Ban Johnson, Walter Walker, and so many of the members of the generation that grew up in the shadow of the Civil War. Harry also had the requisite skill—while still a teenager, he earned a place on a baseball team sponsored by the local Board of Trade and then joined one of the city's top amateur clubs, the Unions.

According to one later account, he enlisted in the army around this time but deserted shortly after reaching Fort Leavenworth. In order to prevent imprisonment, this source reported, Decker claimed to be insane and served a short stint in an asylum in Chester, Illinois. There is, however, no confirmation of this account.

In any event, baseball success continued to come easily to Harry— perhaps too easily. In 1884, while still a teenager, he had shown enough promise to be signed to his first professional contract with Evansville. That year was a chaotic one, with the upstart Union Association challenging the two established major leagues (the National League and the American Association) and refusing to recognize the contracts of their rivals. This defiance created a wealth of new opportunities, and Harry Decker was one of the beneficiaries, soon catapulting to the major leagues with Indianapolis of the American Association and then jumping his contract to join the Kansas City franchise of the Union Association.

Along the way he developed a reputation for cocky self-assurance. During his stint with Evansville he was sometimes referred to as "the Adonis," and on one occasion, when asked to umpire a game on a hot day, he requested a chair, fan, and umbrella. As late as 1886 he continued to play without wearing gloves, a choice that by then was so uncommon that a sportswriter chided that Decker would change his ways "when he has paid for a little experience by broken fingers, etc."

While many players broke their contracts to sign with the Union Association, no one else was quite as brash. According to a baseball man, Decker was catching a game for Indianapolis one day when Ted Sullivan and "Peek-a-Boo" Veach of the Kansas City franchise arrived and seated themselves behind the backstop: "in the second or third inning, Veach held up a big role [sic] of one dollar bills. 'Oh, Deck!' he called, 'look here.' When Decker's eyes sighted the wad and the nod he was wild to get out, and fable says he stuck out his finger and got hurt in the sixth inning, so he could hurry up and join Ted and Peek-a-boo. He jumped, too!" In the

Harry Decker seemed poised for major league stardom as a catcher and was on his way to achieving great wealth after patenting the first catcher's mitt. Instead he baffled detectives from coast to coast with his bizarre schemes and his penchant for changing "his name each time he boards a train." He left behind an even more tangled web of mysteries that frustrates baseball historians to this day. *(Library of Congress)*

course of doing so, Decker left behind debts to his landlady, washerwoman, and several friends who had trusted him. At season's end the Union Association went out of business. While most contract breakers were forgiven, Decker was one of the few to be placed on baseball's blacklist.

These were troubling signs, but Decker's acts are more understandable in light of the unusual circumstances. Talented catchers, as we have seen, were often treated as folk heroes, and there is no question of Harry Decker's skill. One of his early managers would later compare him to catching great Charley Bennett before adding with regret, "If Decker had pursued a different course he would now be in demand by the best clubs in the country." Considering his talent and the adulation he received at so young an age, Decker's self-indulgent tendencies are hardly surprising.

The 1885 season compounded that problem. The blacklist forced him to play outside of organized baseball, and he started the season with a semi-professional club in Keokuk, Iowa. The mood in the city was a recipe for trouble: "Baseball was a great craze in Keokuk at that time, and the members of the crack home club were veritable heroes." No one received more adoration than the charming young catching star, and trouble ensued.

Decker's eye was caught by a fifteen-year-old girl named Angeline "Annie" Burns, and soon the "pretty little black-eyed belle" was carrying Harry's child. News reports had the couple making an attempt to elope, causing considerable scandal, but in fact Harry and Annie were married in Keokuk on July 16, 1885. The next spring the couple became the parents of a baby girl.

A longtime acquaintance who was quite familiar with Harry Decker's shortcomings noted that most people expected that his marriage to the "child bride" would not last long. Yet even he had to acknowledge that "to Decker's credit be it said that the marriage proved to be a genuine one, though at first believed to be otherwise." And most indications suggest that marriage and fatherhood initially proved a stabilizing influence.

The Keokuk club disbanded around the time of Decker's wedding, and he finished the season with a club in Decatur, Illinois. He earned reinstatement to organized baseball that off-season and signed with Macon (Georgia) of the Southern League, where he played the dutiful father. Before one game there he was presented with a baby carriage as a reflection of the devotion he showed to his infant daughter. With his side issues resolved, his talents were once again in demand. Before the season started, the manager of Detroit's National League franchise tried to purchase Decker's contract, but the Macon club wasn't willing to part with him. After two months, however, club management relented and sold him to Detroit.

Decker made an auspicious debut with Detroit on July 2, 1886, earning high praise for his strong and accurate throwing arm. Only a few months after being an exile from baseball, Decker must have again felt on top of the world. He was now part of a juggernaut team that had been assembled at great expense and that looked to be well on its way to winning the National League pennant—at the end of July the Wolverines boasted a formidable 55-14 record. In mid-July the team changed trains in Decatur, Illinois, where many old acquaintances approached Decker in the station and congratulated him on his good fortune.

It didn't last, however. Detroit began to struggle in August, and a shakeup took place. Decker's contract was sold to the lowly Washington club in September, sending him from a club that was still in the thick of the pennant race to one with an abysmal 15-75 record. Even on this lowly squad Decker saw little playing time while his old team was nosed out for the pennant.

Frustrated and bored in Washington, Decker began to exhibit the type of behavior that would become all too familiar. Before a meaningless late-season game in Kansas City, Washington manager John Gaffney received several telegrams warning him of heavy betting on the game and advising him not to use his intended battery of Frank Gilmore and Connie Mack. Gaffney concluded that the telegrams were a ruse by gamblers who wanted him to use a battery that included Decker, so he stuck with his intended lineup and was rewarded when Gilmore pitched a one-hit shutout. Meanwhile Decker played shortstop, where he contributed two hits but also made three errors and was thrown out at home with the game still scoreless.

This chain of events by no means established that Decker was involved in an attempted fix, but the finger of suspicion certainly pointed in his direction. Suspicion grew during the off-season. At season's end Decker apparently learned that he was about to be released, so he went to Washington management and pleaded for another chance by blaming his poor play on his wife's illness. Then he tried to take advantage of uncertainty over where he would play in 1887 by accepting terms offered by Washington, Rochester, and Toronto and receiving advances on each of them. In what would become a recurring trend, these machinations showed a baffling mixture of cunning and folly. The system of advances was rife for exploitation, and Decker's scheme was sure to net him three advance checks; but it was just as inevitable that his course would be discovered and that he would be disgraced. He was so brazen that he tried to cash the advance checks from two of the teams with the same banker, a man who had been a director of the Washington club.

After being foiled in his efforts to con advance money from the first three clubs, Decker next tried to obtain two more checks by representing himself as, first, Cal Broughton, and, second, David Oldfield, both catchers. These efforts failed when the man dispatched to the addresses provided for Broughton and Oldfield found only a vacant lot, then noticed Decker "walking up and down the street, waiting for the mail carrier." The exposure of this latest scam brought to light yet another fraudulent advance that Decker had received from Denver by passing himself off as a catcher named Jack Hayes.

As evidence of his con game mounted, Decker became all the more vehement about proclaiming his innocence. When confronted by a Rochester player, Decker protested that "he had been blacklisted once and did not want to run any chance of again being, and what object would he have in signing two contracts." Yet despite this awareness of the risks he was taking, Decker continued to act with blithe disregard for the consequences. He fired off letters to the editors of the sporting presses in which he devised increasingly far-fetched explanations. Eventually he had the "audacity to claim" that E. H. Decker and E. N. Decker were two different people and that "he never did play with the Washingtons and at the same time . . . that he did play with the Detroits."

Needless to say, no one believed these denials, and Decker acquired "an unsavory reputation." Washington lost interest in retaining him, and it looked as though the young catcher might again end up on the blacklist. But the Toronto club took a chance and purchased Decker's release. He made the most of the opportunity, spending two fulfilling seasons with the International League team. In 1887 his solid batting and capable defensive work helped Toronto capture the pennant. The club slipped back to second in 1888, but Decker posted a team-best .313 batting average. He also appears to have stayed out of trouble both years, and, as described in an earlier chapter, found time to design a mitt that offered more protection to the catcher's hands than ever before.

After the 1888 season Harry Decker's career and life reached a crossroads. Still in his early twenties, his catching skills were very much in demand, and there was every reason to believe he could play baseball for many more years. But while his life must have looked almost ideal to an outsider, there was no mistaking that a bit of the luster was off his career and that Decker was feeling dissatisfied.

Stardom in a top minor league at twenty-three is an impressive accomplishment, but it is still a bit of a comedown for a player who had tasted the major leagues as a teenager. More important, Harry Decker must have believed that he had no chance to recapture the adulation in which he had once basked. For during his five short years as a professional, the prestige of his position had vanished before his eyes. In his first year as a professional he had donned a chest protector described as "a contrivance that likened him to a muffin-maker," only to watch as the catchers who wore that essential piece of equipment began to be perceived as "mere backstops." No doubt he sensed that still more of the prestige of the position was about to be eliminated as a result of the mitt he had helped create and of rules like the brand-new one that legalized substitutions.

The Philadelphia Phillies had offered him a contract for the 1889 season that represented another, possibly final, chance to achieve National League stardom, but Harry Decker had several good reasons to consider giving up baseball. There is strong evidence that his marriage was strained by his constant travel, specifically by rumors that he was unfaithful while on the road. One source suggested that he had once abandoned his wife and daughter. His parents appear to have tried to persuade him to give up baseball, no doubt believing that most of their son's problems were the result of the peripatetic baseball lifestyle and that a stable job was all he needed to make him accept adult responsibilities.

Harry Decker spent that winter working as a porter for a wholesale Chicago grocer, a job probably arranged by Phillip Decker in hopes it would ease his son's transition into a new career. A still more promising sign was that Harry Decker and a man named Paul Buckley had started a business to manufacture the catcher's mitt that Decker had devised. The two men appear to have busied themselves getting everything ready so they could begin production of the mitt as soon as the all-important patent was received.

This was an extraordinarily promising enterprise. A number of ballplayers, including A. G. Spalding and Al Reach, had already made fortunes manufacturing sporting goods, and Decker now held an exclusive patent on a standard piece of baseball equipment. Although other catchers would later try to take credit for the mitt, contemporary notes in *Sporting Life* were unequivocal in crediting Decker with its invention and in predicting large profits. The correspondent R. M. Larner praised Decker's "inventive genius" and referred to the mitt as "his improved catcher's glove or laced glove, which is now so popular with the leading catchers of the country" and as "this glove, which is now worn universally by catchers, and has, in fact, become indispensable." Francis Richter, editor of *Sporting Life*, added that Decker's patent "is sure to be profitable, since the glove is bound to come into universal use and further improvement seems impossible." Yet there were signs that Decker was already losing interest, as he had so little concern for the valuable patent that he risked losing it by failing to pay the minor fees associated with the application.

Decker had the intelligence and resourcefulness to capitalize on the patent by making improvements to the mitt and by trying his hand at other inventions. Once again, however, the question was whether he would bother to try. At some point, possibly during this hectic winter, he created an improved version of the turnstile that attracted the investment interest of Reach and Philadelphia co-owner John I. Rogers. But, as was so often the case, there are two wildly different versions of what happened next. The *New York Times* would later describe Decker as "the man who invented the turnstile used in all the base ball parks, race tracks and fair grounds of the country." A special correspondent to the *New York Sporting Times*, however, told a very different tale. He claimed that Decker "came around with a turnstile register. He intended to have it patented. He exhibited it everywhere. Some of the newspapers wrote nice things about it. Al Reach examined it closely and praised it. John Rogers thought it a great thing and [teammate "Kid"] Gleason, after he had fingered it an hour, conceded that Decker had 'a great hand.' Secretary [Bill] Shettsline saw a fortune in it, and—But to make a long story short, it was found that Decker had stolen or taken—which ever you please—the register from one of the club's own turnstiles. He had filed off the inventor's name and painted on his own." In light of later developments, either sequence of events is entirely possible.

This eventful winter also brought great personal tragedy when Decker's two-year-old daughter died. One must always be cautious when speculating about the effect that such a loss has on a person, especially one with as many failings as Harry Decker. Yet Decker had once been an affectionate father, and it seems likely that he was deeply affected by his daughter's death.

Whatever his reasons, when the time came to make a decision about his future, Harry Decker—like so many other young men of his generation—chose the dream of catching glory over the wishes of his family and the prospect of a stable but tranquil life. While choosing baseball did not necessarily mean giving up the new business, it would be difficult to put his energies into both endeavors. Within a few months of joining the Philadelphia club, Decker did indeed choose to drop out of his partnership with Paul Buckley. Three months later, on August 6, 1889, the valuable patent was finally received, but by then Buckley had decided that he could not go it alone. Eventually the patent was sold to A. G. Spalding's sporting goods firm, which successfully manufactured "Decker's Patented Glove" for many years. The mitts were sometimes even referred to as "deckers," but their namesake reaped few if any of the financial rewards.

Harry Decker spent the next two seasons in the National League but saw only limited playing time in Philadelphia. In 1890 he was traded to Pittsburgh, where he became a regular starter in the major leagues for the first time. Unfortunately Decker would later maintain that the most notable event of his stint in Pittsburgh came when he was struck in the head by a pitch thrown by Brooklyn's Bobby Caruthers.

Whether it was the result of this beaning, or his daughter's death, or some form of underlying mental illness, or too much time on his hands in strange cities, or some combination thereof, after the 1890 season Harry Decker's life and career began a rapid decline. The existence of a third major league that year, the Players' League, had been one of the factors that had enabled him to finally become a major league regular. When that league folded after the season, the number of jobs in the majors was sharply reduced, and Decker was one of the casualties.

In 1891 he signed to play for a minor league club in New Haven, where his reputation for womanizing preceded him. "Some one suggests that the New Haven girls will give E. Harry Decker a rousing reception," noted sportswriter O. P. Caylor, adding sarcastically, "Probably. But that's not the vital question. What will E. Harry give the New Haven girls? Harry is very generous, you know, and when he meets a few girls who believe in reciprocity without protection there is likely to be increase of commerce. . . ."

Before the season could begin, his saga took a new twist when detectives arrived from Philadelphia to arrest him. Decker was charged with an impressive array of crimes, including the seduction of an underage girl named Jessie Dancer who had worked for Decker & Buckley, stealing a suit of clothes from his former roommate, and forging the names of Philadelphia owners Colonel John I. Rogers and Alfred J. Reach (his would-be business partners in manufacturing the turnstile). This litany of crimes again reveals Harry Decker's disconcerting tendency to betray those closest to him.

While trouble wasn't new to Decker, the nature and the extent of these accusations shocked even those who were aware of his earlier indiscretions. An unsympathetic acquaintance who commented sarcastically that "Harry Decker is again in trouble, that is, Harry is always in trouble," was also quick to add that "Harry has hitherto had his troubles confined to escapades with the gentler sex."

Most of the parties involved were willing to settle for restitution. The New Haven team's lawyer predicted that the forgery charge was the only one that would come to trial. Meanwhile Decker vehemently denied all the charges, telling anyone who would listen that he was the victim of an attempt to cheat him out of the proceeds of his invention.

Most of the charges were indeed quietly resolved. By the time Decker's trial on the forged checks and stolen clothes came around, restitution had been made on his behalf—presumably by his father—and Decker was discharged after his guilty plea. Annie Decker, however, was not as willing to forgive and forget, and she sued for divorce, citing infidelity.

She soon relented, but the catcher's troubles continued to mount. In June he was arrested again and charged with using forged checks to pay his tailor's bill. This was followed by allegations that a New Haven teammate had generously loaned Decker money and let him stay at his house, and that Decker had repaid the favor by stealing from him.

Once again Decker denied any wrongdoing. He wallowed in self-pity, telling one reporter, "I think I am a most unfortunate man. It seems to me that if I merely look at a girl she fancies me so much that a breach of promise suit is the result. I never flattered myself that I was invincible, but I am gradually arriving at that conclusion from the force of events." In a letter to one of the sporting presses he repeated the hollow claim that he had been "very unfortunate of late; more so than the average man." As before, he blamed all his trouble on others who had been "trying to push me down" and tried to use his wife and daughter to justify his behavior. In light of his chronic infidelity and erratic support, the latter excuse was understandably viewed as hypocrisy.

The criminal charges were eventually dropped, suggesting that Phillip Decker had once again taken out his checkbook. But Harry's behavior had now turned him into a pariah in the baseball world. He was released by New Haven in mid-June, and a *Sporting Life* correspondent expressed doubt that he would ever play baseball again. This prediction proved correct; Decker had finally succeeded in ruining his promising catching career. Although he was still several years shy of his thirtieth birthday, he never again played a professional game.

He returned to Philadelphia and found work as a sewing machine agent, but made few sales calls. He spent most of the next six months hanging out at a local billiard hall and became an expert at the game. He also wrote more bad checks and found other ways to run afoul of the law. He realized several hundred dollars by reprising his old scam of writing to baseball managers under assumed names and asking for advances, then having the checks mailed to a vacant lot. Eventually, with the threat of prosecution hanging over his head, Decker fled town.

After Annie Decker forgave her husband yet again, the couple moved in with Harry's parents in Chicago. But Decker was soon up to his old tricks. He attempted to marry a different woman while using the ludicrously transparent alias of H. Milton Decker, and was charged with bigamy. More accusations of forgery and larceny soon followed. Decker no longer seemed even to be trying to avoid detection. According to one account, "Decker's hallucination is that he owns the City of Chicago. He was in the habit of entering saloons and ordering wine for everybody present and then walking out with the belief that the place belonged to him and he could give away his own wares if he saw fit." It was as though Harry Decker had replaced the dream of becoming the next Nat Hicks with an aspiration to become Robin Hood.

The legal system was baffled about what to do with such a man. Before one of his trials, he was examined by medical authorities and found to be insane. He was sent to an institution in Elgin, but within a month he was pronounced cured and given his release. The frustrated Chicago prosecutor reinstated the charges, explaining that "he believed Decker insane, but if the Elgin Asylum managers persisted in turning him loose he didn't know what he could do with the man." While in jail awaiting his day in court, Decker suffered three more apparent attacks of insanity. At trial his parents promised to keep him institutionalized until he was cured, and on that understanding he was returned to Elgin.

But once more the asylum found nothing wrong with Decker, and before long he was back on the streets and getting into trouble. By the following spring he was facing charges of stealing a horse, of renting a $75 bicycle and not returning it, and multiple counts of forgery. Once again he was able to avoid a long sentence. He acted as his own attorney on one of the charges, and perhaps his smooth talking helped him stay out of jail. A more likely possibility is that Phillip Decker again made restitution. Soon came new charges that suggested Harry's same disregard for getting caught. He tried to pay his rent by presenting two bad checks, and, after being released on bond, was rearrested for forging A. G. Spalding's name on a check. By this time his long-suffering wife had finally exhausted her patience and obtained a divorce.

In 1896, after five years away from baseball, Decker tried to return to the sport as player-manager of an independent club in Decatur, Illinois.

Even by his standards, the attempt was notable for its gall and for the inevitability of failure and arrest. According to a local attorney, Decker "went there without a penny and didn't have a penny when he got ready to move away. With not a cent in his pocket and no prospect of getting a cent, he went to the Decatur Lumber company and contracted a bill for $800. He rented the ground on North Edward street, enclosed the place, built a grand stand, hired players, ran excursions to neighboring towns, had a band at the games every Sunday and conducted the business like a man who had money to burn. By some hocus pocus of financiering he managed to keep afloat for several months. Decker said to a friend that all this business was easy. When he made up his mind as to what he would do, he studied the question, laid out his plans and then proceeded to carry them out on the strength of his supreme nerve."

No sooner had the season begun than Decker and another man became embroiled in a bizarre dispute over who was actually managing the club. Then Decker abruptly skipped town. When he was arrested in Chicago and brought back to Decatur, a sadly familiar story of attempted check forgery emerged. After his arrest, it was generally assumed that Harry's parents would bail him out, as they had so often done before. But they had finally run out of patience, and they declined to make good on the check or to post Harry's $500 bond. So the matter proceeded to trial at the Peoria courthouse, which, in an odd coincidence, Phillip Decker had helped build.

At the trial Decker again acted as his own attorney, presenting a remarkable defense on a technicality of the charge. "While the indictment charged him with forging one name, the check itself showed another and a different name, and therefore the check could not properly be offered as evidence." With the check inadmissible, there was no case against Decker, and he was acquitted. A reporter commented that Decker "is well posted in the law governing such cases. That is why he was acute enough to spell the name incorrectly when he wrote it on the check."

Yet if the crime was indeed carefully premeditated, as the reporter believed, what an extraordinary act! The brazen method ensured that Decker would be caught, arrested, humiliated, and never be able to do business in Decatur again. And, even if he was able to get off on a technicality, all he had realized was $37. Committing such a crime is perplexing enough, but *planning* such an act seems incomprehensible.

In any event, Harry Decker's apparent cleverness would blow up in his face. He was rearrested and charged instead with fraud and running a confidence game. At the new trial, Decker was represented by two highly respected lawyers, suggesting that his parents had had a change of heart and were trying to help him avoid a long penitentiary sentence. Harry now maintained that "he did not remember signing the check. He said he was kicked by a horse a number of years ago and has since then had many lapses of memory and done things for which he was not responsible." The jury deliberated the case for two days before returning with a conviction. According to the statute, he was sentenced to two to fourteen years in the penitentiary.

Harry Decker served his time in Joliet Prison from January 1897 to September 1905. It was an extraordinarily harsh punishment for forging a $37 check, especially considering that he had been summarily discharged for worse crimes. After years of avoiding the consequences of his acts, Harry Decker was finally forced to do so.

During his stay in Joliet he showed his old dexterity and resourcefulness. He applied himself to the trade practiced by his father (and his maternal grandfather), becoming an expert carpenter and cabinetmaker. He also received another patent on an inflatable glove and convinced prison guard George J. Stiteley to file the patent. Upon his release he appears to have made a short-lived attempt to go straight: there is a single listing of Earl H. Decker, contractor, in the 1906 Joliet city directory.

But before long Harry was back in trouble again. He was accused of forgery in Peoria but "managed to evade arrest and went to Chicago. There he was involved in some trouble with a woman. He left that city before he could be apprehended on the second charge." He next surfaced in Sacramento, where he found work as a brass finisher at the Southern Pacific Railway shops and, typically, proved expert at his trade. He appears to have stayed out of trouble while in Sacramento, but in one telltale sign that he was plotting something, he underwent an operation to remove an identifying cyst from his forehead.

In July 1907 a man calling himself Earl H. Davenport arrived in Los Angeles and began courting a beautiful young woman named Maud McNeil. The relationship progressed so quickly that he wrote to her father to request her hand in marriage. The newcomer had no obvious means of support, but he spent money with reckless abandon. Each day he and his sweetheart showed up at the Oakwood Hotel in Arcadia armed with a sackful of money to play the slot machines. After playing rapidly and carelessly, he would hand out coins with the same cavalier attitude. Regulars at the hotel figured he must be a millionaire.

But it was just Harry Decker's latest scam. His work as a brass finisher had acquainted him with the basics for counterfeiting. He arrived in Los Angeles with the dies and molds necessary to simulate quarters and half-dollars. Then, using an alloy of silver and a gas stove borrowed from his landlady, he created coins that looked deceptively like the real thing.

They were not quite perfect, however. While the likeness was pronounced "exceptional," Decker's coins were a trifle lighter than the genuine article and could be cut to pieces with a pocket knife. These identifying traits soon had detectives on his trail. They arrested him at his rented rooms, where they discovered his counterfeiting apparatus stored in a locked trunk.

Despite overwhelming evidence, Decker maintained that he had been given the counterfeit coins by a mysterious stranger. After further investigation, the detectives concluded that his experiments with the slot machines had been just a dry run and that Decker was planning to flood the city with bogus currency.

As with so many of Decker's crimes, his actions seem to defy rational explanation. He had gone to great trouble and showed great skill in manufacturing the counterfeit coins. The scheme had every prospect of working and making him wealthy if he showed even a bit of restraint. Instead he proceeded to do everything possible to attract attention to himself and thus ensure that he would be caught.

Several people continued to believe in Decker's innocence. In jail he had a steady stream of attractive young female visitors who "sent him flowers, cake and pie, until he was obliged to enlist the service of the County Jail tailor to enlarge his waistband." The most faithful follower was a heavily veiled young beauty who used an alias but was in fact Maud McNeil. She continued to proclaim his innocence and did her best to get him out on bond.

Disentangling the counterfeiter's identity proved the most difficult task for the detectives. They determined he had been using at least three different aliases, but they could not get him to reveal his real name. Only when a photograph of the con man was published in a Los Angeles paper did the manager of his old ball club in Keokuk come forward to identify Decker. The clue enabled detectives to unravel still more of the ex-ballplayer's troubled past, yet somehow they concluded that Decker was one of his aliases and that his real name was Earl H. Alexander.

The detectives also informed Maud McNeil that Decker had a wife in the East, at which time Maud disappeared. It is not clear whether the wife in question was Annie Burns or a different woman named Annie Frantz, who was sometimes referred to as Decker's wife, or yet another of the women who always flocked around him. By the time of Decker's trial in April, even he had concluded that it was futile to maintain his innocence. Even so, the trial produced a surprise twist as physicians attested that "Alexander" was dying of tuberculosis. He agreed to plead guilty in exchange for being allowed to serve his four-year sentence in Arizona.

Once Decker was in Arizona, his tuberculosis vanished. Even when behind bars he remained irresistible to women and received as much mail as all the other inmates put together. Decker again proved an industrious prisoner, studying carpentry and creating "cabinet work that was a marvel to all."

He was released in August 1911 and returned to California, where he soon paid a visit to one of the secret service operatives who had arrested him, to promise that he would begin a new life. Decker got a job working for a Pasadena-based contractor named G. Lawrence Stimson and rented a room from a widow named Jane Lawton.

His new landlady was anything but naive. Her late husband had been a Harvard-educated judge and the superintendent of schools in Solano County, California. The couple had met while she was a school principal there and, even after marriage and three children, she continued to work at the state insane asylum in Napa. She was deeply impressed by her new tenant, who struck her as "in every way a gentleman of culture and refinement. He was reticent to a marked degree and told us little concerning his past life. He evidently has been raised in a good family."

Jane Lawton accordingly had no reservations when her tenant began courting her unmarried daughter, Frances, a forty-two-year-old schoolteacher. Decker showed that, by any name, he still "possess[ed] the remarkable faculty of inducing girls of respectable antecedents to fall head over heels in love with him." The couple was married in May 1912. Within months Harry Decker had squandered his new wife's savings, borrowed more money from various relatives, and deserted her. In November he presented a worthless check to a grocer but avoided prosecution by making good on the amount. Then in December he passed another flurry of forged checks using a variety of names that included a couple of especially audacious choices—that of Stimson, his former employer, and that of C. B. Mathewson, one of the U.S. marshals who had arrested him for counterfeiting. One of the many forged checks was to cover the rent at the apartment where his estranged wife still lived.

Naturally detectives were soon knocking on her door, and she was glad to help them.

The detectives learned that Decker had "dropped out of sight," but as usual he wasn't making a great effort to cover his tracks. After abandoning his wife, he became convinced that a sailor was paying inappropriate attention to her. Using a telegram bearing the name of his favorite foil, U.S. marshal C. B. Mathewson, he lured the sailor to meet him at the docks in San Francisco. Purportedly Decker intended to kill the sailor and then commit suicide, but instead he was attacked by four sailors and left with a broken nose and facial lacerations. He then returned to Los Angeles, where he checked into the King Edward Hotel under yet another assumed name and began using his talents at billiards to rack up steady winnings. By January, Decker was again behind bars.

Detectives learned that he had been planning to resume his efforts to counterfeit half-dollar coins and had rented a small shack behind a bicycle shop as his base of operations. But a raid on the shack did not turn up any counterfeiting tools. So the police turned to the press, providing a list of the prisoner's many known aliases and explaining, "The man's true name is not known. . . . The nearest that federal, State, county or city officers can come to his actual identity is that he comes of a wealthy and respected Pittsburgh family."

Publication of Decker's story and picture prompted many others to come forward with their stories. Eleven forged checks surfaced in all, including one from a milliner who had parted with a custom-made Bird of Paradise hat. Decker had told her that he was buying the hat for his wife, but instead it appeared on the head of another young woman. Tales like this led the press to dub Decker the "Don Juan of Shaven Head."

The landlord of a lodging house on Florida Street also recognized the photo as being one of his tenants. Upon inspecting the man's room, detectives found a trunk filled with "metal, a can of plaster of paris, tongs, a plumber's torch, and other paraphernalia used in counterfeiting silver coins." Harry Decker had been caught in the act once again. As a trial date approached, it became clear that little defense could be mounted. In addition to the mountain of evidence, Decker reportedly "made a species of confession," though in yet another bizarre twist he "indignantly" denied detectives' claims that he had posed as a street revivalist after coming to Los Angeles.

He did, however, receive support from an unexpected quarter. "It is true that he dissipated my daughter's money and he also made away with some of my money," his mother-in-law Jane Lawton told a reporter, "but I have made up my mind to pocket the loss and let it go at that. . . . His actions since we have known him convinced both my daughter and myself that at times he is mentally unbalanced." Perhaps at her urging, when the case came to trial in June "an effort was made to have the man examined by physicians in order to show that his longing for wives in every town and his careless way of signing other persons' names, was due to an engorged brain." When the judge saw the length of Decker's rap sheet, however, he "refused to allow any such waste of effort on the part of the doctors" and sentenced Decker to three years in San Quentin.

On June 19, 1913, "Earl Henry Davenport" arrived at San Quentin to serve his latest sentence. Prison records reveal little of his doings over the next two and a half years, though curiously his occupation is listed as pharmacist. He was released on October 19, 1915—and vanished. Despite the diligent works of generations of baseball researchers, not a trace of his whereabouts after 1915 has been discovered.

The known facts about Harry Decker's life end there, and everything else remains speculation. Did he finally reform upon his release from prison? Did he adopt another alias and finally elude detection? Or did his death soon follow? Those questions are mysteries that researchers are no closer to solving.

It is even more unlikely that we will reach a definitive solution to the underlying enigma of Harry Decker. The problem is not so much the absence of clues; instead there is an abundance of clues that point in so many different directions as to create nothing but endless confusion. There are, for instance, several distinctive patterns in his crimes. Despite their extraordinary number, they run on a very narrow track—never once was he charged with an act of violence, nor is there anything to suggest he was an alcoholic. Several incidents did occur at saloons or billiard halls, but that was where men like Decker spent their spare time, and he was never once described as being drunk.

Then there is the fact that his crimes required considerable premeditation and planning, yet were often executed in a way that ensured that he would be caught. One of the detectives who pursued him claimed that Decker's "method of working . . . [was] to pass about $500 worth of bad checks and then go on to some other town." That is certainly what a man committing these types of crimes would be expected to do, but it was rarely how Decker in fact behaved. Instead, after writing a flurry of bad checks, he usually stayed around town and seemed to make a perverse effort to draw attention to himself. It was as though he really did suffer from what an observer had called the "hallucination . . . that he owns the City . . . and he could give away his own wares if he saw fit."

His motivations are equally perplexing. Over and over he would commit a crime to realize only a few dollars while recklessly jeopardizing his freedom and his reputation. And to what end? If he really wished to get rich, why not stick with the glove-making partnership that had every prospect of making him wealthy? When an intelligent and inventive man is repeatedly arrested for such stupid, self-defeating acts, it seems as though those acts must be some sort of cry for help.

But if Decker wanted help, why didn't he accept it from the many people who offered it? He was surrounded by people who wanted to help him overcome his demons. His father spent a great deal of money, and probably strained friendships and business relationships, in trying to straighten out Harry's wrangles. His first wife gave him far more chances than any man deserves, and his last known mother-in-law was extraordinarily forgiving. Numerous other friends reached out to him, and countless women showered him with affection. Yet he betrayed every single one of them, with the extent of his betrayal often proportionate to the faith shown in him.

So any analysis of his crimes must end with the same basic dilemma that a jury wrestled with in 1897. Did he suffer from mental illness all along (and is that what attracted him to catching)? Did Decker's exposure to foul balls, along with other blows to the head, cause an "engorged brain" and contribute to his bizarre behavior? Did his catching skill and extraordinary way with women give him such a bloated sense of entitlement that he thought he could get away with anything? When his goal of attaining heroism on the baseball diamond faded, were his crime sprees an attempt to recreate that thrill? Or was he just a pathological liar who habitually chose wrong over right?

Many who knew him were adamant that Decker knew exactly what he was doing. After the unsuccessful insanity plea at his 1897 trial, an observer commented, "Decker ought to shine in the proper channel. He is as sharp as a tack, but he never sees anything but a dishonest way of applying his shrewdness. He is a fit subject for the penitentiary." One of the Pinkerton detectives who brought Decker to justice maintained, "I know it is customary in some circles to always describe a criminal as 'one of the most dangerous men in the country.' But this trite phrase well applies to [Decker]. Our records showed he has passed at least twelve years of his life in prison. He comes of a good family. He is intelligent and is able to earn a better salary than I can. . . . But he has the bad streak in him that makes him prey upon society. He is a fairly skillful forger, but his forte lies in his ability to beguile trusting women and shop-keepers." Yet to the many people who were drawn to him, some form of insanity was the only explanation for the actions of this enigmatic man. And some, including as intelligent and sophisticated a woman as Jane Lawton, continued to believe so even after he had betrayed their trust.

While the specific causes of Decker's actions must remain unknowable, his troubled life and those of so many of his fellow catchers were a symbol of the catcher's position in transition. During the mid-1870s the catcher had been perceived as indispensable and was treated accordingly. Over the next decade and a half that status slowly eroded, and catchers struggled to adjust. Some embraced a new model of the catcher as thinking man, but many rebelled against surrendering their special status. And in most cases they found that their prestige made others reluctant to address their misconduct. This in turn encouraged them to continuing choosing their own path and led them to become desperadoes or rebels without a cause.

The catcher of the 1870s had embodied a wide range of characteristics— the pious "Deacon" White and the devil-may-care Bill Craver apparently had little in common. Yet when the game started, all these traits coalesced into a warrior whose skill and courage you needed on your side. By contrast, there was nothing that unified thinking men like Doc Bushong and Connie Mack with the likes of Charley Hoover and Harry Decker. The catcher of the 1870s had been a hero who inspired admiration and a desire to emulate. The catcher of the 1880s was a schizophrenic being who evoked puzzlement and concern.

12

The 1890s: "An Era When Most of the Catchers Were Pot-Bellied and Couldn't Get Out of Their Own Way"

"The modern catcher is a wax doll. The catcher of twenty years ago was a hero and an iron man."—Adrian "Cap" Anson

WHILE THE TWO preceding chapters have described the catcher of the 1880s as a schizophrenic entity, they did so by giving short shrift to the three greatest catchers of the decade, Charley Bennett, "Buck" Ewing, and Mike "King" Kelly.

Bennett probably resolved the dilemma posed by the position's changing requirements better than anyone. He rose to prominence in the 1870s and had every bit as much courage as any of the legendary tough-guy catchers of those years. According to one account, Bennett "declared that only a 'sissy' would use a padded glove with the fingers and thumb cut off. During one of the games in which he figured[,] a foul ball split the left thumb of Bennett's hand from the tip right down to the palm. The flesh was laid open right to the bone. A doctor who examined it immediately told Bennett that it would be necessary for him to quit the game until such time as the thumb healed sufficiently. The physician pointed out that unless Bennett did so, he might suffer new injuries to the thumb or that blood poisoning might set in which would cause him the loss not only of the thumb but perhaps a hand or an arm. But despite all the doctor's caution Bennett remained in the game catching day after day with his horribly mangled finger. He kept a bottle of antiseptic and a wad of cotton batting on the bench and between innings would devote his time to washing out the wound. Several times during the first two weeks other foul tips or wild pitches would catch him on the mangled thumb and reopen the wound. But undaunted, Bennett stayed in the game risking probably the loss of the hand or the arm simply for the glory of playing the game." Many other similar stories were told about how "Bennett would play, heated with his passion for the game, until the blood from his hands would stain the ball."

And there is plenty of additional evidence attesting to Bennett's bravery. His hands became such "gnarled monstrosities" that a photograph showing his swollen joints and grotesquely misshapen fingers became an emblem of nineteenth-century baseball. Yet with the stoicism that characterized his generation of catchers, that picture was the only one ever taken of Bennett's hands, and even that he agreed to allow only because of his friendship with the reporter who wrote the accompanying article.

Despite his courage, Bennett did not share the "dark suspicion" that Ban Johnson and so many of his contemporaries felt toward protective equipment, and he was a pioneer in the use of chest protectors and mitts. He even welcomed rules changes designed to reduce strikeouts—before the 1887 season he expressed pleasure that "Nine men will play the game this season, and not [just] the pitcher and catcher." Charley Bennett was unusual in not taking these things personally, as most of his fellow catchers did feel threatened by the torrents of change that buffeted them.

Mike Kelly found a very different way of reconciling the dilemma faced by the catchers of his era. If everything that has been written about Kelly were true, he would have single-handedly invented every trick ever played on a baseball diamond. One article alone credited him with having "invented the 'Kelly short route'" (by which he ran straight through the pitcher's box to get from first to third base), with having carried a "supply of bird shot in his mouth" to simulate the sound of foul tips, and with having found a new way to create "a dilemma when he got caught in run-downs between bases. He would hop up and down like a jackrabbit, hoping to stop the ball with his body or head, while trying to reach the base and safety." The piece also cited what is probably the best-known Kelly story: that he was taking a day off one day, but when he saw a foul ball that catcher "Pop" Tate could not get to, he cried out "Kelly in for Tate" and caught the ball to retire the batter.

These are marvelous stories that must be taken with a great deal of salt. The last story cannot have happened as described (since substitutions were not permitted without the opposing captain's consent during the years when Kelly and Tate were teammates), and there is no proof that it occurred at all. The other incidents probably happened, but it is unlikely that Kelly was breaking new ground when he used any of these tactics.

Despite the exaggeration, Kelly deserves credit for finding a promising way to unify the competing models of the catcher of the 1880s. His imaginative penchant for devising new tactics suggested the thinking-man catcher, but Kelly also kept alive the tradition of the position being played by men who were at their best under pressure. As a teammate put it, "He played not by rules or instruction, but by instinct, and to him belonged the degree of perfection, that faculty known as baseball sense. I never knew Kel to hesitate in a close play. Before the play ever came up he seemed to have anticipated it, and instantly did the right thing." Meanwhile his reckless disregard for the rules revealed an affinity to both frontiersmen like Daniel Boone who became a law unto themselves, and to the desperado catcher. "Baseball rules," recalled another contemporary, "were never made for Kel."

Kelly was a remarkable all-round athlete who dazzled observers with his throwing arm, his defensive prowess, his stalwart bat, and, perhaps most of all, his brilliant baserunning. No less impressive was his near contemporary, Buck Ewing. Kelly's major league career lasted from 1878 to 1893, and Ewing's from 1880 to 1895, and the two men have much in common. Both had such an astonishing range of talents that credible observers have declared each to be the greatest *player* of all time. They are the only two nineteenth-century catchers enshrined in the Hall of Fame.

Neither man, however, could provide an enduring replacement for the dying tough-guy model of the catcher. They ultimately failed not for lack of ability but because they had too much ability. Catchers had been indispensable during the 1870s, and every team hoped to find a man with the unique combination of skill and courage necessary to meet the requirements. But Ewing and Kelly, probably the two best all-round ballplayers of their generation, were often considered too valuable to use behind the plate. Neither man caught in even half of his major league appearances, and both came to be used more as utility players than anything else. It was an especially telling commentary as to how far the status of the catcher had fallen.

Part of the reason for this highly unusual usage of Kelly and Ewing (see Appendix 1 for details) was that injuries prevented them from catching. Ewing, in particular, was plagued by injuries. When Johnny Ward claimed that

Buck Ewing, left, and Mike "King" Kelly are the only two nineteenth-century catchers enshrined in the Hall of Fame, and credible arguments have been made for each man as the greatest player of that century. Yet it was a sad commentary on how far the prestige of the catcher's position had fallen that Ewing and Kelly were both moved to other positions, and that neither superstar ended up playing even half of his major league games behind the plate. *(National Baseball Hall of Fame Library)*

Ewing was the game's best catcher, a Detroit paper retorted sarcastically: "Bah! It's Bennett; Ewing plays seven games a month and lies around the rest of the time because the skin rubbed off his shins." To some old-timers this inability to play through injuries was a symptom of moral weakness. One of them remarked with disdain, "Ewing never saw the day he could catch with Flint. In these days of the game the players have more of a chance to do looking-glass or shape-playing, and when Silver was at his best he had to work. While I like to see intelligence in players, I am not a bit struck on the calcium-light methods of some very prominent players, who I am told, affect embossed slippers, bathing gowns, novels and cigarettes." Kelly, meanwhile, was said to have "often remarked that 'if he had such [battered] hands as "Charlie" Bennett he wouldn't catch a game of ball for a whole church full of millionaires with their entire wealth stuffed in their pockets!'" Another reporter noted that when Kelly did catch, he "stands half bent and seems to be laboring under the most painful sensation of nervous expectation until the ball is pitched. He holds his hands directly in front of his face and keeps up a continual rubbing of the palms that is sufficient to make a sensitive person uneasy."

But whether Ewing and Kelly were in fact softer than their predecessors wasn't really the issue. The main reason for their unusual using patterns was far more upsetting to the self-image of catchers: these two greats often played other positions not because they were injured but in order to prevent them from getting injured. In effect they were considered *too valuable* to be catchers, at least as long as a competent "backstop" was around.

That was the legacy that Kelly and Ewing passed along to the catchers who reached the major leagues in the late 1880s and 1890s. Predecessors like Jim White and Doug Allison had inspired countless boys to aspire to work behind the plate. The example of Kelly and Ewing caused a new generation to hope that someone would see their work and assign them to a safer position. As a consequence, the catcher's prestige during the 1890s plummeted to a point lower than ever before.

Throughout the 1890s the catcher embodied Matthew Arnold's potent image of a wanderer trapped between two worlds, one dead and the other powerless to be born. Some sought to create a new model for the catcher while others tried to breathe new life into the old model. Neither approach had much success, so promising catchers continued to follow the examples of Ewing and Kelly by shifting to other positions.

Hughey Jennings was the perfect example of a player who might have been a catching immortal had he been born a generation earlier. Blessed with agility, a powerful throwing arm, and boundless energy, he had all the requirements for a great career when he arrived in the majors in 1891. Instead he was converted to shortstop to make better use of his skills, and went on to a Hall of Fame career. Talented athletes like Jacob Stenzel, Hugh Duffy, and Bobby Lowe also started as catchers but were moved to positions that made better use of their abilities. George Winkelman was a less gifted athlete, but he may have provided the best summary. Winkelman was initially signed as a catcher, but as he later admitted, he found the risks too great and chose instead to "try the safer outfield and pitching positions."

Other great athletes left baseball altogether. Frank Ives grew up dreaming of a career as a catcher, and that goal seemed within reach in 1887 when he signed his first professional contract. The following year he was playing for a club in the northern Michigan resort town of Petoskey when a well-known Chicago billiard player came to town, expecting to earn some easy cash from "men who thought they could play billiards." Instead Ives handily beat the visiting pool shark, who returned to Chicago with empty pockets but a marvelous tale to tell about this "boy wonder." At season's end the young catcher was talked into leaving baseball for billiards, and within a few years he was recognized as the world champion, though he still enjoyed showing off the "several crooked fingers" that were souvenirs of his ball-playing days. In his new sport, Ives's greatest rival was Jacob Schaefer, who had also been a star catcher and captain of the local baseball team while growing up in Leavenworth, Kansas.

Notably it was in 1891, with catchers leaving the position in droves, that Stephen Crane gave up baseball for good. And while his later mentions of the game seemed fond, there were surprisingly few of them. Also perplexing is Crane's claim that football had inspired the battle scenes in *The Red Badge of Courage*, since he had less experience in that sport. Crane did have an interest in the maneuvers of football players, so perhaps the parallels to battlefield strategy made this seem a better metaphor. But another plausible explanation is that by the mid-1890s Crane knew that only those who had once played the position really understood what it had once been like to be a catcher.

Many new developments contributed to the prestige of the position hitting rock bottom during the 1890s. After years of tinkering with the rules to little effect, the new code adopted in the late 1880s had finally made the catcher's position safer—just when the new equipment was having the same effect. Before the 1887 season, pitchers were banned from taking a running start, since this practice, in the words of Henry Chadwick, "was alike dangerous and intimidating to the batsman and very costly in the wear and tear on the catchers, especially when playing up close behind the bat. The question was how to check this reckless speed without giving the batsman too great an advantage, and the committee solved the difficulty by the adoption of the appended rule." Six years later another important step toward reducing the "wear and tear on the catchers" moved the pitcher back to his current distance of sixty feet, six inches from home plate.

It is hard to overstate the cumulative effect of so many rapid changes. In 1886 the catcher's position had lost some of its prestige as a result of the introduction of masks and chest protectors, but it still required extraordinary courage and skill. The catchers of 1886 faced an onslaught of pitches delivered by large, powerfully built men who took running starts and launched the ball just fifty-five feet away from home plate. Moreover

they did so with equipment that remained primitive: masks and chest protectors were still being refined while gloves afforded so little protection
that men like Harry Decker declined to wear them at all.

By 1894 the picture was entirely different. Pitchers now stood some
five feet farther away and, instead of taking running starts, were forced to
keep one foot anchored to the ground. Catchers, meanwhile, were now
protected by increasingly effective masks and chest protectors and were
wearing pillowlike mitts that seemed to do all the work for them. Many of
the men who had been catchers before 1887 had a hard time thinking of
the 1894 version of the catcher as being the same position.

Before the 1887 season Doug Allison, who was now forty and hadn't
been a major league regular in a decade, declared that "although not having any practice, he thought he could go in and catch and bat as well under
[the new rules] as he ever did." Old-timers were always making claims like
this, but it was Allison's reasons that made his assertion plausible. Naturally he mentioned that the new equipment had made the catcher's position much easier to play. But the primary factor he cited was the new
restrictions on pitching deliveries, "under which balls are not so difficult
to handle as they were under the old rules." The following year a credible
source claimed that the venerable Jim White—who was now forty and
hadn't caught regularly in nearly a decade—might be moved back behind
the plate and paired with Jim Whitney, whose "hop, step and jump" delivery had lost its terrors as a result of the rules changes.

These new rules in turn led to new strategies that reinforced the trend.
As scoring skyrocketed, less importance was attached to trying to manufacture runs, which naturally reduced the emphasis on having a catcher who
could gun down base runners. Drop balls had been popular at the outset
of the 1890s, but when pitchers were moved farther from home plate they
began to aim instead for the upper reaches of the strike zone. By the end
of the decade, pitching in the bottom half of the strike zone was rare, a
development that diminished the value of having a catcher who could keep
difficult low balls from getting past him. In the same way that the pitcher's
greater distance from home plate and the elimination of running starts had
made the catcher's courage and reflexes less crucial, so too the skills once
deemed essential to the catcher were all seeming less important.

Meanwhile the only enhancement of the catcher's role had come as a
result of the 1893 rule change that moved the pitcher back some five feet,
since this put a premium on a catcher who had the agility to scramble out
in front of the plate and field bunts. Even this change resulted in a net

loss for the catcher's position. When catchers fielded such bunts they lost valuable time in whirling around before throwing to first base, so most managers instructed their third basemen to field bunts whenever possible. Catchers who had shown the dexterity to handle bunts were moved to third base. Established catchers like Lave Cross, Doggy Miller, Charley "Duke" Farrell, Heinie Peitz, and Tom Daly were all converted to third basemen for at least one season during the early to mid-1890s, thereby robbing the position of more athleticism.

The futility that catchers must have felt as a result of these developments was symbolized during an 1892 game when a college catcher literally decided it would be best to let pitches roll to the backstop. Yale catcher Walter Carter, who was sure the Princeton batter would try to bunt even though there were no runners on base, "left his place behind the bat, and, wearing his mask and pad, stood about thirty feet from the batsman, just inside the third base line." His maneuver spoke volumes about how irrelevant the catcher had become.

These demoralizing changes to the catcher's position evoked parallels to the broader societal trends that were depriving frontiersmen and cowboys of their ways of life and were turning thousands of proud artisans into workers who essentially tended machines. The spirit-crushing feeling of being replaced by an inanimate object was rendered with special poignancy in 1894 as a result of the actions of Lave Cross, one of the catchers considered too athletically gifted to remain behind the plate. When asked to cover third base, Cross brought his catcher's mitt with him and provoked an outcry. Henry Chadwick denounced this ploy as "making a travesty of skilful infield play" while Tim Hurst quite accurately predicted, "Why, it will be so after awhile that a player will provide himself with a fan-like contrivance which he will open when he sees a hard grounder coming toward him." Catchers who read these words must have felt very much like the artisans who were being supplanted by machines and the cowboys whose lifestyle was vanishing along with the open-range style of ranch.

After the 1894 season the National League passed a rule limiting the gloves of all players except the catcher and first baseman to ten ounces in weight and fourteen inches in circumference. This ended the uproar, with one sportswriter expressing relief that fielders could "no longer take refuge behind 'pillows,' but are allowed only plain kid or buckskin gloves." Yet the fact that catchers were still allowed to wear these "pillows" underscored the belief that the catcher's equipment performed the most difficult tasks for the man hidden beneath that equipment.

This perception was cemented at the end of the 1888 season when the rules-makers decided that a caught foul tip—once the epitome of catching skill—would no longer be an out. In part, as we have seen, that rules change was made because of catchers who made deceptive noises to simulate a foul tip. Yet it was no coincidence that the change was effected at the end of a season that had seen the catcher's mitt spring into prominence. According to the sportswriter John H. Gruber, "an element of pure luck or ill luck, depending on the viewpoint, guided the whole proceeding [of catching a foul tip]," and fans accordingly "growled and grumbled at the injustice of the rule."

Dissatisfaction with the role played by the catcher's equipment grew as the 1890s brought improvements to his gear. As early as 1890 catchers could choose a mitt known as the "perfect pillow," which was "made of the choicest Plymouth buckskin. A continuous roll or cushion, tightly packed with curled hair, is firmly stitched around the palm, forming a deep hollow." Alternatively they could try the "flexible glove," a mitt composed of the "choicest buckskin" and "thoroughly padded with chinchilla. The padding extends from the wrist to the finger tips, but there is a break at the roots of the fingers forming a sort of hinge by which the fingers are practically separate from the hand."

Improvements such as these increased the perception that the mitt did the catching by itself. In fact, catching a baseball with the mitt was not as easy as it looked, but by the time Lave Cross brought his catcher's mitt with him to third base there was a widespread belief that the mitt "made it impossible" to miss a hard-hit grounder or drop a fly ball. Cross did nothing to dispel this belief, once causing fans at New York's Polo Grounds to laugh in startled amazement when he caught a high foul and then turned the mitt upside down to show that he could do so without dropping the ball. It was all very well for Cross to make light of the ease of catching with a mitt, as he never returned to catching (eventually playing more than seventeen hundred major league games at third base). For the men who continued to play behind the plate, however, this perception was no laughing matter.

The mitt thus proved a great balm to the catcher's hands but offered cold comfort to his already wounded pride. In the 1880s catchers had begun to be referred to as backstops and wind-paddists, metaphors that implied they were becoming synonymous with their equipment. The 1890s saw that process reach its logical conclusion in the idea that the equipment could replace the man: the mitt could catch the ball for him, and

EVOLUTION OF A CAT-CHER.

Early sportswriters loved to describe early catchers as being "quick as a cat." But the introduction of the mask robbed the catcher of this distinction, and these masked men were soon referred to in much less flattering terms. Particularly insulting were jokes about the catcher wearing a muzzle or a bustle (an item that supported a woman's underclothing) on his face. *(Library of Congress)*

if it didn't, the chest protector would stop it. The mitt, readers of the 1890 article that championed the virtues of the "perfect pillow" and the "flexible glove" were informed, was now "recognized as indispensable in the paraphernalia of the big back stop." How many of the readers of that article grasped the irony that it had once been the catcher himself who was indispensable?

Nor was the adjective in the phrase "big back stop" accidental. The success of Lew Brown and Silver Flint had created a brief vogue for the large catcher in the late 1870s, but the trend proved short-lived because agility was still the catcher's most important attribute. After the introduction of the mitt, however, the catcher began to strike observers as "a mere backstop, inserted to break the impact of pitched balls against the grand stand planks." Now the "ideal catcher" came to be "considered a mountain of beef and bone, something that could stand any kind of knocks and, as long as he was successful as a battering ram, mattering not what his other qualities might be."

Predictably, the catcher of the late 1880s and the 1890s became much bigger than his predecessors, in many cases unmistakably fat. The Little Joe Roches and Shorty Ewells were long gone; in their place were the likes of "Fatty" Briody, "Jumbo" Harding, and "Tub" Welch. Just as predictably, the increase in the catcher's girth was taken as confirmation that catchers

---

no longer possessed much athletic skill. Jocko Milligan, claimed a sportswriter in 1891, "will not slide. He would be a fool if he did, for his fat hangs in rolls."

Some observers found tactful ways to describe this new development. A Baltimore sportswriter wrote of the team's catchers, "[George] Townsend and [Wilbert] Robinson are noticeable for heavy-set frames and great avoirdupois, although they are only of medium height." And some tried to rationalize this development, arguing that "a heavier man is better able to stand against the shocks of reckless runners to the home plate." But most onlookers found just another sign that the catcher was not what he once had been. Thus many accounts included blunt references, including one that described Philadelphia's Jack Clements as "a fat, bronzed young man, who makes it hard for folks in the front row of the stand to see the game while he is catching."

Obviously not all catchers had grown fat overnight, but it sometimes seemed that way from the amount of attention paid to their bulging waistlines. One sportswriter later called this "an era when most of the catchers were pot-bellied and couldn't get out of their own way." This perception gave small, agile men such as Stephen Crane yet another reason to abandon their dreams of becoming catchers.

Hidden behind the equipment that seemed to do his job for him, the catcher of the 1890s was both anonymous and interchangeable. As we have noted, the rules changes of 1889, 1890, and 1891, prompted by the Ewing injury, made the catcher literally interchangeable with a replacement who could enter at any time. Now the improvements to his equipment and its prominence suggested something still worse—that he could be replaced by *anyone* who donned the gear. As Murnane put it in 1891, the new equipment caused catchers to "[grow] up like mushrooms in a meadow." Fans likewise came to perceive the catcher as "a mere machine to stop the curves the pitcher throws and the batter misses." Once the catcher had been one in a million, but now it seemed that anyone could do his job.

Since his job was now perceived as being easy, the catcher attracted attention only when he failed. In 1891 a minor league team in New Haven endured a disastrous road trip that the club's directors blamed on excessive drinking. Not so, replied one of the players, who acknowledged the drinking but maintained, "The truth of the matter is that the work of the catchers was enough to drive any one to drink." He then singled out one of the team's catchers, a man named Theissen, for being "so fat he couldn't reach low enough to touch the runner" when he slid. Meanwhile the team's other catcher, Louis Guinasso, in the tradition of overanxious catchers who "fought" the ball, had been hurt when he tried to reach in front of the plate to catch a pitch and was hit in the head by the batter's swing. The disgruntled player told this story not to gain sympathy for the injured catcher but to show how lacking he was in the basic skills of the position.

Another telling indicator of the reduced prestige of the catcher of the 1890s occurred near the end of the decade when a new rule required the catcher to stand behind the plate throughout all at bats rather than only when a strikeout was near, as many catchers were still doing. In years past, any proposed rule that affected where the catcher could stand would have led to a spirited debate in the press, but this time the rule change attracted little notice. The only comments suggested that it was high time to end "the tiresome delays which occurred many times during the progress of a game by reason of having to wait for the catcher to come up and don his mask, and other paraphernalia." It was yet another sign that the catcher's equipment had forever robbed him of the status of folk hero.

Naturally there were catchers who took note of this dispiriting trend and tried to do something about it. Several, for example, tried to restore the position's traditional association with courage by reversing the trend toward specialization and insisting on playing in every game. In 1890, Chief Zimmer caught 111 straight games, more than doubling the previous record. His record stood only until 1895, when Jim "Deacon" McGuire, probably the best of the decade's catchers, caught all 132 of Washington's games.

Yet neither of these streaks was accorded any respect. One reporter attributed Zimmer's hardiness to the new mitt, which had "been improved until it has assumed the size of a pillow, renders injury impossible and makes almost child's play of mere catching." Even Henry Chadwick, who two decades earlier had been one of the first reporters to advocate hiring more than one battery, remarked before the 1891 season: "In the formation of the club battery teams this season it will not be essential to have so many catchers engaged as it was within the past year or two. The introduction of the protective catcher's glove now in use has had a surprising effect in enabling catchers, facing swift pitchers, to stand the wear and tear of their position even better than under the old rule of the straight arm delivery. Last season single catchers did the brunt of the work behind the bat without difficulty, while in 1888 and '89 a supply of reserve catchers was needed to cover the position properly in the face of the wild, swift pitching then in vogue." Chadwick concluded that it was now more important to have good backups for the second baseman, shortstop, and third baseman than for the catcher.

Still more surprising was the transformation in attitude toward catchers who showed endurance. In the 1870s a catcher who played through injury was invariably commended for his pluck and self-sacrifice. During the 1880s such praise became more measured but was still genuine. In stark contrast, sportswriters of the 1890s began to question the motives of catchers who never took a day off. Tim Murnane commented with apparent disapproval that Zimmer "would go in and catch every day rather than give another catcher a chance to distinguish himself."

When the consecutive-games-played streaks of these men weren't being attacked, they were being ignored. McGuire's feat of catching every game of a season has never since been approached despite the continued improvements to the catcher's gear, but his accomplishment attracted only limited attention at the time. Worse, his feat was so quickly forgotten that less than a decade later a frustrated McGuire had to write to the papers to protest when another catcher's much shorter streak of consecutive games caught was heralded as a record. Instead of restoring the lost prestige of the catcher's position, these streaks were seen as more proof that the catcher's new equipment now took the brunt of the abuse once borne by the man himself.

That brings us to the paradox that was arguably the greatest indignity suffered by the catcher of the 1890s. While he still occupied the most dangerous and injury-prone position on the baseball diamond, his toughness no longer manifested itself in conspicuous forms. Instead of sustaining highly visible injuries that stood as "monuments for work well done," the hardships of the position had become easy to overlook. The catcher now spent much of the preseason doing activities designed for "toughening the hands" for the season's work, as explained in an 1890 article: "Rowing on the machines, climbing the rope, swinging on the flying rings, and hand ball, if there be any court for that excellent game, will all tend toward this end. He should consider, however, that it is not merely toughening the skin of the hands that is desirable, but also hardening the flesh so that [it] is not easily bruised. For this reason he should pass ball without gloves regularly every day. At the outset he should receive no swift balls, and should stop at the first feeling of anything beyond a moderate tingling of the palms. His hands should receive their full preparatory hardening before he goes out into the field, for ordinary carefulness demands that he should do

While apprenticing as an iron molder in Albion, Michigan, Jim McGuire earned a reputation as the "one catcher within a radius of fifty miles" who could handle the deadly fastball and "snake ball" of pitcher Charles "Lady" Baldwin. In the major leagues McGuire set a record that will never be broken when in 1895 he caught all 132 of his team's games. But like most of the catchers of the 1890s, McGuire was overshadowed by his predecessors and got little credit for his accomplishments. *(National Baseball Hall of Fame Library)*

no catching behind the bat after the season commences except with hands thoroughly protected by well padded gloves."

Not surprisingly, inconspicuous forms of pain won catchers little sympathy, let alone the hero worship once accorded them. After all, almost every spectator at a baseball game could remember a day when catchers had it much worse. When the minor league club in Detroit opened a new ballpark in 1896, it was named in Charley Bennett's honor. "Charley Bennett was the idol of the local base ball public," explained a sportswriter, "and the entire country still looks upon him as a model in his line. He was undoubtedly the best catcher that ever played ball, and the unflinching manner in which he took punishment in the days when catchers had very little protection, would pale many that are in the business today." It was a

deserved tribute to Bennett, but it was also a telling symbol of how catchers of the 1890s were overshadowed by their predecessors.

Some articles took less-than-subtle jabs at the manhood of catchers
who donned protective equipment by showing how they looked to the
residents of the heartland. An 1890 article in a Chicago paper described
how a cattle farmer from Montgomery County, Indiana, had come to the
city to sell some livestock and had decided to watch a ball game. Expecting the action to resemble the games of his youth fifteen years earlier, he
is surprised to see things "so queer that he couldn't avoid asking help in
understanding them." He begins asking questions of a young man in "a
moon-on-the-lake pair of pants," and almost all of his inquiries focus on
the catcher's equipment. "What the Samhill's that young feller got onto his
stomach?" he demands when he notices the catcher's chest protector. Next
he asks "if the catcher always wore that buggy cushion on his left hand or
if there was something the matter to-day." Finally his attention is drawn to
the catcher's mask, and again he expresses outrage.

The young man in the moon-on-the-lake pants is unsympathetic to
his complaints, so the cattle farmer turns to a young woman and begins
comparing the heroes of his day to "the current decadence of outdoor athletics in America." She proves a much more receptive listener because, we
are told, she too has grown tired of "the lace and cambric young man of today." Soon the farmer is regaling the entire seating section with his tales of
the days when "We didn't know nothing of gloves and pads and masks and
them things, and we played the game for what they was in it, and because
we wasn't soft enough to be afraid of anything that came our way."

This account hit home because it tapped into one of the most prevalent fears of the 1890s, that a fatal softness afflicted the generation of young
men who had come of age without war, farm work, or other rites of passage
to prepare them for manhood. Countless bottles of ink were consumed
and innumerable hands were wrung in bemoaning young men who struck
their elders as being sickly, effeminate, and out of harmony with nature.
From this perspective, the catcher's new equipment seemed to symbolize
this decline, since it too was out of harmony with nature (which is why
it was farmers who usually voiced these complaints). These comparisons
were terribly unfair to the new generation of catchers, who continued to
exhibit great skill and courage, but they persisted nonetheless.

The catcher's mask, in particular, became the subject of an insulting
comparison. A typical anecdote told of a farmer and his wife who make
a trip to town and are passed by a catcher wearing a mask. The farmer is

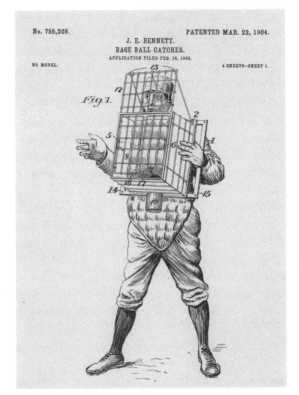

No. 755,209.   PATENTED MAR. 22, 1904.

J. E. BENNETT.
BASE BALL CATCHER.
APPLICATION FILED FEB. 18, 1903.

NO MODEL.   4 SHEETS—SHEET 1.

Fig. 1.

While this extraordinary patented device made no money for its inventor, it demonstrated just how much the prestige of the catcher's position had fallen. It symbolized the popular view of the catcher's equipment during the 1890s—instead of protecting the catcher from injury, it was doing his job for him. *(U.S. Patent and Trademark Office)*

convinced that the man must have been muzzled to keep him from drinking, but his wife is just as sure that he has borrowed his sister's bustle, the wire framework that women wore among their undergarments to support a dress. This comparison seemed more an attempt to humiliate the catcher than to describe a close resemblance. Nonetheless reporters couldn't resist the urge to draw attention to the alleged similarity.

An especially revealing reference appeared in an 1891 article that described an attempt to introduce baseball in Samoa. "The catcher," claimed the reporter, "was a young chief who had once made a visit to New Zealand and while there had seen women's wire bustles displayed for sale in store windows. When handed a catcher's mask at the beginning of the game and its use explained to him, he insisted that it was intended for a different purpose, but effected a compromise by wearing it strapped over his stomach instead of in the manner adopted by the ladies before the bustle went out of fashion." The notion of a Samoan chief being familiar with bustles is ludicrously implausible, but tales like this had force anyway. Their message was that the catcher's mask and the rest of his equipment put him out of harmony with nature. City dwellers like the young man with the moon-on-the-lake pants had themselves lost touch with nature and therefore didn't notice, so it took a farmer or a Samoan chief to point out their incongruity.

Assaults such as these had a predictable effect on the self-images of catchers. It must have been terribly wearying for these men to hear themselves constantly compared to their predecessors in ways that insulted their own courage, skill, and manhood. Many of them had sought to become catchers in order to escape the long shadows cast by the Civil War glory earned by their fathers and uncles. Instead they now found themselves overshadowed by catchers who had earned their badges of courage in ways that were no longer possible.

This disheartening state of affairs may have been best captured in an article in which *Boston Globe* sportswriter Tim Murnane reviewed the work done by catchers during the 1891 season. Murnane began by recalling the glory days of the 1870s, when the position had been dominated by the "natural catcher," a man who could "handle any kind of delivery, and will never find fault with speed or wildness." By contrast, he pointed out that some fifty men had caught in the major leagues that season, and "it is safe to say that the real article was not found in one third of that number." His dissection of the individual strengths and weaknesses of those men made it clear why he felt that way.

Murnane's remarks are striking because he rarely went out of his way to criticize the ballplayers he covered. Like any journalist, he surely knew that scathing criticism of his subjects might make it more difficult to talk with them in the future. Probably more relevant is that having played in the major leagues so recently—he was still only thirty-nine when he wrote this piece, and just seven years removed from his own playing days—Murnane understood that baseball was not as easy as it looked. In later years his likes and dislikes became more pronounced, but even then he remained generous-spirited, never subscribing to the "old fogy" school of ex-players who believed the players of their generation superior to any of their successors.

Thus his assessment of the catchers of 1891 is all the more noteworthy. Boston had entries in both major leagues that year, so Murnane had
the opportunity to watch almost all the catchers in both circuits. He had
unstinting praise for only two, Morgan Murphy and Malachi Kittridge.
He also commended the catching skills of Jack Boyle, Charley Farrell,
and Lave Cross yet noted the sad irony that precisely because of their
skill these players were now spending much of their time at other positions.

His commentary on future Hall of Famers Buck Ewing and King Kelly
was more biting. "Like Buck Ewing," Murnane observed, "Kelly has no
love for fast wild pitchers, and depends more on coaching his man so that
he is sure to know how the ball is coming." He had nothing more to add
about Ewing, who had caught only six games that season, but he proceeded
to offer a lengthy rundown of Kelly's shortcomings. He pointed out that
almost anything was likely to happen with Kelly behind the plate, from a
spectacular throw that surprised a base runner to a dreadful muff—"Mike
Kelly is not a natural catcher and will have more passed balls than any
catcher in either of the major organizations." He also cited Kelly's "in-
difference to condition," a polite reference to the charismatic ballplayer's
well-known drinking problem.

Murnane's opinions of other catchers ranged from lukewarm to dismissive. Charley Bennett, he noted, still did expert work in many areas, but
the aging catcher's arm had lost its zip and he struggled at fielding bunts.
He had largely positive things to say about the work of Tom Daly, Jack
Clements, John Milligan, and Jerry Harrington but also cited the weak
throwing arms of all four men. Con Daily was described as highly skilled
but was downgraded for "not taking proper interest in his work." He even
found many flaws in the performance of Charley Ganzel, despite the fact
that Ganzel's "splendid work" had helped the local National League team
capture the pennant.

Murnane made a particular point of noting how reliant several of the
league's catchers were on their newfangled gear. Dick Buckley, he commented, "is not a graceful workman, but a big, strong fellow, who was
made a valuable man by the introduction of gloves and pads. This New
York man was very quick and threw well to bases, but his hands often gave
out and he was not good in getting after foul flies." Wilbert Robinson was
characterized as "a catcher something after the style of Buckley of the Giants, not pretty to look at but a big man who can stand a heap of work and
handle fast pitching." Of "Doggie" Miller, Murnane said that "with the aid

of mammoth gloves he can stand behind the bat several games at a stretch. While being a good player he is not a man to long for."

Others were similarly damned with faint praise. Pop Schriver was dismissed as "a strong player for the position, but has no head for the game," and Jim Keenan as "a good backstop, but going out of date fast." Meanwhile Chief Zimmer of Cleveland received this appraisal: "While he is a valuable man, his work is not the kind to enthuse his own men or put any fear into the hearts of his opponents."

Murnane's evaluations could be idiosyncratic. It is hard not to notice that his two favorites, Murphy and Kittridge, were both New England Irishmen like himself while both Schriver and Zimmer went on to long careers despite Murnane's lack of faith in their abilities. Yet by and large his judgments of these catchers seem sound, and his belief in the decline of the position was widely shared.

An unidentified old-timer, for example, similarly damned all the 1891 catchers except Ewing with faint praise. He commended Zimmer for his throwing accuracy, only to add, "What ails Zimmer most is the fact that he's a little slow in gettin' the ball away, especially if the base-runner gets a little start on him. Still, he's overcome that fault somewhat. When he first came to Cleveland he had a bad habit of droppin' the third strike. He's over that pretty well now and I think he'll improve a good deal in his throwin' to bases." His comments on other catchers were just as equivocal: "Keenan used to be a good catcher and so did Bennett. . . . Anson's catcher, Kittridge, is handy for a little fellow, and Clements is a very swift thrower, though that left arm is liable to give the ball a tremendous old curve sometimes." Can there be any surprise that it was in 1891 that Stephen Crane abruptly gave up catching?

Through the decade it became increasingly clear that the catcher's potent mystique was a thing of the past. This may have been most apparent in the singular lack of success of the catchers who tried to revive that mystique. We have already seen how the iron-man stints of Chief Zimmer and Jim McGuire were viewed as proof that the catcher's equipment did the brunt of the work. The no-win situation of the decade's catchers was also embodied by Danny Coogan, whose fine play behind the plate at the University of Pennsylvania earned him a major league contract. But it was Coogan's misfortune to play for Washington in the year of McGuire's iron-man performance, so the collegian spent most of his time languishing on the bench.

The opportunity for playing time finally presented itself when a rash of injuries sidelined the team's infielders. Coogan, showing the pluck of old-time catchers, volunteered to fill in at shortstop despite never having played the position before. Not surprisingly, he proved to be the Alamazoo Jennings of shortstops ("his record for consecutive errors in those few hours," claimed one sportswriter, "will never be equaled"). Nonetheless he persevered, playing eighteen games at shortstop and committing thirty errors before the experiment was brought to a merciful end. At season's end Coogan was released, and his career ended without his having had "an opportunity to live down a rather lurid reputation as a shortstop, which he made when he played in that position in an emergency."

Clearly no amount of bravery could free the catcher of the 1890s from the shadow of earlier heroes. The catchers of the 1870s, naked of equipment, had taken bold risks that could not be duplicated, but at least they had been compensated with adulation and acclaim. The 1880s had seen a growing number of catchers take risks that often seemed gratuitous, but at least they attracted notice for doing so. The catcher of the 1890s, so it seemed, could take courageous risks and still be universally ignored.

A telling symbol of the plight of the catcher of the 1890s emerged from a new series of attempts to catch a ball dropped from the Washington Monument. On August 24, 1894, Chicago catcher Billy "Pop" Schriver stood at the bottom of the monument, and, according to contemporaneous sources, became the first man to catch a ball dropped from its summit. Coverage of the feat, however, stressed not his bravery but the opposite trait. Schriver's heart became "faint" and his "nerve forsook him," according to one account, so he made no attempt at all to catch the first ball. Only after the ball rebounded into the air instead of becoming lodged in the ground did the catcher regain his courage, and on a subsequent drop he made the historic catch.

Two years later former teammate Charles Irwin maintained that Schriver hadn't made the catch at all and—typically—managed to blame the catcher's mitt and to deprecate the difficulty of the feat as well as Schriver's courage. Irwin admitted that he hadn't been present, but he claimed that the players who were had told him "that Schriver could easily have made [the catch] had he not been frightened, but that he failed because he was afraid of being injured. Schriver judged the ball easily enough. He got under it, and was just about to handle the ball when he thought about the many stories he had read about the velocity of the ball being so great that it would knock a person's hands off, and he drew back. He stuck out his hand with the big mitt on it, but did not close the other one over it. The ball hit right in the palm of the mitt, and did not strike one whit harder than a high foul fly does. All the players agreed that 'Bill' could have made the catch if he had put out his other hand." Thus, in Irwin's version of events, Schriver's attempt became not only a failure but a parable with pointed messages about the poor catching techniques promoted by the mitt and the cowardice of the catcher of the 1890s.

Fourteen years later, on August 21, 1908, Gabby Street caught a ball dropped from the top of the Washington Monument. The feat was hailed as a first, and Schriver's effort was not even mentioned. It was all too typical of the plight of turn-of-the-century catchers.

Seven years after that, during the 1915 preseason, Wilbert Robinson attempted a still more hazardous feat. Robinson was now managing Brooklyn, and team president Charles Ebbets thought it would be good publicity to have one of his players catch a ball dropped from an airplane. When none of the players seemed anxious to do the stunt, the fifty-one-year-old manager volunteered. His motivation is not entirely clear, but perhaps at some level he hoped to make a statement on behalf of his generation of catchers. Instead he provided yet another symbol that his generation had the requisite courage but lacked the opportunity to prove it.

With his whole team watching, the drop was made, and Robinson correctly gauged the path of the falling object and settled under it. He braced himself for impact and reached out to make the grab, only to find himself knocked to the ground and covered in warm liquid. "Help me, lads, I'm covered with my own blood," cried the alarmed Robinson, believing he had finally achieved his own "red badge of courage." But his players were unable to come to the aid of their manager because they were laughing too hard. The object dropped from the airplane had been a grapefruit, and Wilbert Robinson was covered in its juice.

13

"The Last of the Old Guard of Ball Players"

"[The best athletic sports] are those sports which call for the greatest exercise of fine moral qualities, such as resolution, courage, endurance, and capacity to hold one's own and to stand up under punishment. . . . It is mere unmanliness to complain of occasional mishaps. . . . The sports especially dear to a vigorous and manly nation are always those in which there is a slight element of risk. Every effort should be made to minimize this risk, but it is mere unmanly folly to try to do away with the sport because the risk exists."—Theodore Roosevelt

█ THE FINAL KEY PIECE of the catcher's gear was added on April 11, 1907, when Giants catcher Roger Bresnahan took his position at New York's Polo Grounds for his team's opening-day game. "Bresnahan created somewhat of a sensation," noted the *New York Times* the next day, "when he appeared behind the bat for the start of play, by donning cricket leg guards. . . . The white shields were rather picturesque, in spite of their clumsiness, and the spectators rather fancied the innovation. They howled with delight when a foul tip in the fourth inning rapped the protectors sharply."

Bresnahan was by no means the first major leaguer to wear shin guards, but he was the first to do so openly. Several earlier catchers and infielders had experimented with added protection for their shins but had done so by wearing inconspicuous pads under their uniforms. One big reason for wearing pads under the uniform was that they interfered less when the player needed to run. But it also helped that, as had been the case with the rubber mouthpiece and the first chest protectors, these small guards were worn beneath the uniform where spectators could not see them and "howl."

Hilarity and outrage continued to greet Bresnahan's cricket pads when the Giants took to the road. Bresnahan later recalled receiving an "awful razzing. . . . Fans called me everything from 'Sissie' to 'Cream Puff.'" Two months into the season, Cubs backstop Johnny Kling said that he planned to try similar protective equipment "as soon as I can muster up nerve enough." He explained, "The roasting the rooters gave Bresnahan during the New York series here has taken away my nerve and I cannot muster up courage enough to wear them at home. I guess I will try them away from home first and then it won't be too bad."

Meanwhile Pirates owner Barney Dreyfuss campaigned to have the shin guards banned, and the team's manager, Fred Clarke, backed him up by making an intriguing threat. Clarke was a Westerner through and through, having been born on an Iowa farm in the early 1870s, then as an infant having moved farther west to Kansas with his family in a covered wagon. Clarke would have grown up hearing barbed wire referred to as "the curse of the country," so there was special significance when he vowed to "get even with the New York Club by furnishing his catchers with barbed wire armor." Clarke also threatened to outfit all his infielders with shin guards if Bresnahan's weren't banned.

The Pirates' crusade was seen as the result of the team's bitter feud with Bresnahan's Giants, and it won little support. Fan reaction also abated, making it clear that the day had passed when manly forbearance trumped safety. As most saw it, the only real issue was whether the benefits of added protection offset the hindrance they posed when the catcher tried to run.

Knee joints were soon added to address this concern, and over the next few years shin guards became standard equipment for catchers. The catcher's full regalia—the so-called "tools of ignorance"—was now essentially complete. Although masks, chest protectors, mitts, and shin guards continued to be refined and improved, and minor additions occasionally made, these came to be seen as technical questions rather than philosophical ones. As one sportswriter put it, the acceptance of Bresnahan's innovation established that there was now "no chance for any such interference with a player's right to wear what protection he pleases, provided it is not injurious to other players."

A metaphor that had been fancifully proposed a generation earlier had now become reality. "The great backstoppers of today as they stride back and forth to take their positions behind the bat," one writer observed,

Roger Bresnahan shocked the baseball world by donning cricket-style shin guards for a game at the Polo Grounds on April 11, 1907. The fans "howled with delight" the first time a foul tip bounced off them. Many of Bresnahan's fellow catchers were unwilling to wear them because of the uproar he provoked, but shin guards soon caught on, and, as shown in this picture of Bresnahan, the catcher finally came to resemble a knight in armor that covered him from head to toe. *(National Baseball Hall of Fame Library)*

"remind one of the knights of old, when they strode forth to battle, protected at every point with mailed armor, steel vizor and great gauntlets. The most picturesque, and I might add, statuesque looking figure the writer ever saw was Frank Bowerman, then a member of the New York Giants. When Frank pranced out arrayed in all the newest inventions to protect the catcher, including Roger Bresnahan's awkward but spectacular looking shin guards, he looked fit to stop a freight train, to say nothing of a baseball."

Only a few weeks after Bresnahan's dramatic unveiling of his cricket pads at the Polo Grounds, word came of the death of Nat Hicks. It was a

striking coincidence—the New Yorker who had once embodied the toughness of his generation of catchers had passed away just when another New
York catcher was completing the transition to the new model of the backstop clad from head to toe in protective equipment. The sense that an era
had ended was enhanced by the still-recent memories of the deaths of so
many of the other "tough-guy" catchers who had first dared to stand behind the plate—Bill Craver, Silver Flint, Bob Ferguson, Billy Barnie, Fergy
Malone, and John Clapp had all passed away in the preceding fifteen years.
Several commentators paid tribute to this symbolic changing of the guard
by pointing out that the greater safety enjoyed by the catchers of 1907 had
come at the price of their status as folk heroes.

In June, a month after Hicks's death and as Bresnahan's innovation
was gaining acceptance, a piece written by *Philadelphia Inquirer* sportswriter Edgar Wolfe (who used the pen name "Jim Nasium") consisted of
a purported letter from an old-timer to his son that drew attention to the
connection between the two events. While the letter relies upon deliberate
comic exaggeration, its point is nonetheless important:

"I see my old pal, Nat Hicks, the old Mutual catcher, has passed in his
checks, and the shuffling off, taking place just at the time when there's so
much chin music about catchers wearing shin guards for protection has
started my wheels grinding out some grist which it might be well for you
to store in your garret. If poor old Nat had lived to trim his lamps on Roger
Bresnahan behind the bat fortified behind his shin guards, bird cage, wind
pad and pillow mitt, he probably would have died laughing, anyway. Back
in the seventies Hicks would crawl up under the bat and stop foul tips with
his bare mug and naked mitts, and get cracked over the knot with the willow till he resembled the middle stratum of a cannibal sandwich.

"Back in Hicks' days they didn't have any armor for ball players, the
scrappers didn't put pillows on their mitts and play pussy wants a corner
for six measly little rounds for a decision on points and the mollycoddle
stood about as much chance in sports as a skye terrier in a sausage factory.
The catcher then played in the tall grass up against the backstop, and
Hicks first got next to the idea of taking them off the bat to cut down
base runners doing the sneak act. He'd freeze onto the hottest speed with
his bare mitts, take foul tips in the solar plexus or on his open frontispiece
without wind pad or mask, and his work was so much to the velvet that
the other backstoppers were compelled to do the nervy act, too. They had
to be there with the grit in large chunks. There's a howl going up this year

about the scarcity of catchers, but I'll bet a dollar to a doughnut that if they'd rule out all this modern armor catchers would be as scarce as honest men in Congress.

"Where the high-priced armored pitch stopper of today gets a month's lay-off on salary for a bump on the digits, Hicks would go in on crutches with his mug and mitts done up in slings and deliver the goods. I remember an important game between the Mutuals and the Atlantics, when it was thought that Hicks would be on the shelf, as he was so badly bunged up. Hicks insisted on working that afternoon, and went into the game with his right lamp almost knocked out of his sky-piece and his nose and the port side of his mug hoved out like a bay window on a Brooklyn flat. During the game he was soaked square on the mouth by a foul tip and another landed in the middle of his dining room, besides getting cracked over the know twice with the bat; yet he not only stuck the game out but actually won it with his brilliant work. There isn't a guy wearing spikes today who wouldn't get icicles in his shoes at the bare thought of attempting such a feat.

"I am putting you next to these facts about the old guard catchers because the contrast between their brand of goods and the brand dished up by the present day force of wind-paddists forms a good illustration of how modern improvements have given birth to the mollycoddle germ, which is not only gnawing at the vitals of our athletic sports, but is lapping up the grit and manhood of the whole blamed human race. In the old days, when our forefathers used to tumble out of the hay in the morning and club their breakfasts off the trees, a guy had to be there with the grit or he was planted where the daisies grow. Modern inventions have changed things so that a guy can get his chewing now by cocking his kicks on a desk and pushing electric buttons, and right there is where the mollycoddle germ finds an opening for a knockout punch.

"While our forefathers used to put the bug on the mollycoddle germ by hammering out their shoe nails with a sledge hammer, now they can ship a train load of dirt from the shores of Lake Superior into one of Andy Carnegie's steel mills, and a pale-faced squirt of a slob presses a button and turns it into armored cruisers so fast that the front end may be anything from a sky-scraper to Carnegie hero medals, while the rear end is still real estate.

"Now, I am not knocking against improvements. But I only want to show you that the mollycoddle is a scale which drops from the wheels of progress, and that if we can no longer get immunity from the mollycoddle germ in our daily work, we've got to get [it] in the strenuous outdoor sports, or the whole blamed country will go on the blink.

"But along comes the inventor and he butts into our sports. As a result of his wind pad, mask, shin guards and pillow mitt there's no more immunity for the mollycoddle germ behind the bat. If it hadn't been for the invention of these protectors, we'd still have men in a class with Nat Hicks. Scrappers used to get out on the green and go at each other with bare knuckles, just to see which was the best man, but some stiff, with more brains than grit, invented the boxing glove, and as a result we're raising a bunch of mollycoddle fighters like Jack O'Brien. Thank heaven, these modern improvers will have an awful job to squeeze the mollycoddle into football. If this sort of progress keeps on the mollycoddle in our sports threatens to become a national calamity. John Bull and your Uncle Sam always had the skidoo sign on the other guys simply because their sports were more strenuous.

"There's no telling to what lengths these inventions will go in our national game. The vindication of Bresnahan's shin guards by the president of the National League and Fred Clarke's threat to stick them on the pins of his entire infield opens up new possibilities in the way of base ball uniforms for the future. To offset the advantage gained by these defensive tactics we may soon expect to see base runners equipped with sliding helmets armed with spikes to butt through the defense sliding into the plate on a truck.

"I must close now, son, but I've put you next to these facts, so you can duck the swings of these modern improvements. Kick in and take chances, and be there with the grit and nerve at all stages of the game."

The fictitious old-timer's repeated use of terms like "mollycoddles" and "strenuous" would have been met with a knowing chuckle by *Inquirer* readers, since these were the pet phrases of President Theodore Roosevelt. So too the exaggerated description of the changing nature of the work done at Carnegie's steel mills was carefully crafted to elicit a smile.

Yet these were the slightly uncomfortable chuckles and smiles that come with recognition and empathy. Even though the old-guard catchers themselves were dying out, many Americans still viewed the equipment now worn by catchers with resentment. And many of those Americans, like this old-timer, sensed a parallel between the reduced demands of the catching position and the changes transforming the twentieth-century workplace.

Those same sentiments, along with many of the same revealing word choices, appeared in a 1913 article written under the pseudonym of "Uncle Dud." Uncle Dud and his friend "the colonel" were discussing one of their favorite topics, "the days when baseball was a truly strenuous game, when it took nerve and genuine courage." With little prompting, the colonel snorted, "They're a bunch of mollycoddles and pink tea dudes these ball players of today! . . . Back in the early '80's did you ever see a catcher wear a sofa pillow on his hand or mattress all over his front elevation or armor plate on his shins? No! Of course not; not even a mask, my boy! Infielders and outfielders alike played with bare hands, and a recruit couldn't even get a tryout if he had a straight finger on either paw! Ah, Dudley, my friend, those were the happy days!"

Lest anyone doubt that there were real people who felt as strongly as these fictitious old-timers, consider the 1911 comments of Frank Haggerty, the football coach at Buchtel College (now the University of Akron). Haggerty denounced the "modern foolishness" of going "to a baseball park to see the catcher wearing shin guards. Is it not enough to make the old 'has beens' get the sideache when they behold such a spectacle? In 'ye old times' the receiver wore no mit [sic], or mask, or protector, but little by little these articles came into use, and no one thought to ridicule such steps, but in this day of brains and speed the shin guards act as a hindrance to the activity of the game."

Haggerty blamed Bresnahan for introducing shin guards to protect his legs "from the spikes of such men as [Johnny] Evers and 'Ty' Cobb when sliding home." He acknowledged that their use had become "a fad" but maintained that "you can count all the 'nervy' catchers in both leagues on one hand that use them." He claimed that their use needlessly prolonged the game and led to "dirty work," because the protection encouraged catchers to block the base path and make collisions inevitable. His solution was simple: catchers should "take some nerve tonic and discard shin guards."

Most observers were more realistic than Haggerty and understood that no amount of rhetoric could turn back the clock. Yet the passing of Hicks did cause many less partial onlookers to acknowledge that his like would never be seen again. As the *New York Times* put it, "the last of the old guard of ball players passed away. In the heyday of his glory Hicks's name was as widely known as that of any of the present-day favorites of the diamond, and his renown was better deserved than that of many of the later-day performers. To the enthusiast of the early seventies, when baseball was beginning to gain the firm hold that it has since acquired upon the hearts of the sport-loving American people, Hicks had no equal of the time, while to compare any of the later-day performers with him would be little less than sacrilege."

Spectators shared this outlook. "In the minds of the present-day fans," noted a sportswriter, "a glamour surrounds the old catchers, whose spirit and courage, summed up in the word 'pluck,' they have been taught to admire with a feeling bordering on the supernatural. As for a comparison of the worth of the catchers at hand with those of the 'gloveless' period, that was entirely out of the question, fans being forced to admit the superiority of the gloveless receivers, whether or no."

While some of these sentiments reflected the typical nostalgia for a bygone era, they had a firm basis in reality, as was nicely captured in an article that bore the provocative title of "Backstops Are Deteriorating." The piece acknowledged the "ever-present tendency to magnify the heroic deeds of our ancestors, to compare them with the doings of the current generation, much to the disparagement of the latter, and to sing the praises, vastly magnified, of the great men who have gone before." It traced this tendency back to the days of Homer and then forward to the generations that grew up in the imposing shadows of the men who fought the American Revolution and the Civil War. The article acknowledged that athletics were also affected by the impulse "to magnify the bygone stars and exalt them to a pinnacle of glory such, perhaps, as no merely human individuals could actually gain," with the result that active competitors were sometimes denied their just dues.

But then an important exception was noted: "Nevertheless, when one great department of the game is under consideration there seems to be just reason for singing the praises of the past and comparing the bygone marvels with their successors of today, much to the discredit of the younger generation. That department is the one of mask and pad, of heavy glove and shielding armor—the department of the catcher. The catcher of today, if he approaches the standard attained by the men who did the catching 20 years ago, is a thing of priceless value. He is a player of such worth that any club would give three or four great batsmen or two star pitchers for one catcher of the highest ability."

That was the legacy of Nat Hicks and his generation—a reputation for such incomparable bravery that, thirty years later, catchers were still struggling to live up to it.

14

A New Pitch and a New Crisis

"The 'spit ball' is bound to revolutionize baseball fully as much as the curve ball did twenty [sic] years ago."—Tim Murnane

■ THE PASSING of Nat Hicks and many of the other old-guard catchers elicited deserving tributes to an era when the catchers became folk heroes who stood out in a way that could never happen again. Without demeaning the courage of any man who played behind the plate, there can be no disputing the assessment that it was "little less than sacrilege" to compare the fearlessness and resilience of catchers who wore masks, chest protectors, mitts, and shin guards to their unshielded predecessors. And to many of the old-timers who were appalled by Bresnahan's shin guards, the use of all that equipment was an indictment of the new generation's softness.

Yet by then a viable new model of the catcher had finally begun to manifest itself. That new model would never rival the catcher of the 1870s for toughness, nor would his importance ever again tower over most of the other players on the field. It was, however, a synthesis that enabled the tough-guy catcher to coexist with the thinking-man catcher, that had room for both the beliefs of the Frank Haggertys and Teddy Roosevelts and those of Henry Chadwick, and that even helped bridge the gap between the Puritans' deep suspicion of heroism and the admiration so many Americans felt for rugged individualists like the frontiersman and the cowboy. This new model finally struck the delicate balance necessary to prove enduring, and at last catchers were freed from the shadow of predecessors whose feats could not possibly be duplicated.

Many elements of this new ideal were strikingly familiar and reflected the many similarities between the events that revolutionized baseball in the 1870s and those that occurred during the first decade of the twentieth century. Scoring declined significantly in the first five years of the new century, a trend generally attributed to a rules change that made any foul with less than two strikes count as a strike. Predictably, lower scores prompted a revisit of many of the little things that again began to seem crucial, especially skills like a catcher's ability to throw out base runners, prevent passed balls, and field bunts.

Then a new pitch emerged that afforded an especially close parallel with the 1870s. During the 1904 and 1905 seasons the spitball, a pitch known by only a few, suddenly became a weapon used with great effectiveness by scores of major league pitchers, just as had happened with the curveball in 1874 and 1875. The pitch seemed magical and unfair, just as the curve had three decades earlier, because it dove sharply away from the batter as soon as he began his swing. As had happened with the curve, some players and observers suggested that it would only be fair to allow frustrated hitters to leave the batter's box to pursue it. In another close parallel to the curve, there were those who suspected that the spitball was merely an optical illusion. As Malachi Kittridge observed, "Lots of people wouldn't believe a ball could be curved until it was proven to them. It's the same way with the spit ball."

Batters, however, knew all too well that the spitball was real, and many were ready to panic after the 1904 season saw one American League pitcher after another begin expectorating on the baseball, thereby adding a lethal new pitch to his repertoire. "The batsmen of the American League," noted Tim Murnane, "say that it is utterly impossible to hit the [spitball] square as it breaks in so many different ways just as it reaches the plate. The ball is sent about waist high and usually shoots or drops. . . . The batters claim that it will ruin the batting." What they found especially frustrating was that the American League had adopted the foul strike rule in 1903, just in time for the arrival of a pitch that defied being hit squarely.

The reduction in scoring produced by the spitball was one important factor that placed renewed emphasis on the finer points of catching, but even more important was the pitch's pronounced tendency to dive downward and elude catchers. This made it yet another pitch that was highly valuable with a skilled man behind the plate but useless if one could not be found. After a decade and a half of pitchers working high in the strike zone, catchers who could handle such a delivery were in very short supply.

Thus a familiar cycle recurred. More and more pitchers learned how to throw the spitball, at first mostly in the American League, but soon in the senior circuit as well. By 1905 it had become so essential a part of the pitcher's repertoire that, according to one sportswriter, "You are not in it these days if you are a pitcher without the spit ball." Batters continued to find the pitch all but unhittable, and batting averages, already in a tailspin since the advent of the foul strike, continued to plummet. Like the curve-ball a generation earlier, the pitch was seen as a great equalizer, offering a woebegone franchise the hope that it could be transformed into a winner if only it could find a pitcher who could control it and a catcher who could handle it. The 1908 season produced epic pennant races in both leagues, leading one sportswriter to conclude, "If the spit ball were eliminated I believe the pennant races would not be so close, especially in the American League."

Yet finding a pitcher who could control the spitball and a catcher who could receive it was not easy. One of the popularizers of the pitch, Frank Corridon, discovered it in 1901 while experimenting with a "wet ball more in a manner of fun than anything else. To my surprise one ball took a sudden break just before it reached the catcher and landed against his shins. What he said I guess you can figure out for yourself." Corridon found it easy to continue to get the sharp break but initially concluded that trying to control it was "a hopeless task." After "months of patience and practice," he finally began to learn how to get the pitch over the plate, but the direction of its last-second break remained unpredictable. The experience of other pitchers was similar, with the result that catchers who tried to handle the spitball during its breakout season of 1904 liked it no better than had the catcher whose shins had stopped Corridon's first experimental pitch.

"The catchers dreaded it," reported Johnny Evers and Hugh Fullerton, "because it was hard to handle, and harder to throw." As Lou Criger put it, "the constant shooting of the ball bangs a catcher's hands all up, and when throwing to bases the catcher is likely to make a wild throw as the result of a slippery spot on the ball." With the curveball, at least, a catcher who had been warned that one was coming could anticipate its trajectory and usually handle it cleanly. The spitball, by contrast, seemed to have a mind of its own. As an exasperated Malachi Kittridge explained, "It comes straight toward you like a slow ball, and then it breaks. No pitcher can tell where it will break or how it will break. No catcher can tell."

Kittridge's sentiments were shared by "Red" Dooin, who was described as being "one of the best-natured fellows in the world, but the one subject that makes him fly off at a tangent is the spitball. 'It's rotten,' was his verdict, given in very hearty emphasis, 'and it is really harder on the catcher than it is on the batter. Very few pitchers have any sort of control over the thing, and it has ruined some catchers completely. Besides being the hardest kind of a ball to catch, it is almost impossible to make any kind of an accurate quick throw with it. Don't say spitball to me. It's a bad noise.'"

The problems caused by the pitch were demonstrated in dramatic fashion by the first dominant spitballer, Jack Chesbro. Chesbro won an American League record forty-one games for New York in 1904, but his pitch often proved as uncatchable as it was unhittable. Kittridge spoke for all receivers when he commented, "If Chesbro says he can tell [where and how the spitball will break], he's fooling, that's all. Chesbro can't tell any more than the man in the moon." This contention was borne out on the last day of the season when one of Chesbro's spitballs sailed over the head of catcher Red Kleinow, who watched helplessly as the game and the pennant were lost.

Kleinow's predicament gained added heft from the fact that he was New York's back-up catcher and was in the lineup on that fateful day only because Chesbro's constant use of the spitball that year had sidelined the game's most indomitable catcher, Jim McGuire, with repeated hand injuries. The issue recurred the following spring when Chesbro tried to prepare for the upcoming season by practicing with the catchers at Harvard, only to be forced to stop after breaking the finger of one of the school's catchers and the wrist of another. So the spitball was once again forcing catchers to deal simultaneously with damaged egos and bodies.

Even Bresnahan's decision to don shin guards in 1907 was a response to the new pitch. When asked the oft-repeated question, Bresnahan replied: "Why did I devise them? That's easy. On the pitching staff of the Giants there are four men who throw a very speedy and very deceptive drop ball [the spitball, in most cases]. . . . In 1906 I received such a battering about the legs that I made up my mind it would be a service to the team if it were possible to devise something to assist in putting an end to it." Yet the new piece of equipment addressed only the symptoms; it proved much more difficult to do anything about the roots of the problem. Foreshadowing what would happen with the knuckleball, in 1907 "Nig" Clarke of Cleveland tried to have a special catcher's mitt designed for catching the spitter. Others just threw up their hands. Some managers concluded that the pitch's many drawbacks outweighed its benefits and prohibited their pitchers from using it. Fittingly, it was Jim McGuire who in 1910 became the first manager to prohibit his entire staff from throwing the spitball.

The difficulties and indignities that the pitch caused catchers led many observers to initially "maintain that the introduction of the spitball has had much to do with the decadence of catchers." One sportswriter went so far as to write that "The catcher is a lowly and gazelle-like receptacle for the elusive spit ball, the dizzy floater and the paralyzing in-shoot, and carries more defensive apparatus than an armored cruiser."

But instead of his equipment transforming the catcher into an inanimate object, the difficulty of corralling the spitball created renewed appreciation for his skills. As managers became aware that a pitcher who could throw a wicked spitball was of little use without a catcher able to handle the pitch, the indispensable status once enjoyed by the catcher began to return.

Within a few years the aura of magic surrounding the spitball dissipated, much as the furor over the curveball had quieted by the end of the 1870s. The spitter remained an effective pitch, but it ceased to be a dominant one when batters learned to gauge its trajectory. Even more than had been the case with the curve, once the new pitch began to dip, it was a good bet that it would miss the strike zone. Batters began to take more and more spitballs, which led to more wild pitches and placed a still greater premium on the catcher's ability to keep the elusive pitch in front of him. It is small wonder that Jim McGuire issued his no-spitball edict in 1910.

Yet by then an impressive array of new pitches had begun to appear that added to the frustration of batters and catchers. While each was a new invention, all were the result of the feverish experimenting that followed the spitter's success, and all were designed with the hope of mimicking its late, sharp, downward break. Indeed, these pitches had enough in common with the spitball that they were sometimes collectively referred to as "dry spitters." They all caused catchers to tear their hair out.

One of the most notable of the new pitches was the knuckleball, which, as its name implies, was at first gripped with the knuckles. One of the pioneers of the delivery was Eddie Cicotte, who became so expert with it that the veteran catcher Lou Criger marveled: "The way Cicotte uses it, it's the best slow ball I ever caught. And it's also the hardest slow ball to handle that was ever sent up to me." That was nothing, however, compared to the astonishment occasioned in 1908 when Ed Summers started using his fingernails to grip the ball, as today's knuckleballers almost invariably do, and began to produce the results that still baffle hitters and catchers.

As his teammate Wild Bill Donovan noted, Summers's new pitch was "not only impossible to hit, but almost as hard to catch. I have seen him warming up with Ira Thomas, who was then with Detroit, and almost every other ball would land in the pit of Ira's stomach or break his glove and strike his knee or shin. The ball would frequently come up to the plate, break first to the right, then to the left, and then suddenly duck downward. When the batter hit it, an accident had happened. . . . I was telling Clark Griffith about it and he gave me the hoarse huzza. So one day I got Griff to put on a big mitt and warm up with Summers. He tried and finally succeeded in catching one ball out of four. The others either landed on his shin or up around his chest. When he finally quit he had this to say: 'No batter can hit him, but neither can his catcher catch him if he uses that ball. I could almost swear it broke two ways at the same time.'" Grand Rapids manager Bobby Lowe tried to catch "five or six of the finger-tip balls and [he] failed to catch a single one, being hit on the back of the hand with one and missing one other completely, though it lodged in the pit of his stomach." The pitch made Summers virtually invincible, and in 1908 he won twenty-four games. More important, as these accounts dramatically illustrate, the knuckleball was another pitch that was only effective if a catcher could be found to handle it.

It was the spitball, however, that continued to exert the most influence, simply because so many pitchers used it while few could master the knuckleball. Several other lethal new pitches proved even more difficult to control. Christy Mathewson's celebrated "fadeaway" was highly effective for him, but few others could get the hang of it. Mordecai "Three-Finger" Brown's missing right index finger forced him to develop some unique grips that baffled hitters. The forkball was also invented and used by several pitchers in the immediate aftermath of the "spitball year" of 1904, but none of them truly mastered it.

Despite the limited number of pitchers who were able to benefit from these offerings, the impressive results obtained by Summers, Mathewson, and Brown caused experimentation to continue. It soon became clear that the easiest way to get the ball to dip deceptively was to scuff or deface it. Most pitchers used this tactic in moderation to get a little movement on the ball, since otherwise they couldn't control the pitch, but a few went further. The most notable was Russell Ford, who in 1910 surreptitiously began using a pitch that became known as the emery ball. Like Corridon, Ford was still a minor leaguer when he accidentally discovered what would become his signature pitch during a 1908 warm-up session. While using a ball that had been damaged by striking a wooden upright behind the plate, he noticed that it took a peculiar dip that made it very difficult to hit. Subsequent experiments confirmed that the ball would continue to react in the same way. Nonetheless Ford at first gave up on the pitch, concluding, like Corridon, that it could neither be controlled nor caught.

But a year later, with his career at a crossroads, he took it up again and found that by rubbing emery paper against the ball he could produce the characteristic dip. His success that year earned him a promotion to the major leagues, where he posted a 26-6 record in 1910. He had meanwhile kept the nature of the pitch a secret by leading everyone to believe it was just a particularly effective spitball. Even his teammates were kept in the dark, with one exception—his catcher (and roommate), Ed Sweeney. Like every other unhittable pitch, the emery ball was of no value without a catcher who could control it.

Ford recorded twenty-two victories in 1911, but then his bubble burst. Sweeney held out that spring, and no other catcher on the team could hold the pitch. As John McGraw put it, "Many attributed Ford's poor showing in the early part of last season to the fact that Sweeney did not report until late because he was holding out for more money. He got it." Then Ford hurt his arm and lost his effectiveness. Finally, in 1913, another pitcher, journeyman Cy Falkenberg, picked up the secret of the pitch and experienced the same sudden success that Ford had enjoyed. But Falkenberg was not discreet about what he was doing, and the secret soon leaked.

The 1914 season saw many pitchers begin to feature the emery ball, to the great frustration of puzzled batters. "I experimented with that delivery this season," claimed Grover Cleveland Alexander after the year, "and frankly, I don't think that I would ever lose a game if permitted to use it. This shoot, which is thrown by roughing a spot on the ball with a piece of emery paper, is simply a corker. It will go in or up, down, or out for a yard, the direction of the slant depending on the position in which you hold the rough spot. . . . It placed the batter under a hopeless handicap." Alexander was also quick to note that the new weapon was just as baffling to catchers: "Honestly, it would take such an upward shoot before reaching the batter that the backstop would sometimes have to jump into the air and make the catch."

Presumably Alexander was exaggerating, and batters and catchers would gradually have grown accustomed to the emery pitch, as they had with the curve and the spitball. But they never had that chance. At the end of the 1914 season the emery ball became the first specific pitch ever banned by a major league.

Pitchers responded to the prohibition by devising a barrage of new ways to scuff baseballs so that they would nosedive unpredictably. Catchers took a beating as a result; as Bob O'Farrell recalled, "Those were the days when catching was really rough. There were so many off beat pitches then, you know. Like the spitball, the emory [sic] ball, the shine ball. You name it, somebody threw it. . . . A catcher's life wasn't easy."

The success of the scuffed-ball pitchers was uneven, but finally in 1920 the game's rules-makers decided to ban the spitball and all of its offshoots. By then the brilliance of pitchers like Mathewson and Brown, along with the shorter-lived success of men like Chesbro, Summers, Ford, and Falkenberg, had convinced everyone of the value of pitches with sharp downward breaks.

It was just as evident that catchers had been both the victims and the beneficiaries of this trend. They were victims because, just as in the 1870s, they suffered a great deal of pain. The prestige of their position, however, had begun a dramatic revival. Before the 1908 season a headline proclaimed, "Good Catchers Are Few and Far Between; Managers Have Pitchers to Spare, But Backstops Who Are Onto All the Tricks of the Game Are Not to Be Had for Any Price." The article elaborated: "The cry now is for good catchers. They are more in demand than good pitchers. They simply are not to be had. Three years ago pitchers were as scarce as the oysters in Park Row soup, but today you couldn't throw a stone down Broadway without hitting some big league twirler who had 'speed, plenty of curves, the spit ball, and a good head.'. . . During the recent 'Old Glory' sale of ball players at the Waldorf everybody was reaching out for catchers, while pitchers were a secondary consideration. They were so plentiful as to be swapped in pairs, and a few infielders and outfielders had to be tossed in for good measure to bring down a good throwing catcher who knew his business."

Despite the fact that the sudden scarcity of catchers and corresponding excess of pitchers coincided closely with the advent of the spitball, this sportswriter depicted the cause of this phenomenon as a mystery. "Just why this is managers don't pretend to know," he reported, "but it's true, just the same. . . . The only plausible explanation for this scarcity in catchers, according to Billy Murray, manager of the Phillies, is that the demand for pitchers was so great several years ago that a large majority of players began developing themselves into pitchers. In this flurry for twirling talent the catchers were almost forgotten."

A few observers recognized that it was no coincidence that the renewed discussion of the shortage of catchers had begun in 1904, the year in which the spitball became the most talked-about new pitch since the curveball. At the close of that campaign an astute sportswriter offered this analysis: "A dozen years ago a man who could hold any pitcher's delivery, had a good wing to prevent base stealing and could hit occasionally, could draw a catcher's salary." Throughout the 1890s, he noted, the perception continued that it was now possible to fill the catcher's position with a man of ordinary abilities. These years instead saw a "great demand for pitchers," which produced an effect reminiscent of the days when men like Fred Gunkle and Alamazoo Jennings had managed to get tryouts during major league games: it became "a common remark that any stranger could sign a contract for a good salary if he even told a manager he could pitch some."

Thus between the early 1890s and the middle of the next decade, great athletes were advised to become infielders or outfielders while players with great arms devoted themselves to pitching. Catchers, by and large, were perceived as players who had failed at those more glamorous positions. By the start of the new century, Tim Murnane's dismissive evaluations of the catchers of 1891 had hardened into a consensus.

This was especially true of Jim McGuire, Chief Zimmer, and Charlie "Duke" Farrell, three of the catching stalwarts of the 1890s. It was hard for most to forget that McGuire and Zimmer had both served stints as backups to the great Charley Bennett in Detroit during the 1880s, only to be found wanting even in the role of benchwarmers, and released. Meanwhile an article with the provocative title of "Backstops Are Deteriorating" pointed out that "Charlie Farrell, who was only second or third catcher on the old Chicago team, developed into a great backstop and was a star for years after his contemporaries had left the game." Like so many of his contemporaries, Farrell further damaged the catcher's image when he was able to retain his starter's job even after falling badly out of shape.

The shortage of new catching talent, however, was not perceived as a problem until 1904, the year of the spitball. "The dearth of catchers is most marked," wrote the same sportswriter after the close of that watershed season. "One can not count on his fingers the catchers who have not some pronounced weakness in their department of the game. When such men as Duke Farrell, Jim McGuire and Joe Sugden can not only play, but 'make good' on some of the fastest teams in the world, it is proof that young players have been trying for other positions, to the damage of the stock of backstops." Meanwhile there suddenly seemed to be "a plentiful supply of pitchers on the market."

To continue his analogy, the catcher "market" was already overdue for a correction when the spitball emerged. Suddenly, inconsistent pitchers like Chesbro, Ed Walsh, and "Doc" White were elevated to star status, and the already "plentiful supply" of hurlers became a glut. Meanwhile, as we have seen, the difficulty of catching the new pitch transformed the shortage of good receivers into a crisis. "It would be worse than useless," explained trainer Frank Newhouse in the middle of the 1904 season, for a pitcher "to be a past master of curves, drop balls and swift straights if the catcher was unable to receive and hold the delivery . . . it is the man behind the bat who is the real hero of the game."

Before the end of the decade, the "remarkable scarcity of catchers" had become a universally accepted truth. "I wonder where the catchers will come from in a few years more?" asked Patsy Donovan rhetorically. "Where on earth are we going to get real catchers, genuine maskmen of the time the old-time fans used to see parading with the big chests and the jovial grin?. . . The visible supply of catchers in the two best leagues is so short and so inferior." Another sportswriter observed, "When a new catcher of Billy [Killefer]'s merit is discovered, there is as much rejoicing these times as of old when the one sheep was safely tucked back into the fold with the other ninety and nine. Catchers are rare birds these days."

The difference between the relentless bashing of catchers that had been the rule until 1904 and this new insistence on the scarcity of good catchers may not seem terribly important. At a superficial level, both ways of stating the problem are quite similar. Yet there is a crucial distinction. Before the advent of the spitball, references to the lack of catching talent usually implied that anyone with the skills to be a great catcher ought to be used at another position. Now the message had changed, and addressing the lack of good catchers was again considered such a priority that it was worth using great athletes in the position.

With each passing year the consequences of the shortage became more noticeable. By 1908, at the National League's annual meeting, "pitchers bobbed up in the corridors as frequently as the holes in a sweitzer [Swiss] cheese" but attracted little interest. Meanwhile such clubs as "Boston, Cincinnati, St. Louis, Philadelphia and Brooklyn were all looking for good backstops, and with the exception of Boston, who landed [Frank] Bowerman, they went home disappointed." Perhaps more telling than the fact that four teams were unable to find a satisfactory catcher is that Bowerman would be considered an acceptable solution. In addition to being a thirty-nine-year-old journeyman, he was available specifically because he had been so unhappy as a backup to Roger Bresnahan in New York that he provoked dissension.

Desperate cries began to be heard, yet efforts to meet the shortfall were slowed by a couple of daunting realities. The first, as we have seen, is that an entire generation of young ballplayers had been discouraged from taking up catching. Second, the position still caused great pain and suffering without a corresponding amount of recognition. "Good receivers are few and far between," noted a sportswriter in 1908. "Probably the chances of injury and the thanklessness of the job make youthful baseball aspirants steer clear of the catching position. Go out and catch a good game and you are credited with doing what you are paid for. Have a few passed balls and make a wild throw or two, and the populace rises up and howls it's a shame such a good pitcher can't get a little support." As Johnny Evers and Hugh Fullerton pointed out, it was "small wonder that the men who might make really great catchers prefer some other position where the risk is not so large."

By this time major league teams were employing scouts to find promising players instead of waiting for the right man to show up on their doorsteps. Yet the increasingly desperate managers who were dispatching their best talent hunters in search of catchers kept hearing a disheartening refrain. In 1905 the game's best-known scout, Ted Sullivan, reported that he had been scouring the country for three months but found good catchers and infielders in short supply. In ensuing years, as the focus shifted more and more toward catchers, the answer remained the same: "The real classy backstop is a rare bird. Nearly all the managers in the major leagues today are hotfoot after good catchers, but the scouts unite in saying that only a small percentage of young men aspiring to places on the big clubs are trying to get jobs as catchers." This was quite a comedown from the days when it was the fondest wish of so many boys to become catchers.

With scouts insisting that the pickings were so slim, clubs began to stockpile catchers—another parallel to the 1870s. "Look over the list of great catchers in the big leagues today," explained a commentator in 1910, "and you can count them on your fingers. All the clubs have two or three wind paddists, and to judge by this number one would think that all must be good or else they would not be kept on the payroll. Such is not the case, however, for the clubs are [not] prone to part with them for fear of not being able to secure one as good owing to the scarcity of backstops."

The only long-term solution was for gifted young athletes to turn their attention again to catching. Connie Mack recognized this and commented, "The best advice I can give a young man who aspires to make a great name on the diamond is: 'Practice and study catching. Become a second Buck Ewing.'" Such counsel from one of the game's most influential managers was another step toward ending the practice of shifting talented young receivers to other positions, as—ironically—had been the case with Ewing.

Gradually all the attention being paid to the catching shortage earned the position a new respect. After years of deprecating catchers, expert observers were forced to take a new look at the position and were surprised by what they found. "Much of the scarcity of good timber," concluded a typical one, "is due to the greater requirements to make a successful catcher with the development of the science of baseball." "The game has changed so much in the last decade," added Johnny Evers and Hugh Fullerton in 1910, "that the heavy increase in the duties thrust upon the catchers has not only diminished the supply but overtaxed the physical capacity of all except the extraordinary men. The position has become so vital to the game, and its duties so numerous and trying, that it is difficult for one man to carry them all with any degree of success."

The result of this reexamination was a new model of the catcher that suited the new century. And while the new standard lacked some of the heroic flair and panache of the old school of catchers, it was, finally, a model that could endure.

15

An Enduring New Model

"The bushes are full of players who can stand behind the bat and catch all kinds of speed, curves and spit balls, high, low or wide; who can throw fast and true to second base—if nobody gets in the way—and, in fact, can perform all the duties the public believes are required of the catcher. But the mechanical art of catching is of least importance. The star catcher is the real brain center of his team when it is on the defensive. Usually the man behind the mask plans out every play made in the field. . . . What the quarterback is to the football team the catcher is on the diamond."—*Albany Evening Journal* (1911)

◼ THE EARLY YEARS of the twentieth century witnessed another dramatic transformation in the role of the man behind the plate. The immediate impetus was the emergence of the spitball in 1904 and 1905, followed in quick succession by other evasive pitches like the knuckleball and the emery ball. A familiar pattern reemerged: catchers who could handle these pitches were found to be in short supply, and the baseball world was soon abuzz with talk about the scarcity of qualified catchers.

Analysis of the reasons for that shortage ensued, and it yielded some surprising conclusions. It became apparent that the downtrodden image of the catcher of the 1890s had never been fair, that many of the perceived shortcomings of those "backstops" were just the result of being measured against the incomparable toughness of the catchers of the 1870s. It also became evident that recent changes in the rules and strategies were leading to a subtle but significant expansion of the catcher's role. Clearly the time was right for an enduring new model for the catcher.

The prospect that this new model might become permanent was enhanced by the passing of so many of the subscribers to the old school of catching. Not only were Hicks and so many of his contemporaries dead, so too were most of the sportswriters who had witnessed their feats of courage. Henry Chadwick died in 1908, less than a year after writing his obituary of Hicks for the *New York Times*, and he had outlived many of his peers. The few veteran scribes who survived, finding that most readers could no longer relate to the early days of baseball, had either to adapt or to retire. Al Spink, for instance, gave up the *Sporting News* at the turn of the century, writing about baseball again only in his 1911 book *The National Game*, in which he paid eloquent tribute to "the days when it took pluck and bull dog courage to fill the catcher's place."

These departures were a loss for the game's history, but they must have come as a relief to the rising new generation of catchers. Finally they would no longer have to suffer derogatory references to their inability to measure up to the toughness of catchers who had not worn masks, mitts, and chest protectors. Instead they could be compared to the much-maligned catchers of the turn of the century.

Unlike the catchers of the two preceding decades, these men no longer felt overshadowed by the inimitable example of Hicks and his ilk. For them, old-time catchers were men like Connie Mack, who had tried unsuccessfully to create a thinking-man catcher in the 1880s and who were now applying their cerebral approach to managing. So they were able to reintegrate the two threads—the thinking-man catcher and the tough-guy catcher—that had split apart after the advent of equipment.

When observers began taking a fresh look at the catching position, they saw that it still required great toughness. This had been true all along, but the catchers of the late 1880s and 1890s had earned little recognition because of the inevitable comparisons to their predecessors. Twentieth-century catchers were at last freed from this burden and began earning deserved praise for their courage.

This welcome change was conveyed with particular force in a witty 1909 article in a Washington newspaper that informed its readers:

"A baseball catcher is a cross between a bomb-proof [shelter] and an octopus. His duty is to stand up for nine innings each day and be shot at by a six-foot pitcher with shoulders like a coal digger, and a baseball for a bullet. He must catch this baseball instead of allowing it to perforate him and return it to the human seige [sic] gun. His job is like that of the octopus because he is not supposed to let anything get past him.

"Being a catcher is pleasanter than trying to capture Port Arthur, but not much. The catcher is supplied with a half bushel of mitten for one hand with which to stop the ball. It is a favorite trick of the pitcher, however, to heave the ball on the off side of the catcher and make him stop it with his bare hand. In this manner a catcher soon acquires a bunch of fingers which look as if they had been braided up and frozen that way. No man who has been a baseball player can ever hope to be a good piano player unless he learns to play with his feet.

"The catcher is the armored cruiser of the baseball diamond. He wears a mask to prevent him from trying to catch foul tips with his teeth and a chest protector stuffed with wind to keep stray balls from burrowing into his thorax and spraining his vermiform appendix. Thus armored he is required to crouch behind the batter, brush the bat out of his eyes, watch the bases, dig wild balls out of the atmosphere, keep the opposing players from sliding home by letting them slide into his ankles with their spiked feet and quarrel with the umpire besides running half a block over small boys after a foul ball every inning. Some men do this for pleasure. But then, others dive off the Brooklyn bridge for pleasure too.

"There have been some very great baseball catchers but none of them have been elected president and most of them have died young. Unless a catcher carefully removes all the baseballs that have been shot into his system, he is likely to become a hopeless invalid at a very early age and to be compelled to retire from baseball altogether or even play on the Washington team."

The comic touches in the article no doubt elicited a chuckle from readers, but as with the Jim Nasium piece, this was humor with a message. And that message was unmistakable: you may not be used to thinking of the catcher as tough, and may even have heard old-timers belittling today's catcher, but take a closer look and you'll see just how tough the position really is.

Others made the same point in a more straightforward manner. The baseball trainer Frank Newhouse, who came to the sport from boxing and knew all about toughness, rejected the notion that the catcher's new equipment had eliminated the need for courage. "Even when well protected by a strong mask, a stoutly compressed protector and a heavy glove," he insisted, "there is more danger in a 'foul tip' or a 'cross' ball than the spectator realizes." The hazards, Newhouse pointed out, remained great: "In the past five years many young catchers have suffered such serious injury that they have been obliged to retire from the game for weeks at a time." After citing several examples, he concluded, "the wonder is not that catchers are hurt behind the bat, but that more are not hurt. For [of] all positions on a team it is the man behind the bat who continually runs the greatest risk."

Philadelphia Phillies manager Hugh Duffy claimed in 1906 that catchers had a new badge of courage. Instead of the deformed fingers that had long served as "monuments for work well done," Duffy pointed to a different part of the body. "Did you ever know the mark of the star catcher?" he asked rhetorically. "Fingers with knots on them? Not at all. They are the signs of poor catchers, for your good catcher will seldom get his fingers in the way of foul balls to the extent in that he gets badly damaged. No, the mark of the good catcher—the sign of the man who gets a quick start after everything and is ready to make a throw in any direction—is a set of turned-in toes." Duffy explained that his catcher, Charlie "Red" Dooin, was now pigeon-toed, though, "previous to becoming a catcher his feet pointed out as straight as those of any Indian. But as soon as he began getting the hang of the inside work of catching his toes began to get his feet in position to make a quick start either to the right or to the left. Now, when Dooin walks along the street you get the impression that he is liable to step on his own feet every moment—and the fact that he has made a star catcher out of himself is responsible for this condition."

This part of Duffy's claim was corroborated by catcher Steve O'Neill's description of how he prepared to spring out of a stoop or crouch to throw to bases or field bunts. According to O'Neill, "When ready to receive the pitch I favor having the right foot just a little back of the left foot, say a matter of about four inches. I have found that such a position enables the catcher to get the ball away much more quickly than when standing with both feet even up. Getting the ball away quickly means everything to the catcher."

Duffy's belief that good catchers were no longer subject to hand injuries, however, does not stand up to scrutiny. According to Newhouse, "even in the best ordered game [the catcher's] hands have to undergo a terrible bruising. . . . You will often observe if you are a devotee of the game that all ballplayers have one or more broken or twisted fingers, but the most crippled of the lot are the hands of the catcher. Just notice the throwing hand of any of them and you will see how all the knuckles are enlarged and distorted." After the 1908 season, Billy Sullivan was described as "a real hero. He begged permission to catch the final game in Cleveland although two rows of stitches had been removed from his right thumb only the day before. . . . The nature of his injury must have made his work agony, but he stuck to the job." And George Gibson, universally recognized as one of the best defensive catchers of the early twentieth century, reported: "Catching's a pretty rough deal and you better love it or do something else for a living. Every finger on my right hand has been broken at least twice. I have two sons, George and Bill, both of whom are medical doctors in Pittsburgh, and one of them once X-rayed that hand. He couldn't believe the number of times each finger had been broken." Catchers hadn't traded mangled fingers for turned-in toes—many of them now had both.

Other parts of their bodies continued to take unusual abuse, which the new breed of catchers endured with as much courage as any of their predecessors. Bill Killefer reached the big leagues in 1909 and in one of his first games was struck in the collarbone by a foul tip. Umpire Billy Evans "felt certain that Killefer's collarbone had been broken. I told him this and suggested that he go to the bench. He refused to do so and insisted on finishing out the inning. The inning was a long one and twice Killefer nipped men stealing by wonderful throws to second. At the end of the session he went to the bench, sat down and practically fainted away. A doctor was called and it was found that the collarbone had been broken. How the youngster ever continued playing when so badly hurt I cannot imagine. Those two throws to second must have caused great agony."

Catchers also now had a new way to prove their fortitude because of the increasing number of home-plate collisions. As late as the 1880s, collisions between fielders and base runners had been rare and had attracted much negative comment. During the 1890s fielder interference became rampant, but it usually involved standing in a runner's way rather than initiating contact. Tim Murnane complained in the middle of that decade, "The league rule makers would do the game a big favor by allowing the runner to get home without having to push the catcher out of the way."

But in the new century, with scoring once again scarce, catchers began forcing base runners to go *through* them in order to reach home plate. In a 1902 account, sportswriter Ren Mulford, Jr., described Cincinnati base runner Harry Steinfeldt arriving at home plate well in advance of a relay throw, only to find St. Louis catcher John O'Neill "squatted over the plate as if he owned it." By the time Steinfeldt was able to touch the plate, the ball had arrived, and he was called out. Mulford noted that interference could have been called, but added that "there isn't an umpire in the land who enforces that section [of the rulebook] if he can dodge it."

Naturally such tactics continued and became a new way for catchers to demonstrate their courage. "Catcher [Fred] Abbott, of the Phillies, is

a good plate blocker," read an approving 1905 note. "He fears no man."
Jimmy Callahan said of Bill Carrigan's skill at plate-blocking, "You might
as well try to move a stone wall." Catchers had finally found a way to turn
the slighting references to them as "backstops" into a compliment.

The advent of shin guards further encouraged plate-blocking since
catchers' shins were now protected from the runner's spikes. To some extent, indeed, the greater incidence of this tactic was used to justify the new
equipment. Tough-nosed Detroit catcher Charley Schmidt, for example,
rejected Roger Bresnahan's cricket-style shin guards and instead chose "an
elaborate suit of armor on his left leg . . . concealed under his uniform." He
went to considerable lengths to emphasize that the new piece of "armor"
was of no use in preventing wild pitches or injuries on foul tips, insisting
that he wore them only to protect himself against base runners' spikes. The
new equipment and the old tough-guy mentality thus worked in concert
to encourage plate-blocking, and soon the tactic was looked upon as a job
requirement. As a sportswriter put it in 1914, "the practice has developed in
the last couple of years to such an extent that on close plays a catcher who
does not plant himself in the lines is not considered as doing his duty."

Even with head-to-toe protection, plate-blocking took great courage
and created a grave new risk of injury. As Newhouse explained, "[The
catcher] is in danger from the pitcher and in danger from the batsman,
while he is just as likely to suffer injury in a scrimmage when a runner
is making a wild dash for the home plate. . . . In a recent game on Puget
Sound one of the runners while sliding to base struck his head against the
leg of the baseman. Concussion of the brain resulted, while the man at
the bag was scarcely less badly bruised. These, of course, may be said to be
the exceptional injuries, but nevertheless they are risks which the catcher
has to take in even a greater degree than any other player on the team.
This accident could have been avoided had the baseman not been so 'set'
as the phrase goes in baseball parlance, which means that he should not
have stood so rigidly at the bag, but have allowed his body that freedom of
movement and laxity that would have insured him giving ground in such
a heavy impact, and so saved both the runner and himself. The observance
of this rule devolves particularly on the catcher, for unless he 'sets' himself
properly at all times, whether catching the batter out or the runner at the
home plate or in throwing to bases, he is likely to strain himself or be injured in some such mix-up as I have described."

Some catchers took advantage of the new equipment to initiate contact. "When a man is coming home from third base," explained Red

Dooin, "the only way to get him is to dive for him and reach him before he reaches you. I stand a little inside of the line, and when I get the ball, lunge my whole body at the runner. Then he can't hurt you, for with shin guards and a heavy chest protector, the catcher is pretty safe. When I first caught, I used to stand to one side and try to tag the runner as he came down the line, or just as he went by, but one summer while I was playing ball in the mountains I noticed a big, husky football player. He never tried to tag a man, but just dove for him, and he seldom missed. After I had seen him work I made up my mind that that was the game for me, and I have always kept it up." Perhaps it was no coincidence that the football player mentioned by Dooin came from "the mountains," since it once again seemed reasonable to compare the catcher to American heroes like the frontiersman and the mountain man.

The new unity of the thinking-man catcher and the tough-guy catcher was made especially apparent by the signals that catchers now flashed to pitchers. Here too a subtle but important change had occurred. As noted earlier, when signals first began to be used to communicate pitch selection, there were differing views as to who should initiate them. Then sign-stealing emerged as a threat, and in the 1890s it became customary for catchers to originate the signs since they could more easily conceal their signals. Neither the signs nor the efforts to conceal them were very sophisticated, however, with the result that sign-stealing remained widespread.

Twentieth-century catchers responded by taking new precautions, the most notable and the most painful one being the catcher's crouch. Most nineteenth-century catchers had stooped, but—despite the example set by Bushong—crouching remained rare until the twentieth century. The catchers of the new century had a number of reasons for rethinking their fielding stance, including the new emphasis on the spitball and on low-ball pitching in general. The primary reason, however, was that the crouch helped a catcher give his signals confidentially. As a 1909 article explained, the catcher "must guard against the batsman peeking back to catch his code. That is why the backstop stoops in calling for balls . . . by crouching he shuts out all possible vision of the batsman." Catchers were forced to crouch still lower a couple of years later when word leaked out that the Athletics had stolen "the signs of big Ed Sweeney, catcher of the Yankees, by having one of the A's players hide behind the water cooler on his stomach. When the backstop gave his signals, he dropped his fingers to the ground and they were clearly visible from beneath the cooler."

The crouch caused the catcher new and different forms of physical discomfort—aching backs and, as explained by Hugh Duffy, pigeon toes. But at the same time it served to emphasize the variety of his contributions to his team. He was again earning respect for the way he sacrificed his body while catching pitches, absorbing foul tips, blocking home plate, and crouching to hide his signals. His ability to spring out of that crouch at a moment's notice also showed that the potbellied catcher of the 1890s had given way to a far more agile model.

Signals also drew attention to the need for catchers who could outthink the other team. With the catcher being scrutinized from so many different angles and by so many different opponents—two base coaches, the batter, his teammates on the bench, and as many as three base runners—it was not always possible to keep the signal concealed. Meanwhile the increasing variety of pitches being used was causing signals to become more complex and was making it still more important to keep them secret. So catchers began encoding their signals by such methods as flashing two different signs with their fingers and using some other way to let the pitcher know which one mattered. When these signals still proved too easy to decipher, the next step was combination signs, by which a series of "visible movements, such as spitting on the hands, hitching up the trousers, pulling at the cap," were relayed.

Former catcher Connie Mack's teams became noted both for relaying indecipherable signals and for their ability to intercept other teams' signs. Once sportswriters and fans became aware of the importance of this cat-and-mouse game, and of the catcher's central place in it, they had another reason to see the catcher in a new light. As one sportswriter wrote in 1910: "the catcher, so the majority of the fans think, is a mere machine that stops the curves thrown by the pitcher the batter misses. . . . The great catcher must be a thinker, an inventor, a man who would make a success of any business calling for a level head."

This growing awareness of the importance of the catcher's signals was accompanied by new recognition of the value of many other little things done by catchers. A 1913 article pointed out that where a catcher held his hands after giving the signal was one of the "little knacks about catching which separate the really great from the ordinary first-class type." It noted that some catchers simply held their glove in the spot where they wanted the pitch to be delivered, a habit that could be noticed by the batter out of the corner of his eye. Thus "Johnny Kling probably was the greatest of modern catchers in concealing what he desired. He would move his knee slightly, indicating the spot he wanted the ball to strike. And he did it in so skillful a manner the batter or the coaches couldn't wise up."

Before long, article after article was recounting in great detail the little things that catchers did. Lengthy descriptions appeared of the footwork used by the catcher to shift from his crouch into a throwing position. Particularly intense scrutiny was given to elements requiring teamwork, such as the various strategies for thwarting a double steal, as well as to descriptions of how a catcher signaled a pickoff play "by turning his mitt over and back rapidly" before the pitch and how he and the baseman then had to synchronize their movements in order to successfully execute the play. Detailed explanations told how catchers applied tags to runners as they slid into the plate and of how the catcher's ability to gain the "friendship and confidence" of the umpires might help a pitcher "get the corners." Readers were regaled with descriptions of how a catcher might try to settle down a struggling pitcher by stopping to retie his shoe or adjust his chest protector. Sometimes these little items were so subtle that it almost seems as though a public relations campaign aimed to attract candidates to fill the shortage of catchers. A decade or two earlier, nothing the catcher did could earn him respect; now reporters seemed to be trying to outdo one another in detecting the value of infinitesimal actions.

Yet it was easy for sportswriters to make a convincing case for the importance of all these "little knacks" because there was so little scoring and so many plays were being used to try to push across a run. The hit-and-run play became a staple of early-twentieth-century offenses and drew attention to the catcher's thinking process. If he anticipated it and called for a pitchout, the day would probably be saved, but if not the batting team might be on its way to a big inning. The squeeze play sprang to prominence in 1905, and it too focused attention on the catcher's ability to outthink the opponents.

Specifically, the squeeze compelled catchers to make wise decisions about when to call for pitchouts. This emphasis was unprecedented because, while pitchouts were not unheard of in the nineteenth century, they were used to give the catcher a better chance of throwing out a base-stealer and were viewed with suspicion. Just as it was believed that a true catcher should be able to handle any pitch without being warned what was coming, so too nineteenth-century thinking was that a competent catcher ought to be able to throw out a base-stealer without the advantage of a pitchout. Calling for a pitchout was therefore seen as an admission of weakness.

The sudden rash of hit-and-run plays and squeeze bunts forced a change in perspective, because the pitchout was the best way to thwart both tactics. As a sportswriter explained in 1908: "A good catcher must, of course, be a good receiver and thrower, but it is with men on bases that a catcher is required to display judgment. He must know the game and realize when his opponents are going to do a certain thing and block their play. The hit and run game, for instance, can only be broken up by the catcher. He must know when the base runner is going to steal, and in order to prevent the batsman from helping the runner, he wastes the ball, which means to have the pitcher pitch it out of reach of the batsman, so that he cannot hit and at the same time gives the catcher a clear throw to second or third, as the case may be." If a catcher called for a pitchout and foiled the opponent's plan, his wise decision made him a hero. Even if he called for one and no play was on, fans and sportswriters understood that he was trying to outthink the other team and were likely to give him credit for the attempt. Baseball was becoming a chess match, and it was the catcher who made the pivotal decisions.

As umpire Billy Evans put it, "Baseball is largely a game of trying to outguess the other fellow. Each side is trying to do the unexpected, and at the same time attempting to keep up its defense by constantly doing its best to anticipate what the other fellow really intends to do. Perhaps there is no cog in a baseball machine that plays a more prominent part in the team's success or failure than the catcher. A good, brainy catcher is invaluable in breaking up the best laid plans of the opposition. Fandom doesn't realize the importance of the part a 'heady' receiver plays in the grand old game of 'hit 'em where they ain't.'" Johnny Evers and Hugh S. Fullerton echoed Evans's contention, declaring that "mechanical mistakes form no criteria by which to judge a catcher. His greatest errors are those of judgment, his worst blunders are the ones the spectators never see."

Evans added that the outcome of games now hung in the balance as these maneuvers and countermaneuvers were being made: "So great is the power of the backstop in directing the play of a team, that it is possible for him to tangle up the contest in more ways than one, if outguessed by the opposition." Just as important was the corollary: a catcher who outthought the other team could lead his side to victory, and could even receive credit for doing so.

Once fans and observers recognized the number of crucial decisions being made by the catcher, the next point that needed to be established was that heady catchers relied upon more than mere guesswork. Some

Diminutive Ray Schalk became the epitome of the new breed of thinking catchers of the teens. As Schalk explained, possessing "baseball brains" didn't necessarily make a man an intellectual: "[A man] might know a lot of philosophy or Greek literature and be a frost on foul flies. . . . I used to play in the minors with a graduate of a well known university who was a brilliant scholar and good natural athlete. But he was positively the limit in playing baseball. He would do the most incomprehensible things. In fact he was impossible." *(National Baseball Hall of Fame Library)*

catchers in fact did little more than guess, as was explained by a sportswriter in a revealing 1909 article. He noted sarcastically that those receivers used "the 'rule of three,' apparently" when calling pitchouts—in other words, they signaled for one on every third pitch. Those catchers' teams were usually beaten by ones whose catchers used a more sophisticated decision-making process. The sportswriter concluded that it was this latter group of catchers "whose worth is recognized by their managers, and who are getting the money. The average fan does not detect this difference in backstops, but the wise manager does." Articles like this showed that heroism had returned to the catching position but in a new form: the catcher didn't need to endure pain to be considered a hero.

Catchers were delighted by this new understanding of the importance of what became known as "baseball brains," and they did their best to encourage it. Naturally none of them were willing to admit that they used the "rule of three," so they occasionally tossed in subtle hints showing that they belonged to the group of catchers who made smart decisions. Malachi Kittridge, for example, explained that with teams now relying on the hit-and-run and squeeze play for so much of their offense, "If they strike a dub catcher on the opposing team their work is easy. If they strike a wise fellow back there it's all up. I guess I have broken up a hundred attempts to win a game on the hit and run play." Kittridge also was at pains to explain that making the right decision was not mere guesswork: "The catcher has to watch every move on the diamond. He has to foresee an attempt of the opposing side to pull off a hit and run play or get a stolen base. This consequently keeps his mind working every minute. If he thinks the hit and run is coming off he simply signifies the pitcher to 'pitch out' and if he doesn't nail the man at second he will at least break the play. It is often up to him to have a batter 'walked' to prevent anything spectacular coming off. . . . Give me a good set of catchers and a good fielding club and you can take all the sluggers you want. In the long run we will beat you out."

In similar fashion, Hall of Fame catcher Ray Schalk gave a lengthy description of his thought process that used such phrases as "watched like a hawk," "have the dope," "proved to me how foolish," "use judgment," "study," "we rehearsed all of the batters," "on the lookout," and "the winning percentage," but never once used the word "guess." Fellow catcher Steve O'Neill did use that word but was careful to emphasize that an attentive catcher could hold guesswork to a minimum. "Watch the batsman and base runner in trying to outguess them," he counseled. "The runner on first invariably tips off the catcher when he intends to go down. Knowing this, the catcher can call for a pitchout, thereby increasing his chances to spoil the steal of second or the hit-and-run."

With pitchers increasingly relying on catchers to make these decisions, the man behind the plate began to be viewed as the brainy half of the partnership. The comments of catchers frequently reinforced that perception. New York Giants catcher Jack Warner made pitchers sound like willful children in need of guidance when he commented: "A new pitcher may probably have some pet curve or drop which he has worked successfully in the minor league. Let him have his way, and he will want to toss this favorite curve to every batsman that steps to the plate. He may fool the players for a while, but when they get the hang of this curve it's all off with the youngster. The first principle in developing a new man is to teach him to get command of the ball. Good control of the ball is essential to a pitcher's success. After he has learned to put them over or around the plate as you signal for him to so, the hardest part of a catcher's work is done. If the pitcher insists upon using his pet curve too often, he must be broken of the habit. . . . If a youngster has a good curve or raised ball, the thing is to develop this curve until he masters it to perfection. Then he should be taught to change his pace; that is, use the same motion in delivering the ball, but change the curve. . . . A pitcher to be successful must work in harmony with the catcher. The man behind the bat is generally in a better position to know the weakness of certain players, and if the pitcher follows the catcher's instructions the chances are in many cases they will gain their point." In effect the pitcher was once again being likened to a wild horse that needed to be broken, while the catcher was the skilled rider who instilled control and discipline.

Other commentators were more subtle but made a similar point. "The catcher rather than the pitcher is the real mainspring of a baseball machine," explained one sportswriter. "Stationed behind the batsmen, he has greater opportunities than the pitcher for observing what a certain batter can and cannot hit. Knowing the man with whom he works, he can tell if his curves are breaking right, can make him work slowly when inclined to hurry and can make him hustle when he is inclined to slowness." Ray Schalk stressed the importance of careful observation: "Keep mixing them up on a batter and before you give your signal to the pitcher watch the batter—watch how he grips the bat, how he stands and where you think he's going to try to hit it." Schalk's choice of words again serves to portray the catcher as a man who made well-reasoned decisions and was a student of the game, rather than one who called pitches at random. Johnny Evers and Hugh Fullerton developed the point further, explaining that a catcher had to carefully consider at least three different variables: "Besides first hand knowledge of a batter's possibilities, the catcher must look closely each time he comes to bat, first to see what kind of a bat he carries; second, to observe the position of his feet and body, upon which positions the direction of his hit depend, and third to see how he is gripping his bat, in order to guess his designs."

The point hammered home by all these depictions was that the catcher was not a man who guessed what pitch might fool the batter; instead, in the Daniel Boone model of heroism, he carefully analyzed a complex situation that involved multiple variables and then used his experience to make an informed decision. Just as Boone's intelligence had been differentiated from book learning, and just as the cowboy relied upon "horse sense," and just as Ulysses S. Grant possessed the knack of making decisions with bullets flying all around, so too the "baseball brains" of the catcher were a very different thing from educational qualifications. "A catcher must have baseball brains," Ray Schalk explained. "It isn't enough to say brains, you must add the adjective 'baseball' to describe what you mean. . . . [A man] might know a lot of philosophy or Greek literature and be a frost on foul flies . . . I used to play in the minors with a graduate of a well known university who was a brilliant scholar and good natural athlete. But he was positively the limit in playing baseball. He would do the most incomprehensible things. In fact he was impossible."

Schalk acknowledged that players at every position had "baseball brains," citing infielders Hans Wagner and Nap Lajoie and outfielder Ty Cobb as examples. It was at his own position, however, that Schalk insisted this aptitude was essential: "the catcher, above all men, must have a good baseball brain. . . . The catcher, much more than the pitcher, holds the game in the hollow of his hand. The catcher, much more than the pitcher, is the keystone of the baseball arch." The catcher was regaining both his indispensability and his status as the heir to self-taught natural philosophers like Daniel Boone.

It also mattered that the catcher had not usurped the responsibility for making these decisions but had assumed them because practical factors such as his proximity to the batter made him better qualified for the role. As one manager explained, the catcher "is in a position to see everything on the field. He must try to outguess the enemy hitters by telling his pitcher how to cross them at critical moments."

In the 1880s the rigors of the position had meant that catchers were often given more days off than pitchers. As late as 1888, Johnny Ward suggested that when a battery duo worked in tandem, it was the *catcher* who might need extra rest: "to be able to work regularly with one pitcher through an entire season, catching every day when he pitches, a catcher will more than once find his powers of endurance strongly taxed." By the new century, everything had changed. The advent of the mitt and the decision to move pitchers farther from home plate had enabled many catchers to carry heavy workloads. By contrast, the new distance had put a tremendous strain on pitchers' arms, so teams began to use three or four starters on a regular basis, and to have several additional hurlers on hand for relief duty. This enabled catchers to acquire a much greater familiarity with the tendencies of opposing batters, and reinforced their role as principal decision-maker. As Pat Moran noted, "The catcher, owing to the fact that he works in almost every game, knows the weaknesses of the various batters, and the pitchers set great store on this very thing."

These factors in turn influenced how signals were perceived. During the 1880s, as we've seen, catchers were the originators of signals, but pitchers frequently overruled them by shaking them off (or even by throwing a different pitch). The decision about which pitch to throw was effectively a joint one. These new developments, however, meant that by the twentieth century it was the norm for the catcher to make the final call and to receive the credit (or blame) for doing so. By 1917, Billy Evans could write: "Rarely does a pitcher take the initiative. . . . As a rule the twirler leaves it up to his catcher, particularly if the backstop is a brainy receiver. There are many catchers who resent the shake of the head by the pitcher, signaling he does not want to pitch the ball the catcher called for. Some of the more sensitive backstops feel such action is being shown up before the crowd. I know many catchers and pitchers who have a working agreement not to shake the head negatively when failing to agree with the catcher. The desire to change the signal is made known in some other way, either by stepping off the rubber, or making it appear he didn't catch the sign when first given." Once catchers had prided themselves on being able to handle any pitch without knowing what was coming; now, as Evans's comments suggest, they took similar pride in deciding which pitch to call.

The sense that the pitcher was once again the dependent member of the battery increased with the emergence of each elusive new pitch that could only be handled by a skilled catcher. As Connie Mack explained, "A catcher can make a pitcher look good or bad, especially if the pitcher is a young fellow." He vividly illustrated this by describing a scouting trip he made to watch a pitcher named Lefty Russell. Russell was paired with a young catcher, and Mack saw some potential but was unsure of whether the pitcher had a good enough curveball until veteran catcher Ben Egan replaced the youngster. "As soon as Egan went behind the bat," Mack recounted, "there was a wonderful change in 'Lefty.' Right away Russell began to use his curve, and I made up my mind then and there that I had to have that 'southpaw.'"

With pitchers relying so heavily on catchers, some teams began to hire receivers as the game's first pitching coaches. Before the 1906 season, ageless catcher Jim McGuire was put in "charge of the pitchers of the Highlanders who are working at Hot Springs." During the next two decades every man who was identified as a major league pitching coach—Wilbert Robinson, Joe Sugden, Jack Ryan, Charley "Duke" Farrell, Dan Howley, Lou Criger,

Pat Moran, and Grover Land—was a former catcher. Several of these men used the position as a stepping-stone to a successful managerial career, beginning a still-thriving tradition of ex-catchers being disproportionately likely to become managers.

At the same time there was new recognition of the many other responsibilities that were handled by the catcher—and, in particular, to the thought process behind them. Several catchers helped to revive the hustling play of backing up potential overthrows at first and even at third base. A couple of catchers brought back Nat Hicks's trick of calling for a deliberate passed ball. Some new twists were added, most notably a scheme devised by Phillies catcher Morgan Murphy in 1900 by which a man stationed outside the ballpark used binoculars to steal the opposing catcher's signals, with an electrical buzzer buried near third base to relay them to the base coach. (The scheme was detected on a rainy day when someone found it odd that a Phillies coach kept standing with his foot in a puddle.)

Catchers even began to earn recognition for functions they had always handled. A 1904 article reported, quite inaccurately, "Formerly the catcher signaled to the pitcher only. Today his signals govern not only the pitcher, but the infield decidedly and the outfield in lesser degree." Now that more fielders were being deployed to handle bunts, new attention was paid to the advice the catcher gave to the teammate who fielded the ball. Steve O'Neill explained, "The catcher should always tell the pitcher at what base to make a play, when a ground ball is hit to him. Particular care must be taken to do this on a sacrifice play, where one or more chances are offered to retire a player. The catcher has the play in front of him, the pitcher has his back to it. The coaching of the catcher is most important." Catchers were similarly earning new recognition for their skill in throwing to the bases. Charley Schmidt convinced sportswriter Ernest Lanigan that a statistic should be introduced to measure catchers' success rates in nabbing base-stealers, and the numbers that Lanigan compiled were widely reprinted. When Bill Bergen gunned down six would-be base-stealers in a 1909 game, the accomplishment was widely hailed (and the figure was inflated to seven in the retelling). This must have irked Charley Farrell, who had thrown out eight base-stealers in an 1897 game but whose feat had received little acclaim and had long since been forgotten.

Although the early-twentieth-century catcher was not the center of attention as the receiver of the 1870s had been, the careful observer could see he was again the center of the action. "The catcher is 'the man behind the gun' in scientific baseball," noted one sportswriter, "but, like the trainer of a great racehorse, he seldom receives the credit that is due him. He is constantly doing work for which the thinking spectator gives him little or no credit, but which is of the first importance to the team. The first class catcher judges from the batsman's actions what he is likely to do and communicates his knowledge to the pitcher and to the rest of the players by means of signals. He watches the base runners in order to keep the twirler informed of what is going on, and signals when to throw to catch a man napping. He backs up the first or third baseman on long throws from the field and in general is the right man in the right place at all times."

Perhaps most important, catchers no longer felt haunted by the need to live up to an inimitable model of toughness. This was aptly symbolized when Nat Hicks, shortly before his death, went to watch his son Bill catch for the semipro Hoboken Xenias. Bill Hicks was worried that his father would be disgusted by the changes to the catching position, since, as he put it, "I had a glove and mask, which was a lot more than he ever used." Instead the grizzled veteran's paternal instincts carried the day—"he took one look at me behind the plate and said, 'My god, he'll be killed.'"

All these developments suggested that the process of reconciling the tough-guy and thinking-man schools of catching had finally begun. This in turn allowed the catcher's old mystique to reappear. To be sure, the catcher's image had been updated and modified to take into account baseball's new "scientific" status. Nonetheless a surprising number of the components of the new mystique were familiar.

Catching again came to be regarded as a mysterious craft, which could truly be mastered only by a select few artisans. "Here and there an exceptionally great catcher is to be seen," remarked one account, "a man who is a marvel at taking the rifleshot of the pitcher, throwing to bases, chasing the foul flies and engineering the game as only the great catcher can really do." As of old, players talked about the "natural" catcher who could effortlessly accomplish what others could not do at all. Jack Warner, for instance, was said to "[handle] the delivery of the different pitchers with equal ease. As the saying goes, he could sit in a rocking chair and catch the balls, so apt is he with his hands." According to Honus Wagner, Ray Schalk was "the most natural catcher of them all. He actually makes the work look easy."

There was again talk about how the subtle nature of the catcher's craft made it difficult to judge a catcher from afar. "How are you going to tell a good catcher?" Schalk asked rhetorically in a 1917 article. He proceeded to discuss the question at some length without actually answering it. He dismissed all statistics because "they haven't any direct connection with good, bad or indifferent catching as such." He was just as insistent that nobody could judge a catcher unless they had played the position: "Most of [the catcher's] work, the most important part of his work, is hidden from the spectators' eye. The man in the stands can seldom follow what is going on in the catcher's brain."

This point was made in even more dramatic fashion in 1911 when Connie Mack was asked whom he considered to be the game's best catcher. He shocked reporters by naming Ira Thomas, who was considered to be "below the average as a mechanical catcher." Mack acknowledged that "the batting and fielding averages aren't any too complimentary to [Thomas]. Probably a dozen men can throw to bases better than Ira; he isn't fast, and he isn't a great receiver, but nonetheless I would rather have Thomas behind the bat than any catcher in the game. I'll tell you the reason. Ira can get more out of a pitcher than any catcher I know of." Catching was once again so mysterious a craft that a catcher's work could be judged only by a fellow practitioner.

This in turn led to the reemergence of the corresponding idea that, in the tradition of Doug Allison and Billy Holbert, a catcher might have a misleading outward appearance but an inner worth that would manifest itself when he was put to the test. Sometimes all he needed was a chance to play regularly. At one minor league stop, Lou Criger at first saw little playing time because the team already had a couple of more experienced catchers. So he "sat on the bench a long time . . . until these vets got banged up one day, whereupon the tenderfoot went in and killed off six men stealing second." The slightly built Bill Killefer had an even harder time when the Philadelphia Phillies brought him up from the minors. According to Grover Cleveland Alexander, his new teammates "took a look at him and almost decided not to let him even sit on the bench. Catchers then were usually big, strapping fellows of the type of Roger Bresnahan, and Killefer weighed less than 150 [pounds]. They did let him have a little corner of the bench at last." But eventually "they had to let Killefer try his hand. And when they let him get in there they never could get him out." Alexander and Killefer soon became one of the game's greatest batteries.

Others were stuck at alternate positions until they were given a chance behind the plate, at which point their true value became immediately apparent. Billy Sullivan, for instance, was a shortstop "until an accident left his team without a catcher. Without any previous experience he was put in to catch and found it was his natural position." Roger Bresnahan was a pitcher until he popped off to John McGraw about the team's lack of a good catcher. McGraw angrily retorted, "If you are so smart, why don't you go in there and catch?" So Bresnahan did just that, with familiar results: "The first ball Joe [McGinnity] threw hit me on the finger, and it shows the marks to this day, but I went ahead, and caught the rest of the game. I never pitched another championship game. From that time on I was a catcher. I never thought catching was hard."

What all these descriptions have in common is the idea that a catcher's real merit could be gauged only when he was under pressure. Jack Warner, wrote one sportswriter approvingly, "is not afraid to make a play even in the most dangerous situations and he has won many a game and choked off many a batting rally of his opponents by a quick, heady throw to first, second or third, catching some too anxious base runner 'napping.' It is just this courage, this grit he shows in tight places, that has made Warner as solid as he is with the baseball loving public. 'Take a chance every time' is his watchword. There are some catchers who enjoy reputations as stars who develop a yellow streak in pinch situations, and, through fear of making an error, will not take a chance. But Warner is not of that caliber." Another scribe was more succinct: "The catcher is 'the man behind the gun' in scientific baseball."

Renewed faith in the notion that a catcher's inner strength might be hidden behind a deceptive appearance led to the revival of other familiar concepts. Most notably, the potbellied catchers of the 1890s faded as the position again became accessible to men of various shapes and sizes. The crouch, in particular, made it essential for the catcher to be able to spring from his haunches and into action, which helped bring back the smaller, agile catcher of old.

These slighter men did have to overcome considerable initial skepticism about their ability to endure the punishment of the position. Charlie "Red" Dooin, for example, weighed only 110 pounds when he started college at St. Xavier's (now Xavier University) in Cincinnati around 1898. The captain of the baseball team took one look at him and declared that he didn't want any "little runts" around. Breaking into professional baseball proved even more difficult, as one manager after another sized him up and said, "Why, my boy, I want a catcher, not a jockey." But when given a chance, Dooin proved his worth, and in 1902 he began a fifteen-year major league career.

Similarly the appearance of diminutive Jimmy Stephens at the spring training camp of the St. Louis Browns in 1907 "caused the wise ones to laugh outright. He was a mere strip of a boy and had not yet attained his

majority. He weighed 125 pounds and was as shy and backward as a girl."
Yet like the catchers of old, the "little lad" proved a "revelation" with his
throwing and ability to handle "the terrible shoots of the giant [Jack] Powell and [Fred] Glade with ease," which "immediately won him a place in
the hearts of the St. Louis fans." Ray Schalk likewise had to confront the
stereotype that a catcher needed to "possess brawn" before being given the
chance to prove himself. Once given the opportunity, Schalk emerged as
one of the greatest of defensive catchers.

The success of these small catchers was more than just an opportunity
for specific men; it earned new respect for the athletic demands of the
position. As noted by Grover Cleveland Alexander, Bill Killefer was yet
another catcher who had a hard time earning a chance in the major leagues
because of his slight build. When Killefer developed into a defensive standout, however, it led to a reexamination of some of the stereotypes about
the catcher that had sprung up as a result of the introduction of protective
equipment. "The catcher now is more than a mere backstop," concluded
the writer of one especially perceptive article, "inserted to break the impact
of pitched balls against the grand stand planks. . . . The time has gone by
when the ideal catcher was considered a mountain of beef and bone, something that could stand any kind of knocks and, as long as he was successful
as a battering ram, mattering not what his other qualities might be. . . .
The old iron man has given way to the more delicate structure of steel and
Killifer [sic] is one of that sort, built on graceful lines, but able to give and
take with the best of them."

Another familiar notion that reemerged was the depiction of the
catcher as a man who, in the tradition of frontiersmen like Daniel Boone,
was ill at ease in the big city. This image was often artificially cultivated,
as was especially clear in the instance of Roger Bresnahan, who became
known as the "Duke of Tralee" on the basis of oft-repeated tales about how
he was born in Tralee, Ireland, and came to the States as a "mere broth of a
lad." Some of these accounts had Bresnahan developing his strong throwing arm by hurling square potatoes in the Irish countryside. In fact the
star catcher had never spent a day of his childhood in Ireland, having been
born after his parents had immigrated to Toledo, Ohio.

The concept of the catcher having to complete a rite of passage was
also revived. Jack Warner contended that a ballplayer became a big leaguer
only when he displayed the necessary character traits. "The players in the
big leagues," he maintained, "are seasoned and understand the game thoroughly. They execute plays in an easy, graceful manner that is a revelation

to most of the new men." By contrast, Warner argued that "young ball-players breaking in the big leagues . . . unless they are cool and nervy, fight the ball in trying to duplicate the same plays, and generally with disastrous results." Sound familiar?

Warner's manager, the legendary John McGraw, suggested a way to test for these traits. Like many managers, McGraw found himself "besieged by a lot of well meaning persons who think that they can play ball and insist on being tried out personally by McGraw." Yet the Giants manager was still attached to the nineteenth-century belief that a natural ballplayer might be lurking behind the most unlikely of appearances and couldn't bring himself to dismiss such applicants. So he devised "a scheme to rid himself of the extra work. Taking an ordinary fielder's glove, he cut out the padding from the inside, leaving the single layer of leather over the palm of the hand. When an ambitious young person requested a session, the manager would take down the glove in question and hand it to the candidate. Then McGraw would carelessly deliver a few dozen tobacco inshoots, and the victim, knowing he had a glove, would persevere till his hands were puffed to the size of Westphalian hams. It is a fact that not one of the young men who have worn Dr. McGraw's patent catching glove ever asked for a second trial." As with the descriptions of Jim Whitney's pitching and of Silver Flint's first session with a young pitcher, this account clearly evokes the method a cowboy used to break in a horse.

Also reappearing was the old notion that a catcher didn't necessarily have to excel at other aspects of the game. As Patsy Donovan put it, "Now-adays a catcher is supposed to be simply a catcher—a sort of privilege[d] character. . . . He is there to catch and not to hit, run bases or stir up the game like a red-tailed demon." A sportswriter in 1909 enumerated instances of starting catchers who were feeble hitters and "mere lumber on the paths." The most dramatic example was Bill Bergen, the younger brother of Marty, who made weak-hitting predecessors such as Holbert look like sluggers. Bill Bergen had sufficient at bats to qualify for the batting title in 1909 despite a brutal .139 batting average, then outdid himself two years later by hitting .132.

This, of course, was not a new development, and the only thing truly new was some of the imaginative explanations for the ineptitude of catchers in other facets of the game. Weak-hitting Malachi Kittridge, for example, contended that "catchers, as a rule, do not hit well, because they have so much on their minds. When they go to the bat they are generally exhausted mentally and physically." Meanwhile several catchers offered new reasons why so many receivers lacked foot speed. Frank Snyder maintained that the "ice wagon catcher of the present" was the result of the "continual crouching position, which . . . is very tough on the legs until he gets used to it. And when he does get used to it it merely means that certain muscles in his legs have become hardened and these muscles don't favor his running any." Conversely, Larry McLean argued: "Some of the critics say the crouching position has resulted in the slowness of our limbs, but it's more the fact that we stand rooted like large shot towers, or Gibraltars, or other majestic, noble institutions, through so long a period with the armor helping to push our feet down into the soil. How can a man help getting slow when he is practically set and fixed in one spot?" Kittridge cunningly tried to have it both ways. According to a 1914 article, he had come to believe "that a lot of catchers ruin whatever speed they may have when young by their method of squatting before every pitched ball to give the pitcher the signal. When he was a catcher, Malachi did not do that so much as the modern backstop does, because in those days the catcher did not stay close under the bat except when there were two strikes or three balls called, or runners on the bases. But Kit uses it as an alibi for his own slowness just the same."

These rationales, however, no longer mattered much, since it was once again accepted that a catcher's defensive prowess could offset any drawbacks in other facets of the game. "In most cases," observed a sportswriter in 1909, "the catcher of today is weak at the bat, slow-footed and useless when running bases, and unable to render a good account of himself in any other position. And yet, so important is the catcher's task all this is forgiven in the modern catcher, and if he is an artistic specialist behind the bat he is eagerly engaged at an enormous salary."

Yet while catchers didn't need speed on the bases, they did have to be quick. This paradox was nicely captured by the example of Bill Killefer. Early in his career, Killefer was speedy enough to steal quite a few bases in the minor leagues, so it is possible that his nickname, "Reindeer Bill," was originally intended as a compliment. But after years of crouching he became so slow that fellow catcher Benny Bengough maintained, "Neither of us could run any faster than Yertle the Turtle. That's why they called him 'Reindeer Bill.'" Even then, however, Killefer remained quick on his feet, prompting sportswriter Hugh S. Fullerton to revive a once-popular simile. Fullerton described Killefer as "one of these hustling, agile, cat-like moving catchers that have become so popular in modern baseball."

In a limited way, the position again offered a beacon of opportunity to members of racial minorities. The 1880s had seen a significant number

As a Native American, John Tortes "Chief" Meyers had to overcome prejudice just to reach the major leagues. One minor league pitcher tried to embarrass him by crossing him up, so Meyers responded by no longer giving signs and catching whatever was thrown. Although nearly twenty-nine when he reached the majors with the Giants, Meyers became Christy Mathewson's favorite catcher and played in four World Series. *(National Baseball Hall of Fame Library)*

of African Americans playing professional baseball alongside whites, with catcher Moses Fleetwood Walker being among the most prominent and the only one to get an extensive chance to play in the major leagues. But as the decade drew to a close, men of color were slowly dropped from the rosters of organized baseball. One of the last to be let go was Walker, and, as suggested earlier, it was no coincidence that his release occurred at the same time the introduction of the catcher's mitt was robbing great defensive catchers of their value.

By the twentieth century the odious color line was being enforced too strictly for exceptions to become common, even in the case of an outstanding defensive catcher. Yet the reemergence of the position's prestige and the belief in the scarcity of good catchers did lead to a few instances in which prejudice was overlooked. An African-American catcher named Bill Thompson spent the entire season in the Twin State League in 1911 without encountering problems. While the Twin State League had not signed the National Agreement that would have made it a part of organized baseball, the circuit did maintain a good working relationship with the leagues that had signed, making the lack of controversy over Thompson's presence noteworthy. Two years later another team in the same league tried to use an African-American pitcher, only to be met with their opponent's refusal to take the field.

An even more interesting example involved the Native American catcher John "Chief" Meyers. When Meyers made his professional debut with Harrisburg in 1906, one of the team's pitchers tried to make him look bad by crossing him up. Meyers responded in the same way that Fleetwood Walker once had: "After that I didn't give him any signs at all. Because I was on my own then, I wasn't expecting anything, and I could catch him. 'What's the matter, you're not giving any signs?' he yelled in at me. 'What's the use?' I said. 'You go ahead and pitch.' And I caught him." Meyers earned his teammates' respect and went on to a long and successful major league career.

Another time-honored belief that returned to prominence was that of a mystical bond between pitcher and catcher. Not surprisingly, it was on the Philadelphia Athletics, managed by former catcher Connie Mack, where this was most evident. The eccentric southpaw Rube Waddell and the catcher Ossee Schreckengost comprised the best-known duo and, as in the fabled combinations of old, Schreckengost seemed to be the perfect complement for a pitcher whose offerings tormented other receivers. As Billy Evans put it, "Any catcher who has caught 'Rube' in recent years will tell you that he is a hard man to handle for a dozen different reasons. Yet ask Schreck about 'Rube,' the man who caught Waddell when he was in his prime, when he was the terror of all batsmen, and he will tell you that Waddell was the easiest proposition to catch, of any man he ever worked behind."

Mack continued to use such pairings after both Waddell and Schreckengost departed. In 1910 the Athletics won the World Series although their three pitchers with the most victories each preferred to work with a different catcher. One of these duos, spitballer Cy Morgan and catcher Paddy Livingston, afforded an especially good example of the striking parallels between the spitball era and the curveball era of three decades earlier. When asked about his battery mate many years later, Livingston explained that Morgan was unable to win when any other catcher worked. "You see, Cy was a right-hander who threw a spitter," he added, "and the ball broke down and away; I'd stop it with my bare hand most of the time." Then, by way of illustration, he held up his twisted hands and gnarled fingers.

The Athletics were far from alone in reviving these once-common partnerships. The 1910 season also saw Russ Ford ascend to stardom while using Ed Sweeney to catch his elusive emery ball. Another famous duo was Cy Young and Lou Criger, who worked together for a decade and "belonged together like ham and eggs." When they were finally separated, after some four hundred games together, Young commented sadly, "I've pitched to [Criger] so long that he seems a part of me, and I am positive no one will suffer from the departure more than I. . . . It means that I have to learn a great deal about the batters, features to which I had heretofore paid no attention."

A final development that helped restore the prestige of the catcher involved his equipment. The 1880s and 1890s had seen steady increases in the extent and prominence of the catcher's equipment and a corresponding belief among "many spectators" that the once-dangerous position had become "largely a mechanical one, a sinecure because of the chest protector, mask and large padded mit [sic]." Although shin guards had come along in 1907 to complete the ensemble, the "howls" they caused were soon offset by a reduction in the size of mitts.

According to Steve O'Neill, catchers gradually began to abandon the notion of "the bigger the glove the better." He explained: "I have used any number of models, and find by experience that a small glove is much better suited to the varied uses the catcher must put it to. A big glove is really a hindrance in handling a slow hit ground ball in front of the plate. A small pocket that is well broken in retains pitched balls much better than the larger pocket of the big glove. In touching a runner, the smaller, more compact glove enables the catcher to get a firmer grip on the ball, thereby greatly eliminating the chance of dropping the ball after having touched out the runner." The use of smaller gloves sent the welcome message that catchers were again relying upon their skill rather than upon a mitt so spacious that it reminded old-timers of a fishing net.

Together these developments worked to reestablish another familiar idea: the belief that a good catcher was indispensable. By 1904 it was "a much mooted question as to which is the most important to a team—the catcher or the pitcher." As the effects of the spitball and the other new pitches began to be appreciated, the catcher steadily gained respect. It became accepted wisdom that a club had little "chance to win a pennant without the service of two high class catchers." In 1907, Malachi Kittridge commented, "Show me a ball club with a catcher who uses his head, whether he can hit a balloon or a bass fiddle or not, and I will show you a club that is one, two, three in the race. . . . No club ever won a championship without a good catcher." As a catcher, Kittridge was naturally biased, but countless others echoed his claim. An article the following year observed, "[John] McGraw and Clark Griffith have often said that the catcher is the most important and responsible man on a ball team, and they are right. No championship was ever won without a good catcher, and no world's championship was ever won without a wonderful catcher." Another sportswriter concluded that, "The catcher is, all things considered, the most valuable player on the club. He coordinates the various parts of the baseball machine. . . . More clamor greets the appearance of the new star twirler. More interest centers in the great batter. But all managers know the worth of a clever catcher and realize that a star back stop is one of the rarest finds in baseball." Perhaps Fred Clarke put it most succinctly: "A good pitcher can win games, but a great catcher can win pennants."

As these comments suggest, the catchers of the 1910s did not overshadow their teammates as earlier receivers had. Only occasionally were there stories that attached mythical attributes to the new breed of catchers. This was best epitomized by Larry McLean, who, in addition to being the largest player of the day, also had an outsized appetite for liquor and an infectious *joie de vivre* that recalled earlier catchers such as Mike Kelly, Silver Flint, and Lew Brown. McLean became a "popular idol" among Cincinnati fans, who told stories about the giant catcher collaring a murder suspect or swimming the Ohio River so as not to arrive late to the ballpark. Yet the likes of McLean soon faded and were replaced by less colorful but more dependable receivers such as Ivy Wingo. Within a few years of the departure of McLean, Wingo became so popular with Cincinnati fans that they signed a petition to demand that he not be traded.

In the new model, the catcher no longer exhibited the extraordinary feats associated with his predecessors. While still a hero, he now embodied a form of heroism that seemed attainable to a new generation of urban youngsters. He became an Everyman who, to the extent that he stood above his teammates, had earned that elevated status by dint of dedication, careful observation, patience, determination, and leadership.

A very welcome result of this new role was that the early-twentieth-century catcher did not become cloaked in the suspicion that had plagued the catcher of the 1870s. One exception did occur when Boston's Lou Criger was offered a bribe to throw the 1903 World Series by a gambler who told Criger he had been selected "Because you are the only one capable of turning the trick." But while the catcher again played a pivotal role, baseball had achieved a delicate balance so that no player could single-handedly decide the outcome of a game. Incidents like Criger's did not become a trend, and indeed, as the infamous Black Sox scandal later showed, it became necessary to bribe most of the team to ensure a fix.

The catcher's renewed status was reflected in a wealth of new metaphors used to describe him. They downplayed the notion that he was born with superhuman traits and emphasized instead that he had taught himself to be a leader of men. Johnny Evers and Hugh Fullerton commented, "Catching is the pivotal position and the most important in baseball. The catcher is the director or transmitter of all messages, the key-board used by manager or pitcher to flash orders to all others." Malachi Kittridge added, "The catcher is the keynote and director general of the defensive side of baseball." Another sportswriter found a different analogy: "the catcher is as important in a baseball team as the quarter back in a football team. In football the quarter back is the field general when his team is on the offensive. In baseball the catcher is the general on the defensive." Bozeman Bulger maintained that "The catcher is the pivot of a baseball team. Every play revolves around him while his team is on the defensive." And according to Miller Huggins, "A good catcher is the quarterback, the carburetor, the lead dog, the pulse taker, the traffic cop and sometimes a lot of unprintable things, but no team gets very far without one."

Being compared to a carburetor or a pulse taker was a big improvement after the insulting metaphors of the 1890s, but it was still a far cry from the superhuman, godlike attributes once associated with the catcher's position. The man behind the plate could never again bask in the knowledge that by assuming his position he became the beau ideal of an entire community, who filled the "small boys with awe and admiration" and made female hearts flutter. Never again would he stand apart from the other players as the early catcher had done (literally as well as figuratively, now that he was required to stay directly behind the plate through the at bat).

Yet as the new analogies to carburetors and traffic cops suggest, the catcher's contributions were again being acknowledged. The catcher's less prominent position came to be perceived as a sign that he was underrated. "The tendency is to give the pitcher and the men back of him too great prominence," wrote one sportswriter. "Their work is out in the open, where everybody can see it. The catcher's best work is done out of sight, where nobody but the pitcher can see it, carefully concealed from the enemy." "The catcher stands there behind the bat inning after inning and game after game," remarked another sportswriter, "taking a pounding and filling a less spectacular role than any other member of the nine. His work is not as showy. Superficially viewed, he is more of a dray horse than any of his fellows, but in reality he is a great power in the team's success, though often he doesn't come in for as much credit as the players who work more in the open, so to speak." Just as important, because the new model of the catcher seemed attainable, it also proved enduring.

Perhaps nothing did more to cement the new model than the World Series of 1914, 1915, and 1916, each of which was a showdown between teams managed by former catchers. Nor was it the same men over and over: five different catchers managed their teams to pennants in these three years, with only Bill Carrigan capturing more than one flag. Just a decade earlier, when the spitball came to the fore, Connie Mack had been the only former catcher managing a major league club. (Between 1904 and 1906, Mack was responsible for all but one of the major league managing wins achieved by former catchers. See Appendix 2 for details.) Now, in addition to a renewed emphasis on having a good catcher behind the plate, it was also apparent that "catchers are more in demand as managers than any other players in the big league."

As former catchers became entrenched in major league dugouts, they naturally placed a premium on finding heady players to use behind the plate. In 1922 sportswriter Joe Vila reported that scouts who had been dispatched to discover young catchers were returning with the discouraging news that "the natural quality of inexperienced backstops was the poorest in many years." The definition of a "natural" catcher, however, had changed dramatically: "There were numerous mechanical catchers of fair skill, they declared, but no really smart recruits—'receivers' with baseball brains."

Vila added that the best catchers in the major leagues were now considered to be men like Schalk, O'Neill, Cy Perkins, and Frank Snyder, who "not only possess mechanical skill, but also are well equipped with gray matter. They possess a complete knowledge of the weak points of every batsman and, in that way, they are able to coach their pitchers with successful results. 'I'd rather have a brainy catcher with ordinary ability than a wonderful mechanic with an empty head,' said a big league manager during a fanning bee last winter. 'The catcher is the kingpin. He is in a position to see everything on the field. He must try to outguess the enemy hitters by telling his pitcher how to cross them at critical moments. Watch Schalk, O'Neill, Perkins and Snyder closely and maybe you'll discover the headwork they use in directing their pitchers. These fellows know how to steady their boxmen when under fire and they also inspire the other players with confidence.'" At long last the thinking-man catcher and the tough-guy catcher had morphed into a single coherent model.

With catchers again gaining the respect that had been denied the "backstops" of the 1890s, new applicants came to the position with more realistic goals. In the 1890s the catching position had lost talented play-ers like Bobby Lowe, who began his professional career as a catcher but switched positions because he wanted to see action on a daily basis. Now the reverse was happening. Ray Schalk started out as an outfielder but, as he explained, "I wanted more work, I wanted to be right in the thick of every game, where I could see what was going on." His sentiments were echoed by another Hall of Fame catcher of a later generation—Roy Cam-panella recalled that "catching appealed to me as a chance to be in the thick of the game continually."

Once, aspiring catchers had expected to be the center of *attention*. Now they were content with aiming to become the center of the *action*, and to play a crucial but understated role. This less glamorous but more realistic goal enabled the new model of the catcher to become an enduring one.

16

The Catcher's Legacy

"A good catcher is actually a receiver. He receives the ball rather than catches it. The good ones always take the ball in; the poorer ones go for it."—Catcher-turned-manager Charlie Fox

IN THE ninety-some years since the new model became established, the catcher's position has by no means been static. Its prestige has seen ebbs and flows, declining when Babe Ruth ushered in the home run revolution and rebounding when lower scores brought base-stealing back to the fore. New equipment has continued to emerge from time to time, including the helmet, Paul Richards's enormous glove for catching the knuckleball, the neck guard, the hockey-style mask, and the Knee Saver®. Renewed efforts to capture the paradoxes of the position have produced new catchphrases like the "tools of ignorance" along with memorable sayings such as Casey Stengel's description of the decision to draft Hobie Landrith and Rocky Marciano's mother's purported declaration that "I didn't raise my son to be a catcher." Countless catchers have come and gone, including greats like Johnny Bench, Mickey Cochrane, Josh Gibson, Bill Dickey, and Roy Campanella, men of distinction like linguist and spy Moe Berg and Yankee catcher-turned-congressman Pius Schwert, wits like Bob Uecker and Joe Garagiola, countless men who achieved more fame as managers than as catchers, and unique figures like Yogi Berra. Through the years, the enormous shadow once cast by the incomparable catchers of the 1870s gradually disappeared, and even their once hallowed names faded from memory. This enabled some twentieth-century catchers to indulge in their own nostalgic boasting as they grew older, by making disparaging and usually exaggerated statements to the effect that "baseball was a more virile pastime when [I] used to stand behind the plate."

Yet while the catcher's position has been far from static during these years, it has remained relatively stable, especially when compared to the years chronicled in this book. If an old-time catcher could watch a game played today, he would be amazed by many of the changes that have taken place and be envious of the improvements made to the catcher's gear. But at the same time he would feel a sense of recognition and kinship when he concentrated his attention on the man behind the plate. He would soon notice that the catcher is still a man who provides leadership to his teammates (though his role places him among them, not above them) and endures pain (though usually not an unbearable amount). He would also be pleased to find that the catcher still stands as the embodiment of such virtues as stoic fortitude, leadership, teamwork, and courage.

Our old-time catcher would nod his head approvingly if he could hear Bob Boone giving this description of the art of pitch-calling: "You watch. You watch every hitter, everything he does. If he moves his feet, what's he trying to do? Where's his weight when the ball gets in the hitting zone? Then, what does your pitcher have? Where's he at? Then, what's the exact situation we're facing—it's everything that determines what you do." He would be pleased if he had the chance to hear a recent catcher such as Joe Ayrault explain, "The key to having soft hands is not closing the glove, but letting the ball close the glove for you." Comments like that would enable him to realize that, even wearing a mitt, a good catcher still understands how important it is to learn not to "fight the ball."

And he would take particular satisfaction if he could witness those rare moments where the catcher gets special recognition for his receiving ability, such as in 2006 when Red Sox management traded away knuckleball-catching specialist Doug Mirabelli, only to admit their mistake by hastily reacquiring him, then flying him back to Boston and getting a police escort to rush him to Fenway Park in time for one of Tim Wakefield's starts. That police escort was the ultimate tribute to the principle that, as Casey Stengel put it, "You have to have a catcher or you'll have a lot of passed balls."

The catcher has become an institution and is treated as such—respected, familiar, and, all too often, taken for granted, but at least his value to a ball club is recognized by his teammates and by knowledgeable observers. It was not always thus.

I think it's also appropriate to credit the catcher with an important contribution to one of the least appreciated and least understood revolutions of the twentieth century. Reverend Jonathan Crane's denunciations of baseball and his 1869 prediction that the new interest in the game would soon fade because "everyone connected with it seems to be regarded with a degree of suspicion" now seem extreme. In fact he was not out of step with his times.

Other fathers of his generation held the same reservations about baseball, and the idea of a son trying to make a living at the game was viewed with particular alarm. William Clift, a Connecticut minister and contemporary of Jonathan Crane, created an idealized fictional farmer named Tim Bunker and put the following words in his mouth: "Base ball, as we used to play it when I was a boy at school, was a very healthful recreation. It was a change from sedentary habits that the boys needed. . . . But what do people want of it whose lives are already full of labor? It can only add to their weakness, and detract from the interest and pleasure that every man should take in his daily toil. After a man has spent three or four hours in a game, he is pretty well used up for the day, and is in rather poor trim for work next morning. Base ball, as it is played now, is getting to be a great nuisance. It seriously interferes with the business of life. . . . [The local ballplayers] are not such men as I should want my [son] Jim to associate with. Some of them are what they call gentlemen's sons, with plenty of money and no business, which is very bad. Others have business, and neglect it to play ball, which is still worse. Some are average farmers and mechanics, rather green at the play, not yet spoiled, but in a fair way to be. Others are confirmed loafers, rather seedy, and far on the downhill road."

This suspicion of baseball remained strong throughout the nineteenth century. As we have seen, Charley Bennett was far from alone in becoming a catcher "against his father's wishes"; others played under aliases or succumbed to parental disapproval and refused to play professional baseball. Still stronger was the related concept that no respectable father would let his daughter marry a ballplayer. Even in social circles, the ballplayer's status was dubious at best. "In the early days of baseball," noted one observer, "a cyclone center was a more desirable guest in a hotel than a ball team away from home."

Yet in the early twentieth century this perception changed, and soon baseball came to be viewed as a respectable profession. Many factors played a role in this dramatic shift, including tangible ones like the passage of time and baseball's transformation into a lucrative profession. More than anything else, however, the impulse for that change was a corresponding shift in attitude: baseball ability, long thought of as an impressive but ultimately trivial skill, came to be considered a profession in the artisan tradition. It is, I believe, no coincidence that that new outlook emerged at the same time that the tough-guy and the thinking-man catchers finally blended into a unified model.

The reservations of men like Jonathan Crane were based upon the belief, passed down from the Puritans, that the passage from boyhood to manhood was completed by taking on a profession that made a positive and demonstrable contribution to the betterment of society. The athlete, however, seemed to make no such transition. As the fictional farmer Tim Bunker put it in 1868, being "a first-rate farmer . . . means cheaper bread and meat for the nation. To be a good mechanic is praiseworthy. It means better homes for the people, and better tools to do their work. But to be a first-rate ball player . . . what does it amount to?" He accordingly concluded that baseball "makes good ball players, but bad farmers and mechanics, bad husbands and fathers."

These were legitimate concerns, and they continued to trouble many Americans even after the next three decades saw baseball grow in popularity and emerge as a lucrative business. The ability of ballplayers to earn impressive salaries still didn't address the underlying issue pinpointed by the words of Bunker: "I believe in the division of labor and in new kinds of business, but it is a question whether [base ball] is going to add anything to the common wealth or happiness."

Thus even in the 1870s, when the catcher's courage and skill were inspiring awe among boys, he made no real progress with the fathers of these boys. An athlete still struck these men as someone who refused to assume adult responsibilities, and indeed there was no tradition of athletics as a profession with redeeming social values. Popular sports like boxing and football were appallingly brutal, so the few American professional athletes were boors like the boxer John L. Sullivan. Alternatives like rowing and track and field were more elegant but remained raw exhibitions of strength and speed, without any suggestion of the development of character or the intellect of a profession. Even in Europe the professional athlete remained a rarity and a figure who made people uncomfortable. Professionalism was well known in cricket, for example, but it was restricted to men from working-class backgrounds; somehow, cricketers from upper- and middle-class backgrounds earned large amounts of money but retained their amateur standing.

The place of athletics in American society therefore continued to be circumscribed. Athletics were a fine thing in youth and even in college, but then a man had to move on to more serious pursuits. If he persisted in athletic pursuits, it was a reflection on his character. A caring nineteenth-century father might allow his children to admire an athlete, but he wouldn't let his son become a professional athlete and he certainly wouldn't permit his daughter to marry one. Calling an athlete a hero would have seemed still more inappropriate to such men—after all, a hero achieved a serious moral purpose such as saving lives while an athlete merely won a game.

The strength that this perception still held at the close of the nineteenth century is dramatically illustrated in the example of Teddy Roosevelt. Roosevelt was celebrated for his admiration of the strenuous life, Western culture, and warfare, and for his willingness to put his big-city responsibilities on hold to pursue one of these courses. His formation of "Boone and Crockett Clubs" to encourage "energy, resolution, manliness, self-reliance, and a capacity for self-help" left no doubt about who his heroes were. Even his famous slogan, "Speak softly, but carry a big stick," was taken straight from the playbook of the frontier hero.

Yet what is less remembered is that Roosevelt, in the tradition of the Puritans, approved of manly conduct only when he could justify its usefulness, so he could not accept the part of the Boone model that valued adventure for its own sake. His attitude toward sporting endeavors thus remained closer to Jonathan Crane's than to Stephen Crane's. "It is a good thing," Roosevelt maintained at the turn of the century, "for a boy to have captained his school or college eleven, but it is a very bad thing if, twenty years afterward, all that can be said of him is that he has continued to take an interest in foot-ball, base-ball, or boxing, and has with him the memory that he was once captain. A very acute observer has pointed out that, not impossibly, excessive devotion to sports and games has proved a serious detriment in the British army, by leading the officers and even the men to neglect the hard, practical work of their profession for the sake of racing, foot-ball, base-ball, polo, and tennis—until they received a very rude awakening at the hands of the Boers. Of course this means merely that any healthy pursuit can be abused."

For Teddy Roosevelt, as for most members of his generation (he was born in 1858), an athletic competition was either a blood sport or, as he famously put it, it was just for mollycoddles. As his biographer Edmund Morris aptly observed, "Roosevelt was sanguine in every sense of the word, physiological and psychological. . . . [His wife] Edith told him, 'Theodore, I wish you'd do your bleeding in the bathroom.'"

Not surprisingly, Teddy Roosevelt and Stephen Crane viewed one another suspiciously. While Roosevelt admired some of Crane's writing, he was perplexed by the attraction that the younger man felt for the unconventional. After reading Crane's short story "A Man and Some Others"—which defied the conventions of the Western tale by ending with the death of the outnumbered underdog—Roosevelt wrote to Crane to suggest that he "write another story in which the frontiersman shall come out on top; it is more normal that way." So too Teddy Roosevelt and his generation could never really see a sport as a fitting pursuit for a man unless it involved a genuine risk of bloodshed.

But the succeeding generation came to look at sports differently. While its members undoubtedly continued to recognize that baseball games were not as serious as war, they also came to understand that boys who grew up when no war was taking place needed heroes just as much as any other generation. Once they themselves became parents and saw that baseball could be used to teach their sons valuable lessons, they learned to embrace it.

As this book has tried to suggest, a key reason for that development was the growing perception of the catcher as a man who might win a game by outthinking the other side. It was, I believe, no coincidence that only after the tough-guy and thinking-man models of the catcher came together in the early twentieth century were American men able to overcome their discomfort that an athlete was someone who didn't accomplish anything tangible. That new outlook was in turn part of a broader societal trend that finally saw the resolution of an old dilemma.

In 1905 a man named Daniel Carter Beard founded an organization to teach boys the skills of the frontiersman within a socially acceptable context. He named it "The Sons of Daniel Boone," but after a few years he merged his organization with another to form the Boy Scouts of America. That merger was a symbol that Americans no longer saw heroic traits as being in conflict with wholesome ones, which in turn enabled the American hero to become a permanent institution.

One of the results of this new outlook was acceptance of the idea of the athlete as a role model. Accompanying that transformation was the growing sense that baseball had become a profession in ways that transcended its financial rewards—that once a ballplayer grew too old to perform athletically, he could become a coach or manager and pass the knowledge he had accumulated along to the next generation. In turn, it became more common for spectators at sporting events to offer audible advice to far-away players who couldn't possibly hear them. Fathers in particular began to use events that occurred during the ball game as object lessons for their sons and eventually for their daughters. No doubt they knew that their children were more enthralled by the action and didn't pay attention to everything they were told, but they hoped that some of it would sink in and in particular that it would give their sons a better understanding of what it meant to be a man. A model of athletic heroism had finally emerged that could be reconciled with traditional values. Fittingly, the embodiment of that ideal was the catcher.

If Reverend Jonathan Crane could be brought back to life and shown the prominent role that baseball plays in twenty-first-century America, he would initially be dismayed. But upon further examination perhaps he too would ultimately see some value in the lessons that baseball allows parents to teach kids and would overcome his suspicion. And maybe he would come to understand that the now-familiar motif of parents playing catch with their children is one that embodies the same ideals he held dear.

Afterword:
The Man the Hall of Fame Forgot

WHEN JIM WHITE PLAYED

The baseball cranks all sneer at me,
And poke a lot of fun,
Because I tell of plays they made
In the days of seventy-one
And yet, who cares for fun and sneers?
By gum, I know I'm right!
Somehow the game ain't played the same
As 'twas by old Jim White.

They talk about their great Lajoie,
And Wagner and McVeigh [sic];
To hear 'em yarn, you'd think, by darn,
Nobody else could play.
And yet I often call to mind
Those scenes of wild delight
When 'cross the fence some hit immense
Was smashed by old Jim White.

And Lordy! How old Jim could catch!
He'd stand and dodge the bat
'Thout mask or mitt—it took some grit
To catch great speed like that.

He'd nail 'em high and scoop 'em low—
It was a thrilling sight;
No player dared—he'd be too scared—
To catch like old Jim White.

So when you sing of modern stars
Don't call the old 'uns slow;
They knew the game and played it too
Some fifty years ago.
And while o' course, the players now
Are men o' grit and might,
Somehow the game ain't played the same
As 'twas by old Jim White.
                              —Dale Lancaster

■ Most of the early catching greats were dead by 1904, when the advent of the spitball and the subsequent adoption of shin guards helped pave the way for a new model for the position. Yet one—the greatest of all nineteenth-century players, in my estimation—did live to witness these pivotal years and then to see an additional three decades of change in the position he had once defined.

Even as a young man, Jim White had displayed many of the traits usually associated with the end of life. His stoic reserve was so pronounced that one sportswriter was moved to write: "Placid, like a frog-pond on a moonlit evening; quiet as the growth of grass upon a hero's tomb; unassuming as the innocent cow that munches the wholesome cud, is the theologian of the profession, honest Jim White. Years have passed; pennants have been won and lost; the grand stand even has changed, and the Boston & Providence Road has found some new cars, but Jim is all himself, the same genial, simple-hearted private he was in days of yore, when Spalding skimmed the whirling sphere and Harry's ample form loomed up in center-field. Faithful James! he remains where others have perished." Those words were written in 1884, seven years before White finally hung up his spikes.

White's serious countenance had earned him the nickname "Deacon" and led to the perception that he was "scarcely one who would be taken for an athlete." The passage of time only increased this impression, and when he showed up at one reunion of old-time ballplayers it was politely suggested to him that he was at the wrong event. (Perhaps White displayed his battered fingers to show that he did indeed belong.)

Some quiet souls become garrulous in old age, but Jim White continued to hide his light under a bushel. In retirement he kept his opinions to himself as baseball turned into a lucrative business—and as his old battery mate, A. G. Spalding, earned fabulous profits off the sport. He lived his final years in the small Illinois communities of Mendota and Aurora, where some of his neighbors were unaware of his extraordinary accomplishments. When asked, however, the old catcher had stories to tell and souvenirs to display.

Those reporters who did seek him out were treated to the same candor for which Jim White had always been known. For many old ballplayers, their era will always remain the golden age and later players are only pale imitations. White, however, knew that this was nonsense.

When he was well into his eighties, his old catching teammate Connie Mack invited him to see his Philadelphia Athletics play in Chicago. It was the first major league game that White had witnessed in fifteen years, and he had the good fortune to watch Mack's star pitcher, Lefty Grove. With characteristic forthrightness, White acknowledged afterward that the skill of twentieth-century batters and pitchers surpassed the work done by the stars of his day. Yet there was no false modesty about Jim White, and he was quick to add, "But I don't think you have any better fielders now than we had in those first days of the game. We had to learn to field bare-handed and that took a lot more skill than your fielders need with gloves."

When Mack joined him, White expressed awe at Grove's pitching and exclaimed, "Imagine a batter trying to hit that speed while standing just 45 feet from the pitching box!" His old teammate smiled knowingly and then said aloud what both men were thinking: "And imagine a catcher trying to hold those pitches bare-handed." The reporter who had been fortunate to witness the exchange closed his account by explaining, "Both Mack and Jim White are old-time catchers with gnarled fingers as trade-marks."

*

In 1939 the National Baseball Hall of Fame and Museum opened its doors in the pastoral New York town of Cooperstown. The location was the decision of a commission put together in 1905 by White's old battery mate, A. G. Spalding, with the mission of determining baseball's origins. The commission did little digging into the question; instead Spalding convinced the members to take the uncorroborated word of an elderly man and to consecrate Abner Doubleday as the inventor of the game and Cooperstown as its birthplace.

Despite the shaky basis for the setting, the Hall of Fame had a golden opportunity to recognize one of the game's greatest and most admirable pioneers. Jim White, now ninety-one, had learned to play the game in a rural New York setting very much like Cooperstown and had blossomed into one of baseball's first superstars. He had collected the first hit in the first major league game ever played, and remained one of the game's brightest stars for two decades, leading his teams to six pennants and defining its most important position. Just as important, he had been a hallmark of integrity during an era in which, as Jonathan Crane put it, "everyone connected with [baseball] seems to be regarded with a degree of suspicion." As much as Jim White had done to fill the lads of Stephen Crane's generation "with awe and admiration," perhaps a still more important contribution was the role he played in convincing their fathers that baseball could be played honorably.

The opening of the Hall of Fame's doors prompted the nonagenarian's hometown newspaper to start a campaign to enshrine him, and it wrote optimistically that there was "little chance . . . that White's name will be omitted when the next group of diamond immortals is named next month." White himself apparently got his hopes high.

But when the day rolled around, the electors looked at a called third strike. The Old Timers' panel chose Spalding, Cap Anson, Candy Cummings, Charley Comiskey, Buck Ewing, and Charley Radbourn, all long dead. Members of the Baseball Writers' Association of America voted for a wide range of recent stars while completely ignoring the game's pioneers. Ballots were cast for the likes of Otto Knabe, Charlie Irwin, Dickie Kerr, and Chick Fraser. Catchers who received a vote or two included Ossee Schreckengost, Bill Carrigan, Heinie Peitz, and, unbelievably, Marty Bergen. Yet not a single ballot was cast for Jim White, who was not even invited to the opening of the Hall. He died a few months later, reportedly deeply disappointed.

In the years since, a fair number of his contemporaries have been inducted, many of them far lesser players, while White remains on the outside. In 2008, White was short-listed for induction—an encouraging sign that he may yet be chosen—but was not ultimately selected. Thus there are still only two nineteenth-century catchers who have been enshrined for their record as players—in the ultimate irony they are Mike Kelly and Buck Ewing. Both men were worthy choices, to be sure, but they also embody the years when it became accepted that a great ballplayer was too valuable to be used exclusively as a catcher.

Yet while White's absence from Cooperstown is a grave injustice, it makes sense in a curious way. He was the greatest catcher of an era when the feats of catchers were so incomparable that they could not be incorporated into the game's history. A generation of catchers tried to escape from their outsized shadows and failed miserably, so later generations have instead decided on a sad but inevitable course. In order to gain recognition for the skill and courage of the catchers of their day, without being subjected to comparisons to stalwarts such as Joe Leggett, Nat Hicks, Jim White, Charley Bennett, and Silver Flint, those early greats have been forgotten.

Appendix 1: The Shift of Catchers of the Late 1880s to Other Positions

FOUR MEN in baseball history have played at least twenty-five major league games at catcher, first base, second base, shortstop, third base, and the outfield. It is the sort of feat that one might expect to be accomplished by an obscure utility player, and that is an apt description of one of the four men: turn-of-the-century journeyman Charley Dexter. Yet the other three were great talents whose wanderings reflected both their versatility and the dwindling value of a good catcher. The first two were Hall of Famers Mike Kelly and Buck Ewing; the third was Jack Doyle, who came up in 1889 and played mostly catcher in his first few years but was ultimately shifted to positions where injuries would be less likely to remove his bat from the lineup.

Ewing (debut 9/9/1880): p, 9; c, 636; 1b, 253; 2b, 51; ss, 34; 3b, 127; lf, 9; cf, 34; rf, 193

Kelly (debut 5/1/1878): p, 12; c, 583; 1b, 25; 2b, 54; ss, 90; 3b, 96; lf, 2, cf, 8, rf, 742.

Dexter (debut 4/17/1896): p, 0; c, 116; 1b, 76; 2b, 41; ss, 39; 3b, 79; lf, 8; cf, 159, rf, 235.

Doyle (debut 8/27/1889): p, 0; c, 176; 1b, 1,043; 2b, 127; ss, 53; 3b, 50; lf, 13; cf, 45; rf, 76.

Others of the era with similar usage patterns:

Lave Cross (debut 4/23/1887): p, 0; c, 324; 1b, 7; 2b, 60; ss, 65; 3b, 1,721; lf, 13; cf, 34; rf, 72.

Heinie Peitz (debut 10/15/1892): p, 4; c, 960; 1b, 75; 2b, 74; ss, 11; 3b, 79; lf, 4; cf, 0; rf, 7.

Charley "Duke" Farrell (debut 4/21/1888): p, 0; c, 1,003; 1b, 106; 2b, 0; ss, 13; 3b, 290; lf, 48; cf, 22; rf, 39.

George "Doggie" Miller (debut 5/1/1884): p, 0; c, 636; 1b, 22; 2b, 51; ss, 83; 3b, 243; lf, 146; cf, 68; rf, 96.

Jack Boyle (debut 10/8/1886): p, 0; c, 544; 1b, 455; 2b, 7; ss, 44; 3b, 52; lf, 6; cf, 2; rf, 7.

Appendix 2: Number of American League and National League Games Managed by Former Catchers, 1899–1920

1899	157 (Buck Ewing)
1900	63 (Buck Ewing)
1901	273 (Connie Mack, George Stallings)
1902	220 (Connie Mack, Wilbert Robinson)
1903	276 (Connie Mack, Chief Zimmer)
1904	173 (Connie Mack, Malachi Kittridge)
1905	152 (Connie Mack)
1906	149 (Connie Mack)
1907	262 (Connie Mack, Jim McGuire)
1908	312 (Connie Mack, Jim McGuire, Fred Lake)
1909	967 (Connie Mack, Jim McGuire, Fred Lake, George Stallings, Roger Bresnahan, Billy Sullivan, Frank Bowerman, Harry Smith)
1910	1,083 (Connie Mack, Jim McGuire, Fred Lake, George Stallings, Roger Bresnahan, Red Dooin, Jack O'Connor)
1911	480 (Connie Mack, Jim McGuire, Roger Bresnahan, Red Dooin)
1912	613 (Connie Mack, Roger Bresnahan, Red Dooin, Johnny Kling)
1913	548 (Connie Mack, Red Dooin, George Stallings, Bill Carrigan, Branch Rickey)
1914	942 (Connie Mack, Red Dooin, George Stallings, Bill Carrigan, Branch Rickey, Wilbert Robinson)

1915   1,216 (Connie Mack, George Stallings, Bill Carrigan, Branch
        Rickey, Wilbert Robinson, Pat Moran, Lee Fohl, Roger Bres-
        nahan)

1916   937 (Connie Mack, George Stallings, Bill Carrigan, Wilbert Rob-
        inson, Pat Moran, Lee Fohl, Ivy Wingo)

1917   779 (Connie Mack, George Stallings, Wilbert Robinson, Pat Mo-
        ran, Lee Fohl)

1918   635 (Connie Mack, George Stallings, Wilbert Robinson, Pat Mo-
        ran, Lee Fohl)

1919   777 (Connie Mack, George Stallings, Wilbert Robinson, Pat Mo-
        ran, Lee Fohl, Branch Rickey)

1920   928 (Connie Mack, George Stallings, Wilbert Robinson, Pat Mo-
        ran, Branch Rickey, George Gibson)

Notes

Full citations of many sources appear in the Selected Bibliography.

INTRODUCTION: A GENERATION IN SEARCH OF A HERO

page

xi "You have to have a catcher or you'll have a lot of passed balls": This quotation was reportedly occasioned by the Mets' decision to make well-traveled thirty-one-year-old catcher Hobie Landrith their first choice in the 1961 expansion draft. When I tried to pin down the date and precise wording of Stengel's remark, however, I found that it did not appear in print at the time, and at first I was unable to find any citations of it that preceded his death. This made me skeptical of the legitimacy of the quotation until Bobby Plapinger did some impressive research on this topic. He uncovered the earliest known published version of the quotation, which appeared in the 1966 book *Backstage at the Mets*, written by Mets broadcaster Lindsey Nelson (with Al Hirshberg). On page 64, Nelson mentions the drafting of Landrith and then writes, "Later, when I asked Casey Stengel why the Mets started with a catcher, he replied with typical Stengel logic. 'When ya build a ball club,' he said, 'ya gotta start with a catcher, 'cause if you don't you'll have all passed balls.'" Since this appeared only five years after the events in question, it seems unlikely that Nelson had misremembered or fabricated it. In addition, Plapinger notes that Jack Lang, who was covering the Mets for the *Long Island Press* at the time of the expansion draft, also claimed in his 1987 book *The New York Mets: Twenty-Five Years of Baseball Magic* that Stengel had made the statement. Most persuasively, Plapinger contacted longtime New York sportswriter and Stengel biographer Maury Allen, who maintained that he had heard Stengel make the comment, or something along those lines, on many occasions. None of these sources provide definitive information about the exact wording, date, or circumstances of Stengel's remark, but it now seems clear that he did in fact make it. I also appreciate the efforts of Warren Corbett, Scott Schleifer, Cliff Blau, Bill Deane, Cary Smith, and the late Jules Tygiel, all of whom made helpful responses to a query I posted on this subject on the SABR-L listserv.

3 he took a dim view of dancing, tobacco, opium, alcohol, billiards, chess, and novel-reading: Quoted in R. W. Stallman, *Stephen Crane: A Biography*, 5. Jonathan Crane opposed

novels because he feared they might create "a morbid love of excitement somewhat akin to the imperious thirst of the inebriate."

3 "everyone connected with it seems to be regarded with a degree of suspicion": Quoted in Stallman, *Stephen Crane*, 14.

3 "home from school or play . . .": Stanley Wertheim and Paul Sorrentino, *The Crane Log*, 31.

4 "It was his pose . . . puzzled so many": Harvey Wickham, "Stephen Crane at College," *American Mercury* 7 (March 1926), reprinted in Paul Sorrentino, ed., *Stephen Crane Remembered*, 66.

4 The specific source of this statement is dubious . . . : This statement comes from Thomas Beer, *Stephen Crane: A Study in American Letters*, 52. Beer was Crane's first biographer, and his was the only biography written while a significant number of Crane's contemporaries were still alive. Unfortunately Beer's sources are not documented, and recent research has established that even direct quotations in Beer's biography cannot be trusted to be authentic. The result is a paucity of reliable source material and, since most later biographers used Beer as a key source, it casts doubt on their works as well. I have done my best to base my comments solely on sources other than Beer but have made this one exception since this sort of boast was so much a part of being a catcher during those years. The necessity of excluding most of Beer's biography has forced me to omit some highly intriguing material linking Crane to baseball. For example, according to Beer, Crane said of his years at the military school: "But heaven was sunny blue and no rain fell on the diamond when I was playing baseball. I was very happy there" (53). I am grateful to Paul Sorrentino for helping me sort through these confusing issues; any misrepresentations that remain are my responsibility and not his.

4 There is even reason to suspect that Stephen dreamed of a career as a professional baseball player . . . : According to Beer, Crane confided in a letter to a friend that he dreamed of a career as a professional ballplayer, even though "ma says it's not a serious occupation" (Beer, 52). Crane scholars now doubt the authenticity of this letter, and there is no incontrovertible evidence that Crane expressed a goal to play professional baseball. He did, however, hint at such an ambition in another letter: "They used to say at Syracuse University . . . that I was cut out to be a professional base-ball player. And the truth is that I went there more to play base-ball than to study" (Stanley Wertheim and Paul Sorrentino, ed., *The Correspondence of Stephen Crane*, 231–232, from Crane to J. Herbert Welch in late April–May 1896, as quoted in an article by Welch). In addition, as quoted later in this chapter, teammate Mansfield French recalled that Crane followed and loved to discuss the "newspaper reputation" of the "leading professional players of the day."

5 He took great pride in being the catcher of the school baseball nine . . .: Abram Lincoln Travis, "Recollections of Stephen Crane" (1930 manuscript), reprinted in Sorrentino, ed., *Stephen Crane Remembered*, 61. Another teammate, Clarence Peaslee, recalled that Crane "stood up [i.e., close] to the plate like a professional." Clarence Loomis Peaslee, "Stephen Crane's College Days," *Monthly Illustrator and Home and Country* 13 (August 1896), 27–30; reprinted in Sorrentino, ed., *Stephen Crane Remembered*, 84. William J. Ryczek, in *Blackguards and Red Stockings*, 16, attests that it was not uncommon for catchers to use chemical preparations to harden their hands. See also the description of the extract used by famed National League catcher Silver Flint, published in the *New York Sunday Mercury* on June 19, 1880, and quoted at the end of Chapter 3.

5 "motley crowd of baseball enthusiasts": Ernest G. Smith, "Comments and Queries," *Lafayette Alumnus* 2 (February 1932), 6; reprinted in Sorrentino, ed., *Stephen Crane Remembered*, 71.

5 He hoped to make the varsity team . . . : John Berryman, *Stephen Crane*, 20; Stallman, *Stephen Crane*, 26. Crane received no grade in three of his seven classes, primarily because of excessive absences.

5 "never seemed to be particularly interested . . .": Peaslee, "Stephen Crane's College Days," 85.

5 "would not be cramped . . .": Berryman, *Stephen Crane*, 24; Stallman, *Stephen Crane*, 30.

5 "I went to Lafayette College . . .": Letter to John Northern Hilliard, dated January 2, 1896, in Wertheim and Sorrentino, ed., *Correspondence of Stephen Crane*, 166–167.

5 the student newspaper was predicting a bright future: *Syracusan*, February 2, 1891. Many Eastern colleges had indoor cages for winter practice, and Syracuse must have had something of the sort. (*Boston Globe*, March 8, 1885; *Outing*, April 1890; Walter C. Bohm, "College Baseball," *Los Angeles Times*, May 21, 1893.)

5 "must have been among the first . . .": Mansfield J. French, "Stephen Crane, Ball Player," *Syracuse University Alumni News* 15 (January 1934); reprinted in Sorrentino, ed., *Stephen Crane Remembered*, 77.

5–6 "He should have worn white stockings . . .": French, "Stephen Crane, Ball Player," 78. Another classmate recalled Stephen as "a wiry, slender youth, under the average height, with a complexion almost yellow, and very large and expressive eyes. I remember that he did not have one of the old gray 'Varsity suits, but wore a crimson sweater, buff-colored trousers and a pair of broken patent-leather shoes." Peaslee, "Stephen Crane's College Days," 84.

6 "seemed to bound back with every catch": Peaslee, "Stephen Crane's College Days," 84–85.

6 "always 'froze on to the ball,' . . .": Carl F. Price, "Stephen Crane: A Genius Born in a Methodist Parsonage," *Christian Advocate* (New York) 98 (July 13, 1922), 866–867; reprinted in Sorrentino, ed., *Stephen Crane Remembered*, 22.

6 . . . wore only a simple padded glove on his left hand: French, "Stephen Crane, Ball Player," 78.

6 "He would not stand on his two feet . . .": French, "Stephen Crane, Ball Player," 77.

6–7 "He played ball with a fiendish glee . . .": French, "Stephen Crane, Ball Player," 77–78.

7 The local press also took notice . . .: *Syracuse Daily Standard*, April 21, 1891, 6, and June 2, 1891, 6; *Syracusan*, May 4, 1891; Stallman, *Stephen Crane*, 28.

7 "loved to talk baseball . . .": French, "Stephen Crane, Ball Player," 2–3.

7 "baseball masks and bats . . .": Peaslee, "Stephen Crane's College Days," 84.

8 he even wrote the first draft of a novel: Stallman, *Stephen Crane*, 32.

8 withdrew from Syracuse: It is sometimes reported that Crane failed most of his courses and was dismissed from Syracuse. In fact the school did not give grades at the time, leaving it unclear whether his withdrawal was voluntary.

8 "I did little work at school . . .": Wertheim and Sorrentino, ed., *Correspondence of Stephen Crane*, 99, letter to John Northern Hilliard, possibly written in February 1895, originally published in *New York Times*, Supplement, July 14, 1900, 466.

8 "We met occasionally thereafter to 'pass ball,' . . .": Hamlin Garland, "Stephen Crane as I Knew Him," *Yale Review* 3 (Spring 1914), 494.

8 Garland agreed to read the younger man's novel . . .: The novel, *Maggie: A Girl of the Streets* (1893), is still considered a first-rate work.

9 "all his knowledge of battle had been gained on the football field": Garland, "Stephen Crane as I Knew Him," 498.

9 "I see that they are beginning . . .": Wertheim and Sorrentino, ed., *Correspondence of Stephen Crane*, 196, letter dated February 2, 1896, to Ripley Hitchcock.

9 "unconsciously working the detail of the story out through most of his boyhood": Willa Cather, "When I Knew Stephen Crane," in *The World and the Parish: Willa Cather's*

Articles and Reviews, 1893–1902, ed. William M. Curtin (Lincoln: University of Nebraska Press, 1970), 766.

10 "dreamed of battles all his life . . .": Stephen Crane, *The Red Badge of Courage* (1895), in *Great Short Works of Stephen Crane* (New York, Harper & Row, 1965), 5–6.

11 Like Crane's, his devoutly religious parents . . .: *Marietta* (Ohio) *Times*, December 3, 1928.

11 "to see a game at the old Cincinnati grounds . . .": Tim Murnane, *Sporting Life*, March 10, 1906; quoted in Eugene C. Murdock, *Ban Johnson: Czar of Baseball*, 13.

11 "surely had a wicked inshoot . . .": AP dispatch, July 28, 1927; quoted in Murdock, *Ban Johnson*, 248.

11 Byron split his hand . . .: Paul Eaton, "When Ban Johnson Went to College," *Sporting News*, October 27, 1927.

11 "By the finish of the season . . .": Ban Johnson, as told to George Creel, "Slide, Kelly, Slide," *Saturday Evening Post*, April 12, 1930, 17.

11 "The only thing I wore to protect myself . . .": Ban Johnson, as told to Creel, "Slide, Kelly, Slide," 17.

11 He did allow himself a pair of fingerless gloves . . .: AP dispatch, July 28, 1927; quoted in Murdock, *Ban Johnson*, 248.

11 "I viewed the mask with dark suspicion . . .": Ban Johnson, as told to Creel, "Slide, Kelly, Slide," 17.

11 . . . little inclination to apply himself to schoolwork: Murdock, *Ban Johnson*, 14. One classmate recalled him as "the kind who did well in the studies that interested him, but placed no great strain on his mental dynamo for those that did not." Eaton, "When Ban Johnson Went to College."

11 "The first person who caught my eye . . .": Eaton, "When Ban Johnson Went to College."

11–12 The dirty uniform became one of his signatures . . .: AP dispatch, July 28, 1927; quoted in Murdock, *Ban Johnson*, 248.

12 Another youngster known as Wallie . . .: For more details on Walker, see Peter Morris, "Walter Walker: One of Baseball's Odd Lives," *National Pastime* 15 (1995), 97–99.

14 . . . the Native Americans with very different ways of life: Richard Slotkin notes that the "Indian was the antithesis of the European—dark-skinned, pagan in religion, tribal in politics, seminomadic in economics, with a moral system that seemed to sanctify pleasure taking and self-gratification." Richard Slotkin, *The Fatal Environment*, 53.

14 a disastrous war with the natives: King Philip's War of 1675–1676 devastated the New England settlements. As Richard Slotkin notes, the war was the costliest one in American history when measured in proportion to the population. Slotkin, *Fatal Environment*, 55. The war caused most of the emigrants, particularly the New England Puritans, to lose faith that conversion was possible. Slotkin calls the resulting alienation the "anxiety of the emigration trauma." Richard Slotkin, *Regeneration Through Violence*, 40–41, 118.

14 Polar opposites increasingly dominated the Puritans' worldview . . .: As Richard Slotkin explains, the Puritans' literary genre of choice was the captivity tale in which a member of their community was snatched from safety and held prisoner. Such narratives left no room for active heroism, and even when the Indian Wars were addressed in Puritan literature, "God, never man, is the hero, and the community is the central subject" (92). This message was reinforced by sermons that offered a similarly narrow view of their surroundings. Slotkin, *Regeneration Through Violence*, 94–115.

14 "Beyond the rim of settlement . . .": Slotkin, *Regeneration Through Violence*, 87.

15 "coveted after the earth . . . all for land and elbow-room": Quoted in Slotkin, *Regeneration Through Violence*, 86.

15 "utopian district, freed at once of the Indian menace and the corruptions of the city": Slotkin, *Fatal Environment*, 71. Crevecoeur's depiction of his life on the farm was just as idyllic: "I am but a feller of trees, a cultivator of land, the most honourable title an American can have. I have no exploits, no discoveries, no inventions to boast of; I have cleared about 370 acres of land, some for the plough, some for the scythe; and this has occupied many years of my life. I have never possessed, or wish to possess anything more than what could be earned or produced by the united industry of my family." J. Hector St. John de Crevecoeur, *Letters from an American Farmer*, 206.

15 "be the design of Providence . . ." and "The conquest of the New World . . .": Slotkin, *Regeneration Through Violence*, 213. As another example, Slotkin cites William Byrd, who "portrayed himself as a hero in the wilderness—the man who controls all situations, imposes restraints on whites and Indians, passes judgment on the mores of Indians and frontiersmen, and speaks with the voice of reason" (222).

15–16 "a state approaching nearer to that of nature . . .": Crevecoeur, *Letters from an American Farmer*, 205.

16 With middle ground untenable, it became inevitable that the American hero . . .: Slotkin contends that the Puritans responded by developing "a heroic myth in which representatives of colonial culture could engage in struggle with the Indians, become in the process quite close to the Indians, and yet emerge as spiritually regenerate heroes of Christian civilization." Slotkin, *Fatal Environment*, 62.

16 Boone was a complex man, and portrayals of him differed widely . . .: See John Mack Faragher's *Daniel Boone* for the best effort to sort fact from myth in Boone's life. Slotkin, *Regeneration Through Violence*, 398–409, provides a good summary of the key issues.

16 "a code of natural laws from the wilderness": Slotkin, *Regeneration Through Violence*, 310, 410.

17 "I can't say as ever I was lost . . .": Faragher, *Daniel Boone*, 65. Boone once said that his hunting companion John Stewart was always in the right place at the right time, and the compliment is an apt summary of the quality that made Boone a model of heroism. Faragher, *Daniel Boone*, 76.

17 "might have accumulated riches . . .": Quoted in Henry Nash Smith, *Virgin Land*, 54.

17 "As civilization advanced, so he, from time to time, retreated": Quoted in Smith, *Virgin Land*, 54. James Fenimore Cooper similarly referred to Boone's eternal quest for "the renewal of enjoyments which were rendered worthless in his eyes, when trammeled by the forms of human institutions." Quoted in Smith, *Virgin Land*, 59. Like many tales about Boone, this image was grossly exaggerated and misinterpreted. In fact Boone was a sociable man who lived in a household of as many as twenty, and his tendency to retreat was the obvious response of a hunter, since wild animals instinctively avoid human settlements. The related image of Boone as a man of action, not words, was also born of necessity. Like any hunter, he appreciated that silence was essential in order to avoid scaring off the prey. Less obviously, the ability to hold one's tongue was just as important in combat. Eighteenth-century battlefields became engulfed in gunsmoke, making it impossible to see the enemy and aim effectively. So combatants engaged in "blackguarding"—taunting the other side from the safety of cover in hopes of eliciting an angry retort that would make it easier to pinpoint a location and take aim. Faragher, *Daniel Boone*, 196–198.

18 . . . Boone's philosophy was closer to that of the Native Americans: Slotkin, *Regeneration Through Violence,* 307.

18 their reverence for the hunter as a man who had attained oneness with nature: By contrast, in Christian and European myth the hunter was traditionally seen as an "accursed figure," despite the value of hunting, because stalking his prey meant becoming too much like the prey. Slotkin, *Regeneration Through Violence,* 307. Faragher, in *Daniel Boone,* 20, notes that there was a practical component to this perception of the hunter as well—it was rare for emigrants to have any experience as hunters because hunting in Europe was generally restricted to the nobility. As a result, American hunters learned the craft from Native Americans.

18 As Americans rushed westward . . .: Davy Crockett was the most notable example. As Slotkin puts it, "[The] contemplative Boone gave way to the violent, garrulous, slaughter-loving David Crockett." Slotkin, *Regeneration Through Violence,* 308.

18 "Defining courage exclusively as a virtue . . .": Martin Green, *The Adventurous Male: Chapters in the History of the White Male Mind,* 5.

18 . . . the discernment and good sense to make such decisions: Late in his life Boone acted as a frontier judge. It was said that he held court beneath the shade of a large elm tree and "governed more by *equity* than *law.*" Faragher, *Daniel Boone,* 285–286.

19 The cowboy was a man who lived his life by a rigorous but unwritten code of behavior . . .: David Dary, *Cowboy Culture,* 124, 278–279, for his code of behavior; 54 for his skills; 281 for his avoidance of artifice; 164 for his "horse sense."

19–20 The cowboy needed first of all to break the horse . . .: Dary, *Cowboy Culture,* 48–49; the quotation ("the harder . . .") is from H. T. Lilliencrantz, "Recollections of a California Cattleman," *California Historical Society Quarterly* 37 (1959), 341.

20 "the idea of human supremacy," "incompetent horsemanship upon his back," "the recollection of the lariat's spilling ability," and "fear of leather": Philip Ashton Rollins, *The Cowboy: An Unconventional History of Civilization on the Old-Time Cattle Range,* 292–293.

20 . . . the cowboy and his horse could work in perfect harmony . . .: In *Cowboy Culture,* Dary describes the complex interactions between horse and rider that were necessary to perform each of these tasks effectively; for cattle roping, see 58; for bear hunting, 64–66; for battle, 6 and 12.

20 When separated from his horse . . .: Erwin Gustav Gudde, ed., "Edward Vischer's First Visit to California," *California Historical Society Quarterly* 19 (1940), 205–206; quoted in Dary, *Cowboy Culture,* 59–60.

20 Part of the lore of the cowboy . . .: Dary, *Cowboy Culture,* 14, 197.

20 "On horseback, the cowboy is a picturesque figure; afoot he is a waddling swan": J. W. Sullivan, "Cattle Range Work," *Los Angeles Times,* June 5, 1892, 11.

20 "A cowboy is a man with guts and a horse": Quoted in Douglas Branch, *The Cowboy and His Interpreters* (1926), (reprint, New York: Cooper Square, 1961), 32.

20 "the occupation of the cowboy in this hemisphere . . .": Dary, *Cowboy Culture,* 275.

20–21 When the subject was a real person . . .: This was particularly well illustrated by an episode during which the most famous of the mountain men, Kit Carson, admitted that he and his companions went on a long drinking spree. But this didn't suit his mythologizers, who turned a blind eye to such indiscretions and instead encouraged readers to "Think of such a man as Kit Carson, with his native delicacy of mind; a delicacy which never allowed him to use a profane word, to indulge in intoxicating drinks, to be guilty of an impure action; a man who enjoyed, above all things else, the communings of his own spirit with the silence, the solitude, the grandeur, with which God has invested the illimitable wilderness." Even Carson became embarrassed by the tendency of such champions to lay it on "a leetle too thick." Smith, *Virgin Land,* 85–86.

Smith notes that Daniel Boone (who was related to Carson by marriage) also objected to idealized depictions of him (102–103).

21 just transferring a man to the West was enough to bring out heroic qualities: As Henry Nash Smith observes, "By the 1890's the Western novel had come to hinge almost entirely upon conflicts between detectives and bands of robbers that had little to do with the ostensibly Western locales." Smith, *Virgin Land*, 92.

21 "the major idols of America have been men of good will . . .": Dixon Wecter, *The Hero in America*, 11.

21 "Typically the hero of the fairy tale . . .": Joseph Campbell, *The Hero with a Thousand Faces*, 36–38.

22 dime novels served up an abundance of highly implausible plot twists: An inherent contradiction with plots featuring characters in disguise was having them speak in ways appropriate to their stations. The disguise plot became so prevalent that Henry Nash Smith remarked that many novelists followed the principle "that both the sons and daughters of parents who speak a pronounced dialect are themselves free of dialect if they are involved in a love affair." Smith, *Virgin Land*, 98.

22 This led to even more blatant plot contrivances: Henry Nash Smith notes that in order to keep dime-novel hero Deadwood Dick from domestication, his love affairs became "hopelessly confused. He has been married several times: one recorded wife sells herself to the devil and becomes unfaithful to him, another is killed, he is menaced by lovesick female villains, he fruitlessly courts Calamity Jane, he is subsequently the object of her hopeless devotion, and in the end he marries her." Smith, *Virgin Land*, 101.

22 "an occupation like those of vigorous, primitive pastoral peoples . . .": Theodore Roosevelt, *Ranch Life and the Hunting Trail*, 6.

23 Ulysses S. Grant . . .: Edmund Wilson, "Northern Soldiers: Ulysses S. Grant," in *Patriotic Gore*, 131–173.

24 "achieves and accumulates wealth not through drudgery and self-denial . . .": Slotkin, *Fatal Environment*, 68.

24 Ben Franklin took a pummeling from those who associated him primarily with the notion of equating wealth with virtue: Franklin of course was a multifaceted man of diverse achievement. But by the mid-nineteenth century the message of self-improvement in his *Poor Richard's Almanac* had begun to dominate his reputation. Some found this image of Franklin appealing, but others were troubled by it, as is nicely captured by Twain's parody. In light of Franklin's rich sense of humor, he would undoubtedly have laughed heartily at Twain's comments. See the chapter on Franklin in Wecter's *Hero in America* and Gordon S. Wood's *The Americanization of Benjamin Franklin* for detailed discussions of the fascinating ups and downs of Franklin's reputation.

24 "of a vicious disposition . . .": Mark Twain, "The Late Benjamin Franklin," *The Galaxy*, July 1870, 138.

24 novelists like Dickens and Thackeray: Charles Dickens's *David Copperfield* revolved around the question of whether the title character would prove to be the hero of his own life. William Makepeace Thackeray's *Vanity Fair* was subtitled "A Novel Without a Hero," and he went still further in *Henry Esmond*, offering an extended examination of the proposition that "no man is a hero to his valet."

25 "but the catcher has almost complete control . . .": John Montgomery Ward, *Base-Ball: How to Become a Player*, 65.

26 As late as 1856, any player who caught a ball might be referred to as a "catcher": For example, *Porter's Spirit of the Times* of December 6, 1856, 229, referred to Knickerbocker first baseman Lewis Wadsworth as "a catcher of almost unerring accuracy" and to third baseman Samuel Yates as "an excellent catcher," with the context of these and other

references making it clear that what was being described was the ability of these players to catch the ball while playing positions other than catcher.

1. IN THE BEGINNING

27 "He who would occupy the post of honor . . .": "Bob Lively," "Base Ball: How They Play the Game in New England," *Porter's Spirit of the Times*, December 27, 1856, 276–277.

27 By the end of the 1850s there were only two versions of baseball with enough structure to stand a realistic chance of becoming a national standard: Other versions were still being played, most notably a game known as "town ball," which was more widely played than was the Massachusetts Game. But town ball and the other versions lacked standard rules, making it virtually impossible that any of them could be adopted as a national standard.

28 They also eventually denounced as childish . . .: By the time the Knickerbockers decided that the "bound rule" should be abolished, control of the game's rules had passed to a body known as the National Association of Base Ball Players. Thus while the Knickerbockers could and did lobby to have the rule changed, they no longer had the power to change it themselves.

28 "As the excitement of the game intensified . . .": Chadwick Scrapbooks, unspecified 1879 article from the *Cincinnati Enquirer*.

28 "could not break themselves of the habit . . .": *Janesville Daily Gazette*, February 8, 1905, 5.

29 This represented a dramatic change from all previous bat-and-ball games . . .: David Block, "How Slick Were the Knicks?," Chapter 6 of *Baseball Before We Knew It*.

29 clubs often stationed two or three catchers, or "behind men," back of home plate: According to an article in the *Boston Globe*, March 27, 1888, 5, the third catcher was known as the "shacker." But James L. Steele, in "How the National Game Developed: Some Baseball Reminiscences," *Outing*, June 1904, 334, claims that "shacker" was a synonym for "scout" or "scoot"—the term that designated all the players other than the pitcher, catcher, and basemen. Quite possibly both articles are right, as terminology often varied.

29 "found himself crawling among those thorny bushes . . .": Steele, "How the National Game Developed," 335.

29 "Some of the players had a knack of shortening up their bat . . .": James D'Wolf Lovett, *Old Boston Boys and the Games They Played*, 132.

30 "A tick and a ketch / Will always fetch": "Old Baseball: The Game as the Boys Used to Play It," *Indianapolis Sentinel*, April 3, 1887.

30 "right to knock the ball with his bat . . .": "Lively," "Base Ball," 276–277.

30 . . . catchers in the Massachusetts Game typically stood closer . . .: "Lively" in "Base Ball," 276–277, stated that catchers in New England typically stood three or four paces behind the batter, and his recommendation was three paces. There are different interpretations about the distance designated by a pace, with some believing it was equivalent to a yard and others believing it was less. Either way, it is clear that the New England catcher stood much closer to the batter than did his New York counterparts, and probably cut the distance about in half.

30 "reach forward and take the ball from before the bat": *Boston Globe*, March 27, 1888, 5.

30 "could about pick a ball off a striker's bat": Lovett, *Old Boston Boys*, 129.

30 "received a broken arm by a striker . . .": *Boston Globe*, March 27, 1888, 5.

30 "sometimes got a bad blow from the bat . . .": Lovett, *Old Boston Boys*, 131.

31 "stop[ped] with a solid *smack* in the catcher's hands" and "I have frequently heard the catcher . . .": "Lively" in "Base Ball," 276–277.
31 "The two best players upon each side . . ." and "The finest exhibition of skill . . .": "Lively," "Base Ball," 276–277.
31 "a good pitcher and catcher alone are not sufficient to win a match": *New York Atlas*, July 31, 1859, 1.
31 "The day has gone by . . .": *New York Atlas*, August 28, 1859.
31 "too slow and lazy a game . . .": "How Baseball Began—A Member of the Gotham Club of Fifty Years Ago Tells About It," *San Francisco Examiner*, November 27, 1887, 14. Similarly a Philadelphia town-ball player explained in 1858 that the members of his club preferred that game to cricket because it kept all the players involved in the action. *New York Clipper*, July 31, 1858.
32 foul tips were rare occurrences in this version: In an 1857 game between two New York clubs, for instance, it was considered noteworthy that the Continental Club's batters "were not used to striking such balls as [Baltic pitcher Ed] Brown pitched to all appearances, and tipped many of them—this is where the Continentals made their poorest playing." *Porter's Spirit of the Times*, July 18, 1857.
32 "could stop a ball with his shins . . .": "Modern Base Ball Playing," *Cornell Era*, reprinted in *Trenton Daily State Gazette*, November 10, 1870.
32 Even in the New York version, pitcher and catcher were generally viewed as key players: In 1859, for example, a New York sportswriter declared that the catcher, pitcher, and first baseman played the most important roles and that the first two were "selected for their peculiar skill." *New York Herald*, October 16, 1859.
32 "bad blood between rival teams": Lovett, *Old Boston Boys*, 131.
33 "the foolishness, fancy airs and smart capers . . .": *New York Atlas*, July 3, 1859, 5.
33 "Mr. DeBost's fondness for display . . .": *New York Atlas*, July 31, 1859.
33 The decisive triumph of the New York Game was the result of a combination of factors . . .: See Peter Morris, *Level Playing Fields*, xvi–xvii, for a detailed discussion.

2. THE CATCHER AS TOUGH GUY

35 "There is a ground sparrow's nest . . .": *Milwaukee Daily Sentinel*, June 16, 1877, 2.
37 Pitchers soon began intentionally delivering wild offerings . . .: Peter Morris, *A Game of Inches*, vol. 1, entry 3.3.1, 180–181, and entry 3.3.2, 181–185. The advent of the latter tactic had the immediate effect of increasing the prominence of the pitcher and catcher. After an 1863 game, a sportswriter (probably Henry Chadwick) complained about "all the heavy work laying between the pitchers and catchers, the efforts of the former apparently being devoted to the intimidation of the batsman by pitching *at* them instead of for them as the rules require." *New York Clipper*, October 17, 1863.
37 he was occasionally referred to as the "behind" or "behind man": The use of the noun "behind" to refer to the catcher was never common, despite its appropriation by the modern recreators who play "Vintage Base Ball." Both were, however, used on a few occasions in descriptions of both the Massachusetts Game and the Knickerbockers' game. For example, an article in the *Spirit of the Times* on September 22, 1855, remarked that "[Charles] Debost, as behind man, has no equal." Far more common was to use "behind" as an adverb to describe the catcher's positioning (e.g., Smith played behind the plate).
38 The catcher's ability to handle speedy deliveries became crucial . . .: Henry Chadwick, for instance, wrote in 1868 that with a swift pitcher, "the catcher must pay attention to stopping the ball and to catching sharp tips from the bat, than anything else, for passed balls are one of the expensive results of swift pitching, and sharp tips are pretty difficult to hold, from swiftly delivered balls." Henry Chadwick, *The Game of Base Ball*, 31.

38 It had also become essential for the catcher to be able to handle fast pitches cleanly
. . .: As Chadwick explained, it was "very difficult to hold a swiftly pitched ball in time
to throw it to second base to cut off a player, while with slow pitching it can be done
with comparative ease by an active and expert catcher." Chadwick, *Game of Base Ball*,
32.

38 "both the strikers and catchers will have to pad themselves up like cricketers do": *Brooklyn Eagle*, October 7, 1863.

39 His ability to catch a pitch makes it legitimate . . .: In the early years of baseball a catcher
could complete a strikeout by catching the ball on the first bounce, but some sort of
catch has always been required. Even the current rule that batters cannot run to first
on a missed third strike with less than two out if it is occupied did not come into effect
until later.

39 "You have to have a catcher or you'll have a lot of passed balls": See the very first note in
this Notes section for a discussion of the origins of this quotation.

39 Leggett's role in Creighton's development . . .: James Wood, as told to Frank G. Menke,
"Baseball in By-Gone Days," part 2, syndicated column, *Marion* (Ohio) *Daily Star*,
August 15, 1916.

39 In a three-game all-star series . . .: *Brooklyn Eagle*, March 15, 1896. Four days later the
Eagle published a letter in which veteran sportswriter William Rankin pointed out several mistakes in this article. Rankin noted, for instance, that the game actually occurred
on June 5, 1862, rather than in 1863 as stated by the first author. But Rankin confirmed
that it was considered necessary to replace Creighton when Chapman's injury occurred,
a detail that is also substantiated in a game account in the *Eagle* on June 6, 1862.

40 New York catchers typically stood in an upright position: See my *A Game of Inches*, vol.
1, entry 4.2.1, 203–208, for a full discussion of the evidence on this topic and on the
evolution of catcher positioning.

40 Many of them moved nearer to the plate . . .: Some New York Game catchers of this
period even stationed themselves directly behind the plate, but they did so only when
the pitcher intended to deliberately toss pitches too wild for the batter to reach. This
odd strategy was devised in response to the tendency of batters in this situation to stand
at the plate without swinging until a wild pitch allowed the base runners to advance.
But it backfired so often that the *New York Atlas* of October 27, 1861, recorded sarcastically that a runner had advanced from first base to third base as "the usual penalty of
catcher standing directly behind [the batter] to receive the ball pitched over the batter's
reach." Elsewhere in the same issue appeared a reference to another catcher "who came
up behind the batter to catch balls not intended to be struck at, —a system which so
often ends in a man on first base getting to third base or perhaps home, in the absence
of a bulkhead [backstop], which it is to be hoped will be done away with by the next
Convention."

40 They would also move noticeably closer . . .: Even Henry Chadwick, generally a strong
advocate of safety and caution, counseled in 1860, "when a player has made his first
base, the Catcher should take a position nearer the striker, in order to take the ball from
the pitcher before it bounds." *Beadle's Dime Base-Ball Player*, 21.

40 "proved so great a success . . .": Francis C. Richter, *Richter's History and Records of Base
Ball*, 220. According to Rankin, Boerum pioneered the practice at the suggestion of
Atlantics president William V. Babcock.

40 "so close to the batter, as to hardly give him any room . . .": *Brooklyn Times*, July 20,
1860; reprinted in Howard Rosenberg, *Cap Anson 3*, 9.

40 "It was not until Creighton . . .": Henry Chadwick, "The Catchers," *New York Clipper*,
December 30, 1876.

40 As they did so, Leggett's courageous positioning attracted praise and even awe: When the Excelsiors paid a visit to Baltimore in 1860, the amazed locals proclaimed him "the first to ever take fly-tips close behind the bat." William Ridgely Griffith, *The Early History of Amateur Base Ball in the State of Maryland*, reprinted in *Maryland Historical Magazine* 87, no. 2 (Summer 1992), 204. Two years later the ballplayers of Boston took careful note of how Leggett "caught on a bound except when a man was on third base, and then he went up behind the bat." *Boston Journal*, February 22, 1905.

40 A number of Brooklyn catchers . . .: According to the *Brooklyn Eagle* of August 18, 1864, Howard "rather astonished" a crowd in Hoboken with a "peculiar style" that involved stationing himself "close behind the bat." Boston audiences got another peek at the daring technique in 1865 when Frank Prescott Norton, playing for a visiting Brooklyn club, "caught up behind the bat when there was a man on any base, and on a bound when the bases were free." *Boston Journal*, February 22, 1905. Candy Cummings was quoted in the *Brooklyn Eagle* on April 26, 1896, 17, as saying that Jewell "was the pluckiest man I ever saw behind the bat. I often told him he would meet with an accident, but he stood right under the bat with no protection whatever." A. H. Spink, in *The National Game*, 92, cites Ferguson's practice of standing close to the batter.

41 Fergy Malone: Spink, *National Game*, 92.

41 "I began to believe it possible to get close up to the bat . . .": *Daily Kennebec Journal*, January 4, 1908, 4.

41 catchers in towns like Rochester, New York, and Detroit . . .: Rochester catcher John Morey was also said to "get under the bat and catch the hot delivery without even dodging." Quoted in Priscilla Astifan, "Baseball in the Nineteenth Century," *Rochester History* 52, no. 3 (Summer 1990), 15. University of Michigan student George Dawson played for the Detroit Base Ball Club in the summer of 1868 and startled onlookers by "standing close to the batter" in order to hold opposing base runners near to their bases. *Detroit Advertiser and Tribune*, September 10, 1868.

41 "stepping back, so as to intimidate the catcher . . .": *Cincinnati Daily Times*, July 10, 1868. A batting line was created that year in hopes of ending this practice, but it was not enforced.

41 "one of the finest catchers in the community . . .": Chadwick Scrapbooks, circa 1861. Masten moved to Washington, D.C., in hopes of regaining his health but died in 1864 at the age of thirty.

41 "puffed up and exceedingly painful . . .": James L. Terry, *Long Before the Dodgers*, 144.

41 Hicks served briefly in the New York Infantry's Fifteenth Regiment: Hicks never filed for Civil War pension benefits, so there is no definitive evidence that this service record belongs to him. But there appears to be no other man of that name and age who it could be, and there was a family tradition that Hicks served as a Union drummer boy. *Hudson Dispatch*, August 29, 1961; Hicks Hall of Fame file.

42 "Since the secession of Hicks . . .": *New York Clipper*, August 21, 1869.

42 he never forgot the version played in Massachusetts: For Cummings's recollections of playing the Massachusetts Game and moving to Brooklyn, see "First Pitcher to Curve Ball: Cummings Tells How He Made Discovery Which Revolutionized the Game," syndicated, *Duluth News Tribune*, September 14, 1913.

42 Cummings would give many different accounts of his experiments: See Morris, *Game of Inches*, vol. 1, entry 3.2.3 on the Curveball, 118–136, for a detailed discussion.

42 The most colorful version had him throwing seashells at the beach: See, for example, Arthur Cummings, "How I Curved the First Ball," *Baseball Magazine*, September 1908, reprinted in Roger Kahn, *The Head Game: Baseball Seen from the Pitcher's Mound* (New York: Harcourt, 2000), 18–21.

42 "Every day I would be at it . . .": Elwood A. Roff, *Base Ball and Base Ball Players* (self-published, 1912), 226. Roff wrote to Cummings and received a lengthy letter in response, which he reprinted in this book. There were many published versions of the origins of Cummings's curveball, so it is dangerous to give more weight to one account than to others. But many of the versions were filtered through sportswriters who often left out key details such as these in order to streamline their accounts. In contrast, Roff appears to have published Cummings's long letter verbatim.

42 some frustrated batters complained they should be allowed to leave the batter's box in pursuit of it: In the *Owosso* (Michigan) *Weekly Press* of August 8, 1877, for instance, a ballplayer complained bitterly about an umpire who called strikes on curveballs that ended up out of reach of the batters, yet told them they could not leave the batter's box to chase the elusive pitch. Despite the humor, this lament also suggested why pitchers were resented by many for having gained power by suspect means, whereas the catcher was admired because he did things in a straightforward manner.

42 Others simply despaired of ever being able to hit the unhittable pitch: According to Harvard ballplayer James Tyng, when his club first faced a curveball pitcher in 1875: "Out of the first nine men at the bat eight, I think, were unable to hit the ball. We had no idea what was the trouble, except that the bat and ball seemed to have a repulsion for each other which we could not overcome. About the fifth inning one of our men, who had been standing behind the catcher, came back with the announcement that the balls were curving away from the batsman. There was a general exodus on our part to the backstop to watch this unheard of phenomenon. Sure enough, there were the balls coming in for the middle of the plate and curving off beyond the reach of the bat." *Harper's Weekly*, quoted in *New York Times*, June 10, 1900. In the preceding year a Boston batter facing a curveball pitcher for the first time "made thirteen futile attempts to hit the ball and then congratulated the young man on his success." *Sporting Life*, March 5, 1898.

43 "If a catcher can be found to hold him . . .": *New York Sunday Mercury*, April 24, 1880, about Amherst College left-handed pitcher Willard Sawyer, who did indeed prove proficient enough—once he found a good catcher—to pitch in the major leagues.

43 "Cummings' crazy curve" and "believed in the possibility of pitching a curve ball": Roff, *Base Ball and Base Ball Players*, 226.

43 Cummings gave specific credit to Hicks in two accounts of the origins of the pitch: "First Pitcher to Curve Ball"; *Brooklyn Eagle*, April 26, 1896, 17. Cummings also gave many accounts that did not mention Hicks, but Hicks was the only professional catcher he ever singled out.

43 "The Hicks technique behind the plate . . .": Arthur Daley, "Catching Revolutionary," *New York Times*, June 24, 1946, 26.

43 "the side bias imparted to the ball . . .": *New York Clipper*, December 14, 1873, 293. Chadwick, however, was not as impressed with the curve, sniffing that the pitch was "practically useless in its effect on the batting."

43 Bobby Mathews, the only other professional pitcher who mastered the underhand curveball: Cummings maintained that the only pitchers besides himself who mastered the curve while the underhand delivery requirement was still in effect were Mathews and two college stars, Charles Hammond Avery of Yale and Joseph McElroy Mann of Princeton. *Sporting News*, December 29, 1921. While some of Cummings's statements about the curve are contradicted by other evidence, this assertion was confirmed by many other contemporaries. Morris, *Game of Inches*, vol. 1, entry 3.2.3, 118–136. Hicks and Mathews worked in tandem in 1875 with New York and in 1877 with Cincinnati. "Of the new players engaged by the Mutuals for this season all played well except Hicks, the catcher, who was completely out of form. However, as this is the first game

of the year, and as Matthews' [sic] peculiar delivery bothers all catchers more or less for the first few games, there is an excuse for the bad play shown by Hicks yesterday." *New York Times*, April 11, 1875, 12. Yet they obviously worked out their difficulties quickly, as Hicks and Mathews signed as a pair to play with Cincinnati in 1877. *Chicago Tribune*, July 30, 1876, 3. Hicks appears to have first gotten together with Mathews after the 1870 season, when Hicks traveled to Baltimore to work with the diminutive pitcher. Hicks Hall of Fame file, unidentified clipping. This suggests two intriguing possibilities—either that Hicks taught the pitch to Mathews or, more likely, that Mathews had begun to develop his curve but knew that he would need Hicks in order to be able to use it.

44 "No matter how swift . . .": *New York Clipper*, December 28, 1872. Chadwick made the same argument in the *Brooklyn Eagle*, August 13, 1872.

44 Harry Wright tried to persuade Nat Hicks to play with the Red Stockings in 1870: *New York Clipper*, March 26, 1870. Hicks instead joined the National Club of Washington, and he appears there on the 1870 census as a treasury clerk—a job offer that lured many ballplayers to the nation's capital. At some point that year he moved on to Baltimore and began working with Mathews.

45 "exactly five shutouts prior to 1870": John H. Gruber, "Scoring Rules," *Sporting News*, November 4, 1915.

45 baseball's first recorded shutout at the hands of Jim Creighton: *Brooklyn Eagle*, November 10, 1860.

45 an increasing number of clubs responded by opting for the "dead ball": There was no standard baseball until near the end of the decade, so in 1870 the home club usually chose the ball to be used.

45 even Harry Wright would advocate livelier baseballs: *Detroit Post and Tribune*, January 4, 1879. See also *Chicago Tribune*, November 12, 1876, 7, in which Wright made suggestions for rule changes that would increase scoring.

46 the prevalence of passed balls: In the early days of baseball, the term "passed ball" did not imply that the catcher was at fault as it does today. Any pitch that got beyond the catcher was called a "passed ball," regardless of whether it did so because of the pitcher's wildness or the catcher's mishandling of it.

46 Even catchers like Hicks who played close to the plate still did not crouch, though many did stoop slightly: An 1871 article noted of the Red Stockings' Allison: "In standing close to the bat, too, he takes a ball hot from the pitcher, while perfectly upright. Most catchers take a stooping position." *New York Clipper*, January 21, 1871. Johnny Ward added, "all assume a stooping posture, bending forward from the hips, in order better to get to a low as well as a high pitch. Some, like [Con] Daily, of Indianapolis, crouch almost to the ground, but such a position must be not only more fatiguing, but destroy somewhat the gauging of a high pitch." Ward, *Base-Ball: How to Become a Player*, 68. See Morris, *A Game of Inches*, vol. 1, entry 4.2.2, 208–210, for a more detailed discussion of the origins of the crouch.

46 Some of Hicks's contemporaries believed he was the first catcher to stand directly behind the batter: "Behind the Bat with 'Nat' Hicks," *New York Times*, May 12, 1907, S4. Early sportswriter William Rankin correctly denounced "that fake about Nat Hicks being the first man to play close up behind the bat." *Sporting News*, September 9, 1909. But the testimony of Hicks's contemporaries is nonetheless important evidence of the key role he played in popularizing this positioning.

46 "created a sensation by catching behind the bat . . .": "Behind the Bat with 'Nat' Hicks," S4. The article's author is not given, but Arthur Daley later maintained that Chadwick had written it. Daley, "Catching Revolutionary," 26.

47 "very badly hurt forefinger": *New York Clipper*, June 14, 1873.

47 "struck in the face with a sharp foul tip": *New York Times*, July 4, 1873, 2.

47 "it was not thought by any . . .": *New York Times,* July 5, 1873, 5. Hicks was playing for the Mutuals of New York against the Atlantics of Brooklyn, but the account was not an example of hometown favoritism; that day's *Brooklyn Eagle* similarly gushed, "Such a plucky exhibition of catching has never been witnessed as that of Hicks in this game. Despite his injury of Thursday, and another severe blow in the face yesterday, beside a blow from a carelessly slung bat he faced the music bravely."

47 "sharp fly tip catches": *Brooklyn Eagle,* July 5, 1873, 3.

47 "The punishment the stout-hearted and thick-skinned Hicks absorbed . . .": Daley, "Catching Revolutionary," 26. Hicks's knee injury did not in fact end his career, but it handicapped him throughout the 1876 season and probably played a large part in his decision to retire in the middle of the 1877 season. Chadwick, "The Catchers."

47 the only injury that kept Hicks out of action: Ryczek, *Blackguards and Red Stockings,* 110; *New York Clipper,* August 2, 1873; the incident occurred in a game played on July 24, 1873.

47 "baseball's original tough guy": Daley, "Catching Revolutionary," 26.

48 "almost wholly unable to earn a support . . .": William Craver Hall of Fame file, copy of Civil War invalid pension application, dated June 28, 1892.

48 "disciple of Joe Leggett": *New York Clipper,* December 14, 1872, 293.

48 William "Cherokee" Fisher, who pitched with "cyclonic speed" but little control: *Brooklyn Eagle,* April 26, 1896, 17; *Chicago Tribune,* April 11, 1875, 16.

48 "worked together that day . . .": *Chicago News,* reprinted in *Cleveland Plain Dealer,* June 10, 1888.

49 "The captain of a nine . . .": *Ball Player's Chronicle,* August 8, 1867, 6.

50 "obstinate fits . . .": *New York Clipper,* December 21, 1872.

50 His Troy club was plagued by rumors of shady dealings . . .: William Ryczek, *When Johnny Came Sliding Home,* 226; *Chicago Tribune,* February 17, 1878. Craver also created the only blemish on the perfect season of the 1869 Red Stockings of Cincinnati by pulling his Troy team off the field with the score tied. He was ostensibly protesting a decision by the umpire, but many believed that it was an excuse to save Troy's backers from losing their large wagers on the outcome. The umpire declared the game forfeited to Cincinnati, but Harry Wright preferred to regard the game as a tie and considered the club's record to be fifty-seven match victories and one tie.

51 being publicly assaulted by a gambler in 1876, suggesting a double cross: *New York Clipper,* June 17, 1876, 92; Ryczek, *Blackguards and Red Stockings,* 211. The incident occurred before New York's game on June 6, 1876.

51 Craver was banned for life: Throughout these troubles, Craver continued to have his defenders, especially in Troy. When he was expelled in 1870, a Troy newspaper dismissed the allegation as "a trumped up charge." Craver Hall of Fame file, 1871 article from unidentified Troy newspaper. Henry Chadwick was less emphatic but seemed inclined to give Craver the benefit of the doubt, noting that his accuser had little credibility. *New York Clipper,* December 14, 1872, 293. Later another Troy journalist would even write of Craver's lifetime ban that "he was barred from the National League for putting batters out with a trick foul tip." Craver Hall of Fame file, article from an unidentified Troy newspaper, June 17, 1901. And Troy's entry in the International Association tried to sign him in 1878 despite the preceding year's scandal. That August the International Association's judiciary committee voted to reinstate him, and it was reported that he would become captain of the Haymakers. *New York Sunday Mercury,* August 17, 1878.

51 Hicks was a far less notorious character than Craver, but he too was the subject of occasional rumors and innuendos: The rumors that flew about Hicks and other catchers will be discussed in a lengthy note in Chapter 6.

51 "The necessity for a rule of the kind . . .": *New York Clipper,* November 25, 1871.

51 "played so close to the bat . . .": *Cincinnati Enquirer*, September 10, 1875.

52 "one of the pluckiest catchers . . .": "Murnane's Baseball," *Boston Globe*, January 27, 1907, 30.

52 "with a singular 'assist' . . .": Rankin Scrapbooks, describing a May 16, 1880, game between the Knickerbocker and Bay City clubs.

52 "with vast thoughtlessness . . .": *California Spirit of the Times*, December 13, 1879.

52 "our catcher worked through a game with the blood dripping from his bruised hands . . .": Stanley B. Cowing, early player for the Niagaras of Buffalo, quoted in the *Kalamazoo Evening Telegraph*, March 26, 1906.

52 "was struck on the end of his little finger . . .": *Terre Haute Evening Gazette*, April 16, 1883.

52 "with bursted hands and blood trickling down his arms . . .": "Base Ball Players of Salisbury Past and Present," *Wicomoco News*, August 13, 1903.

52 "but would not give in and caught through the game . . .": *Washington Post*, February 10, 1884.

52–53 "The veterans of the diamond field smiled . . .": *New York Sunday Mercury*, November 15, 1879.

53 "knotted and twisted joints," "monuments for work well done," and "how often he had been 'put to sleep' . . .": *Daily Kennebec Journal*, January 4, 1908, 4. A photo of Allison's hands appeared in J. Ed Grillo, "Allison, One of Baseball's Pioneers, Tells How the Great Game Was Played Forty Years Ago," *Washington Post*, January 12, 1908, S3.

53 "false prudence which dotes on health and wealth is the butt and merriment of heroism": Ralph Waldo Emerson, "Heroism," in *The Collected Works of Ralph Waldo Emerson,* vol. II, *Essays: First Series,* 149.

53 the cowboy, who was similarly known for having disfigured hands: Dary, *Cowboy Culture*, 31. The cowboy's mangled hands remain one of his trademarks; John R. Erickson, in *The Modern Cowboy* (Denton: University of North Texas Press, 1981), 10, writes, "A cowboy's hands tell the story of his work. You rarely see one with delicate hands. Most often the fingers are thickened by constant use, the palms rough enough to snag on delicate fabrics, the top side scarred and scabbed, and the nails bearing evidence of abuse."

54 "plucky, facing the hottest delivery and taking his knocks and bruises like a man": Unidentified clipping, Jack Chapman Scrapbook, National Baseball Hall of Fame and Museum.

54 "Larry Corcoran gave me this . . .": *Cleveland Plain Dealer*, April 2, 1888.

55 "I saw Flint get a hard one . . .": *Washington Herald*, July 4, 1909, 13.

55 "hands were so broken up . . .": Byron E. Clarke, "Catchers of the '70s Were Stars in the Game," *Atlanta Constitution*, December 1, 1907, C2.

55 "each member, of course, shook hands with the President . . ." and "The gnarled fingers of the old catcher . . .": Both of these tales appear in Flint's obituary in *Sporting Life*, January 23, 1892, 9. Intriguingly, one note claimed that President Grover Cleveland's own political career had received a boost from his having been a catcher during the early days of baseball. The note, which appeared in the *Cincinnati News Journal* on April 22, 1883, and was said to have originated in the *Philadelphia Press*, stated that Cleveland's election as governor of New York "depended largely and with reason upon his artistic work behind the bat during his more active sports twenty years or so again." I have, however, not been able to find any confirmation of this assertion.

55 "mangled hands . . . frequent subjects of sport photography . . .": Guy M. Smith, Danville, Ill., "He Could Catch Anything," typescript in McGuire file, Hall of Fame.

55 many of the fingers on his gnarled hands . . .: *Albion Evening Recorder*, August 2, 1932.

55–56 "It was one of the wildest pitches Bill ever made . . .": Smith, "He Could Catch Anything."

56 "Things were going along swimmingly . . .": *Wilkes-Barre Times*, February 3, 1898, as told by early ballplayer Tom Taylor.

56 "hand had lost so many finger nails . . ." and "'Mart' was a hero in purpose . . .": T. Z. Cowles, *Chicago Tribune*, May 26, 1918.

56–57 "massive lines of a battleship . . .": this anecdote about Mart King is from W. W. Aulick, "One Hundred Notable Figures in Baseball: Mart King, Who Scorned All Precautionary Measures," *Auburn Citizen*, March 10, 1911.

57 "A finger nail torn from its roots meant nothing to him . . .": T. Z. Cowles, *Chicago Tribune*, May 26, 1918.

57 "with the knuckles, which become bruised . . .": *Boston Globe*, August 5, 1886, 5.

57 "into his palms a mixture of alcohol, lemon juice, and rock salt . . .": *New York Sunday Mercury*, June 19, 1880.

57–58 "hand became split or a finger broken . . .": *San Francisco Chronicle*, reprinted in *Sporting News*, December 30, 1909, 2.

58 "On a hot day . . .": Tip Wright, "Rusie Was the Best," *Wilkes-Barre Times Leader*, March 7, 1910, 13.

58 "My head has been so sore . . .": Wright, "Rusie Was the Best," 13. O'Rourke apparently is referring here to the consequences of being hit by pitches while batting, but of course the damage done by a foul tip could be at least as severe.

3. THE CATCHER AS INDISPENSABLE

59 "The backstop in a team was everything then . . .": T. W. B., "Then—'Johnnie' Clapp—Now," *Elmira Telegram*, June 5, 1904.

59 Most clubs were simply lost if their catcher couldn't continue: For example, a member of the Charter Oaks of Hartford recalled a game against the Pequots of New London in which his team was ahead until a foul ball struck team catcher Gersh Hubbell in the face and knocked him out. The account concludes by stating with an aura of inevitability that with no catcher able to take Hubbell's place, the Charter Oaks were beaten. "Baseball Here Forty Years Ago," by Major Julius G. Rathbun, a "muffin" player for the Charter Oaks, Chadwick Scrapbooks, c. 1907.

60 "The regulation ball . . .": *New York Times*, March 12, 1876, 2.

61 "proved to be the best . . ." and "'Carley' Moon volunteered . . .": *Janesville Daily Gazette*, February 22, 1905, 2.

61 "The catcher wore no mask, gloves or pad . . .," "it looked to me . . .," "striking at balls . . .," "Allen's catching . . .," and "had not recovered . . .": *Janesville Daily Gazette*, February 25, 1905, 2.

62 "possessed the ability . . .," "but his pardonable fear . . .," "no catcher seemed available," "having no catcher . . .," "something had to be done . . .," "These two games," "refused to catch," and "hands were a sight to behold": *Janesville Daily Gazette*, March 1, 1905, 2.

62–63 "if we could have traded . . .," "he had his usual . . .," "our nine was becoming . . .," and "It seems almost incredible . . .": *Janesville Daily Gazette*, March 6, 1905, 2.

63 "A first class battery would have helped us . . .": *Janesville Daily Gazette*, March 9, 1905, 5.

63 "played in every game during the season . . .": *Janesville Daily Gazette*, April 17, 1905, 2.

64 a club from Chicago arrived in Muskegon . . .: *Muskegon Journal*, August 20, 1878.

64 "IMMENSE ATTRACTION! . . .": *Evansville Journal*, June 4, 1877.

64–65 "if catcher 'Joe' had not . . .": *Pontiac Gazette*, September 25, 1874.

65 "would bring a curve pitcher . . ." and "the curve in the pitching . . .": *Clinton* (St. Johns, Michigan) *Independent*, August 21, 1879.

65 . . . he calmly explained that the two men were jilting Detroit . . .: *Detroit Advertiser and Tribune*, September 2, 1876.

65–66 "Now Mr. Sullivan! come back! . . .": *Detroit Free Press*, September 9, 1876, under the pseudonym "M. Pyre."

66 Boston . . . dominated the first professional league, the National Association: Boston won the 1872, 1873, 1874, and 1875 pennants, though White did not arrive until 1873.

66 "if anybody hits Brad clean . . .": *Louisville Courier-Journal*, reprinted in *St. Louis Globe-Democrat*, March 25, 1877, 7.

66 there was talk of letting Cap Anson catch: The *New York Sunday Mercury* of September 9, 1876, reported that if White left, Anson, "who likes the position," would catch for Spalding. But if the Chicago management ever considered using Anson as its primary catcher, the plan was shelved after Spalding decided to give up pitching and concentrate on managing the club.

67 "to catch Bradley requires . . .": *Boston Globe*, June 13, 1877.

67 "his superior has not been seen . . ." and "requires a catcher": *New York Clipper*, June 30, 1877, 107.

67–68 "half the strength of a pitcher's play . . .": William Rankin Scrapbooks, clipping from unspecified source.

68 "McVey's hands were . . .": *St. Louis Globe-Democrat*, May 13, 1877, 7.

68 "was not, is not, and never can be a catcher . . .": *Chicago Tribune*, October 28, 1877, 7.

68 "The Chicago players are very unfortunate . . .": *New York Times*, September 5, 1877.

4. THE CATCHER AS ONE IN A MILLION

69 "Who would be a candidate for the governorship . . .": *Boston Transcript*, reprinted in the *Lake Superior* (Minnesota) *News*, December 5, 1878.

69 "McVey is a catcher who . . .": *New York Clipper*, December 21, 1872.

70 "I used to travel with the Nationals and Olympics . . .": *Buffalo American*, reprinted in the *Daily Kennebec Journal*, December 9, 1907.

70 "used to fill the small boys with awe and admiration . . .": *Sporting Life*, January 12, 1887, 2.

70 "one of the greatest catchers whom . . .": Lovett, *Old Boston Boys*, 225–226. In like fashion, at a parade for the American Association champion Mets after the 1884 season, it was catcher Billy Holbert who "seemed to be the most popular," even though Holbert had as usual struggled to keep his batting average over the .200 mark. *New York Times*, October 28, 1884, 5.

70 "In the old days the boys . . .": The quotation continued "then in the pitcher's box, then the infield and after that the outfield." "Few Good Catchers," *Fort Pierce* (Florida) *News*, June 11, 1909.

70 "against his father's wishes": Letter from Bennett's nephew, George W. Porter, September 28, 1960, Charley Bennett Hall of Fame file.

70 "a perfect model . . .": Maclean Kennedy, "Greatest Backstop of Them All Was the Detroit Boy, Charley Bennett," *Detroit Free Press*, March 30, 1913, 20.

70 "quite a bevy of girls were looking at him . . .": *New York Clipper*, July 10, 1875.

70 "just too brave for anything . . .": *Denton Journal*, June 7, 1884.

70 "one bad fault . . .": William Rankin Scrapbooks, clipping from unspecified source, dated April 17, 1869.

71 "the star backstop . . ." and "was considered more or less of a joke . . .": Both examples from Kennedy, "Greatest Backstop of Them All Was the Detroit Boy, Charley Bennett," 20.

71 "When we heard of the professional game . . .": Clarence Darrow, *The Story of My Life*, 171–178.

71 John Clapp returned to represent the town in key matches . . .: The game between Ithaca and Binghamton occurred on July 17, 1875. *Ithaca Journal*, December 19, 1904; W. Lloyd Johnson, *DeWitt Historical Society Newsletter*, Summer 1983. On another occasion, an Elmira team tried to hire Clapp for a key game against Binghamton, knowing that Clapp's allegiance was with Elmira. Alas, Clapp's major league owner had already pledged to let the Binghamton team borrow Clapp for the game. So, as Clapp put it, with great reluctance he had "to play with the enemy. It was like taking [the Elmira team's president's] heart out before his own eyes. I did not want to go to that game anyway, and wished myself back again in New York. But I was working for a salary, for bread and clothes for my family. I had no choice." T. W. B., "Then— 'Johnnie' Clapp—Now."

71 good catchers came in a wide variety of shapes and sizes . . .: Mills's six-foot-two-inch, 165-pound frame was said to give him "an advantage over all other catchers, in his long reach." *Brooklyn Eagle*, August 15, 1868. John Montgomery Ward added in 1888, "the size of the candidate seems not to be of vital importance, for there are good catchers, from the little, sawed-off bantam, [Joseph 'Chick'] Hofford, of Jersey City, to the tall, angular [Connie] Mack, of Washington, and Ganzell [Charley Ganzel], of Detroit. Still, other things being equal, a tall, active man should have an advantage because of his longer 'reach' for widely pitched balls, and on account of the confidence a big mark to pitch at inspires in a pitcher." Ward, *Base-Ball: How to Become a Player*, 66.

72 Only fat men were not seen behind the plate in the 1870s . . .: For example, Scott Hastings was noticeably overweight when he reported at the start of the 1876 season, and it was reported that he "will need a good deal of reduction before he can fill his place well; but if he does take the trouble to train down, he can make a high record, as he is nimble enough." *New York Sunday Mercury*, March 25, 1876.

72 "One thing that must be remembered . . .": "Modern Ball Hard for Defense," *Bellingham Sunday Herald*, February 27, 1910, 8.

72 "Some players catch with the fingers pointing toward the ball . . .": Ward, *Base-Ball: How to Become a Player*, 69.

72 "a model for catchers in his style . . .": *New York Clipper*, December 30, 1876.

73 "seemed to be endowed with the ability . . .": *Syracuse Courier*, reprinted in the *Cleveland Herald*, September 17, 1869.

73 "White behind the bat is just simply perfection": Randolph, the New York correspondent for the *Chicago Tribune*; reprinted in *St. Louis Globe-Democrat*, June 1, 1875.

73–74 "the skill or 'knack' required . . ." and "The fact of the bat . . .": Essay on catching by "Doc" Bushong in N. Frederick Pfeffer, *Scientific Ball* (Chicago, 1889), 51–52. It will be recalled from Frank L. Smith's description of his efforts to tutor young catcher Abe Allen that the "weakness of watching the bat instead of the ball" was one of Allen's great shortcomings.

74 "get the ball before it reaches him": *Sporting News*, June 16, 1894.

74 "should not 'fight the ball' . . .": *New York World*, reprinted in *Milwaukee Journal*, April 19, 1900.

74 "muffed four foul tips . . .": *Cleveland Herald*, September 17, 1869. This perception appeared as early as 1860 when a game account recorded that a catcher for a New York amateur club had been able to catch almost every foul ball and foul tip that came his way as a result of having "got his courage up." *New York Atlas*, September 9, 1860.

74 "ambitious but youthful back-stops . . .": John Doyle, "Catch the Curves," *Duluth News Tribune*, May 13, 1894, 5. Similarly, in the June 16, 1894, article from *Sporting News* cited in the previous paragraph, the fault of "fighting the ball" was attributed to "over-anxiety."

74 "one day a foul tip struck me in the throat . . .": "George Wright Recalls Triumphs of 'Red Stockings,'" *New York Sun*, November 14, 1915, section 6, 4.

75 "The most important lesson I ever learned . . .": Quoted in Bill O'Neal, *Encyclopedia of Western Gun-Fighters* (Norman: University of Oklahoma Press, 1979), vi.

76 "gnarled and his fingers crooked . . .": "Billy Sunday and Deacon White, One-Time Teammates, Meet After Separation of 35 Years," *Elmira Star-Gazette*, September 18, 1924.

76 "Part of a catcher's effectiveness . . .": "Chicago exchange," reprinted in *Rocky Mountain News*, November 26, 1883, 2.

76 Fleetwood Walker was sharing tips . . .: *Oberlin News-Tribune*, December 28, 1945; cited in David W. Zang, *Fleet Walker's Divided Heart*, 37.

76 "As for the catcher . . ." and "retired in 1870 . . .": Will Irwin, *Collier's*, May 15, 1909.

76 Another aspiring catcher named Jim Mutrie . . .: *Sporting Life*, December 9, 1885, 2.

76 "showed himself a born catcher . . .": "After 22 Years," *Atlanta Constitution*, May 27, 1888, 5.

76 "cool, quiet manner": From an 1870 description of Jim White's work in the *New York Times*, reprinted in the *Cleveland Herald*, August 18, 1870.

76–77 "When foul tips were 'out' . . .": Clarke, "Catchers of the '70s Were Stars in the Game," C2. Another sportswriter referred to "the windmills which serve the Chicago catcher [White] as hands." *Boston Times*, June 4, 1876.

77 "greatest natural catcher that I ever saw . . .": A. G. Spalding (as told to Tim Murnane), "Mike Kelley [sic] Refused $10,000 When He Was Broke," *Boston Globe*, December 24, 1905, SM4. Henry Chadwick extended the metaphor beyond the breaking point in an 1874 article in which he wrote that White was "as agile in his movements as a cat, and as plucky withal as a bulldog," and that he "does not know how to growl." *New York Clipper*, December 19, 1874.

77 "A catcher should not stand . . .": Ward, *Base-Ball: How to Become a Player*, 68.

77 "a system of protecting their heads and breasts with their arms": Will Irwin, *Collier's*, May 15, 1909.

77 "quite an art for a catcher . . .": *Boston Globe*, April 24, 1904, 24; the writer is not specifically identified, but Murnane made this point on a number of occasions, and I feel safe in assuming he was the author.

77 "head would always go in the opposite direction . . .": Tim Murnane, "Work Behind the Bat," *Boston Globe*, October 25, 1891, 23.

77 "We have never seen his superior . . ." and "With him it is simply bull dog perseverance . . .": *New York Clipper*, December 14, 1872, 293.

77–78 "It is, of course, plucky . . .": *New York Clipper*, December 19, 1874. In this article, Chadwick maintained that Jim White and Bill Craver embodied the two different methods of catching then in vogue. White, he wrote, "yields to the ball" and thereby "saves his hands" while Craver "stops the ball abruptly, and, therefore, feels the full force of the blow."

78 "from any position that he might be placed in . . .": Sam Crane, "Buck Ewing," (Fifty Greatest series) *New York Journal*, January 20, 1912.

78 "could throw to second like a shot . . .": "After 22 Years," *Atlanta Constitution*, May 27, 1888, 5. The writer added that "Biggers couldn't always catch hold [of Cassin's throws], and when they passed him, as they frequently did, they would be sure to give the center

fielder a long chase up along the carriages on the hill." Obviously Casey Stengel's maxim about catchers applied to second basemen as well.

78 "fingers gave way . . . forming a sort of spring box . . .": *Cincinnati Enquirer,* January 2, 1899.

78–80 "The catcher not only has to make . . ." and "throwing to second base. . .": Essay on catching by "Doc" Bushong in Pfeffer, *Scientific Ball,* 52. Interestingly, sportswriter Bugs Baer later argued that this tendency of batters to interfere with catchers was the reason left-handed catchers became virtually extinct by the end of the nineteenth century: "Right-handed batters would easily balk [the left-handed catcher] when he attempted to put the subpoena on a baserunner. He had to step out to right-field when throwing to second and also had to do a sun dance when tossing to third. He could whale away at first base all he wanted without competition." Of course left-handed batters could also do this to a right-handed catcher, but at the time there were significantly more right-handed batters. By the time Baer wrote this article in 1923, left-handed batters had become far more common and he concluded, "there doesn't seem to be any reason against left-handed catchers." But by then right-handed catchers had become a tradition. Syndicated column, *Detroit Free Press,* April 17, 1923. Baer's argument is only a partial explanation of this trend; others are discussed in my *A Game of Inches,* vol. 1, entry 4.1.3, 199–200, including the fact that sporting goods manufacturers didn't make mitts for left-handed catchers.

80 "No other position poorly played . . .": Essay on catching by "Doc" Bushong in Pfeffer, *Scientific Ball,* 52–53.

80 Many early catchers were extraordinarily feeble hitters: As another indication that an inept hitter could still aspire to become a major league catcher, six of the seven weakest-hitting nonpitchers who played at least 150 major league games in the nineteenth century were catchers: George Townsend (.469 OPS), Rudolph Kemmler (.462), Tom Dowse (.459), Billy Holbert (.454), Bill Traffley (.450), and Phil Powers (.428). Charles Sweasy at .430 was the only noncatcher to play that many games and contribute so little offensively. Another catcher, George Baker, had the lowest OPS of any nineteenth-century player who appeared in at least 100 games, easily beating out handicapped pitcher Hugh "One Arm" Daily.

80 "bunt and run act": *Wilkes-Barre Times,* February 3, 1898, obituary of Dan B. Loderick.

80 Wilbert Robinson was a legendary lead-foot: Astute Boston left fielder Tommy McCarthy, for example, took advantage of Robinson twice during the same game. On the first occasion, McCarthy let a routine fly ball drop and was then easily able to start a double play. Later a similar situation arose, and Robinson tried to avoid the same fate by edging off of second base. So, as "Robbie's" teammate John McGraw later recounted with malicious glee, "instead of trapping the ball, McCarthy caught it on the fly, threw to second, and again a double play was completed. Those of us who were on the bench almost rolled off with laughter over Robbie's break, but he was as sore as a man can get." *Sporting Life,* April 7, 1906.

80 "must have been left out over night": *Detroit Free Press,* May 8, 1887.

81 "acquired such speed . . .," "a large number . . .," "sufficiently enthusiastic . . .," "compelled to retire in short order," "if he could catch . . .," and "Devlin was just beginning to pitch . . .": *St. Louis Democrat,* January 17, 1875.

81 "Hastings was the only man who could catch him": *Chicago Tribune,* April 1, 1894.

81–82 "throw a fast one . . .," "a puzzling curve . . .," "hardier than a pine knot," "a pair of hands . . .," and "catch anything and anybody": Smith, "He Could Catch Anything."

82 "This past season Allison caught finely . . .": *New York Clipper,* December 21, 1872. Similarly, Mike McGeary was regarded as a first-rate catcher when paired with the right

pitcher, but, according to Henry Chadwick, he "does not excel in the position until he becomes thoroughly familiar with the style of delivery of his pitcher." *New York Clipper*, December 14, 1872, 293. Some believed that this new dynamic affected even the great Jim White. When White rejoined Boston after the 1876 season, some naysayers believed that he would not be able to adjust to the hard throwing of Tommy Bond after so many years of handling the slow, strategic pitching of Spalding. There were even rumors that White's contract called for him to catch only when his brother was pitching, and not for Bond. But the *St. Louis Globe-Democrat* disputed the notion that White could not catch Bond, pointing out that he had previously caught speedballer Al Pratt and maintaining that "White, with a little practice, can support any man that ever pitched a ball as well as any catcher in existence." *St. Louis Globe-Democrat*, October 3, 1876, 7. White did indeed spent most of the 1877 season playing first base or the outfield, but that was mostly the result of Boston having the luxury of also having Lew Brown, and White did catch Bond from time to time.

82 "the honor of catching for Cal. Hawk . . .": Kennedy, "Greatest Backstop of Them All Was the Detroit Boy, Charley Bennett," 20.

82 "Nobody will pay . . .": *Cincinnati Enquirer*, reprinted in *Bismarck Tribune*, June 26, 1889. The other two players were John Reilly (who was the source of this account) and Joe Sommers, both of whom went on to successful professional careers. Presumably it didn't help Ewing's cause that Al Jennings, whose disastrous 1878 attempts to catch major league pitching are discussed in the next chapter, was also an amateur from Mill Creek.

82 "You get this boy . . .": Crane, "Buck Ewing."

83 "securing the services . . ." and "Another important adjunct . . .": *Chadwick Scrapbooks*, letters from Chadwick at the *Brooklyn Eagle* office, dated January 8 and January 15, 1872.

84 A Boston director was sent to his hometown . . .: *New York Sun*, January 13, 1889.

84 "The wisdom of having two regular catchers . . .": *New York Clipper*, May 4, 1872, 37.

84 "it being next to impossible to employ . . .": *New York Clipper*, December 14, 1872, 28.

84–85 "he cannot pitch with justice to himself . . .": *New York Sunday Mercury*, May 18, 1878.

85 "the good or bad taste of hanging up such pictures . . .": *Chicago Tribune*, May 5, 1878. Nolan continued to be known as "The Only Nolan" for the remainder of his career.

85 Another common belief was that a left-handed catcher was better suited to work with a fellow southpaw: Left-handed catchers were also believed to be better suited to catching a right-handed pitcher who threw an "in-curve" or "in-shoot"—a pitch that tended to move in the opposite direction from a curveball. The belief in pairing pitchers and catchers based on their throwing hands became much more pronounced after the emergence of padded gloves in the 1880s. The *Detroit Free Press* of May 2, 1884, for example, reported that "[Dupee] Shaw's left-handed out-shoots are responsible for [Walter] Walker's sore hand. With a right-handed pitcher, the catcher can do most of the stopping with his left hand, protected by a thickly padded glove. Such a glove cannot be worn upon the right hand as it renders accurate throwing impossible." Similarly the *Washington Post* of March 23, 1884, noted that Ed Trumbull would be paired with John Humphries, "since a left-handed catcher can handle an in-curve more easily," leaving Henry Morgan to catch Bob Barr.

85 Others suggested that a catcher's size . . .: The *Washington Post* of June 15, 1884, for instance, maintained that John Hanna was "too short" to work with Bob Barr, and suggested that he would do better with John Hamill. Another well-known duo of the early

1880s, Robert Black and Kid Baldwin, became known as the midget battery because both were very small men.

85 "no catcher can play . . .": *New York Clipper*, December 21, 1872.
85 "first and second mate": "Lively," "Base Ball," 276–277.
85 "Critchley and Keenan . . .": *Auburn Evening Auburnian*, March 20, 1879, 1.
85–86 Charles Getzein and Ed Gastfield: *Detroit Free Press*, May 13, 1884.
86 Connie Mack was one of several ballplayers to marry the sister of his battery mate: Several pitchers married a sister of their catcher, including Dick Conway, who married the sister of George Moolic in 1888 (*Detroit Free Press*, April 14, 1888), Ed Morris of Pittsburgh, who married the sister of Fred Carroll in 1884 (*Detroit Free Press*, April 28, 1884), and Jack Powell of the St. Louis Browns, who married the sister of Jack O'Connor in 1902 (*Sporting Life*, November 22, 1902).
86 "In his last moments he was delirious . . .": *Boston Advertiser*, June 13, 1876. Miller's words, sometimes with very slight variations, were quoted in many other newspapers. According to one 1891 article, Miller died because of the aftereffects of being struck by a pitched ball. *St. Louis Globe-Democrat*, reprinted in *Sporting News*, September 19, 1891. This article, however, contained numerous mistakes, and this claim has not been corroborated.
86 "Catchers and pitchers are beginning . . .": *Chicago Tribune*, March 16, 1879.
86 "specialists. Pitcher Smith . . .": Hal Lebovitz, "Zimmer, Oldest Catcher, Leafs Memory Book," *Sporting News*, January 12, 1949.

5. THE CATCHER AS THE MAN IN DISGUISE

87 "Catching is the most elusive position . . .": David Falkner, *Nine Sides of the Diamond*, 289.
87 "arm behind the barn" and "backwood scouts": Kevin Kerrane, *Dollar Sign on the Muscle*, especially 23.
88 "What caliber and speed . . .": Harry Wright correspondence, quoted in David Arcidiacono, *Middletown's Season in the Sun*, 57. Spalding was not a particularly fast pitcher by major league standards, but Wright was undoubtedly comparing him to the semipro pitchers with whom Clapp had previously been paired.
88 "Nearly all of our great catchers . . .": H. L. Rann, "Sidewalk Sketches," *Olympia Recorder*, May 14, 1912.
88 Jim "Deacon" White grew up on a farm . . .: Jim White's cousin Elmer had a brief major league career before dying of tuberculosis at the age of twenty-two. Jim's brother Will had a long major league career as a pitcher, winning 229 major league games.
89 "the cows, watermelons, turnips and such": *Cincinnati Enquirer*, reprinted in *Sporting Life*, January 7, 1885.
89 "It made no difference how anxious . . .": *Cincinnati Enquirer*, January 22, 1899.
89 "The fact is, White is . . .": *New York Clipper*, January 21, 1871.
90–91 "When it came to securing a catcher . . .": *Cincinnati Commercial*, reprinted in the *Chicago Tribune*, April 13, 1879.
91 "a tanned and freckled country boy . . ." and "sat in his hotel room . . .": Allison Hall of Fame file, typewritten note.
91 "was a gawky . . .," "as soon as he began . . .," "young Philadelphia brick-yard player . . .," and "propelled from a catapult": Hall of Fame file for Cincinnati, unidentified clipping, but apparently from the *Cincinnati Enquirer*, and dated by hand as being from March 1887 (precise day not given).

91–92 "One day, when we were in Philadelphia . . .": *Louisville Courier-Journal*, reprinted in *Cleveland Herald*, June 13, 1884. Chase recalled these events as taking place in 1877, but Holbert's major league debut actually occurred late in the 1876 season.

92 His defensive prowess alone . . .: Holbert had the second-lowest OPS during the 1870s of any player to appear in at least 100 games in that decade. The only weaker hitter was Jim White's brother Will, a pitcher whose eyesight was so poor that he was the only player of the era to wear glasses.

92–93 "looking for a catcher . . .": *New York Sunday Mercury*, October 4, 1879. According to Young, these events had happened thirteen years earlier. As Young goes on to note, Force was soon shifted to the shortstop position, which reflects that the catcher's position had not yet attained the preeminence it would have in the 1870s. Indeed, in the 1860s it was not uncommon for a club to move its most agile defensive player back and forth between the catcher and shortstop positions, showing that the two positions were considered of fairly equal value and had the same skill requirements. Dickey Pearce, the man generally credited with developing the shortstop position, played catcher when not playing shortstop. As noted earlier, George Wright was a catcher before a foul tip led him to give up the position and become the game's best shortstop. So Force's shift to shortstop should be taken as just an indication that he was considered more valuable there. Force's play at shortstop was so highly regarded that an 1875 dispute over his services ended up being one of the main reasons for the founding of the National League. On another occasion, Nick Young stated that "Force was the only player in my recollection who approached Wright in trapping the ball." *Toledo Blade*, February 2, 1897.

93 . . . the newcomer simply steps in and makes it look easy: And Allison, originally a cricket player, had virtually no experience as a catcher before his discovery by Joyce. The *New York Clipper* of October 2, 1869, stated that he had played left field for the Masonic of Manayunk for two years but that his experience as a catcher before joining the Red Stockings was limited to eight games as catcher for the Geary club of Philadelphia. Holbert at least had caught for the Peabody club of Baltimore and the Quicksteps of Wilmington before the game that catapulted him to prominence. *New York Clipper*, May 24, 1884.

93 "usual languor . . .": Erwin Gustav Gudde, ed., "Edward Vischer's First Visit to California," *California Historical Society Quarterly* 19 (1940), 205–206; quoted in Dary, *Cowboy Culture*, 59–60.

93 "a plucky, cool sort of fellow . . .": *New York Sunday Mercury*, June 30, 1877. Sullivan was injured and never caught a game in the major leagues, but he did play 112 major league games at first base before his premature death at the age of twenty-five.

93 Allison . . . had been a cricket wicket-keeper: Grillo, "Allison," S3.

93–94 "Green Mountains" and "the catcher of the other club . . .": *St. Louis Post-Dispatch*, August 23, 1884.

94 one of only two major leaguers born in Prince Edward Island: Ship passenger lists show Oxley arriving in Boston as an infant in 1859. Most reference sources list him as the only native of P.E.I. in major league history, but recent research has established that George Wood was also born there.

94 "a farmer and a good one . . .": *Cleveland Herald*, December 25, 1882.

94 "When I work, I work in the rolling mill": *Sporting News*, May 7, 1892, 3.

94 "Tom Sullivan, the catcher . . .": *Sporting Life*, September 10, 1884.

94 "he should not have bought him . . .": *Sporting News*, April 29, 1899.

94–95 "Very well . . ." and "then up came Shorty": *Chicago Tribune*, April 22, 1877, 7.

95 St. Louis catcher Jimmy Adams . . .: Gerard S. Petrone, *When Baseball Was Young*, 34.

95 "once had a good laugh . . .": *Sporting Life*, reprinted in *Washington Post*, February 10, 1884, 8.

96 "A foul tip crippled . . .": *Milwaukee Daily Sentinel*, July 31, 1876, 3.

96 "He was a wonder . . .": *Michigan Alumnus*, November 2, 1922, quoting Frederick K. Stearns, who went on to become president of the Detroit Wolverines of the National League. Bliss was also the man whose work prompted Frank L. Smith to bemoan, "if we could have traded our three catchers for Bliss, the result of the game would have been reversed."

96 "a very quiet man personally . . .": William Rankin Scrapbooks, clipping from unspecified source.

96 "a clerical-looking man, with a tall hat" and "pair of the hardest-looking hands . . .": Boston director Charles H. Porter, quoted in *New York Sun*, January 13, 1889.

96 "Jim White is a steady kind of man . . .": *Cleveland Leader*, reprinted in *Hornellsville Times*, June 28, 1878.

97 The first Native American to reach the major leagues was Tommy Oran . . .: See my profile of Oran in the SABR BioProject (http://bioproj.sabr.org/). Like so many others, Oran got his chance to catch in 1869 when forced to take "the place of John W. O'Connell, who had retired as the Empires catcher on account of broken fingers." Spink, *National Game*, 42.

97 The first Hispanic to play in the National League . . .: A Cuban named Esteban Bellan had played briefly in the National Association.

97 as Joel S. Franks has shown: Joel S. Franks, *Whose Baseball?*, 46. Census data confirm Franks's conclusions.

97 When he first came east in 1882 . . .: *Cleveland Leader*, March 25, April 12 and 14, 1882.

97 "Vincent Nava, known on this coast as 'Sandy' Irwin": *San Francisco Examiner*, January 10, 1887.

98 "a colored Pullman porter . . .": Harry Slye, "Early Days of Baseball in Baraboo—There Were Giant Players in Those Days," *Baraboo Daily News*, June 25, 1925.

98 "a stalwart negro . . .," "a good catcher . . .," and "contrasted strongly": *Elizabethtown Post and Gazette*, May 28, 1903.

98 "was the best catcher . . .": *New York Age*, January 11, 1919, quoted in Zang, *Fleet Walker's Divided Heart*, 43.

98 "his fingers split open and bleeding . . .": Zang, *Fleet Walker's Divided Heart*, 37.

99–100 "Our mail every day . . ." and "Last season, for instance . . .": *Cleveland Herald*, March 31, 1884.

100 He took a train to Cleveland . . .: *Cleveland Plain Dealer*, May 17, 1879.

100 "all that was necessary . . ." and "have to walk back to Chicago . . .": *Cleveland Plain Dealer*, May 18, 1879. For more on Gunkle, see the SABR BioProject (http://bioproj.sabr.org/), Fred Gunkle biography by Peter Morris.

101 "We were all mixed up . . .": Ren Mulford, Jr., "Umpire Jennings: His Name Is Alfred Gordon, but He's Known as Alamazoo," *Idaho Daily Statesman*, January 6, 1892, 5.

101–102 "has umpired an occasional game . . .," "He looked so large . . .," and "When Al pulled on . . .": "The Coming Catcher," *Cincinnati Enquirer*, reprinted in *Milwaukee Daily Sentinel*, August 19, 1878. Caylor intentionally exaggerated Jennings's lack of experience; he had been a well-known local amateur player since the late 1860s.

102 "I read a few lines . . ." and "like wax": Mulford, "Umpire Jennings," 5.

102 "famous record of twenty-six passed balls in one game": *Milwaukee Sentinel*, April 23, 1888.

102 "the awful threat . . .": *Base Ball Gazette*, April 21, 1887. This note was not signed, but Caylor was the editor of this short-lived daily and undoubtedly wrote most if not all

of the notes. Since the author of this note recalled that Golden was the pitcher in that game, it seems safe to assume that Caylor wrote it.

102 . . . there were a host of similar tales: John McGuiness, for instance, filled in for Nat Hicks in an 1876 game but proved "unable to throw to second base" and switched positions with Bill Craver. Later in the game, McGuinness made another attempt behind the plate and this time "was struck in the face and severely hurt by a sharp foul tip." He did at least show his pluck by continuing to catch after a delay of fifteen minutes. *Boston Globe*, May 8, 1876, 3. Hiram Wright was yet another catcher whose major league debut proved a disaster. The base runners of the opposing Detroit team were known for their lack of speed, but they knew enough to challenge the novice in the 1887 game. He proved "a dismal failure as a thrower," prompting the observation that "Wright must be anything but right in his throwing when five of the Detroits—the ice wagons of the League—could steal second on him." *Detroit Free Press*, September 17, 1887; *Sporting Life*, September 28, 1887, 6. Worse was the suggestion that his misplays were the result of being unable to handle the pressure; one account stated that Wright "was nervous . . . and the Detroits ran bases as they pleased." *Sporting Life*, September 21, 1887, 2. Similar fates befell numerous other catching aspirants. Nealy Phelps and Jim Ward both tried to fill in as catcher for the hapless Athletic Club of Philadelphia in 1876; Phelps committed seven passed balls and three errors while Ward was charged with five passed balls and two errors. Infielder Joe Ellick volunteered to catch for the injury-plagued 1878 Milwaukee team but committed three errors and eleven passed balls in two games.

102 Alex Gardner . . .: *Washington Post*, May 11, 1884, which reported that Gardner committed six errors and eleven passed balls; in the official records he was charged with six passed balls.

102 hard-throwing, deceptive left-handed pitcher Dupee Shaw: This description, while obviously exaggerated, captures the spirit of Shaw's pitching motion: "There have been long fought and dangerous disputes about the exact number of motions through which Shaw puts himself before delivering the ball. One man claimed thirty-two, holding that he had counted them. An attempt to give all of them would be foolish. A few will be enough. When Shaw first lays his hands on the sphere he looks at it. Then he rolls it around a few times. Then he sticks out one leg; pulls it back and shoves the other behind him. Now he makes three or four rapid steps in the box. When he does all this he holds the ball in his left hand. After he has swapped it to the right he wipes his left on his breeches, changes the ball to his left again and pumps the air with both arms. Then he gets down to work and digs up the ground with his right foot. Then you think he is going to pitch. But he isn't. He starts in and reverses the programme and does it over again three or four times, and just as the audience sits back in the seats with a sigh, the ball flies out like a streak. Nobody knows how it left his hand, but it did." *St. Louis Post-Dispatch*, June 19, 1886. A later account recalled, "Dupee Shaw, left-handed, was one of the first pitchers to use the 'wind-up' motion of the arm before delivering the ball, and his antics caused much merriment and good-natured joshing wherever he appeared." *Washington Post*, February 11, 1906.

102 "Walker caught . . .": *Detroit Free Press*, April 9, 1884.

103 "about thirty seconds, " "nearly tore Crane's forefinger . . .," and "three errors and two runs. . .": *Boston Globe*, August 17, 1884, 8.

103 Lew Brown, the man who had originally discovered him: Tim Murnane, in "Lew Brown's Last Sleep," *Boston Globe*, January 19, 1889, 1, writes that Brown "was the man who first discovered Dupee Shaw was a pitcher, and prevailed upon him to practice for the box."

103 rookie Ed Crane: Ed Crane later became a pitcher who featured such a blazing fastball that he was known as "Cannonball" Crane. As a rookie in 1884, however, he pitched a few games but was used mostly as a position player.

103 man named Haley . . .: Haley caught two games for Troy in 1880. He was once listed as Fred Haley in the encyclopedias, but this was proved incorrect; Fred Haley was an infielder from West Virginia who played much later. The Haley who caught for Troy was an amateur from Chicago, but his identity has not been established.

103 Kragen, for instance . . .: SABR Biographical Committee newsletter, January/February 2003.

103 because of parental disapproval . . .: Similarly, Clarence Walker of Louisville became the first professional catcher hired to play in Columbus, Georgia, but did so under the name Clarence Leslie because he was "of good family and well connected in Louisville." "Early Days of Baseball in Georgia," *Columbus Ledger*, reprinted in the *Atlanta Constitution*, May 23, 1901, 6.

104 a man named Wright . . .: *St. Louis Post-Dispatch*, August 24, 1888, 8. Wright was last heard from shortly after this incident when he eloped with the daughter of a wealthy farmer from Woodstown, New Jersey, after claiming to be a professional baseball player and a relative of Harry Wright.

6. THE BREAKING POINT

105 "The catcher occasionally gets a hot foul tip . . .": *Boston Globe*, June 3, 1876, 1.

105 a twenty-four-inning scoreless tie between Harvard University and the professional Manchester club: Steele, "How the National Game Developed," 336, reports that Harvard catcher Jim Tyng, the same man who popularized the catcher's mask, recorded thirty-one putouts in the game.

106 "the outward and inner curve . . .": *Manchester Mirror and Farmer*, reprinted in *New York Sunday Mercury*, May 19, 1877, describing pitcher Mike Snigg of Manchester.

106 "got tired of a batter . . .": "Old-Time Base Ball," *Chicago Herald*, July 12, 1890, 11.

106 "constitute the main strength . . .": *Chicago Tribune*, reprinted in *St. Louis Democrat*, May 8, 1875.

106 "if your pitcher . . ." and "the pitcher was . . .": *Boston Globe*, reprinted in *Cincinnati Enquirer*, October 12, 1884. Likewise, the narrator of an autobiographical novel by the famed attorney Clarence Darrow emphasized that baseball was more fun when "The contest was not between the pitcher and the catcher alone; we all played, and each player was as important as the rest." Clarence Darrow, *Farmington*, 215.

106–107 "Four-fifths of the outs . . .": *New York Clipper*, May 1, 1875

107 "nobody on the outside derives . . .": *New York Times*, April 26, 1884, 4.

107 When baseball had been a game in which the contributions of all nine men mattered, fixing a game was a monumental task: The game's first fixing scandal occurred in 1865, and it was New York Mutuals catcher William Wansley who initiated it. But Wansley had to get two teammates to cooperate, and while he told them that he would make all the misplays necessary to ensure the defeat, in fact that did not prove the case. Dean Sullivan, ed., *Early Innings*, 49–53.

107 Many of the fix rumors were baseless, but . . . they were likely to fly whenever a catcher had a bad game: Nat Hicks, in particular, attracted an inordinate number of rumors. For instance, the *Chicago Tribune* of April 11, 1875, 16, noted: "In ridding themselves of Messrs. Hicks and Cummings [the Quakers] discard a bad element, and one that greatly contributed to their ill-success last year." A note at the end of the 1875 season reported: "The Mutual was not strong enough this season to successfully 'hippodrome' [fix games] to a very great extent. Hicks, their catcher, it is said, could tell how many runs their opponents would make in each inning, and his friends used to lay their bets accordingly." *St. Louis Globe-Democrat*, quoted in *Brooklyn Eagle*, November 4, 1875, 2. And the argument between Hicks and Bob Ferguson that left Hicks with a broken arm

began when Ferguson insinuated that Hicks had "sold" the game. *New York Clipper,* August 2, 1873. Henry Chadwick made frequent allusions to Hicks's temperamental nature. In 1872, he wrote of Hicks: "A rather undisciplined temper, however, clouded his judgment on some occasions in the employment of his physical powers." *New York Clipper,* December 14, 1872. Four years later he elaborated that Hicks "probably presented a more striking illustration of the disadvantage the lack of control of temper is to a catcher than any other player in the position in 1876. When cool and collected, and in a good humor . . . few can play the catcher's position as well as Hicks, and certainly none better; but the moment he gets his 'mad up'—and it is very easily roused—then come hurried fly-tips, passed balls and wild throwing to bases, not to any unusual extent except for a catcher of his marked skill, but sufficient to present quite a contrast to his play when his temper is all right." Chadwick, "The Catchers." Nonetheless Chadwick, who was never afraid to suggest that crooked play had occurred, insisted that Hicks was an honest player who had the misfortune of being so good that gamblers assumed the worst on the rare occasions when he let a ball get past him. Following the 1873 season, Chadwick reported that Hicks had gone so far as to get the managers of the Mutual club to write letters clearing his name. *New York Clipper,* February 28, 1874. The development suggests how commonly such rumors flew and how impossible it was to lift the cloud of suspicion, even when it was baseless. As another example, while John Clapp was playing with Cleveland he was offered the phenomenal sum of $5,000 from Chicago bookmakers "to allow one or two 'pass-balls' when one or two men happened to be on base." Clapp turned down the bribe and earned himself the nickname of "Honest John," but what would have become of his reputation if he had just happened to have a bad game that day? (T. W. B., "Then—'Johnnie' Clapp—Now,"; W. Lloyd Johnson, *DeWitt Historical Society Newsletter,* Summer 1983.

107 "but few catchers in the country can stand up . . .": *Cincinnati Enquirer,* reprinted in *Chicago Tribune,* August 19, 1877, 7.

107 "The Lowells need a catcher . . .": *St. Louis Globe-Democrat,* September 24, 1878, 5. Likewise the *New York Sunday Mercury* of June 19, 1880, reported that Troy had just signed Tom Deasley because the club "has had hard luck with its catchers lately. [Bill] Harbridge and [Bill] Holbert have each broken two fingers. [Mike] Lawlor and [Charles] Briody have been tried, but both failed."

108 "stated to them that he was on the auction block . . .": Quoted from an article in the *Chicago Tribune,* November 3, 1878, and in the *New York Sunday Mercury,* November 9, 1878. According to the *Tribune* article, the piece originated in the *St. Louis Spirit* and was based on reminiscences by ballplayer Ed Cuthbert. In the excerpts it was stated that Clapp had received the $3,000 salary "two seasons ago," which leaves it unclear whether these events occurred after the 1875 or 1876 season (since Clapp played for St. Louis in both 1876 and 1877). But since Mase Graffen was the St. Louis representative at the meeting, I believe it occurred after the 1875 season.

108 Hartford responded by signing Allison . . .: Salary figures from an undated clipping from the *Brooklyn Argus,* included in the Chadwick Scrapbooks. The New York franchise was not paying salaries, instead letting its players divide the gate receipts, but it did reach a special agreement in order to sign Hicks and Mathews. These salary figures should not be assumed to be entirely accurate, but I believe them to be reasonably close.

108 Thus Chicago, Hartford, and Louisville entered . . .: The backups in question were Bill Harbridge and Dick Higham for Hartford, Cal McVey for Chicago, Scott Hastings for Louisville, Mike McGeary for St. Louis, and Bill Craver for New York. McGeary and Craver had not caught much during the 1875 season, which is why the totals of their teams lag behind the other three, but both men were highly experienced catchers

who could be relied upon if needed. In contrast, the eighteen men who would catch for Boston, Philadelphia, and Cincinnati had combined to catch only twenty-six major league games in the preceding season.

108 . . . only to have shareholders initially vote down the signing: *Chicago Inter-Ocean*, May 15, 1876, 8. Eventually the club became desperate and did sign Malone. He caught only twenty games, but that was more than any of the other nine catchers the club used that year.

108 even Chicago amateur Patrick Quinn declining Cincinnati's offer: *Boston Advertiser*, May 12, 1876.

109 Cincinnati, which split the workload between three unimpressive rookies: One of Cincinnati's rookies was Dave Pierson, who distinguished himself as "the worst thrower of any of the professionals who stand behind the bat." *Boston Advertiser*, May 24, 1876.

109 "suffering from sore hands . . .": *Chicago Tribune*, July 30, 1876, 3.

109 "to face it at all . . .": *Louisville Courier-Journal*, July 9, 1876.

109 "having no one to hold him had to pitch easier than usual": *St. Louis Globe-Democrat*, August 2, 1876, 8; an account of a 15-7 Louisville loss.

109 "The Athletics again appeared . . .": *Chicago Tribune*, August 6, 1876, 7.

109–110 "The Chicago team has one advantage . . .": *Chicago Tribune*, July 30, 1876, 3.

110 "We no longer see him come up close . . .": Randolph, the New York correspondent for the *Chicago Tribune*; reprinted in the *St. Louis Globe-Democrat*, June 1, 1875.

110 "Some of the best talent . . .": *New York Sunday Mercury*, September 9, 1876.

111 The exception was the new entry from Milwaukee . . .: "1878—Milwaukee, A National League City," an unpublished paper by Dennis Pajot, provides a detailed account of the woes of this team and is the source of the quotations that are not cited.

111 "Golden was not able to pitch with his usual force": *Milwaukee Daily Sentinel*, April 18, 1878.

111–112 "There are a number of persons . . ." and "The simple fact . . .": *Milwaukee Daily Sentinel*, June 5, 1878.

112 "It Is Heart-Breaking; A Good Club Demoralized for the Want of a Catcher": *Milwaukee Daily Sentinel*, June 26, 1878, 4.

112 A similar chorus of laments came from semipro clubs . . .: In one of numerous examples, the *St. Louis Globe-Democrat*, May 14, 1876, 6, described how the Reds' regular catcher, Tom Dolan, was hurt, forcing Packey Dillon to replace him, and, "as [Dillon] could not catch Morgan's swift pitching, Pidge had to let up. The consequence was, the Stars got in fourteen base hits."

112 "brought a paid pitcher . . .": *St. Louis Globe-Democrat*, August 2, 1876, 8.

112 After Northwestern University defeated a rival school . . .: *Tripod*, November 27, 1875; quoted in Arthur Herbert Wilde, *Northwestern University, A History, 1855–1905* (New York: University Publishing Co., 1905), vol. 2, 173 (in a chapter on baseball at the school, written by Wirt E. Humphrey). The losing school was known as the University of Chicago, but it was not the school that now bears that name.

112 When the New York College Association championship . . .: *New York Clipper*, May 28, 1881.

112 "The Amherst College University nine . . .": *Cleveland Herald*, March 9, 1884. There were also a few other incidents of the kind involving catchers. Ten years later the University of Michigan baseball team made an effort to "import" catcher Frank Bowerman, but the school's faculty saw through the ruse and refused him admission. *Boston Globe*, April 2, 1894. And in 1895, future major leaguer Charlie Hickman received ten dollars a month plus his board and books to attend West Virginia University and catch for the school baseball team. John R. Husman, "Charles Taylor Hickman," in David Jones, ed., *Deadball Stars of the American League*, 652.

113 ... pigtail or hindcatcher: For example, the *St. Louis Globe-Democrat* of June 23, 1877, described a May 26 game in Woodbridge, California, with ten players a side, the extra being another catcher. Around the same time the Western Base Ball Club of Topeka, Kansas, designated Frank Waters as their "official pigtail." Chadwick Scrapbooks, clipping from unspecified source. A particularly notable instance occurred in an 1863 game in which eighteen members of the St. George Cricket Club played a baseball nine. The cricket club stationed two future members of the Baseball Hall of Fame behind the plate—Harry Wright stood closest to the batter while his brother George backed him up. Christopher Devine, *Harry Wright: The Father of Professional Base Ball*, 23. While the use of pigtails never became common, it doesn't seem to have ever entirely died out, as is suggested by a reference to them in *Dickson's Baseball Dictionary*, xviii.

113 "The batsman can not hit the ball ...": *Cincinnati News Journal*, April 21, 1884.

7. PROTECTING THE CATCHER'S FACE (BUT BRUISING HIS EGO)

114 "An old man sat in his easy-chair ...": Harry Ellard, "The Reds of Sixty-Nine," in Harry Ellard, *Base Ball in Cincinnati: A History* (Jefferson, N.C.: McFarland and Co., 2004), 120–121.

115 "In these days of scientific base ball ...": *Grand Rapids Democrat*, May 30, 1877. Muffin games featured the weakest members of their respective clubs and were so named because a lot of "muffing" of the ball was sure to take place.

115 "that he was not playing base ball unless ...": *Indianapolis Journal*, June 5, 1878.

115 "Let up on the scientific/ Give us more of play terrific": *New York Sunday Mercury*, August 3, 1878.

115–116 "There is no doubt at all ...": *Cincinnati Commercial*, reprinted in *New York Sunday Mercury*, August 3, 1878.

116 "One of the great objections ...": *St. Louis Globe-Democrat*, May 13, 1877, 7. That same year Colonel John P. Joyce, the Red Stockings director who had discovered Allison, "denounce[d] the underhand throw, and insist[ed] that the old-time, straight-arm pitching will have to be revived." *Cincinnati Enquirer*, reprinted in *Chicago Tribune*, August 19, 1877, 7. The *Enquirer* appended its own endorsement of Joyce's sentiments, noting that "but few catchers in the country can stand up before the present cannonball throwing, and those few are being rapidly battered into oblivion. For one, we would willingly welcome back the old-time pitching and large scores."

116 the National League's reliance on local umpires: The National League used local umpires exclusively in its inaugural season, and at season's end rejected the idea of hiring a traveling staff of professional umpires. Billy McLean was finally hired as the first traveling umpire in 1878, but locals continued to umpire most games.

117 Pitchers simply responded by wearing their belts at deceptively high levels: A. G. Spalding, *America's National Game*, 484; James Wood, as told to Menke, "Baseball in By-Gone Days."

117 "the catcher who faces swift pitching ...": *Chicago Tribune*, November 12, 1876, 7. Henry Chadwick concurred, writing, "We are glad to see that the rule repealing the foul-bound catch was not adopted. It would have materially weakened the play of amateur nines. By and bye, when the game has reached a higher degree of existence, it will be well to consider the subject again. A great mistake was made in supposing that the doing away with foul bounds would lessen the catcher's work. The very reverse would have been the case. It would have doubled the arduous nature of his task, and it would have obliged him to stand up behind the bat all the time. We are surprised that Harry Wright did not see that this would be the result." Henry Chadwick, "The Catchers" (part two), *New York Clipper*, January 6, 1877.

117 "one of two things is probable . . .": *Boston Herald,* reprinted in *New York Sunday Mercury,* December 2, 1876.

118 "mush ball . . . a lively, hard, and uniform ball": *Chicago Tribune,* December 10, 1876, 7.

118 "too soft . . ." and "to make a harder and livelier ball": *Chicago Tribune,* May 17, 1877.

118 "the same degree . . .," "mellowed," "be handled without pain," "by any possible . . .," and "Base balls these days . . .": *Pittsburgh Dispatch,* reprinted in the *Clinton* (St. Johns, Michigan) *Independent,* June 14, 1877.

118 The league was flooded with complaints, making it necessary to bring the softer baseball back on an emergency basis: *Chicago Tribune,* May 17, 1877.

118–119 "mush balls," "out of the diamond," and "a lump of mud rubber . . .": *Chicago Tribune,* September 1, 1878, 7.

119 "Probably Bond has been taught a lesson . . .": Henry Chadwick, "The Catchers," *New York Clipper,* December 30, 1876.

119 "showed no sympathy for his catcher": Joseph Overfield, "Christo Von Buffalo, Was He the First Baseball Cartoonist?," *Baseball Research Journal* 1981, 148; Joseph Overfield, "The First Great Minor League Club," *Baseball Research Journal* 1977, 2.

119–120 "was as stiff as an oak tree . . .": Murnane, "Lew Brown's Last Sleep," 1. Another sportswriter expressed awe that Brown "weighs one hundred and ninety two pounds stripped!" *New York Sunday Mercury,* March 24, 1877.

120 "are even larger than Brown's . . .": *New York Sunday Mercury,* February 23, 1878.

120 "his hands badly bothered . . .": *Chicago Inter-Ocean,* August 7, 1879, 2.

120–121 "hands got sore . . ." and "To this my family . . .": *Philadelphia Press,* reprinted in *Cleveland Plain Dealer,* May 12, 1888.

121 Thatcher later claimed to have experimented with one in the spring of 1876: Spink, *National Game,* 384. See my *A Game of Inches,* vol. 1, entry 9.4.2, 432–436, for a lengthy discussion of the controversy over the origins of the mask. Thatcher's first name was Henry, but Spink incorrectly referred to him as Howard Thatcher, and the mistake was repeated in my book.

121–122 "ridiculed the first time . . ." and "When it made its first appearance . . .": *Philadelphia Press,* reprinted in *Cleveland Plain Dealer,* May 12, 1888.

122 "a cumbersome affair . . .": "When Ball Players Wore Neither Gloves Nor Mask," *Miami Herald,* June 3, 1912, 5.

122 "The near future may bring about . . .": *Providence Dispatch,* reprinted in *Boston Globe,* May 19, 1877.

122 "the new safety uniform of the Harvard base ball nine": Quoted in *St. Louis Globe-Democrat,* March 16, 1877.

122 "There is a great deal of beastly humbug . . .": Quoted in Dan Gutman, *Banana Bats and Ding-Dong Balls,* 186.

122 "that the best protection in base-ball . . .": *Norristown Herald,* reprinted in *St. Louis Globe-Democrat,* March 16, 1877.

122 In column after column Chadwick extolled the virtues of the mask . . .: *New York Clipper,* January 27, 1877; *Brooklyn Eagle,* May 19, June 15, and August 13, 1877.

123 "'rat-trap' and 'the bird-cage'": *Chicago Tribune,* July 20, 1877.

123 "Don't you ever let me see you with that trap on in a game": *Sporting News,* October 30, 1897.

123 "he hasn't mustered up . . .": *Louisville Courier-Journal,* July 6, 1877.

123 "apt to jar the head . . .": *New York Clipper,* April 14, 1877.

123 "constructed of upright bars . . .": *New York Clipper,* January 27, 1877. A retrospective article also commented on how the "broad strips of flattened iron" on Tyng's mask

obstructed the catcher's vision. "When Ball Players Wore Neither Gloves Nor Mask," 5. But even after improvements were made, the impediment to the catcher's eyes remained a problem. For example, as late as 1890 an article probably written by Henry Chadwick entitled "Training the Catcher" (originally published in *St. Nicholas* and reprinted in the *Brooklyn Eagle*, August 4, 1890) recommended that catchers wear their masks during practice: "All his throwing and passing should be performed with his eyes behind its wires, in order that, from becoming thoroughly accustomed to it, it may add no inconvenience to his work." Walter Camp offered the same advice in his 1901 *Book of College Sports* (244–245). And George Gibson reported of his days as an amateur catcher during the final years of the nineteenth century: "Lots of times I didn't even wear a catcher's mask in those days; I couldn't see clearly enough through it, so I'd take it off. And of course many's the day I'd come home with a black eye or a bloody nose." Lawrence S. Ritter, *The Glory of Their Times*, 70. This remains the case to some extent, which is why catchers always remove their masks when chasing a foul ball or in preparation to receive a throw to the plate.

123 "almost as large as a water bucket . . .": Luther Green, "Second Letter from Luther Green on Early Baseball Days," *Thomson* (Illinois) *Review*, March 19, 1931.

123 "put on the cage," "save himself from further injury," and "militated against his catching": Undated clippings, Joe Hornung Scrapbooks, vol. 1, National Baseball Hall of Fame and Museum.

123 "bothers his playing": *Chicago Tribune*, July 26, 1877.

123 "made several attempts . . .": "Catchers Now Pampered in Comparing of Old-Timers," *Auburn Citizen*, June 3, 1918. Hotaling and Powers were playing in the rival International Association while Dorgan, Hastings, and Harbridge were in the National League. While Hotaling seems to have been the first professional catcher to try a mask, it is not clear whether he continued to wear it.

123–124 "The amateur catchers have . . ." and "as a class . . .": *Brooklyn Eagle*, August 16, 1877.

124 "The idea seems to prevail . . .": *New York Clipper*, August 25, 1877.

124 "visited the club room of the Boston nine . . .": *Grand Rapids* (Michigan) *Morning Democrat*, September 4, 1883.

124 "For the first year . . .": *Philadelphia Press*, reprinted in *Cleveland Plain Dealer*, May 12, 1888.

124 "be put on and off in a moment": *New York Sunday Mercury*, September 1, 1877.

124–125 "The catcher's mask is . . .": *New York Sunday Mercury*, September 8, 1877.

125 "we can imagine other sturdy backstops . . .": *Sporting News*, December 2, 1915.

126 more conspicuous than the limited protective equipment that had been worn earlier: Previous equipment, such as the rubber mouthpiece, had been kept hidden from the view of spectators, with the exception of a few players who donned light gloves (and even some of these glove-wearers apparently used flesh-toned gloves to escape notice). By contrast the catcher's mask was, well, as plain as the nose on his face, with the result that the urge to comment on it proved irresistible. See my *A Game of Inches*, vol. 1, entry 9.3.1, 419–421, for an extended discussion.

126 the use of barbed wire to enclose Western ranches increased exponentially between 1874 and 1880: Dary, *Cowboy Culture*, 315.

126 "in nearly each instance where the fences were erected . . .": Dary, *Cowboy Culture*, 330.

126 sabotage of barbed-wire fences led to violent conflicts in several Western states: Dary, *Cowboy Culture*, 319–331.

126 "*not* in harmony with the land": Dary, *Cowboy Culture*, 308.

126 "the curse of the country": Dary, *Cowboy Culture*, 319.

126 "devil's hatband": Dary, *Cowboy Culture*, 308.
127 "was 'booed' until he took it off in disgust": *San Francisco Chronicle*, reprinted in *Sporting News*, December 30, 1909, 2.
128 "Base ball is one of the healthiest games . . ." and "now procured a mask . . .": *Easton Star*, July 2, 1878. The article was signed by "Wes," but his identity is not clear according to Marty Payne, who drew my attention to this article.
128 even this staunch opponent of risk-taking endorsed the new positioning in certain situations: *New York Clipper*, December 1, 1877. Chadwick remained dubious about the value of having the catcher close to the plate with two strikes or on low pitches, but had begun to endorse it with runners on base.
128 This latter rule change was reversed after one season, but within a few years . . .: The foul bound was permanently abolished in 1883 by the National League and in 1885 by the American Association.
128 "the pitcher a guide": *Atlanta Constitution*, May 16, 1885.
129 "gave up trying to fight the pitchers . . .": *Detroit Free Press*, March 31, 1895. The National League finally allowed pitchers to use overhand deliveries in 1884, and the American Association followed suit in 1885. Even before then, however, most pitchers were getting away with such deliveries, and catchers were forced to resort to drastic measures.
129 "The twirler was allowed . . .": *Ottumwa* (Iowa) *Courier*, March 16, 1903.
129 "hop, step and jump" and "Whitney, with his long legs . . .": *Washington Post*, February 11, 1906.
130 "champion catcher of St. John, New Brunswick," and "was in good form . . .": *Cincinnati Enquirer*, March 31, 1884.
130 its reserve team: Reserve teams were formed by several clubs in the existing professional leagues in 1884, primarily in hopes of keeping players away from their newly formed rival, the Union Association.
130 "Boston's new pitcher . . .": *Detroit Free Press*, April 21, 1881, 1.
130 "With the batsman in position . . .": Joe Hornung Scrapbooks, National Baseball Hall of Fame and Museum, clipping of game account of Boston's 4–0 victory over Buffalo on May 10, 1881, from unspecified newspaper.
130–132 "Whitney made several wild pitches . . .": *Philadelphia Press*, reprinted in *Haverhill Bulletin*, May 8, 1885, 3.
132 "In the fifth inning . . .": *Cleveland Herald*, April 20, 1883.
132 Nor was it unheard of for early masks to break when struck hard enough: *Kalamazoo Telegraph*, June 21, 1879.
133 suffered a serious enough injury that he was allowed to leave the game: As will be discussed in greater detail later, until 1889 a substitute was typically allowed to enter the game only if the other side's captain agreed that the injury was serious enough.
133 "a foul tip nearly knocked off his right leg . . .," "each tried to pull . . .," and "reduced his pace": *Detroit Free Press*, September 27, 1884.
133 "the wilds of Canada": Murnane, "Lew Brown's Last Sleep," 1.
133–134 "No man had ever been found . . .," "nobody else could hold . . .," and "He is the fastest pitcher . . .": *Boston Globe*, October 17, 1887, 8.

8. "A LOT OF FOOLS IN THE CROWD LAUGH AT HIM"

135 "With the pillows allowed at the present time . . .": T. H. Murnane, "Murnane's Baseball," *Boston Globe*, February 25, 1906, 38.
135 A catcher named William Clare . . .: *Sporting News*, February 3, 1910.

135 "crude but very substantial shield . . .," "the slightest jar," and "for fear of fans . . .":
Maclean Kennedy, "Charley Bennett, Former Detroit Catcher, Inventor of Chest Pad,"
Detroit Free Press, August 2, 1914. *Leslie's Illustrated Weekly* printed a similar article on
October 15, 1914, which is quoted in Vince Staten, *Why Is the Foul Pole Fair? (Or,
Answers to Baseball Questions Your Dad Hoped You'd Never Ask)* (New York: Simon &
Schuster, 2003), 263. For contemporaneous reaction to Bennett's chest protector, see
Morris, *A Game of Inches*, vol. 1, entry 9.4.5, 436–438. According to one later account,
Bennett "declared that the foul tips hit him so hard on the breast that the flesh was
pinned against his ribs and later on he could feel it tear away." "Catchers Now Pampered in Comparing of Old-Timers." But the author of this article is not identified,
and Bennett, like other catchers of the era, typically downplayed his injuries, making
me skeptical that he made this assertion.

136 Then a Hartford inventor named William Gray . . .: Bennett believed that his own
"home-made affair" was the inspiration for Gray's invention. Kennedy, "Greatest
Backstop of Them All Was the Detroit Boy, Charley Bennett," 20. For more on Gray,
see the profile I wrote of him for the SABR BioProject (http://bioproj.sabr.org/bioproj
.cfm?a=v&v=l&bid=1573&pid=19540).

136 "O'Rourke put the thing on . . .": *Cleveland Herald*, April 10, 1884; *National Police
Gazette*, April 19, 1884.

136 "This most useful piece . . .": *Sporting News*, November 1, 1890.

136 "the catcher who refuses . . .": *Brooklyn Eagle*, June 1, 1884.

136 "The chest protector is coming into general use . . .": *Sporting Life*, July 23, 1884.

136 "Green Mountains": *St. Louis Post-Dispatch*, August 23, 1884.

138 "If only the poor lad . . .": Quoted in Gutman, *Banana Bats and Ding-Dong Balls*, 192.

138 "the only catcher in the country . . .": *Cranbrook* (New Jersey) *Press*, August 19, 1892.

138 "renders it impossible . . .": This copy appeared in full-page ads in most of the annual
Spalding's Official Base Ball Guides issued during the 1890s.

138 "McKenna, the catcher of the Nationals . . .": *Cincinnati Enquirer*, May 29, 1884.

138 "looks like a back-stop when he wears the body protector": *Columbus Dispatch*, May 21,
1884. The perception that Kemmler resembled a backstop was no doubt enhanced by
his unusual bulk. According to the *Dispatch* of March 18, 1884, he stood five feet eleven
inches and weighed 206 pounds, making him one of the largest players of the era and
the heaviest man on the team by nearly 20 pounds.

138 The term "backstop" had almost always been used to refer to the fence located behind
the catcher . . .: *Dickson's Baseball Dictionary* is the most authoritative source for first
usages, but of course new citations are sometimes found that antedate what had been
the earliest known usage. I have discovered an 1878 instance of the word "backstop"
being used to refer to the catcher—the May 31 issue of the *Cincinnati Enquirer* noted
that "Jim [White], too, never did a finer day's work behind the bat, as his record shows.
He threw to bases like a shot, and was a perfect back-stop." But this usage is clearly
a positive one, and it is the only example I have found before 1884. When the use of
Gray's Body Protector became widespread, it quickly became common to designate the
catcher as the "backstop," with connotations that were much less flattering. The term
"receiver" also originated around this time—the earliest citation is from 1885—and it
suggests the same passivity as the term "backstop." Yet it does not appear that the term
was intended to have negative connotations, since it is a very accurate description of
the technique always practiced by skillful catchers. As catcher-turned-manager Charlie
Fox put it, "A good catcher is actually a receiver. He receives the ball rather than catches
it. The good ones always take the ball in; the poorer ones go for it." Quoted in David
Falkner, *Nine Sides of the Diamond*, 289.

139 "a contrivance that likened him to a muffin-maker": *Evansville Journal*, August 3, 1884. This journalist at least added that Decker didn't do any "muffing," but the fact that he felt the need to point this out suggests how unflattering a simile it was.

139–140 "a little fellow named . . .," "Cox galloped . . .," "For the next few minutes . . .," and "At last one policeman . . .": Dan Brouthers, article that appeared originally in the *New York World*, reprinted as "'Entertaining the Umpire' in the Early Days of Baseball," *Washington Post*, July 8, 1917, SM5.

140 "With the advent of the pad and big gloves . . .": Murnane, "Work Behind the Bat," 23.

140 "No two fingers of a professional baseball catcher point in the same direction": *New York Journal*, reprinted in *San Francisco Bulletin*, August 27, 1885.

140 "so pounded out of shape . . .": *Boston Daily Globe*, June 9, 1885.

140 "presented by a young lady with a manicure case . . .": *American Sports*, reprinted in *Cleveland Herald*, April 23, 1883.

141 "really no protection at all": *Albion Evening Recorder*, August 2, 1932. One exception was Bill McGunnigle, who during the 1870s tried to protect his sore hands by wearing a pair of bricklayer's gloves that were made of hard leather. During practice he found that he could not throw effectively while wearing them, so he cut off the fingers. Jim Tyng, the Harvard catcher who popularized the mask, reportedly saw the gloves and modified them by adding lead to the lining. *New York Sun*, April 27, 1890. But other catchers seem to have concluded that such gloves interfered too greatly with the throwing motion, and they did not become popular.

141 "Catching a swift pitcher . . .," "lay down rules . . .," and "a difficult task . . .": "King Catchers," *St. Louis Post-Dispatch*, August 14, 1886, 12. This article did maintain that a hierarchy of catchers still existed, citing Bennett and Bushong as the game's two best catchers and also mentioning familiar names like Silver Flint, King Kelly, Buck Ewing, and Kid Baldwin, but it was much less definitive about differentiating the great catchers from lesser ones than would have been the case until a few years earlier.

141 several well-known catchers . . . began using beefsteaks in their gloves: McGuire's use of a beefsteak is mentioned in Smith, "He Could Catch Anything"; Zimmer's in Lebovitz, "Zimmer, Oldest Catcher, Leafs Memory Book"; Robinson's in Jack Kavanagh and Norman Macht, *Uncle Robbie*, 4; and Criger's in a letter from his son Harold in the Criger Hall of Fame file, dated July 4, 1970. Several other sources, including "When Ball Players Wore Neither Gloves Nor Mask," 5, also mention the practice.

141 Others, including "Doc" Bushong, preferred padding their gloves with sponges: *San Francisco Examiner*, December 12, 1887.

141 Still others resorted to stuffing grass or cotton batting into their gloves for extra protection: "When Ball Players Wore Neither Gloves Nor Mask," 5.

141 "gloves more suited for a four-round knocker-out than to a baseball player": "King Catchers," 12.

141 "made of a piece of pine board . . .": *San Antonio Express*, March 15, 1925.

141 "a three-pound lead plate": *Baltimore American*, August 22, 1886. Baltimore catcher Chris Fulmer initiated the use of the lead plate, and fellow catcher Tom Dolan followed his example. No explanation was given as to how it was possible to secure the ball. Thanks to Marty Payne for drawing this to my attention.

142 "the big mit . . .": Tim Murnane, "Ball Players May Use Armor," *Salt Lake Herald*, October 6, 1907.

142 Many catchers therefore continued to keep padding on both hands to a minimum and removed the fingers from the gloves on both hands: *Cleveland Leader*, April 2, 1884.

142 "stiff cowhide, jointed at the bottom . . .": *Cleveland Leader*, April 4, 1884. These two articles could have been describing different gloves, but it was probably the same one.

142–143 "caused a general laugh . . .": "When Ball Players Wore Neither Gloves Nor Mask," 5.

143–144 "do most of the stopping . . .": *Detroit Free Press*, May 2, 1884.

144 Some sources credit "Doc" Bushong . . .: See Morris, *A Game of Inches*, vol. 1, entry 4.4.1 on "One-handed Catches," 233–237, for a full discussion.

144 "left-hand glove" and "a conglomeration of ragged buckskin . . .": *Sporting News*, September 27, 1886.

144 "I have learned that in receiving . . .": *Brooklyn Eagle*, November 16, 1888. An obituary of Bushong maintained that he was eventually "prevailed upon to wear a small quilted pad over his chest, but never would wear a glove or mask." *Utica Saturday Globe*, August 22, 1908. But this was clearly not true, though, as we have seen, Bushong was slow to start wearing the kid gloves used by catchers before the mitt emerged.

144 "to show that one hand was sufficient to catch a pitched ball": "When Ball Players Wore Neither Gloves Nor Mask," 5.

144 "only one glove, as he can throw better with one bare hand": *St. Louis Post-Dispatch*, June 17, 1886. A 1913 account, however, suggested that Bennett had earlier begun wearing "a thin kid glove on his left hand with the fingers cut." *Detroit Free Press*, March 30, 1913.

144 "the most prominent catchers demonstrated . . .": *New York Sun*, April 27, 1890.

145 "the catchers learned with marvelous speed to take the play upon the fat, safe palm": "Modern Ball Hard for Defense," 8.

145 A couple of catchers later claimed . . .: See Morris, *A Game of Inches*, vol. 1, entry 9.3.2, 421–426, for a full discussion.

145 "I took the glove I was then wearing . . .": Charley Scully, "'Father of the Catching Glove' Admits Split Finger Fifty Years Ago, With Twin Bill Ahead, Was 'Mother,'" *Sporting News*, February 23, 1939. At another point, Gunson told a somewhat different version in which he made a few innovations before the Decoration Day doubleheader but then made further improvements to the mitt: "I stitched together the fingers of my left hand glove, thus practically making a mitt; and then I caught both games. It worked so well that I got to work, took an old paint-pot wire handle, the old flannel belts from our castoff jackets, rolled the cloth around the ends of the finger, and padded the thumb. Then I put sheepskins with the wool on it in the palm and covered it with buckskin, thus completing the mitt." Quoted in Gutman, *Banana Bats and Ding-Dong Balls*, 178.

145 "swelled and bunged" and "a mattress made in the style of a glove . . .": Ticket broker Kid Bernstein, quoted in "Intended for Joke Was Original Mitt," *Fort Wayne Sentinel*, March 2, 1910, 8. Decker went on to get the first patent on a catcher's mitt, and his story is told at length in Chapter 11 of this book. There is one error in Bernstein's story: he identified the pitcher as speedballer Ed "Cannonball" Crane, who in fact left Toronto after the 1887 season, while Oldfield did not join the team until 1888. But this is the kind of mistake that is easy to make after the passage of twenty years and does not discredit the account.

145 "putting a circle of wire around it . . .": *Sporting News*, December 30, 1926.

145 "the first good one": *Minneapolis Journal*, reprinted in *Sporting News*, May 28, 1914.

146 the luxury of carrying ten or at most eleven players: As late as 1879, Chicago's practice of "hiring two high-priced and experienced men as substitutes" was singled out for being unusual. *Chicago Inter-Ocean*, June 12, 1879, 3. Most clubs got by with one paid substitute, sometimes supplemented by a groundskeeper who could fill in if an emergency occurred. See my *A Game of Inches*, vol. 1, entry 6.2.1 on substitutes, 305–306, for more details.

146 "give any manager in the country . . .": *St. Louis Globe-Democrat*, July 7, 1883, 4.

146 Cincinnati won a fierce bidding war for Bill Traffley . . .: *Rocky Mountain News*, May 14, 1883, 2.

146 The Northwestern League club in Bay City . . .: *Bay City Tribune*, February 14, 1884.

146–147 Before the 1887 season, Harry Wright . . . signed no fewer than six catchers: *St. Louis Globe-Democrat*, February 10, 1887.

147 "created a sensation by wearing an immense glove . . ." and "declared that his hand . . .": *New York Sun*, April 27, 1890.

147 "stuffing to the glove and covering it with patches of new leather . . .": John H. Gruber, "The Gloves," *Sporting News*, December 2, 1915.

147 "perfect[ing] a movement of the left wrist . . ." and "during an entire season . . .": "When Ball Players Wore Neither Gloves Nor Mask," 5.

147–148 "Bushong's method . . .": "King Catchers," 12.

148 "My advice to youngsters . . ." and "I do not think catching is dangerous . . .": Doyle, "Catch the Curves," 5.

150 "The fat mitten stopped the runner . . .": "Decline of Running: Why Fewer Sacks Are Stolen Now Than Formerly," *Kansas City Star*, January 14, 1905.

151 "in the latter part of 1888 came the big glove into use . . .": *Cincinnati Enquirer*, January 2, 1899. The other article, published in 1910, similarly noted that as soon as mitts appeared on the scene, "the stolen base records began to go. The coming of the big glove, in short, meant a cinch for catchers, and meant the death of baserunning. When the catcher had to take the pitch in the thin, leather tipped glove, the shock of the first ball drove him back and made his hands give way to save the bump. This gave the runner an elegant start and saved him on the slide. With the big glove, the catcher could come forward with the reception of the pitch and snap the ball like lightning, beating the runner right along." "Modern Ball Hard for Defense," 8. Another factor was that discarding the second glove made it easier for catchers to throw out runners. As one observer explained, "With the right hand gloveless catchers gradually learned to throw to bases with greater speed and accuracy than ever before, for a ball thrown with a gloved hand naturally traveled slowly and without the proper aim." "When Ball Players Wore Neither Gloves Nor Mask," 5.

151–152 "Louisville has a wonderful catcher . . .": *Louisville Courier-Journal*, March 9, 1890.

152 "I can kill myself in one year pitching . . .": *New York Press*, December 17, 1909.

152 "retired from the game inveighing against an effete civilization . . .": Aulick, "One Hundred Notable Figures in Baseball."

153 "[Craver's] reputation is not first-class . . .": Charles Chase, quoted in the *Chicago Tribune*, March 4, 1877, 7.

153 Allison, who never again caught regularly: Allison did catch nineteen games in 1878, but after that he caught only two more major league games.

153–154 "went behind the bat but fifteen times . . .": *Sporting Life*, January 23, 1892, 9.

154 "If they're going to dress me up like a deep-sea diver it's time for me to quit": Michael Daisy, "When Commissioner Guiney Was Also DAC Baseball Great," *DAC News*, October 2007, 72. The comment was reported by Detroit Athletic Club teammate and longtime Detroit mayor John C. Lodge, who claimed that Guiney made the statement in 1889. If so, Guiney must have had second thoughts, as he returned to catching for the DAC in the 1890s. Lodge gives a slightly different version of the remark in his memoirs. (John C. Lodge, *I Remember Detroit*, Detroit: Wayne State University Press, 1949), 53. Guiney attended Assumption College with Walker, and the two were later teammates on the DAC baseball club.

154 "in times past . . ." and "the really good catcher . . .": Essay on catching by "Doc" Bushong in Pfeffer, *Scientific Ball*, 52.

154 Walker spoke at a convention of African-American Masons . . .: *Sporting Life*, August 30, 1913, describes the talk at the Masons' convention. Zang, in *Fleet Walker's Divided Heart*, 37, confirms that Walker usually caught bare-handed, occasionally donning lambskin gloves.

155 "leather back, thus preventing the back of the hand being hurt" and "impossible to break the fingers": Both ads appeared in the *New York Sporting Times*, June 20, 1891.

155 "a sufficient bulwark to make it impossible . . .": *New York Sun*, April 27, 1890.

155 "with this glove such a thing . . .": editor's note appended to R. M. Larner, "Decker's Glove," *Sporting Life*, May 3, 1890.

155 With a few exceptions, substitutions had never been allowed in baseball . . .: See Morris, *A Game of Inches*, vol. 1, entry 6.2.1, 305–306, and entry 6.2.6, 313–314, for a detailed discussion.

155 "the interest had been destroyed . . .": *Chicago Tribune*, August 29, 1886, 3.

155 A war of words continued in the press for weeks . . .: Philadelphia owner John I. Rogers indignantly accused Chicago of a litany of unsporting tactics, including "Objecting to the substitution of a new player for one manifestly injured in the game, as in the subject of this inquiry, and the hundreds of other unmanly, unchivalrous, and unsportsmanlike acts and deeds which have so often disgusted the lovers of fair play and honorable rivalry in athletic contests." *Chicago Tribune*, September 22, 1886. The *Chicago Tribune*, however, contended: "There seems to be a disposition among a good many people to criticize Capt. Anson for his refusal to permit the changing of catchers, and blame him for the entire delay. Base ball is played on its points, and the element of sentiment or chivalry does not and should not enter into the question in any shape whatever. Capt. Anson knew that McGuire's hands were sore when he went in to play, and, believing that they had not been seriously injured in the game (the umpire sustaining him in this opinion), he insisted that McGuire should play the game out. He was simply claiming his rights." *Chicago Tribune*, August 29, 1886, 3.

156 A strikingly similar incident occurred two years later . . .: *Chicago Tribune*, September 13, 1888, 3.

156 "The most radical change made in the playing rules . . .": Henry Chadwick, *Evansville Journal*, April 27, 1889, 7.

156 "doing away with the style of play . . .": *Brooklyn Eagle*, November 8, 1885.

9. THE THINKING-MAN CATCHER

158 "Heroism feels and never reasons . . .": Ralph Waldo Emerson, "Heroism," in *The Collected Works of Ralph Waldo Emerson*, vol. II, *Essays: First Series*, 148.

159 "the proper thing to do at the right moment": *Daily Alta California*, September 26, 1869; quoted in Paul Dickson, *The Hidden Language of Baseball*, 31.

159 Henry Chadwick naturally seized on this trend, and by 1867 he was instructing pitchers to attempt pickoffs only when signaled to do so by the catcher: *Ball Player's Chronicle*, June 20, 1867.

159 "the 'headwork' in strategic play . . .": *New York Clipper*, October 28, 1871.

159 "if the pitcher is familiar . . .": Henry Chadwick, *Chadwick's Base Ball Manual*, 14–15.

159 So most catchers ignored this part of Chadwick's advice . . .: An exception neatly proves this rule. In 1869, Dickey Pearce reportedly "kept his eye on the striker, and let [pitcher Tommy] Pratt know just where to deliver the ball." *National Chronicle*, May 15, 1869. Note, however, that this description makes it explicit that the purpose of the communication was to offer advice as to which location would be most difficult for the hitter, not to help the catcher do his job.

159 "Deacon Jim White was the greatest natural catcher . . .": A. G. Spalding (as told to Tim Murnane), "Mike Kelley [sic] Refused $10,000 When He Was Broke," *Boston Globe*, December 24, 1905, SM4. Spalding was mistaken about when White joined Boston, as this actually occurred after the 1872 season.

160 The ultimate compliment that a cattleman could pay . . .: Dary, *Cowboy Culture*, 280–281.

160 Thus almost no one but Chadwick referred to the catchers of the 1870s using such signals: The only references that I have found to signals being used in the 1870s to convey information about the pitch (as opposed to the type used by Flint) were after the fact. Tim Murnane, for instance, credited Charles Snyder of Louisville with originating such signals in 1877, while H. G. Merrill cited Little Joe Roche of the 1876 Crickets of Binghamton. *Sporting News*, July 16, 1908. Meanwhile a *Boston Globe* reporter suggested that pitcher Jim Devlin had started their use. Quoted in *Sporting Life*, July 1, 1893.

160 "It is said that Flint . . .": *Boston Globe*, May 18, 1879.

160 "There is nothing at all mysterious . . .": *Chicago Tribune*, May 25, 1879.

160–162 "in nine cases out of ten . . .," "down to the corner . . .," "swelled to twice their normal size," "dared not squeal," and "the fourth day . . .": *Sporting Life*, January 23, 1892, 9. According to the article, this pitcher went on to major league stardom, but his identity was not revealed.

162 "I try to learn my pitcher's delivery . . .": *St. Louis Post-Dispatch*, July 30, 1893.

162 When Baltimore began using signals . . .: *Cincinnati Enquirer*, May 3, 1885; reported by researcher David Ball and reprinted in Frederick Ivor-Campbell, "When Was the First? (Part 4)," *Nineteenth Century Notes* 95:3, 4 (Summer/Fall 1995), 12.

162 "Get a telephone": *Detroit Free Press*, May 13, 1887.

162–163 "If you use your pipes . . .": *St. Louis Post-Dispatch*, April 10, 1898; recounted by teammate Gus Weyhing, who also disliked McCloskey's system. McCloskey is the same man who claimed a role in the development of the catcher's mitt.

163–164 "The modern catcher is equally important . . .," "cool, level head," "pluck and endurance," "that the strong points . . .," "true catcher should . . .," and "In these days, it has become . . .": "Chicago Exchange," in *Rocky Mountain News*, November 26, 1883, 2.

164 "Until within a few years . . .": Ward, *Base-Ball: How to Become a Player*, 53.

164 veteran pitchers like Charley Radbourn and Bill Hutchison were continuing to give signs into the 1890s: See Morris, *A Game of Inches*, vol. 1, entry 1.27, 47–49.

164–165 "work together as a team . . .": *Brooklyn Eagle*, July 28, 1881, 3.

165 "catchers would catch nothing but . . .": *Dayton Journal*, August 14, 1889.

165 In the years immediately after the advent of the curveball, if the pitcher and catcher exchanged pitch information at all, it was the norm for the pitcher to let the catcher know what was coming: For example, curveball pioneer Arthur "Candy" Cummings, who retired in 1878, later recalled: "we used to have signals, but our catchers did not take care of them as they do now. I did all this myself, and they were so simple, too, that no opposing batsman got on to them for that reason." *Sporting News*, February 20, 1897.

165 "by shutting my eyes . . .": *St. Louis Post-Dispatch*, July 30, 1893.

165 "head 'yes' or 'no' pretending the catcher is calling them": *Milwaukee Daily Journal*, April 25, 1891, Thanks to researcher Frank Vaccaro for drawing this to my attention.

165 "it has always been my practice . . .": *New York Sun*, May 6, 1888.

165 "The catcher calls for the kind of ball . . .": *St. Louis Post-Dispatch*, August 12, 1894.

165–166 "is a better plan when the catcher is a cool and experienced man": *Boston Globe*, June 26, 1886.

166 "More than ever before . . .": *Spalding's Official Base Ball Guide, 1890*, 45.

166 "The 'pairing' of pitchers and catchers . . .": *New York Sun*, May 6, 1888.

166–167 "combination," "as varied as the moves . . .," "the catcher should have . . .," and "new wrinkles being introduced . . .": Tim Murnane, "How the Stars Play Combinations," *Boston Globe*, March 10, 1889, 22.

167 An 1885 rule change that legalized flat bats . . .: Morris, *A Game of Inches*, vol. 1, entry 2.2.1, 76–81, and entry 9.2.4, 411–412.

167–168 "throwing to short-stop . . .": *New York Clipper*, December 20, 1879. Because of a typographical error, the final sentence read, "When the ball [sic] swiftly thrown and accurately returned, the play invariably yields an out; but it must be is [sic] understood by signal to be done effectively." In the text I have moved the word "is" to its correct location.

168 "There is little difference . . .": *Baltimore American*, April 28, 1889.

168 "The great number of games . . .": Essay on catching by "Doc" Bushong in Pfeffer, *Scientific Ball*, 51.

169 "once a man got to first base . . .," "The modern principle . . .," and "we didn't play . . .": *Sporting News*, October 30, 1897; see Morris, *A Game of Inches*, vol. 1, entry 6.6.1, 349–350, for more details on the origins of one-run strategies.

169 "shrewdly" and "stepped into the trap": *Chicago Tribune*, May 19, 1870. According to Sam Crane, Buck Ewing also used this trick. Crane wrote that Ewing "was so confident in his ability to head off base runners that even when the speediest of players were on the bases I have seen him very often have passed balls purposely and throw the balls away from him to entice a runner to try for a base." Crane, "Buck Ewing."

169 "looked like cold-blooded murder . . .": John H. Gruber, "You're Out," *Sporting News*, February 17, 1916.

169 Craver was known for trying this tactic . . .: *National Chronicle*, May 29, 1869.

169–170 "turned about carelessly . . .": *Cincinnati Enquirer*, April 24, 1877.

170 tricks struck Americans of the era: the contempt with which they could be regarded was nicely captured by a former ballplayer who wrote, "In the scrub games tricks were often resorted to for advantage. . . . These antics prevented the exercise for which the game was instituted and had no good effect." *Boston Journal*, March 6, 1905.

170 "unworthy of a fair and manly player": *New York Clipper*, October 30, 1875. And Tim Murnane wrote in the *Boston Globe* of May 14, 1908, that "No Boston player has been allowed to attempt the trick since Harry Wright declared it was unsportsmanlike and an insult to the spectators." See entry 4.4.10 in my *A Game of Inches*, vol. 1, 249–253, for more details on the hidden ball trick.

170 "a batter would swing at a ball . . .": Connie Mack, "Memories of When the Game Was Young," *Sporting Life* (monthly), June 1924.

171 "had a way of snapping his fingers . . .": *Boston Globe*, January 17, 1915.

171 Mike Kelly tried snapping a rubber band: *St. Louis Post-Dispatch*, September 16, 1888. See Morris, *A Game of Inches*, vol. 1, entry 11.1.11, for a more detailed discussion of the topic.

10. THE CATCHER AS DESPERADO

172 "I often used to wonder . . .": Judge Fred E. Crane, son of early ballplayer Fred W. H. Crane, quoted in *Brooklyn Eagle*, April 8, 1934.

173 "rather more proud of my base ball ability than of some other things": Wertheim and Sorrentino, *The Crane Log*, 169.

173–174 "Large bat manufacturers . . .": *New York Clipper*, April 26, 1879.

174 Typical was Wesley Blogg . . .: *Williamsport Sunday Grit*, March 18, 1888.

174 "with remarkable agility, often smoking a cigar at the same time": Slye, "Early Days of Baseball in Baraboo."

174 "Little Hunter of Saginaw . . .": *Grand Rapids Eagle*, August 10, 1883. The *Grand Rapids Daily Democrat* of August 7, 1883, similarly chastised Hunter for employing the "grand stand racket."

174–175 A notable example occurred when the Washington Monument . . .: *Sporting Life*, January 14, 1885; *Washington Herald*, reprinted in *Sporting Life*, January 21, 1885.

175 "the deed was accomplished . . .": *Haverhill Bulletin*, May 8, 1885, 3.

175 "cannon would stand": Murnane, "Lew Brown's Last Sleep," 1.

175 he was offered a job as an inspector of fireplugs: "This Fan Recalls When A's Made 850 Runs in 19 Games," *Philadelphia Inquirer*, March 12, 1922, 19, 21, reminiscences of longtime baseball fan Edward N. Haith.

176 "The wound ran . . .," "Well, maybe . . .," and "Due to his weakened . . .": James J. Corbett, "In Corbett's Corner," syndicated column (King Features), *Macon Daily Telegraph*, January 3, 1919.

176 there is corroboration from a reliable enough source: The same basic account appears in Spink, *National Game*, 91, with some minor differences and is attributed to Al Reach's brother Robert, a credible source.

176 There is also plenty of evidence that Dockney . . .: Tim Murnane, for example, referred to Dockney as a "grand catcher" in the *Boston Globe*, February 22, 1900.

176 He became the subject of colorful stories . . .: *Washington Post*, August 15, 1909.

176 "to play ball every afternoon . . .": *Philadelphia Times*, reprinted in *Sporting Life*, October 24, 1891.

177 "stabbed by a drunken man . . .": *Brooklyn Eagle*, May 25, 1868.

177 facing charges of larceny: *New York Times*, March 15, 1871.

177 Sometime in the 1880s he died in obscurity . . .: Dockney's exact date and place of death are unknown, but the *Boston Globe* of January 8, 1893, referred to him as being dead. Despite his lengthy Civil War service, no pension application appears to have ever been filed on his behalf, and efforts to determine exactly when and where he died have been unsuccessful.

177 "a regular, earnest and plucky worker . . .": Henry Chadwick, *New York Clipper*, December 21, 1872.

178 "I was once catcher . . .": *New York Times*, September 9, 1877; *Boston Times*, September 16, 1877; *New York Sunday Mercury*, September 29, 1877. The various newspaper accounts of Barlow's statements differed in many significant particulars, and there is no way to be sure whether Barlow's story changed or whether reporters were inattentive. For example, in the *New York Times* article the injury had occurred four years earlier while the piece in the *Sunday Mercury* stated that it had happened on August 10, 1874.

178 The baseball historian David Arcidiacono notes . . .: David Arcidiacono, "The Curious Case of Tommy Barlow," *Elysian Fields Quarterly*, Winter 2004, 31–44; David Arcidiacono, *Grace, Grit and Growling* (East Hampton, Conn.: n.p., 2004), 95–101.

178 John J. "Rooney" Sweeney's promising career ended prematurely after a series of arrests . . .: *Sporting News*, July 21, 1888; *London Free Press*, June 5, 1890; *Sporting News*, January 16, 1892.

178 had to resign in the face of department disciplinary charges: New York City Fire Department records obtained by researcher Peter Mancuso.

179 "promising amateur" and "an inmate of the Illinois penitentiary . . .": *Sporting Life*, July 24, 1897.

179 detailed profiles of him that regularly appeared in the *Sporting News*: *Sporting News*, April 8 and September 9, 1893; January 20 and October 27, 1894; November 6, 1897.

179 a series of notes detailed the jobs he held in the off-season: *Sporting Life*, February 10, 1894; *Sporting News*, November 28 and December 12, 1896; November 6 and December 4, 1897; February 5 and November 26, 1898.

179 His career was almost derailed before it started: *Sporting News*, February 28, 1891; *Sporting Life*, June 13 and July 25, 1891.

179 serving briefly as captain of St. Louis's struggling National League entry: *Sporting News*, October 27, 1894.

179 committed to a Memphis insane asylum: *Sporting Life*, June 15, 1901.

179 he was last heard from in 1904: *Sporting News*, June 25, 1904.

179 "cool and us[ing] good judgment": *Chicago Tribune*, April 24, 1875.

179 "spree" and "bottle in order . . .": *St. Louis Post-Dispatch*, August 5, 1885.

179 "He is believed by his friends to be insane": *Sporting Life*, May 9, 1887, 1.

179–180 "Hoover is a perfect ringer . . ." and "today's practice . . .": *Sporting News*, reprinted in *Chicago Inter-Ocean*, March 25, 1888.

180 In 1887, Hoover was arrested in Lincoln, Missouri . . .: *Sporting Life*, December 14, 1887; *Sporting News*, December 31, 1887.

180 "on the condition that he was to leave town . . .": *Sporting News*, January 3, 1891, 1.

180 "an out and out desperado [who] carries shooting irons at all times": *New York Sporting Times*, March 7, 1891.

180 The next season saw a drunken Hoover . . .: *Sporting Life*, August 1, 1891.

180 prompted that town's *Sporting News* correspondent . . .: *Sporting News*, August 17, 1895.

180 "broken and gnarled fingers": Researcher Bill Carle tracked down Hoover's prison record.

181 All these men were born in the 1850s or 1860s: Exact dates of birth are not available for many of these men, but the censuses give us a good approximation for everyone but Knowdell. Barlow was the oldest, born around 1852, followed by Sweeney in 1858, Hoover around 1865, Twineham in 1866, and Adams in 1869. There is conflicting evidence about Knowdell's date of birth, with one profile of him making the improbable claim that he was born in 1840. The preponderance of evidence, however, suggests that he was born in the mid-1850s.

182 No professional catcher is known to have died as an immediate result of a foul ball: Robert M. Gorman and David Weeks have, however, documented twenty-four examples of amateur and semipro catchers who died as a direct result of a foul tip or pitched ball in their recent book *Death at the Ballpark: A Comprehensive Study of Game-Related Fatalities of Players, Other Personnel and Spectators in Amateur and Professional Baseball, 1862–2007* (Jefferson, N.C.: McFarland and Co., 2009). Most of these catchers were teenagers, who are more susceptible than adults to dying from such sudden blows because their hearts are not yet fully developed.

182 While none of the four men died as a direct result of brain damage . . .: Waters and Long both committed suicide while Strzelczyk died in a car chase with police. Webster was homeless and suffering from cognitive and psychological disorders when he died of a heart attack. Alan Schwarz, "Expert Ties Ex-Player's Suicide to Brain Damage," *New York Times*, January 18, 2007; Alan Schwarz, "Lineman, Dead at 36, Exposes Brain Injuries," *New York Times*, June 15, 2007.

183 "call into question how effectively . . .": Described in Alan Schwarz, "Study of Ex-N.F.L. Players Ties Concussion to Depression Risk," *New York Times*, May 31, 2007.

183 A disturbing number of National Hockey League players . . .: Research by the *Toronto Star* concluded that since 1996 concussions have forced or played a large role in the retirements of at least thirty NHL players. Prominent players whose careers have been disrupted or ended have included Pat LaFontaine, Eric and Brett Lindros, Keith Primeau, Adam Deadmarsh, Nick Kypreos, Kevin Kaminski, and Jeff Beukeboom. Randy Starkman, "Hockey Concussions Take a Toll" and "Players Put Team Above Health" (two-part series), *Toronto Star*, December 23 and 24, 2007.

183 The international football (soccer) community . . .: See, for example, Fuller, Junge, et al., "A Six Year Prospective Study of the Incidence and Causes of Head and Neck Injuries in International Football," *British Journal of Sports Medicine* (2005), vol. 39, supplement 1, i3–i9.

183 Mike Matheny became the first major league baseball player: Major league umpire Greg Bonin was also forced to retire in 2001 as the result of multiple concussions incurred while working behind the plate.

183 "was struck by a ball on the temple . . .": *Omaha Bee*, reprinted in the *Louisville Courier-Journal*, March 23, 1890.

183 "manifested symptoms of insanity . . .": *New York Sunday Mercury*, November 10, 1877. Lindsley's name was difficult to read in the article and appears to have been spelled "Lendsey," but based on census information it seems to have been Lindsley. He must have recovered to some extent, as he is listed on the 1880 census with his wife and daughter. But by 1900 his wife was not living with him, yet she was still listed as married, suggesting that his health or sanity may again have failed.

183–184 home plate umpire Cal Drummond . . .: Larry R. Gerlach, "Death on the Diamond: The Cal Drummond Story," *National Pastime* 24 (2004), 14–16.

184 "tobacco-industry-like refusal to acknowledge the depths of the problem": Christopher Nowinski, *Head Games: Football's Concussion Crisis from the NFL to Youth Leagues* (East Bridgewater, Mass.: Drummond, 2007); quoted in Alan Schwarz, "Expert Ties Ex-Player's Suicide to Brain Damage."

184 "I'd sniff some smelling salts, then go back in there": Quoted in Schwarz, "Expert Ties Ex-Player's Suicide to Brain Damage." Similarly, NHL player Stu Grimson said of the aftereffects of a concussion: "It's very tempting to play through it. Nobody can see your injury. Only you can really articulate what's going on." Quoted in Randy Starkman, "Hockey Concussions Take a Toll," *Toronto Star*, December 23, 2007. And former NHL star Keith Primeau now looks back on his decision to keep playing after suffering a concussion during the 2000 Stanley Cup playoffs as "the most erroneous decision I ever made." Primeau continues to suffer symptoms from that concussion, and while he still recalls "how proud I was that I played in Game 1 of the conference finals," he is forced to add, "But now, in retrospect, I jeopardized my health." Quoted in Randy Starkman, "Players Put Team Above Health," *Toronto Star*, December 24, 2007.

184 "Dillon, of the Reds . . .": *Pittsburgh Dispatch*, reprinted in *St. Louis Globe-Democrat*, June 30, 1876, 8.

184 longtime catcher Tom Deasley began to display signs of dementia: *Sporting Life*, April 4, 1891.

184 a series of Yogi Berra–esque tales at Deasley's expense: For example, in the *New York Sporting Times* of April 19, 1891—immediately after Deasley's delusional behavior had been reported—Lynch claimed that Deasley had seen a sign in the window of a dry goods store that read "Pitcher's Castoria for sale here," which prompted him to enter the store and ask if they had any "Catcher's Castoria." When the clerk smiled and said no, Deasley "walked out, muttering, 'That's the way, it's all for pitchers—pitchers. Nobody ever thinks of a catcher.'" Two days later, the same periodical published another similar anecdote from Lynch.

184–185 "Waldo Ward was hit twice . . .," "was still dazed," "no one had noticed it," and "and he went down again . . .": *Thomson* (Illinois) *Review*, April 23, 1931.

185 "We understand, as players . . .": Quoted in Schwarz, "Expert Ties Ex-Player's Suicide to Brain Damage."

186 coming to light only recently . . .: The discoveries of most of these men have been announced in the SABR Biographical Committee newsletter: the June 1993 issue for Walker, the November/December 2006 issue for Quinton, and the May/June 2008

issue for both Bancker and Brennan. Whiting appears to have died in 1902, but the evidence remains under review. The lives of each of these men included disturbing suggestions that they too could have suffered from the lingering effects of repeated blows to the head. In an 1875 game, for instance, Marshall Quinton was struck in the head with such force by a foul tip that it rebounded on the fly to pitcher Will Carrigan, who caught it for an out. *New York Sunday Mercury*, January 27, 1877. This horrifying incident, which was recounted without any signs of concern about Quinton's health, received mention only because a similar play involving catcher Billy Holbert and pitcher Jim Devlin occurred in 1876. Was it a coincidence that Quinton's life after baseball was marred by petty crimes and that he too died in obscurity? Quinton was last heard from when the *Trenton* (New Jersey) *Times* of June 25, 1900, reported that he had been arrested for stealing wire. A few years later Quinton died, and when the *Times* reported his death it mentioned that he had once been a well-known catcher, but it managed to give his name erroneously as Mason Quinton. Twenty-eight-year-old Ed Whiting had been a major league regular for three years in 1884 when he was "suspended for insubordination, drinking and careless play." *New York Clipper*, September 20, 1884. Barely more than a year later he was found living with his wife and newborn baby in such destitute circumstances that his old baseball friends had to raise money to help him out. *Sporting Life*, January 20, 1886. John Bancker, a Philadelphia native who caught for several professional clubs, disappeared when he was sent to jail in 1884. Then there was a St. Louis catcher named Gottlieb Doering, Jr., who became a regular at local saloons, where he was noted for his fondness for a song about an Irishman named Brennan. Soon the young catcher became known as Jack Brennan, and it was under that name that he caught in 1884 for the local team that ran away with the Union Association's lone pennant. Two years later, however, came word that Brennan had been arrested for breaking into a freight car. *St. Louis Post-Dispatch*, April 5, 1886. He was soon a free man, and the *Sporting News* maintained that the arrest "taught him a lesson and made him a man." *Sporting News*, October 25, 1886. For years he did indeed stay clear of trouble, returning to catching and then to a career in umpiring, while the *Sporting News* showed its faith in his rehabilitation by allowing Brennan briefly to write a column. But in 1903 that journal had to report that its onetime columnist had been arrested again for an act of larceny committed at a saloon known as "one of the most disreputable joints in Rock Island [Illinois] at the time it was closed." *Davenport* (Iowa) *Leader*, reprinted in the *Sporting News*, November 21, 1903. Yet another example was Horace Phillips, who parlayed a mediocre career as a semipro catcher during the 1870s into becoming one of the best-known managers of the 1880s. But at the height of his career he was struck down by an ailment variously described as brain fever or paresis. He was institutionalized, and over the next five years the sporting press periodically mentioned his descent into madness. Eventually the references stopped and his date and place of death remain unknown.

186 Frank Ringo's drinking problems . . .: *Kansas City Star*, April 12, 1889.

186 "whisky bringing a player absolutely to the gutter": *Washington Post*, December 2, 1895; quoted in David Ball's biography of Baldwin for the SABR BioProject.

186 Baldwin was sentenced to an asylum . . .: *Cincinnati Enquirer*, July 4, 1897; *Sporting News*, July 10, 1897, 4; both cited in David Ball's biography of Baldwin for the SABR BioProject.

186 Billy Earle . . . was hit and nearly killed by a pitched ball in 1896: *Sporting News*, June 6, 1896, 1.

186 Within two years he had become a hopeless morphine addict . . .: *Philadelphia Inquirer*, August 27 and October 28, 1898; *Cincinnati Enquirer*, June 18, 1899; research by David Ball. John McGraw paid for the hospitalization that may have saved Earle's life.

186–187 "his great ability as a catcher . . ." and "He drifted carelessly . . .": *Louisville Courier-Journal*, reprinted in *Wheeling Register*, January 27, 1889.

187 shot to death at the corner of Main and Austin streets . . .: *Dallas Morning News*, January 17, 1889. Adding to the melodrama of the situation, this account recorded that "As Bradley was receiving his death wound the 'Cold Day' theatrical company happened to be passing, and remembering the Curry-Porter killing they took to their heels in great style." The newspapers gave conflicting accounts about whether Bradley had done anything to provoke the attack, but his killer was released after just over a year, suggesting that some extenuating circumstances were found to exist. *Columbus Dispatch*, April 11, 1890.

187 "a beautiful floral base ball mask": *Dallas Morning News*, January 19, 1889.

187 "fits of melancholia": *Sporting Life*, January 27, 1900, 9.

187 "Marty Bergen, the great catcher . . .": *Denver Evening Post*, July 29, 1899, 8. Jacob Morse was just as insistent that Bergen never drank and that he suffered only from mental illness. *Sporting Life*, January 27, 1900, 9. One doctor did attribute Bergen's behavior to "tobacco abuse," but that diagnosis seems far-fetched. Glenn Stout, "Blood Sport," *Inside Worcester*, Autumn 1993, 26.

187 the dual blows seemed to drive him over the edge: See Stout, "Blood Sport," 23–26, for a discussion of the tragedies that precipitated the murder-suicide. The *Boston Globe* of February 13, 1898, provides a description of Bergen's home and family. *Sporting Life*, January 27, 1900, 9, covers the tragedy in great detail.

187 "the best catcher in America . . .": *Cincinnati Enquirer*, reprinted in the *Boston Globe*, July 25, 1899.

188 Entrusted with collecting liquor license payments . . .: Leggett's crime was covered extensively in the *Brooklyn Eagle*, particularly December 20, 1877, 4; December 26, 1877, 4; January 6, 1878, 2; February 9, 1878, 4. Worse, an editorial on December 22, 1877, 2, claimed that Leggett was hired by the city when it was well known that he had previously defrauded the fire department of money. In articles written in 1889 and 1891, Henry Chadwick made clear that Leggett was still alive but added no details. In the first of the two articles, he implied that Leggett had been disgraced but declined, "for old times' sake," to provide details. "Old Chalk" [Chadwick], "Baseball in Its Infancy," *Brooklyn Eagle*, December 15, 1889; "Old Chalk" [Chadwick], "Base Ball Reminiscences," *Brooklyn Eagle*, June 7, 1891, 16.

188 He apparently moved to Texas . . .: Terry, *Long Before the Dodgers*, 25, 29, 143–145. Family genealogical records indicate that Leggett died in Galveston, Texas, in 1894, but no death certificate has been found to confirm that.

11. HARRY DECKER, THE "DON JUAN OF SHAVEN HEAD"

189 "Decker's hallucination is that he owns . . .": *Chicago Tribune*, November 7, 1893, 11.

189 "changes his name each time he boards a train": "Don Juan of Shaven Head," *Los Angeles Times*, January 18, 1913, H1-H2.

190 while still a teenager, he earned a place . . .: *Fitchburg Daily Sentinel*, April 18, 1889.

190 According to one later account, he enlisted in the army . . .: *Peoria Herald*, reprinted in *Decatur Daily Review*, June 11, 1896.

190 "the Adonis": *Evansville Journal*, August 18, 1884.

190 when asked to umpire a game on a hot day . . .: *Evansville Journal*, July 14, 1884.

190 "when he has paid for a little experience by broken fingers, etc.": *Sporting Life*, August 18, 1886, 5.

190 "in the second or third inning . . .": *Sporting Life*, September 13, 1890. The source was Tom Loftus.

191 left behind debts to his landlady, washerwoman, and several friends . . .: *Sporting Life*, September 10, 1884.

191–192 "If Decker had pursued . . .," "Baseball was a great craze . . .," and "pretty little black-eyed belle": *St. Louis Star-Sayings*, quoted in *Decatur Herald-Despatch*, March 28, 1891.

192 News reports had the couple making an attempt to elope . . .: The story of the elopement appeared in *Sporting Life* on July 29, 1885, and in the *Official Baseball Record* on July 31, 1885, and was later repeated in such sources as the *St. Louis Star-Sayings*, quoted in *Decatur Herald-Despatch*, March 28, 1891. But these reports were contradicted by one J. F. Brennan of Jacksonville, Illinois, who wrote to *Sporting Life* as follows: "In your issue of July 29 I see you made mention of an elopement, Mr. Decker and Miss Burns being the parties mentioned. From personal knowledge I will state Mr. Decker has been done an injustice; he was married in the Burnett House, Keokuk, Iowa, July 16th, 1885. He was married with the girl's mother's consent and no attempt at elopement was made." "Not So Romantic After All," *Sporting Life*, August 5, 1885, 1. And county marriage records confirm the basic facts of Brennan's claim.

192 "child bride" and "to Decker's credit . . .": *St. Louis Star-Sayings*, quoted in *Decatur Herald-Despatch*, March 28, 1891.

192 Before one game there he was presented with a baby carriage . . .: *Official Baseball Record*, June 26, 1886.

192 the Macon club wasn't willing to part with him: *Decatur Daily Review*, April 4, 1886.

192 earning high praise for his strong and accurate throwing arm: *Washington Post*, July 3, 1886.

192 many old acquaintants approached Decker in the station . . .: *Decatur Daily Review*, July 18, 1886.

193 Before a meaningless late-season game in Kansas City . . .: *Washington Post*, October 10, 1886.

193 At season's end Decker apparently learned . . .: *Sporting Life*, November 10, 1886.

193 He was so brazen . . .: *Sporting Life*, November 17, 1886, 2; *Sporting Life*, November 24, 1886, 2.

193 "walking up and down the street, waiting for the mail carrier": *Sporting Life*, January 5, 1887, 1.

193–194 The exposure of this latest scam . . .: *Sporting News*, January 22, 1887.

194 "he had been blacklisted once . . .": *Washington Post*, November 10, 1886. The player was Robert Barr.

194 He fired off letters to the editors . . .: *Washington Post*, November 10, 1886.

194 "audacity to claim" and "he never did play . . .": *Sporting Life*, December 22, 1886, 1. Thanks to David Ball for alerting me to this particular bizarre chapter of Decker's life and familiarizing me with the details.

194 "an unsavory reputation": *Sporting Life*, January 5, 1887, 1.

194 the Toronto club took a chance . . .: *Sporting Life*, January 5, 1887, 4.

195 One source suggested that he had once abandoned his wife and daughter: *St. Louis Star-Sayings*, quoted in *Decatur Herald-Despatch*, March 28, 1891.

195 Harry Decker spent that winter . . .: *Sporting Life*, January 16, 1889; *Philadelphia Inquirer*, March 26, 1889.

195 The two men appear to have busied themselves . . .: Although the patent was not received until August 6, 1889, their partnership was listed in the 1889 Chicago city directory.

195 "inventive genius" and "his improved catcher's glove . . .": R. M. Larner, "A Careless Patentee," *Sporting Life*, April 26, 1890.

195 "this glove, which is now . . .": Larner, "Decker's Glove."

195 "is sure to be profitable . . .": Editor's note appended to R. M. Larner, "Decker's Glove."

195 he risked losing it by failing to pay the minor fees associated with the application: Larner, "A Careless Patentee"; Larner, "Decker's Glove."

196 "the man who invented the turnstile . . .": *New York Times*, November 7, 1893.

196 "came around with a turnstile register . . .": *New York Sporting Times*, May 2, 1891.

196 Decker's two-year-old daughter died: *Sporting Life*, February 6, 1889.

196 Decker did indeed choose to drop out of his partnership with Paul Buckley: *Sporting Life*, July 10, 1889.

196 on August 6, 1889, the valuable patent was finally received: U.S. Patent Office, patent #408,650; Gutman, *Banana Bats and Ding-Dong Balls*, 179. Ads for the mitt suggest that it was the back of the mitt, which featured extra thick felt, that differentiated the "Decker patent" glove from its rivals. *New York Sporting Times*, February 21, 1891.

196 Eventually the patent was sold to A. G. Spalding's sporting goods firm: As with so many of the details in Harry Decker's story, there is confusion about the details of the patent's sale. Two 1890 articles maintained that he had sold the rights to A. J. Reach & Company. Larner, "A Careless Patentee"; Larner, "Decker's Glove." The sale to Reach is confirmed by U.S. Patent #450,366 (which can be viewed on the Google Patent Search website). But Spalding's firm was soon marketing the mitt, so presumably the rights were resold. See Gutman, *Banana Bats and Ding-Dong Balls*, 178–180, for more details on the mitt's history.

197 Unfortunately Decker would later maintain . . .: *Sporting Life*, July 5, 1913.

197 "Some one suggests that the New Haven girls . . .": *New York Sporting Times*, March 7, 1891.

197 Decker was charged with an impressive array of crimes . . .: *New York Clipper*, March 4, 1891; *Lincoln Evening News*, March 27, 1891. Coincidentally, onetime National League president Morgan Bulkeley, now the governor of Connecticut, signed the papers allowing the catcher's extradition to Philadelphia.

197 the nature and the extent of these accusations shocked even those . . .: *Sporting Life*, April 4, 1891.

197 "Harry Decker is again in trouble . . .": *St. Louis Star-Sayings*, quoted in *Decatur Herald-Despatch*, March 28, 1891.

197–198 Most of the parties involved . . .: *Sporting Life*, April 4, 1891; *Sporting News*, April 4, 1891; *St. Louis Star-Sayings*, quoted in *Decatur Herald-Despatch*, March 28, 1891.

198 Decker was discharged after his guilty plea: *Frederick News*, April 23, 1891; *Syracuse Sunday Standard*, April 26, 1891.

198 Annie Decker, however, . . . sued for divorce: *Decatur Morning Review*, May 2, 1891.

198 This was followed by allegations . . .: *Sporting Life*, June 20, July 18 and 25, August 1, 1891; *New York Sporting Times*, June 20, 1891. The teammate was named Jack Horner.

198 "I think I am a most unfortunate man . . .": *Sporting Life*, September 27, 1890, quoting Decker's comments to a reporter for the *Pittsburg Press*.

198 "very unfortunate of late . . ." and "trying to push me down": *Sporting Life*, July 18, 1891.

198 the latter excuse was understandably viewed as hypocrisy: *Sporting Life*, August 1, 1891.

198 a *Sporting Life* correspondent expressed doubt that he would ever play baseball again: *Sporting Life*, August 15, 1891.

198 he never again played a professional game: In the spring of 1892, Decker did write to *Sporting Life* to correct an erroneous report of his death and to state that he intended to return to baseball. *Sporting Life*, May 7, 1892. But nothing came of it.

198 He realized several hundred dollars . . .: *Peoria Herald*, reprinted in the *Decatur Daily Review*, June 11, 1896.

199 Decker fled town: *Sporting News*, January 30, 1892.

199 He attempted to marry a different woman . . .: *Sporting Life*, April 15, 1893.
199 More accusations of forgery and larceny . . .: *Sporting Life*, July 1, 1893.
199 "Decker's hallucination is that he owns . . .": *Chicago Tribune*, November 7, 1893, 11.
199 The legal system was baffled . . .: *Chicago Tribune*, November 7, 1893, 11; *Sporting News*, November 11, 1893; *Sporting Life*, November 11, 1893.
199 By the following spring he was facing charges . . .: *Chicago Tribune*, April 28, 1894; *Sporting Life*, May 5, 1894.
199 He tried to pay his rent . . .: *Decatur Daily Review*, December 28, 1894.
199 his long-suffering wife had finally exhausted her patience and obtained a divorce: *Washington Post*, October 14, 1894. Decker's wife then tried her hand at an intriguing project, receiving a patent for a new type of catcher's mitt that was claimed to be far superior to the one pioneered by her husband. *Sporting News*, November 30, 1895. The patent, #550,949, may be viewed by a search of the Google Patent Search website, as can Decker's various patents. Little was heard of Harry Decker in 1895, so he may finally have had to serve jail time on some of these charges.
200 "went there without a penny . . .": *Decatur Daily Review*, January 15, 1897.
200 Decker and another man became embroiled in a bizarre dispute . . .: *Decatur Weekly Republican*, April 16, 1896; *Decatur Daily Republican*, June 4 and 6, 1896.
200 he was arrested in Chicago and brought back to Decatur: *Decatur Daily Republican*, June 8, 1896.
200 After his arrest, it was generally assumed . . .: *Peoria Herald*, reprinted in the *Decatur Daily Review*, June 11, 1896.
200 "While the indictment . . .": The forged check was supposedly signed by Charles Bartson, a former major league pitcher and co-owner of the Peoria team along with Dan Dugdale, an ex-major league catcher and former teammate of Decker. But when Decker forged the check, he transposed two letters in the signature and instead wrote "Charles Barston." Decker then spent a great deal of time in the jail's law library and arrived in court with "an armful of books" to support his contention that, "while the indictment charged him with forging one name, the check itself showed another and a different name, and therefore the check could not properly be offered as evidence." *Decatur Review*, November 24, 1896.
200 "is well posted . . .": *Decatur Review*, November 24, 1896.
201 "he did not remember signing the check . . .": *Decatur Daily Review*, January 8, 1897.
201 he was sentenced to two to fourteen years in the penitentiary: *Decatur Weekly Republican*, January 14, 1897; *Sporting Life*, January 16, 1897.
201 Harry Decker served his time . . .: One reason for the lengthy stay was an unsuccessful 1896 escape attempt, made with two other prisoners, while Decker was awaiting trial. *Decatur Evening Bulletin*, July 31, 1896.
201 becoming an expert carpenter and cabinetmaker: "Seize Alleged One O' Names," *Los Angeles Times*, January 14, 1913, H1.
201 He also received another patent . . .: U.S. Patent Office, patent #812,921, filed November 15, 1904, awarded February 20, 1906.
201 "managed to evade arrest . . .": "Striped Past of Alexander," *Los Angeles Times*, October 17, 1907, H9.
201 In July 1907 a man calling himself Earl H. Davenport . . .: Sources for Decker's first stay in Los Angeles are "Just Threw Money Away," *Los Angeles Times*, August 14, 1907, H1; "Conviction Seems Certain," *Los Angeles Times*, August 22, 1907, H5; "Veil Is Up in Jail Mystery," *Los Angeles Times*, September 27, 1907, H1; "Dims the Romance," *Los Angeles Times*, October 24, 1907, H1; "Striped Past of Alexander," H9; "Ill and Deserted," *Los Angeles Times*, March 25, 1908, H5; "Seize Alleged One O' Names," H1; "Don Juan of Shaven Head," H1-H2.

202 "sent him flowers, cake and pie . . .": "Don Juan of Shaven Head," H1-H2.

203 Even so, the trial produced a surprise twist . . .: "Ill and Deserted," H5; "Death Before Freedom," *Los Angeles Times*, April 28, 1908, H5. Decker began his sentence in the Territorial Prison in Yuma but was soon transferred to the Florence Territorial Prison.

203 "cabinet work that was a marvel to all": "Don Juan of Shaven Head," H1-H2. Decker is listed as a carpenter and inmate at Florence Territorial Prison on the 1910 census, under the name of E. H. Alexander.

203 he soon paid a visit . . .: "Try 'Don Juan,' Forgery Charge," *Los Angeles Times*, June 10, 1913, H7.

203 His new landlady was anything but naive . . .: "Woman Argonaut Crosses Divide," *Los Angeles Times*, October 14, 1916, II3.

203 "in every way a gentleman of culture . . .": "Man's Career a Dual One," *Los Angeles Times*, January 15, 1913, H5.

203 "possess[ed] the remarkable faculty . . .": "Don Juan of Shaven Head," H1-H2.

204 "The man's true name is not known . . .": "Seize Alleged One O' Names," H1.

204 "Don Juan of Shaven Head": "Don Juan of Shaven Head," H1-H2.

204 . . . Harry Decker had been caught in the act once again: "Don Juan of Shaven Head," H1-H2; "Try 'Don Juan,' Forgery Charge," H7.

204–205 "It is true that he dissipated my daughter's money . . .": "Man's Career a Dual One," H5.

205 "an effort was made . . ." and "refused to allow . . .": "Try 'Don Juan,' Forgery Charge," H7.

205 Prison records reveal little . . .: Researcher Bill Carle obtained Decker's prison records.

205 he was never once described as being drunk: As confirmation, the *New York Sporting Times* of February 7, 1891, reported that Decker had signed a temperance pledge and noted that he had never been a "drinking man." The assertion seems highly credible since several of the other players who took the pledge, including Silver Flint, were described as having had drinking problems.

205 "method of working ..": "Try 'Don Juan,' Forgery Charge," H7.

206 His father spent a great deal of money . . .: *Decatur Daily Republican*, June 26, 1896.

206 "Decker ought to shine in the proper channel . . .": *Decatur Daily Review*, January 15, 1897.

206–207 "I know it is customary in some circles . . .": "Don Juan of Shaven Head," H1-H2.

12. THE 1890s: "AN ERA WHEN MOST OF THE CATCHERS WERE POT-BELLIED AND COULDN'T GET OUT OF THEIR OWN WAY"

208 "The modern catcher is a wax doll . . .": "Backstops Are Deteriorating," *New York Telegram*, reprinted in *Duluth News Tribune*, November 14, 1909.

208–209 "declared that only a 'sissy' would use . . .": James J. Corbett, "In Corbett's Corner," syndicated column (King Features), *Macon Daily Telegraph*, January 3, 1919. A somewhat different version of what seems to be the same event appeared in 1911, when Alfred H. Spink offered this description: "Between each inning [Bennett] would have to sponge the gash in his thumb with cotton soaked in antiseptic which he carried with him in his pocket, in order to remove the corruption which was continually flowing from the wound. This he did in spite of the fact that the doctor warned him that he must either stop playing ball until the thumb had entirely healed, or lose his thumb, or even his arm, as blood poison was liable to set in." Spink, *National Game*, 91. Kennedy, in "Greatest Backstop of Them All Was the Detroit Boy, Charley Bennett," 20, gave a similar account and placed it as occurring during the 1887 postseason series in which Bennett led the National League champion Detroit Wolverines to victory over the American Association pennant-winning St. Louis Brown Stockings. In Kennedy's version: "A heavy cloud of deep gloom and despair hung over Michigan and part of Canada when the news went around that the great Bennett would be unable to play. A physician pronounced the verdict that if Bennett caught another game, his thumb would be in danger of amputation. But Bennett brought himself up to the point where he felt he had to work in the first game of the series, even if he lost a hand."

209 "Bennett would play, heated with his passion . . .": "Stories of Early Base Ball Days Told by Charlie Bennett, King of the Olden Catchers," *Detroit News Tribune*, March 11, 1906. The article also recounted a description by Jim Hart, one of Bennett's former managers, of how reluctant Bennett was to come out of an 1891 game even when the ball became covered in his blood. Hart gave a slightly different version of that game in "Bennett Dead Game," *Sporting Life*, October 1, 1891. A 1909 article was probably also referring to that game in this account: "A bruised finger now drives most catchers to the bench. Bennett and the other veterans had to be forced from the game by managerial order ere they would quit, and in one game Bennett caught with both hands split till the bloadsoaked ball attracted the attention of the pitcher, who literally drove the heroic fellow from the field." "Backstops Are Deteriorating." And in 1918 an unnamed author recalled watching Bennett catch while "blood dripped from his hands." "Catchers Now Pampered in Comparing of Old-Timers," 2. It is possible that the accounts offered by Corbett, Spink, and Kennedy also are derived from the same 1891 game, but this seems unlikely. In addition to Kennedy's claim that he was describing the 1887 postseason series, there are enough differences that I believe they are probably descriptions of separate events.

209 there is plenty of additional evidence attesting to Bennett's bravery: Additional stories about Bennett's courage appeared in an article in *Sporting Life*, January 17, 1894, which described Bennett's career-ending train accident. Bennett lost both his legs in the accident, but he bore the tragedy with characteristic fortitude.

209 a photograph showing his swollen joints and grotesquely misshapen fingers: John Richmond Husman, "Charles Wesley Bennett," in Robert L. Tiemann and Mark Rucker, eds., *Nineteenth Century Stars*, 12; "Stories of Early Base Ball Days Told by Charlie Bennett, King of the Olden Catchers."

209 even that he agreed . . .: Charles W. Bennett Hall of Fame file: letter from Bennett's nephew, George W. Porter, dated July 8, 1960.

209 "Nine men will play the game this season . . .": *St. Louis Globe-Democrat*, April 3, 1887.

209 "invented the 'Kelly short route,'" "supply of bird shot in his mouth," "a dilemma when . . .," and "Kelly in for Tate": Unspecified article reprinted in Petrone, *When Baseball Was Young*, 116–117. A still more preposterous story had Kelly and Ed Williamson pulling off a game-winning double steal in which Kelly, the lead runner, started from third, then suddenly stopped and let Williamson dive between his legs and elude the catcher. Marty Appel, *Slide, Kelly, Slide*, 72.

209 The last story cannot have happened as described . . .: A more plausible version of this story had it happening shortly after the 1889 rule change and had the umpire denying Kelly's ploy. According to that version: "Sitting on the bench one day, waiting for a hangover to heal, he saw a foul fly dropping where his catcher could not reach it. Knowing that the new rule said that substitution could be made 'at any time, on notice to the umpire' he merely bellowed 'Kelly now catching!' and stood up and made the catch. The umpire refused to allow it, even when Kelly showed him the rule. After that they changed the rule." Robert Smith, *Heroes of Baseball* (Cleveland: World Publishing,

1952), 65. In yet another version of this oft-told tale, Morgan Murphy was the catcher when Kelly tried to enter the game, and umpire John Gaffney allowed the out to stand. Mike Kelly Hall of Fame file, source unidentified. And Hugh S. Fullerton would eventually claim that it was Em Gross who invented the ploy.

210 "He played not by rules or instruction . . .": Fred Pfeffer, quoted in Appel, *Slide, Kelly, Slide*, 96.

210 "Baseball rules were never made for Kel": Sam Crane, quoted in Appel, *Slide, Kelly, Slide*, 123.

210 credible observers have declared each to be the greatest *player* of all time: For example, Hall of Famer Mickey Welch proclaimed Ewing "the greatest ball player that ever lived. There may have been better catchers, but for knowledge of the game, knowing just what to do and all-around ability he had them all beat. . . . Ewing certainly was the king of them all and I've yet to see his equal." *Syracuse Post Standard*, July 10, 1901. Another Hall of Famer, Tommy McCarthy, was among the many who considered Kelly "the greatest player I ever knew." Spink, *National Game*, 103.

210 They are the only two nineteenth-century catchers enshrined in the Hall of Fame: This excludes Connie Mack and Wilbert Robinson, who are in the Hall for their managing careers; Jim O'Rourke, who caught 227 games but played many more games at other positions, as well as others who occasionally caught; and Roger Bresnahan and Frank Chance, who started their careers at the close of the nineteenth century but are enshrined for their accomplishments in the twentieth century.

211 "Bah! It's Bennett . . .": *Detroit Free Press*, June 15, 1888, replying to Ward's book. In fact Ward had already anticipated the *Free Press's* response—he described Ewing as "the 'King' of all catchers—when he catches." Ward, *Base-Ball: How to Become a Player*, 67.

211 "Ewing never saw the day . . .": Ned Cuthbert, quoted in *Sporting News*, January 30, 1892.

211 "often remarked that . . .": Kennedy, "Greatest Backstop of Them All Was the Detroit Boy, Charley Bennett," 20.

211–212 "stands half bent and seems to be laboring . . .": "King Catchers," 12.

212 Talented athletes like Jacob Stenzel, Hugh Duffy, and Bobby Lowe: William E. Akin, "Jacob Charles Stenzel," in Frederick Ivor-Campbell, Robert L. Tiemann, and Mark Rucker, eds., *Baseball's First Stars*, 158. Duffy caught in only a handful of minor league games while playing for Hartford at the end of the 1886 season and for Springfield, Massachusetts, at the start of the 1887 campaign, before being shifted to the infield and then to the outfield. *Sporting Life*, October 9, 1897. But he was a catcher when he was discovered and signed. Lowe was a catcher when he began his professional career but requested a switch so he could play every day. *Boston Globe*, October 5, 1891.

212 "try the safer outfield and pitching positions": Joel F. Olesky, "George Winkelman, Baseball Pioneer," *Washington Post*, May 21, 1960, B2. Winkelman, however, was ninety-five by the time he made the admission.

213 "men who thought . . ." and "boy wonder": "A Born Billiard Player's Career," *Philadelphia Inquirer*, December 9, 1894, 24 (based on a sketch in the *Baltimore Sun*).

213 "several crooked fingers": "Death Claims Frank C. Ives," *New York Times*, September 1, 1899.

213 Jacob Schaefer, who had also been a star catcher . . .: *Janesville Daily Gazette*, March 11, 1905. There were at least a couple of other instances of catchers who became better known for their success in other sports. Tom Cotter, who caught for a several amateur and minor league clubs in his native Boston and had a brief major league career, was also reputedly "the best polo player in the country." *New York Sporting Times*, September 26, 1891, 5. And Clarence Terwilliger of Hillsdale, Michigan, was a catcher and

pitcher for several of the best Michigan clubs of the mid-1870s, including being catcher of the Mutuals of Jackson on June 9, 1876, when the club captured the state championship. But Terwilliger turned to rowing at the end of the decade and led the "Hillsdale Crew" to the national championship, which the crew retained for three years.

213 "was alike dangerous and intimidating . . .": Henry Chadwick, "The New Base-Ball Rules," *Lippincott*, May 1887, reprinted in *Louisville Courier-Journal*, April 24, 1887.

214 "although not having any practice . . ." and "under which balls . . .": *Base Ball Gazette*, April 21, 1887.

214 a credible source claimed that the venerable Jim White . . .: *New York Sun*, May 2, 1888. The source was W. W. Nimick, president of the Pittsburgh club. Whitney was pitching for Washington at the time, and White was playing third base for Detroit, but Detroit was short of pitchers and Nimick claimed that Detroit was looking to trade for Whitney and then install the forty-year-old White as his catcher. It sounds unlikely, but in light of the new rules changes it was not inconceivable.

214 By the end of the decade, pitching in the bottom half of the strike zone was rare . . .: This subject is discussed in detail in my *A Game of Inches*, vol. 1, entry 3.3.3, "Keeping the Ball Down," 185–187.

214 the only enhancement of the catcher's role . . .: In addition, the greater frequency of bunting that resulted from this rules change was partially offset the following year by another rules change that made any foul bunt a strike.

215 "left his place behind the bat . . .": *New York Times*, June 23, 1892. The account continued, "If the striker had bunted then, he would probably have been thrown out at first by Carter. The wily Princetonian, however, calmly made two strikes, whereupon the Yale catcher was forced to go behind the bat to catch the third. Then the Princeton man bunted and went safely to first."

215 "making a travesty of skilful infield play": *Spalding's Official Base Ball Guide, 1895*, 121.

215 "Why, it will be so after awhile . . .": quoted in the *St. Louis Post-Dispatch*, July 3, 1894. The first third baseman to play third base while using a catcher's mitt appears to have been William Urquhart of Rochester, in 1891. *New York Sporting Times*, May 16, 1891, 5.

215 "no longer take refuge . . .": *St. Louis Post-Dispatch*, March 3, 1895.

216 "an element of pure luck . . ." and "growled and grumbled . . .": John H. Gruber, "Out for Interference," *Sporting News*, February 24, 1916.

216 "perfect pillow," "made of the choicest . . .," "flexible glove," "choicest buckskin," and "thoroughly padded . . .": *New York Sun*, April 27, 1890.

216 once causing fans at New York's Polo Grounds to laugh . . .: "When Ball Players Wore Neither Gloves Nor Mask," 5.

217 "recognized as indispensable . . .": *New York Sun*, April 27, 1890.

217 "a mere backstop . . .," "ideal catcher," and "considered a mountain . . .": *Sporting News*, August 14, 1913. The article doesn't specify that it is referring to the catcher of the 1890s, but that inference is the only possible one. Symbolically, the 1890s briefly gave rise to at least one new term for the catcher that was as unflattering as had been the synonyms added during the previous decade—according to an 1894 note, "The latest terms to indicate the pitcher and catcher are 'deceiver' and 'retriever.'" *Boston Globe*, April 25, 1894. It didn't catch on, however, perhaps because the era's catchers were not especially proficient at retrieving balls.

218 "will not slide . . .": *New York Sporting Times*, May 16, 1891.

218 "Townsend and Robinson are noticeable . . .": *Baltimore Sun*, March 20, 1891.

218 "a heavier man is better able to stand . . .": Ward, *Base-Ball: How to Become a Player*, 66.

218 "a fat, bronzed young man . . .": *Chicago Herald*, July 8, 1891. Clements was so conspicuously overweight that his hometown paper regularly referred to him as the "big fat catcher" (*Philadelphia Inquirer*, June 25, 1891, August 4, 1893) or the "fat catcher" (*Philadelphia Inquirer*, April 23, 1892). Even the team's secretary, Bill Shettsline, was quoted as calling Clements the "big fat catcher." *Philadelphia Inquirer*, January 20, 1892.

218 it sometimes seemed that way from the amount of attention paid to their bulging waistlines: For example, in the *Chicago Tribune* of July 28, 1891, Malachi Kittridge was referred to as the "fat catcher."

218 "an era when most of the catchers were pot-bellied . . .": Frank Graham, "No Stranger to the Polo Grounds," *New York Sun*, August 26, 1943. Graham was not explicit about which years he was referring to, but the 1890s are the only era he could mean.

218 "a mere machine to stop the curves . . .": "Few Good Catchers."

218 "The truth of the matter . . ." and "so fat . . .": *New Haven Evening Register*, August 6, 1891, 1. Not surprisingly, the player who made these charges was not identified.

219 "the tiresome delays which occurred . . .": Mack, "Memories of When the Game Was Young." See also *Sporting News*, November 5, 1898.

219 Jim "Deacon" McGuire . . . caught all 132 of Washington's games: The *Albion Evening Recorder*, August 2, 1932, claimed that McGuire "caught every inning of 133 consecutive games for the Washington club in 1895." This, however, is not true, as several teammates spelled him for a few innings that year.

219 "been improved until it has assumed . . .": Clipping from unidentified newspaper in Hall of Fame file, dated August 9, 1890; quoted in David Ball's biographical profile of Kid Baldwin on the SABR BioProject website.

219–220 "In the formation of the club battery . . .": *New York Sporting Times*, February 21, 1891.

220 During the 1880s such praise became more measured but was still genuine: The *Evansville Journal* of July 27, 1884, for instance, wrote that Al Strueve "in base ball parlance is known as an 'every day catcher.'"

220 "would go in and catch every day . . .": Murnane, "Work Behind the Bat," 23.

220–221 "toughening the hands" and "Rowing on the machines . . .": "Training the Catcher," originally from *St. Nicholas*, reprinted in *Brooklyn Eagle*, August 4, 1890; the article is unsigned, but its distinctive themes and phraseology suggest that it was written by Chadwick.

221 "Charley Bennett was the idol . . .": *Sporting News*, January 25, 1896, 4.

222 "so queer that . . .," "a moon-on-the-lake pair of pants," "What the Samhill's . . .," "if the catcher . . .," "the current decadence . . .," "the lace and cambric . . .," and "We didn't know nothing . . .": "Old-Time Base Ball," 11.

222 young men who struck their elders as being sickly, effeminate, and out of harmony with nature: For example, in "A Psychic Crisis: Neurasthenia and the Emergence of a Therapeutic World View," in *No Place of Grace: Antimodernism and the Transformation of American Culture, 1880–1920*, 47–59, T. J. Jackson Lears describes the prevalence of neurasthenia among young American men of the late nineteenth century, a disease that was often attributed to that generation's introspection and apparent lack of will. In turn, these symptoms were usually seen as the result of the pressures of city living and "modern civilization." John F. Kasson notes that the leading medical specialist in neurasthenia considered it to be the result of such forces as "excessive brain work, intense competition, constant hurry, rapid communications, the ubiquitous rhythm and din of technology." John F. Kasson, *Houdini, Tarzan, and the Perfect Man*, 11.

222–223 A typical anecdote told of a farmer and his wife . . .: *Arcola* (Illinois) *Record*, reprinted in the *Beverly* (Massachusetts) *Morning Citizen*, November 17, 1888.

223 reporters couldn't resist the urge to draw attention to the alleged similarity: Examples appeared in *Duluth Tribune*, August 8, 1884; *Philadelphia Call*, reprinted in *New Haven Evening Register*, June 8, 1885; *Puck*, reprinted in the *Boston Globe*, July 18, 1886; *Macon Weekly Telegraph*, June 11, 1885; *Aberdeen* (South Dakota) *Daily News*, July 30, 1891; *Cincinnati Commercial*, reprinted in *Raleigh News and Observer*, July 16, 1884; and *Wisconsin State Journal*, July 3, 1885. The *Somerville* (Massachusetts) *Journal* published a poem, reprinted in *Philadelphia Inquirer*, May 24, 1896, that included the lines: "The catcher will stand in his armor of pads/ With a bustle strapped over his phiz [face]/ And when a foul pops up over his head/ He will struggle to see where he is." That so many of these articles were reprinted also testifies to their appeal.

223–224 "The catcher was a young chief . . .": *Chicago Herald*, April 12, 1891, 28.

224–226 "natural catcher," "handle any kind of delivery . . .," "it is safe to say . . .," and the quotations in the ensuing seven paragraphs: Murnane, "Work Behind the Bat," 23.

226 "What ails Zimmer . . ." and "Keenan used to be . . .": John B. Foster, "About Great Catchers," *New York Sporting Times*, May 2, 1891, 9, quoting an unidentified "old ball player."

227 "his record for consecutive errors . . ." and "an opportunity to live down . . .": *Sporting Life*, January 4, 1896.

227 The catcher of the 1890s, so it seemed, could take courageous risks and still be universally ignored: It is even possible to see the tragic case of Leonard Weiker as an example of this predicament. In 1898, Weiker had signed to catch for a minor league team in Mansfield, Ohio. But when the Spanish-American War began, he chose to enlist and lost his life in Santiago, Cuba, on August 1. As the only known professional ballplayer to be a casualty of the war, Weiker's death ought to have earned him acclaim as a hero. Yet he died of yellow fever, and even though the cause of his death in no way lessened his courage, it meant that his sacrifice received only scant coverage. *Youngstown Vindicator*, August 8, 1898; military records of Leonard Weiker of Artillery Co. H8. The only catcher to receive widespread recognition as a hero during these years was Princeton catcher Frederick Brokaw (1868–1891), who lost his life on June 24, 1891, while trying to save three women from drowning. At his funeral the school president called Brokaw a hero and added, "True greatness never comes by seeking. The man who makes distinction an end rarely reaches it; or, if he does, it is not such distinction as the true man values. To take a thought suggested by the game he loved, the man who plays for the eyes of the grand stand is not the man the grand stand is watching. It is the man who is struggling so hard to do his level best in the position in which he finds himself that he has no time to think of what others are thinking of him." Quoted in Henry Chadwick, "Frederick Brokaw," *New York Sporting Times*, July 4, 1891. It was a fitting tribute and also captures the reasons why many observers looked at the catcher as a hero who never tried to draw attention to himself, while having reservations about the pitcher. Brokaw's death took place within weeks of the end of the career of fellow college catcher Stephen Crane.

227 Billy "Pop" Schriver stood at the bottom of the monument, and, according to contemporaneous sources, became the first man to catch a ball dropped from its summit: *Tacoma Daily News*, September 1, 1894; *Baltimore Sun*, August 27 and September 15, 1894.

227 "faint" and "nerve forsook him": *Tacoma Daily News*, September 1, 1894.

227–228 "that Schriver could easily have made . . .": *Philadelphia Inquirer*, September 6, 1896.

228 The feat was hailed as a first, and Schriver's effort was not even mentioned: Lee Allen, *The Hot Stove League*, 99; Jack Kavanagh, *The Heights of Ridiculousness*, 1–24. Catcher Billy Sullivan of the White Sox duplicated the feat in 1910.

228 "Help me, lads, I'm covered with my own blood": Kavanagh and Macht, *Uncle Robbie*, 73-74.

13. "THE LAST OF THE OLD GUARD OF BALL PLAYERS"

229 "[The best athletic sports] are those sports . . .": Theodore Roosevelt in *Harper's Weekly*,
December 23, 1893, 1,236.
229 The final key piece of the catcher's gear: It might reasonably be argued that the jock-
strap was also an essential piece of equipment. Like most pieces of equipment that
remain hidden, however, its introduction was not mentioned when it was first used. We
do know that sporting goods stores were advertising it by the 1880s. Gutman, *Banana
Bats and Ding-Dong Balls*, 227.
229 "Bresnahan created somewhat of a sensation . . .": *New York Times*, April 12, 1907.
229 Several earlier catchers and infielders had experimented with added protection for
their shins . . .: Morris, *A Game of Inches*, vol. 1, entry 9.4.6, 439–442.
230 "awful razzing . . .": *Sporting News*, May 9, 1936.
230 "as soon as I can . . ." and "The roasting the rooters . . .": *Washington Post*, June 17,
1907.
230 "get even with the New York Club . . .": *Boston Globe*, June 2, 1907, 12.
230 the only real issue was whether the benefits of added protection offset the hindrance
they posed when the catcher tried to run: Bresnahan told one reporter that Giants manager John McGraw had initial misgivings, but explained: "McGraw thought they would
interfere with my running, and looked askance at them at the beginning of the year,
but he has changed his mind. . . . Last year my legs were bruised from the knees down,
and part of the time it was all that I could do to walk after a game. That interfered with
my running a great deal more than the shin guards possibly can interfere." *Washington
Post*, May 12, 1907. But some catchers continued to find them uncomfortable and
inconvenient. In 1912 an article reported that Pittsburgh catcher George Gibson and
his backup, Billy Kelly, had both abandoned wearing shin guards. But the change had
nothing to do with Dreyfuss's campaign; instead Gibson cited such practical reasons as
"it takes too long to put the armor on and take it off," and "the guards interfere with
the getting up of speed in going after foul flies." *Sporting Life*, May 4, 1912.
230 Knee joints were soon added to address this concern, and over the next few years shin
guards became standard equipment for catchers: "When Ball Players Wore Neither
Gloves Nor Mask," 5.
230 "tools of ignorance": Unlike most of the well-known terms associated with the catcher's position, the origin of the phrase "tools of ignorance" remains shrouded in mystery.
The *Dickson Baseball Dictionary* presents theories suggesting that it originated in the
1930s with Muddy Ruel or Bill Dickey, but definitive evidence for either claim is lacking.
230 "no chance for any such interference . . .": *Washington Post*, May 16, 1907.
230–231 "The great backstoppers of today . . .": Kennedy, "Greatest Backstop of Them All
Was the Detroit Boy, Charley Bennett," 20.
232–234 "I see my old pal, Nat Hicks . . .": "Jim Nasium" [Edgar Wolfe], "Letters from an
Old Sport to His Son at College," *Philadelphia Inquirer*, June 23, 1907, 4.
235 "the days when baseball . . ." and "They're a bunch of mollycoddles . . .": *Grand Forks*
(North Dakota) *Daily Herald*, January 30, 1913.
235 "modern foolishness," "to a baseball park . . .," "from the spikes . . .," "a fad," "you can
count . . .," "dirty work," and "take some nerve tonic . . .": "Shin Guards and Armor of
the Modern Catcher," *Duluth News Tribune*, April 9, 1911.

235–236 "the last of the old guard of ball players . . .": "Behind the Bat with 'Nat' Hicks," S4.
236 "In the minds of the present-day fans . . .": *Sporting News*, December 2, 1915.
236 "ever-present tendency . . .," "to magnify the bygone stars . . .," and "Nevertheless, when one great department . . .": "Backstops Are Deteriorating."

14. A NEW PITCH AND A NEW CRISIS

237 "The 'spit ball' is bound to revolutionize . . .": T. H. Murnane, "The 'Spit Ball' Fools 'Em—League Action Needed to Help Batsmen," *Boston Globe*, October 2, 1904, 41. Murnane's prediction would prove prophetic, though it's hard to understand why he placed the curveball revolution in the mid-1880s instead of the mid-1870s.
238 During the 1904 and 1905 seasons the spitball . . .: See my *A Game of Inches*, vol. 1, entry 3.2.7, 140–153, for a lengthy discussion of the origins of the spitball. As noted there, the emergence of the pitch in 1904 and 1905 prompted many old-timers to maintain that the spitter had been used by various pitchers in the 1870s and 1880s. The name mentioned most often was Bobby Mathews, and it seems very likely that he used the offering. That would also be consistent with Mathews's frequency in working with Nat Hicks and other catchers known for their knack for handling offerings that broke unexpectedly. There were fewer claims of spitballers in the late 1880s and 1890s, which no doubt reflects that there were fewer catchers with experience in catching low pitches. Incidentally, another of the early pitchers who were later said to have thrown the spitball was Mike Golden, the man whose deliveries mystified "Alamazoo" Jennings. *Chicago Tribune*, reprinted in *Sporting Life*, June 30, 1906.
238 some players and observers suggested that it would only be fair to allow frustrated hitters to leave the batter's box to pursue it: Jimmy McAleer, quoted in *Los Angeles Herald*, August 11, 1907.
238 "Lots of people wouldn't believe . . .": "Anson Doubts Spit Ball," *Washington Post*, December 11, 1904, ST1.
238 "The batsmen of the American League . . .": T. H. Murnane, "Murnane's Baseball," *Boston Globe*, October 2, 1904, 41.
239 "You are not in it these days if you are a pitcher without the spit ball": Timothy Sharp, *Sporting News*, May 6, 1905.
239 "If the spit ball were eliminated . . .": A. H. C. Mitchell, *Spalding's Guide*, 1909; quoted in David W. Anderson, *More Than Merkle*, 124.
239 "wet ball more . . .," "a hopeless task," and "months of patience and practice": *Sporting News*, January 1, 1920.
239 "The catchers dreaded it . . .": John J. Evers and Hugh S. Fullerton, *Touching Second*, 113.
239 "the constant shooting of the ball . . .": Murnane, "The 'Spit Ball' Fools 'Em," 41. On another occasion Criger similarly commented, "The 'spit ball' is a terror to the catchers. My hands were in bad shape most of the time during the season, and I attribute it to the introduction of the 'spit ball' in the pitcher's repertory." *Syracuse Journal*, December 6, 1904.
239 "It comes straight toward you . . .": "Anson Doubts Spit Ball," ST1.
239–240 "one of the best-natured fellows . . .": "Dooin Tells of Catcher's Work," *Winchester* (Kentucky) *News*, October 17, 1908, 2.
240 "If Chesbro says he can tell . . .": "Anson Doubts Spit Ball," ST1.
240 one of Chesbro's spitballs sailed over the head of catcher Red Kleinow: In another slap in the face to beleaguered receivers, Chesbro's widow would later make comments that suggested an attempt to shift responsibility for the wild pitch to Kleinow. Chesbro himself,

however, never said anything of the sort, and according to Jim McGuire, who watched the pitch from the New York bench and knew more about trying to catch Chesbro's spitball than anyone else, "Jack let that old spitter get away from him. There wasn't a chance in the world to stop it. It might just as well have gone over the top of the grandstand." Smith, "He Could Catch Anything." On another occasion McGuire claimed that the pitch had been "so wild that it hit way up on the grandstand." *Albion Evening Recorder*, August 2, 1932. Lou Criger, who by coincidence was the runner who scored on the pitch, was just as emphatic that it was a wild pitch. *Syracuse Journal*, December 6, 1904.

240 Chesbro's constant use of the spitball that year had sidelined . . .: Petrone, *When Baseball Was Young*, 89.

240 breaking the finger of one of the school's catchers and the wrist of another . . .: *Wilkes-Barre Times*, April 7, 1905.

240 "Why did I devise them? . . .": Chadwick Scrapbooks, clipping from unspecified source.

240 "Nig" Clarke of Cleveland tried to have a special catcher's mitt designed for catching the spitter: Petrone, *When Baseball Was Young*, 89.

240–241 it was Jim McGuire who in 1910 became the first manager to prohibit his entire staff from throwing the spitball: Several previous managers had instructed specific pitchers not to use the spitball. Brooklyn manager Patsy Donovan, for example, prohibited Nap Rucker from throwing the pitch in 1907. Petrone, *When Baseball Was Young*, 89. Cubs manager (and onetime catcher) Frank Chance also forbade star pitcher Mordecai "Three-Finger" Brown from using the pitch. Cindy Thomson and Scott Brown, *Three Finger*, 87.

241 "maintain that the introduction of the spitball . . .": "Few Good Catchers."

241 "The catcher is a lowly and gazelle-like receptacle . . .": H. L. Rann, "Sidewalk Sketches."

241 "The way Cicotte uses it . . .": *Detroit Free Press*, March 22, 1908.

242 "not only impossible to hit . . .": *Boston Globe*, March 5, 1915. In addition, according to old-time player Bill Lange, Griffith maintained that the pitch "came to the plate in such peculiar manner that it fooled not only the batsman but the catchers, too . . . [Griffith] couldn't catch half the balls Summers had thrown him in practice." *Detroit Free Press*, March 14, 1909.

242 "five or six of the finger-tip balls . . .": *Sporting Life*, April 11, 1908.

242 Christy Mathewson's celebrated "fadeaway" . . .: Morris, *A Game of Inches*, vol. 1, entry 3.2.12 on the screwball, 161–163.

242 Mordecai "Three-Finger" Brown's missing right index finger forced him to develop some unique grips that baffled hitters: Thomson and Brown, *Three Finger*, Appendix A: "How Did He Do It?," 213–218.

242 The forkball was also invented . . .: Morris, *A Game of Inches*, vol. 1, entry 3.2.9 on the forkball, 155–156.

243 "Many attributed Ford's poor showing . . .": *Idaho Daily Statesman*, March 23, 1913.

243 "I experimented with that delivery . . ." and "Honestly, it would take . . .": Harry A. Williams, *Los Angeles Times*, November 18, 1914.

244 "Those were the days when catching . . .": Ritter, *Glory of Their Times*, 258.

244 in 1920 the game's rules-makers decided to ban the spitball and all of its offshoots: This ban inadvertently inaugurated the home run era—not so much because the old pitches had been that effective, as because eliminating the scuffed ball meant always playing with a fresh ball.

244 "The cry now is for good catchers . . ." and "Just why this is managers . . .": "Good Catchers Are Few and Far Between; Managers Have Pitchers to Spare, But Backstops

Who Are Onto All the Tricks of the Game Are Not to Be Had for Any Price," *Bellingham Herald*, April 18, 1908, 15.

245 "A dozen years ago . . .," "great demand for pitchers," and "a common remark . . .": "Catchers Are Scarce," *Chicago Tribune*, reprinted in *Dallas Morning News*, December 11, 1904.

245 This was especially true of Jim McGuire, Chief Zimmer, and Charlie "Duke" Farrell . . .: McGuire led catchers of the 1890s in games caught, followed by Zimmer. But the fact that McGuire was born in 1863 and Zimmer in 1860 increased the perception of the catchers of the 1890s as men who got their chance only when a better catcher retired or moved to another position. Next on the list of games caught were Wilbert Robinson (b. 1863), Malachi Kittridge (b. 1869), Jack Clements (b. 1864), and Farrell (b. 1866). Clements, Zimmer, and McGuire all reached the major leagues in 1884 while Robinson debuted in 1886, which reinforced the tendency to see the best catchers of the 1890s as having been the journeymen of the 1880s.

245 "Charlie Farrell, who was only second or third catcher . . .": "Backstops Are Deteriorating."

245 Farrell further damaged the catcher's image . . .: Rich Eldred reports that Farrell became as much as sixty pounds overweight. "Charles Andrew (Duke) Farrell," in Tiemann and Mark Rucker, eds., *Nineteenth Century Stars*, 41.

245–246 "The dearth of catchers is most marked . . ." and "a plentiful supply of pitchers . . .": "Catchers Are Scarce."

246 "It would be worse than useless . . .": Frank Newhouse, "Dangers of the Hero Behind the Bat," *San Francisco Call*, June 5, 1904, 14.

246 "I wonder where the catchers will come from . . .": "Patsy Donovan Fears for Game's Future," *Macon Telegraph*, September 11, 1910.

246 "When a new catcher of Billy . . .": Wilson Matthews, *Sporting News*, October 28, 1909. To cite a few more of the countless examples, Washington manager Jimmy McAleer acknowledged in 1910, "We all know how scarce good catchers are." Michael H. Cahill, "Has Strong Catchers," *Washington Post*, March 2, 1910, 8. At the end of the season, another observer reported, "The demand for backstops is vastly greater than it is for great pitchers, hard hitters or fast fielders; infinitely greater, in fact, than is the supply." Tommy Clark, "Good Catchers Sorely Needed in Major Leagues," *Washington Herald*, October 2, 1910, 8.

246 "pitchers bobbed up . . ." and "Boston, Cincinnati, St. Louis . . .": "Good Catchers Are Few and Far Between," 15. There is an odd coincidence between the events described in this piece and the ones that occurred after the 1875 season. As described earlier, in that year St. Louis was the winner of the auction for John Clapp while Boston, Cincinnati, and Philadelphia were the three teams that ended up without an experienced catcher.

246–247 Bowerman . . . had been so unhappy as a backup to Roger Bresnahan in New York that he provoked dissension: Cait Murphy, *Crazy '08*, 29.

247 "Good receivers are few and far between . . .": "Charley Street Most Promising," *Washington Times*, December 29, 1908, 8.

247 "small wonder that the men . . .": Evers and Fullerton, *Touching Second*, 90.

247 In 1905 the game's best-known scout, Ted Sullivan, reported . . .: *Sporting Life*, March 25, 1905.

247–248 "The real classy backstop . . .," "Look over the list . . .," and "The best advice . . .": Clark, "Good Catchers Sorely Needed in Major Leagues," 8.

248 "Much of the scarcity of good timber . . .": "Catchers Are Scarce."

248 "The game has changed so much . . .": Evers and Fullerton, *Touching Second*, 87.

15. AN ENDURING NEW MODEL

249 "The bushes are full of players . . .": "Catcher Is Brain Center of Successful Ball Team," *Albany Evening Journal*, December 18, 1911, 6.

250 Henry Chadwick died in 1908 . . .: Other veteran sportswriters who died in the 1890s and the "aughts" included O. P. Caylor in 1897, Harry Weldon in 1902, and Al Wright in 1905. Even Stephen Crane was dead by 1900.

250 "the days when it took pluck . . .": Spink, *National Game*, 94.

250–251 "A baseball catcher is a cross between . . .": "Essays on Baseball: The Catcher," *Washington Herald*, May 23, 1909, 13.

251–252 "Even when well protected by a strong mask . . .": Newhouse, "Dangers of the Hero Behind the Bat," 14.

252 "Did you ever know the mark . . .": *Wilkes-Barre Times*, October 17, 1906.

252 "When ready to receive the pitch . . .": Steve O'Neill, "How to Play Baseball," *Charlotte Sunday Observer*, June 4, 1922, sec. 3, 1.

252 "even in the best ordered game . . .": Newhouse, "Dangers of the Hero Behind the Bat," 14.

252–253 "a real hero . . .": "Billy Sullivan a Game Player," *Atlanta Constitution*, October 11, 1908, C4; quoted in Trey Strecker, "William Joseph Sullivan," in Jones, ed., *Deadball Stars of the American League*, 484.

253 "Catching's a pretty rough deal . . .": Ritter, *Glory of Their Times*, 73. John J. Evers and Hugh S. Fullerton offer additional testimony to Gibson's fortitude, reporting that "at one time in 1909, George Gibson, in spite of chest protectors, shin guards, and heavy pads, had black and blue spots imprinted by nineteen foul tips upon his body, a damaged hand, a bruise on his hip six inches square where a thrown bat had struck, and three spike cuts. Yet he had not missed a game and was congratulating himself on his 'luck.'" They also cite Pat Moran as an example that, "Under such conditions of wear and tear the wonder is that the supply of catchers even approximates the demand." Evers and Fullerton, *Touching Second*, 89.

253 "felt certain that Killefer's collarbone . . .": *Sporting News*, December 9, 1909.

253 "The league rule makers would do . . .": *Boston Globe*, January 14, 1894.

253 "squatted over the plate . . ." and "there isn't an umpire . . .": *Sporting Life*, August 2, 1902.

253–254 "Catcher [Fred] Abbott . . .": *Sporting Life*, April 15, 1905.

254 "You might as well try to move a stone wall": Quoted by Mark Armour in "William Francis Carrigan," in Jones, ed., *Deadball Stars of the American League*, 432.

254 "an elaborate suit of armor . . .": *Detroit Free Press*, April 30, 1910.

254 "the practice has developed . . .": *Sporting News*, March 5, 1914; see my *A Game of Inches*, vol. 1, entry 4.4.11, 253–255, for more discussion of these examples and more on plate-blocking.

254 "[The catcher] is in danger . . .": Newhouse (boxer and trainer), "Dangers of the Hero Behind the Bat," 14.

254–255 "When a man is coming home . . .": "Dooin Tells of Catcher's Work," 2.

255 sign-stealing remained widespread: *St. Louis Post-Dispatch*, August 11, 1894; *New York Press*, reprinted in *Washington Post*, July 31, 1904.

255 crouching remained rare until the twentieth century: See Morris, *A Game of Inches*, vol. 1, entry 4.2.2, 208–210, for more on crouches. But as late as 1904, Connie Mack was still advising: "when a catcher takes his position he should assume a stooping posture. The body should be well bent forward from the hips, so as to enable the player to handle the ball at any height. Crouching to the ground should not be considered, as a player who insists on so doing will never become a first-class catcher. An easy position should be assumed as far as possible. Where the catcher crouches he is unable to control the er-

ratic flight of the ball." Connie Mack, "How to Play Ball," multipart series, *Washington Post*, March 20, 1904.

255 The primary reason, however, was that the crouch helped a catcher give his signals confidentially: *Sporting News*, April 29, 1909.

255 "must guard against the batsman . . .": *Washington Post*, July 18, 1909.

255 "the signs of big Ed Sweeney . . .": Stan Baumgartner, "Signals," *Baseball Guide and Record Book 1947*, 127.

256 So catchers began encoding their signals . . .: "New Method of Signaling Is Disagreeable for the Catcher," *Duluth News Tribune*, July 20, 1909, 7.

256 "visible movements, such as spitting . . .": Baumgartner, "Signals," 127; *Sporting News*, April 16, 1908. And in 1919, Ray Schalk explained: "Finger signs naturally are the easiest, but add something to the finger signals. Such moves as touching the mask, tossing dirt, rubbing a shoe or spitting in a certain direction will help." Sid C. Keener, "From a 'Mite' into a Star," syndicated column, *Kansas City Star*, July 13, 1919, 13.

256 "the catcher, so the majority of the fans think . . .": Clark, "Good Catchers Sorely Needed in Major Leagues," 8.

256–257 "little knacks about catching . . ." and "Johnny Kling probably . . .": "Great Pitchers Twirl Own Game," *Wilkes-Barre Times Leader*, November 8, 1913.

257 Lengthy descriptions appeared of the footwork . . .: John "Dasher" Troy wrote in 1915 that "Young catchers should always try to be in a position when they receive a ball to get the runner trying to steal a base. Whether the pitched ball is coming above or below the waist, the catcher should always put his left foot forward; let his arm go well back, and throw the ball with the same motion by which he throws his body forward. Never draw the arm up in front, and never take a step after you catch the ball. That is what loses time, and the smallest fraction of a second is what counts. . . . If the ball happens to be pitched as high as the shoulder, or near it, let the hand go back over the shoulder and throw the ball with the full length of the arm. If the ball is pitched on the side of the plate and low, stay in your position, as you may have to take a short step when you throw it." John "Dasher" Troy, "Reminiscences of an Oldtimer," *Baseball Magazine*, April 1915, 78–80. Mickey Cochrane added in 1939, "Mechanically, the first thing a catcher must acquire is a wide comfortable stance behind the plate. Stand with the left foot advanced three or four—perhaps six—inches ahead of the right foot; assume a crouch that does not tighten you up and prevent you from shifting quickly. A catcher should NOT try to stand with his feet in the same PLANE. By standing with one foot behind the other he can shift his balance with agility, eliminating wasted motion for receiving or throwing. The difference between a wide comfortable stance and an awkward one means as much as three full seconds with a man on base, and if he's a fast man that means ten to twenty feet—a put-out or a stolen base. By assuming the stance that fits best, a receiver should shift his feet, catch, and throw in no more than two or three motions . . . it is doubly important that a catcher put all his first thoughts into stance behind the plate. He must have his feet ready to shift easily and quickly." Mickey Cochrane, *Baseball: The Fans' Game*, 42–43.

257 Particularly intense scrutiny was given to elements requiring teamwork . . .: Evers and Fullerton, *Touching Second*, 93–96.

257 Detailed explanations told how catchers applied tags to runners as they slid into the plate: According to an umpire, Billy Sullivan had "everybody beaten, so far as my knowledge goes, in nailing the runner at the plate. . . . The second Billy gets the ball he holds it about two inches from the plate toward third base. If the man slides in he simply has to bump against Sullivan's hand with the ball in it. He can't swerve aside, because Sullivan has him dead. It's the same if the runner comes in standing up. He's a goner. . . . When Sullivan gets the ball while the man is sliding in he is a wonder coming

down on him. It's a wonder to me how he can get that ball over to the side of the plate so fast. I guess long years of practice is what has made him so perfect." Billy Sullivan Hall of Fame file: undated clipping, hand-dated November 1912, quoting umpire Brick Owens following that year's Chicago city series between the Cubs and White Sox.

257 "friendship and confidence" and "get the corners": Evers and Fullerton, *Touching Second*, 97.

257 how a catcher might try to settle down a struggling pitcher by stopping to retie his shoe or adjust his chest protector: Billy Sullivan, quoted in Spink, *National Game*, 390.

257 Sometimes these little items were so subtle . . .: Lou Criger, for example, provided an explanation of how he strove to throw to bases in such a way that the ball "rotates backward and has an upward tendency, while some catchers throw with the thumb exposed and that gives it the downward effect, like the billiard draw shot, a ball that hurts to catch." Steve Krah, "Louis Criger," in Jones, *Deadball Stars of the American League*, 406. And Oscar Stanage, according to a Detroit sportswriter, "threw fast and accurate, but always a light ball. He never moved faster than he had to but he always got there. His lack of wasted motion made him a favorite with pitchers, for he was an easy man to pitch to and he had the ability to steady the twirlers." Jim Moyes, "Oscar Harland Stanage," in Jones, ed., *Deadball Stars of the American League*, 566, quoting a 1920 description by H. G. Salsinger.

257 The hit-and-run play became a staple. . . . The squeeze play sprang: The hit-and-run play had been used quite a bit in the nineteenth century but became much more widespread after 1900. The squeeze play was all but unheard of before 1905. See my *A Game of Inches*, vol. 1, for detailed histories of both plays—entry 5.4.7, 290–293, for the hit and run, and entry 5.4.5, 285–287, for the squeeze play.

257 while pitchouts were not unheard of in the nineteenth century . . .: See my *A Game of Inches*, vol. 1, entry 5.3.11, 280–282, for a history of the pitchout.

258 "A good catcher must . . .": J. Ed Grillo, *Washington Post*, April 25, 1908.

258 Even if he called for one and no play was on . . .: Naturally, this led some catchers to abuse the privilege of calling pitchouts, or "waste balls," as they were then usually called. According to umpire Billy Evans, "There is a major league catcher who is known as the 'waste ball king.' He has a wonderful throwing arm and is proud of it. It gives him pain any time a runner steals a base. With his marvelous whip he really never need call for a waste ball. However, he likes to turn them back a mile, and the players know it. When a runner reaches first all he need do is to take a good lead, and it is a good bet the catcher will call for a waste. The theory on which the opposing players work is that the first two balls are almost certain to be waste balls, if the runner has any reputation for speed. It can easily be seen what a load it makes for the pitcher." Billy Evans, syndicated column, "Catcher Can Make or Break a Club; Brainy Backstop Is Invaluable to Team and Can Bring Results by Properly Directing Pitcher," *Philadelphia Inquirer*, January 21, 1917, 20.

258 "Baseball is largely a game of . . .": Evans, "Catcher Can Make or Break a Club," 20.

258 "mechanical mistakes form no criteria . . .": Evers and Fullerton, *Touching Second*, 88.

258 "So great is the power of the backstop . . .": Evans, "Catcher Can Make or Break a Club," 20.

259 "the 'rule of three,' apparently" and "whose worth is recognized . . .": "New Method of Signaling Is Disagreeable for the Catcher," 7.

260 "If they strike a dub catcher . . .": Malachi Kittridge, "The 'Heady' Catchers Win the Ball Games," *New Enterprise* (Madison, Florida), May 30, 1907, 6.

260 Hall of Fame catcher Ray Schalk gave a lengthy description . . .: Keener, "From a 'Mite' into a Star," 13.

260 "Watch the batsman and base runner . . .": Steve O'Neill, "How to Play Baseball," *Charlotte Sunday Observer*, June 4, 1922, sec. 3, 1.

260–261 "A new pitcher may probably . . .": "Developing Material for the Big Leagues, by Catcher Jack Warner," *New York Evening World*, February 15, 1904, 10.

261 "The catcher rather than the pitcher . . .": "Charley Street Most Promising," 8.

261 "Keep mixing them up on a batter . . .": Keener, "From a 'Mite' into a Star," 13.

261 "Besides first hand knowledge of a batter's possibilities . . .": Evers and Fullerton, *Touching Second*, 90.

262 "A catcher must have baseball brains . . ." and "the catcher, above all men . . .": Ray Schalk, article in *Baseball Magazine*, reprinted as "What Makes a Great Catcher," *Pueblo Chieftain*, October 8, 1917.

262 "is in a position to see everything . . .": Joe Vila, "Major Owners Find Few Young Catchers," syndicated article, reprinted in *Philadelphia Inquirer*, March 31, 1922.

262 "to be able to work regularly . . .": Ward, *Base-Ball: How to Become a Player*, 66.

262–263 "The catcher, owing to the fact . . .": Unidentified article by Moran in *Baseball Magazine*; quoted in Spink, *National Game*, 110.

263 "Rarely does a pitcher take the initiative . . .": Evans, "Catcher Can Make or Break a Club," 20.

263 now . . . they took similar pride in deciding which pitch to call: This sense was aptly summed up in an account that observed, "The first class catcher judges from the batsman's actions what he is likely to do and communicates his knowledge to the pitcher." "Good Catchers a Necessity," *Chicago Tribune*, reprinted in *Duluth News Tribune*, December 13, 1904.

263 "A catcher can make a pitcher look . . .": "Catchers Make or Break Pitchers," *Aberdeen American*, April 29, 1911, 11.

263 "charge of the pitchers . . .": *Washington Post*, February 26, 1906.

263–264 every man who was identified as a major league pitching coach: Morris, *A Game of Inches*, vol. 1, entry 7.2.3 on pitching coaches, 363–364. Pitching coach was still not a formal position, and many clubs did not have one. But these men are the only ones whom I have found described as a major league pitching coach before 1926, and every single one was a catcher by trade. The only exception I've found is Jim Drohan, a pitcher who became a minor league pitching coach.

264 a still-thriving tradition of ex-catchers being disproportionately likely to become managers: See Appendix 2 for details. Pat Moran, one of the many catchers who went directly from behind the plate to the manager's position, commented: "The owners of teams are beginning to see that a man who makes a good catcher must have brains and an intimate knowledge of the game. Consequently, they are beginning to give their catchers the positions on their salary list which they have always filled on the playing field—the office of manager. . . . To my mind the day is almost at hand when we will see every big league team with a catcher as manager." Unspecified article in *Baseball Magazine*, quoted in Spink, *National Game*, 110.

264 the hustling play of backing up potential overthrows: "Good Catchers a Necessity"; for more information, see the entry in my *A Game of Inches*, vol. 1, on backing up.

264 A couple of catchers brought back Nat Hicks's trick of calling for a deliberate passed ball: Hugh Jennings, *Rounding Third*, Chapter 73, credits Charley Schmidt with using this play; Joe Jackson, writing in the *Washington Post* of March 24, 1911, cited several unnamed catchers for a minor league team in York, Pennsylvania. And, naturally, new tricks ensued. Jack O'Connor of the St. Louis Browns, for example, "made big John

Anderson, then with Washington, throw the ball against the pavilion. Jack pretended to be the first baseman and 'Big' John heaved the ball to him. Then Jack sidestepped and let the horsehide roll, while a pair of Brownies scored." Spink, *National Game*, 111.

264 a scheme devised by Phillies catcher Morgan Murphy in 1900 . . .: *Philadelphia Inquirer*, September 18, 1900; Joe Dittmar, "A Shocking Discovery," *Baseball Research Journal* 20 (1991); Christy Mathewson, *Pitching in a Pinch*, 145–148; Rosenberg, *Cap Anson 3*, 306–311.

264 "Formerly the catcher signaled . . .": "Catchers Are Scarce."

264 "The catcher should always tell . . .": O'Neill, "How to Play Baseball," sec. 3, 1.

264 Charley Schmidt convinced sportswriter Ernest Lanigan . . .: Morris, *A Game of Inches*, vol. 2, entry 17.19 on caught stealing, 167.

264 When Bill Bergen gunned down . . .: Joe Dittmar, "William Aloysius Bergen," in Tom Simon, ed., *Deadball Stars of the National League*, 277; the game occurred on August 23, 1909.

264 This must have irked Charley Farrell . . .: Rich Eldred, "Charles Andrew (Duke) Farrell" in Tiemann and Rucker, eds., *Nineteenth Century Stars*, 41; Farrell's feat was accomplished against Baltimore on May 11, 1897.

264–265 "The catcher is 'the man behind the gun' . . .": "Good Catchers a Necessity."

265 "I had a glove and mask . . ." and "he took one look . . .": *Hudson Dispatch*, August 29, 1961. Bill Hicks placed this event as occurring in 1903. Similarly Rufus Woodward, "a barehand catcher of the eighties," made it "his greatest mission" to make a major league catcher of his son. He bought his son a complete set of "professional-looking equipment" at the age of nine, and it was a bitter disappointment to him when the son's failing eyesight forced him to give up catching. Instead the son, Stanley Woodward, became one of the best-known sports editors of the twentieth century. Stanley Woodward, *Paper Tiger* (1963; reprint, Lincoln: University of Nebraska Press, 2007), 7, 17.

265 "Here and there an exceptionally great catcher . . .": "Backstops Are Deteriorating."

265 "[handle] the delivery of the different pitchers . . .": *National Police Gazette*, August 26, 1905, 7.

265 "the most natural catcher of them all . . .": William R. Cobb, ed., *Honus Wagner on His Life and Baseball* (1924; reprint, Ann Arbor: Sports Media, 2006), 137.

265–266 "How are you going to tell . . .," "they haven't any direct . . .," and "Most of [the catcher's] work . . .": Schalk, "What Makes a Great Catcher."

266 "below the average . . ." and "the batting and fielding averages . . .": Frank G. Loman, "The Man Behind the Athletics' Revival," *Sportlife*, September 1925, 83.

266 "sat on the bench a long time . . .": Lou Criger Hall of Fame file, unidentified clipping, circa 1910.

266 "took a look at him and almost decided . . ." and "they had to let . . .": "Alexander Tells Life Story (Part 3)," *Los Angeles Times*, June 29, 1930, E4.

266 "until an accident left his team . . .": Spink, *National Game*, 115.

267 "If you are so smart . . ." and "The first ball Joe . . .": *Sporting News*, April 10, 1930, 4. A similar account of these events appears in Arthur Daley, "Knocking at the Door of the Hall of Fame," *New York Times*, August 31, 1943, 20.

267 "is not afraid to make a play . . .": *National Police Gazette*, August 26, 1905, 7.

267 "The catcher is 'the man behind the gun' in scientific baseball": "Good Catchers a Necessity."

267 the potbellied catchers of the 1890s faded as the position again became accessible to men of various shapes and sizes: As an example that plumpness was no longer accepted in catchers, Allison remarked after the 1907 season that Edward "Tubby" Spencer of the St. Louis Browns was "the best throwing catcher I have seen in many years . . . but he seemed to be too fat to do himself justice." Grillo, "Allison," S3.

267 "little runts" and "Why, my boy, I want a catcher, not a jockey": *New York World*, September 21, 1913, quoting St. Joseph manager Byron McKibbon in 1901. The article also reported that Charles Comiskey, then managing St. Paul, had had a similar reaction to Dooin. A slightly different version of the story appears in Spink, *National Game*, 100.

267–268 "caused the wise ones . . .," "little lad," "revelation," "the terrible shoots . . .," and "immediately won him a place . . .": Spink, *National Game*, 115.

268 "possess brawn": Keener, "From a 'Mite' into a Star," 13. Meanwhile Lou Criger had to overcome multiple handicaps, as he was perceived as being "an old man as baseball goes, not overly strong, [and] a man so skinny he appears in imminent danger of breaking every time he throws to second base." "Charley Street Most Promising," 8.

268 "The catcher now is more than a mere backstop . . .": *Sporting News*, August 14, 1913.

268 "mere broth of a lad": Dick Farrington, "Bresnahan, Former Catching Star, Fighting Back at 60 from Crash of '29, That Turned His Wealth into Want," *Sporting News*, November 14, 1940, 3. While Bresnahan may not have originated these myths, he "did nothing to discourage the use of the nickname until late in his life." John R. Husman, "Toledo's Own 'Duke of Tralee,'" *Toledo Magazine*, August 30–September 5, 1987, 4–7.

268 Some of these accounts had Bresnahan . . .: Roger Bresnahan Hall of Fame file, undated clipping, written by Ed Wray.

268–269 "The players in the big leagues . . ." and "young ball-players . . .": "Developing Material for the Big Leagues, by Catcher Jack Warner," 10.

269 "besieged by a lot . . ." and "a scheme to rid . . .": *Kansas City Star*, March 19, 1905.

269 "Nowadays a catcher is supposed to be simply a catcher . . .": "Patsy Donovan Fears for Game's Future."

269 "mere lumber on the paths": "Backstops Are Deteriorating." Similarly, Forrest Cady of the Red Sox was described as "a big, slow-moving fellow who takes about as long to reach first as it does Cobb to take two bases." Hugh S. Fullerton, "Doping the World Series," syndicated, *Atlanta Constitution*, October 5, 1915, 10.

269 "catchers, as a rule, do not hit well . . .": Kittridge, "The 'Heady' Catchers Win the Ball Games," 6.

270 "ice wagon catcher of the present" and "continual crouching position . . .": John J. Ward, "Baseball [sic] Premier Catcher," *Baseball Magazine*, January 1916, 42.

270 "Some of the critics say . . .": *Lexington Herald*, April 9, 1913.

270 "that a lot of catchers ruin whatever speed . . .": I. E. Sanborn, "Baseball Brains Necessary to Speed," syndicated article, *Anaconda Standard*, July 26, 1914.

270 "In most cases, the catcher of today . . .": "Backstops Are Deteriorating."

270 Killefer was speedy enough to steal quite a few bases in the minor leagues: The *St. Louis Post-Dispatch* of April 5, 1910, also referred to Killefer as being a "fast" runner.

270 "Neither of us could run any faster . . .": *Philadelphia Evening Bulletin*, July 5, 1960.

270 "one of these hustling, agile, cat-like . . .": Fullerton, "Doping the World Series," 10.

270 In a limited way, the position again offered a beacon of opportunity to members of racial minorities . . .: In addition to the examples that follow, catcher Mike Gonzalez also became one of the first Cuban major leaguers. A rather different example of how catching skill could create opportunity was provided by the Bloomer Girls teams. These squads became popular in the early twentieth century, and most of the players were females. But, as Gai Ingham Berlage explained, these teams always "hired one or two male ringers whom they passed off as females." Naturally, the ringers were assigned to play catcher, pitcher, or shortstop. Gai Ingham Berlage, *Women in Baseball: The Forgotten History* (Westport, Conn.: Praeger Publishers, 1994), 34.

272   . . . making the lack of controversy over Thompson's presence noteworthy: Seamus
      Kearney, "Bill Thompson, Pioneer," *National Pastime* 16 (1996), 67–68. The Twin State
      League was based in Massachusetts and Connecticut.
272   Two years later another team in the same league . . .: Brian Turner and John S. Bow-
      man, *Baseball in Northampton, 1823–1953*, 42.
272   "After that I didn't give him any signs at all . . .": Ritter, *Glory of Their Times*, 173; see
      also R. J. Lesch, "John Tortes 'Chief' Meyers," in Simon, *Deadball Stars of the National
      League*, 71.
272   Another time-honored belief that returned to prominence was that of a mystical bond
      between pitcher and catcher: Pairings of pitchers and catchers had never disappeared
      entirely. Yet after having assuming prominence in the 1870s and 1880s, they had fallen
      into disfavor by the 1890s. As late as 1888, John Montgomery Ward could write, "In
      every well-regulated team nowadays the pitchers and catchers are paired, and the same
      pair always works together . . . it is believed that a battery will do better team-work
      where its two ends are always the same." Ward, *Base-Ball: How to Become a Player*, 66.
      But by 1890 a note stated: "Manager [Bill] Barnie will not separate his pitchers and
      catcher into pairs as strictly this year as in the past, but will give each backstop a chance
      to handle all the different styles of delivery. In most of the games, however, [Norman]
      Baker and [George] Townsend, [Sam] Shaw and ['Pop'] Tate, [Les] German and [John]
      Kerins will face each other. Stain [?] will pitch to any catcher who may be available for
      the present." *Baltimore Sun*, April 1, 1890. And, according to an 1898 article, "Manager
      W. H. Watkins of the Pittsburg club believes in keeping a good catcher behind the bat
      as long as he can do good work. He does not believe in the former fashioned scheme
      of alternating players, putting in a backstop every other day. Neither does he believe
      that pitcher and catcher should be coupled up into slated batteries." *Lima Daily News*,
      February 21, 1898.
272   "Any catcher who has caught 'Rube' . . .": "Pitchers Are Superstitious Lot: Many Star
      Slabmen Harbor Weird Imaginations About Certain Catchers," *Philadelphia Inquirer*,
      November 20, 1910, 4.
272   their three pitchers with the most victories each preferred to work with a different
      catcher: According to Evans, Jack Coombs "has always expressed a preference for [Jack]
      Lapp" while Chief Bender "insists that [Ira] Thomas do the catching. . . . [Bender]
      firmly believes that he is far more effective with Thomas working than with any of the
      other Athletics' clever catchers" and that spitballer Cy Morgan was at his most effective
      when working with Paddy Livingston. "Pitchers Are Superstitious Lot," 4.
273   "You see, Cy was a right-hander . . .": Eugene Murdock, "Looking Back at 96," *Base-
      ball Research Journal* 1976, 59.
273   "belonged together like ham and eggs": Lou Criger Hall of Fame file, letter from
      Criger's son Harold, dated July 4, 1970.
273   "I've pitched to [Criger] so long . . .": Quoted in Steve Krah, "Louis Criger," in Jones,
      ed., *Deadball Stars of the American League*, 407. Christy Mathewson likewise expressed
      a preference first for Frank Bowerman and later for "Chief" Meyers. "Pitchers Are
      Superstitious Lot," 4. Jack Chesbro signed with the upstart American League following
      the 1902 season only after receiving assurances that the team would also sign his catcher,
      Jack O'Connor. Dick Farrington, "O'Connor Looks Back at Lajoie's 'Eight Hits' After
      22 Years as Exile from Organized Ball," *Sporting News*, February 23, 1933. In addition,
      as had been the case a generation earlier, many of these partnerships were cemented
      by off-the-field friendships. Waddell and Schreckengost roomed together in the days
      when players shared a single hotel bed on road trips, and supposedly Schreckengost
      had a clause written into his contract prohibiting Waddell from eating animal crackers
      in bed. Ray Schalk similarly stressed the importance of "associating with the pitchers

off of the field . . . talk[ing] over games during the evenings . . . rehears[ing] all of the batters." Keener, "From a 'Mite' into a Star," 13. Red Sox catcher and manager Bill Carrigan also became well known for his belief that "one catcher is better with some pitchers than with others." Fullerton, "Doping the World's Series: The Catchers," 8. In a strategy that recalled the heyday of the tough-guy catcher, his battery pairings were generally designed so that certain catchers worked as often as possible with right-handed pitchers, while other specialized in catching southpaws. Fullerton, "Doping the World Series," 10; T. H. Murnane, "Red Sox Have the Edge in Catchers," *Boston Globe*, October 7, 1915, 9.

273 "many spectators" and "largely a mechanical one . . .": Billy Sullivan; quoted in Spink, *National Game*, 390.

273 "the bigger the glove the better" and "I have used any number . . .": O'Neill, "How to Play Baseball," sec. 3, 1. Bill Bergen of Brooklyn found a novel way to underscore this in a 1910 game in Cincinnati: "When he walked into the catcher's box he carried with him three immense catching gloves. Two were placed on the ground near the plate and the third adorned his left hand. This glove was worn until a Cincinnati player reached first, and then discarded in favor of one of the other gloves. If a pitched ball happened to bounce out of this glove, Bill dropped it and used glove No. 3. Bill explained that gloves Nos. 2 and 3 made it easier for him to start his throws when redlegs tried to steal. He was breaking in glove No. 1." *Fort Wayne Sentinel*, August 30, 1910.

273 "a much mooted question . . .": Newhouse, "Dangers of the Hero Behind the Bat," 14.

274 "chance to win a pennant . . .": "Good Catchers a Necessity."

274 "Show me a ball club with a catcher . . .": Kittridge, "The 'Heady' Catchers Win the Ball Games," 6.

274 "McGraw and Clark Griffith have often said . . .": "Good Catchers Are Few and Far Between," 15.

274 "The catcher is, all things considered . . .": Ward, "Baseball [sic] Premier Catcher," 39. Added Billy Evans: "The crack backstop means everything to a club. It is practically an impossibility to rate his worth." Evans, "Catcher Can Make or Break a Club," 20. And, according to John J. Evers and Hugh S. Fullerton, "There are not ten really first-class catchers in America and the team which lacks one of these ten, no matter how great its strength may be in other departments is doomed to failure before it starts." Evers and Fullerton, *Touching Second*, 87.

274 "A good pitcher can win games, but a great catcher can win pennants": Ward, "Baseball [sic] Premier Catcher," 39. Others who echoed Clarke's claim included sportswriters I. E. Sanborn, who asked readers in 1918 to "look back and see if any team ever won a world's series without a good catcher," and Hugh Fullerton, who remarked in 1920, "There is a saying in baseball that no team has ever won a championship without an extraordinarily good catcher. This is perhaps an exaggeration, but not much of one." I. E. Sanborn, "What's Put Our Cubs on Top? Bill Killefer! That's Answer," *Chicago Tribune*, July 7, 1918, A3; Hugh S. Fullerton, "Bill Killifer [sic] Greatest Catcher in the National," *Atlanta Constitution*, April 8, 1920, 19. At least one sportswriter made such a claim as early as 1907: "Crack pitchers are all right—a baseball team has to have them to win a pennant. Nevertheless teams that have won pennants and have not had capable, brainy catchers are as scarce as hen's teeth." "Catcher's Part in Baseball: First Class Backstops Needed to Win Pennants," *New York Sun*, May 26, 1907, 33.

274 This was best epitomized by Larry McLean . . .: McLean retraced some of Kelly's stops, as he grew up in Boston and spent a long stint in Cincinnati. McLean was nowhere near the all-around player that Kelly had been. But what made the parallel especially close was the regularity with which both men broke training rules and how hard it was

to hold a grudge against them. Both men were dead before the age of forty and were genuinely mourned even by those who had unsuccessfully tried to get them to follow team rules. Of McLean it was said, "He had no enemies, even among those with whom he clashed," a comment that echoed a remark famously made about Kelly—that he "never had an enemy but himself." Mike Lackey, "John Bannerman 'Larry' McLean," in Simon, *Deadball Stars of the National League*, 244; Spink, *National Game*, 104, quoting Jim Hart. Frank "Silver" Flint and Lew Brown, the two men who brought the big catcher to the fore in 1878, also shared this propensity. Both men had severe drinking problems and disturbing tendencies to let down the people closest to them, and both were dead by 1892. Yet both were viewed with great affection by those who knew them, especially the ones they kept letting down. Flint was seen as a man whose spirit simply could not be forced to conform to society's rules. He was practically penniless when he died, but this was attributed to "the wide-open policy he pursued in helping his friends and holding his own end up always kept him close to the shore. . . . He had not an enemy in the world and was always willing to make a divide with a person in need." *Sporting Life*, January 23, 1892, 9. These traits were also symbolized by his wife, who divorced him two years before his death because of his drinking but maintained, "Frank is a good fellow and I'm not going to say one word against him." *Sporting Life*, November 8, 1890. And she even returned to nurse Flint through his final illness. *Sporting Life*, January 23, 1892, 9. Although a native of St. Louis, like so many of the catchers of the era, Flint was portrayed as not being worldly wise. Early in his career he reportedly received a telegram from the manager of a baseball club in Minnesota, asking him how much of a salary he would require to report. Flint replied: "125 a month. Where is Minnesota?" *New York Clipper*, August 23, 1879. Brown was the hard-drinking, hard-living, tough-as-nails catcher who once volunteered to have a cannonball shot at him. When he died at the age of thirty, boxing legend and longtime friend John L. Sullivan sent a "magnificent floral offering." But others saw a very different side. Brown was "of timid disposition," recalled Tim Murnane, and "was never known to have an argument with a fellow player." He added that Brown's "boyish spirits" were never dampened, and that after leaving the major leagues he could often be found playing baseball with boys in the open lots of Boston. Murnane, "Lew Brown's Last Sleep," 1. Perhaps the happy-go-lucky nature of Brown and these other catchers was best encapsulated when Brown's many friends tried to arrange a benefit game for him in 1885. A crowd gathered to pay tribute to the big catcher, but the event had to be rescheduled because it had slipped Brown's mind. *Sporting Life*, November 11, 1885.

274 "popular idol": Lackey, "John Bannerman 'Larry' McLean," in Simon, *Deadball Stars of the National League*, 243.

274 they signed a petition to demand that he not be traded: Jim Sandoval, "Ivy Brown Wingo," in Simon, *Deadball Stars of the National League*, 261.

275 "Because you are the only one capable of turning the trick": Lou Criger Hall of Fame file, clipping from unidentified source.

275 "Catching is the pivotal position . . .": Evers and Fullerton, *Touching Second*, 87.

275 "The catcher is the keynote . . .": Kittridge, "The 'Heady' Catchers Win the Ball Games," 6.

275 "the catcher is as important in a baseball team . . .": "Catchers Are Scarce."

275 "The catcher is the pivot of a baseball team . . .": Bozeman Bulger, "The Science of Baseball (Part 4)," *New York World*, March 20, 1909, 7.

275 "A good catcher is the quarterback . . .": Quoted in Walter Alston, *The Complete Baseball Handbook*; reprinted in Paul Dickson, *Baseball's Greatest Quotations* (New York: HarperCollins, 1991), 193.

275–276 "The tendency is to give . . .": Sanborn, "What's Put Our Cubs on Top? Bill Killefer! That's Answer," A3.

276 "The catcher stands there . . .": "Catcher's Part in Baseball: First Class Backstops Needed to Win Pennants," *New York Sun*, May 26, 1907, 33.

276 "catchers are more in demand . . .": "Second Fitchburg Manager," *Boston Globe*, December 13, 1914, 17.

276–277 "the natural quality . . .," "There were numerous . . .," and "not only possess mechanical skill . . .": Joe Vila, "Major Owners Find Few Young Catchers," syndicated article, reprinted in *Philadelphia Inquirer*, March 31, 1922.

277 "I wanted more work . . .": Keener, "From a 'Mite' into a Star."

277 "catching appealed to me . . .": Roy Campanella, *It's Good to Be Alive*; quoted in Dickson, *Baseball's Greatest Quotations*, 71.

16. THE CATCHER'S LEGACY

278 "A good catcher is actually a receiver . . .": Quoted in Falkner, *Nine Sides of the Diamond*, 289.

278 "I didn't raise my son to be a catcher": Lena Marciano is quoted by Paul Dickson in *Baseball's Greatest Quotations*, 268; Dickson notes that the authenticity of the quotation is dubious. Marciano did, however, aspire to a career as a professional catcher and was good enough to receive tryouts with two Chicago Cubs farm clubs in the spring of 1947 before launching his boxing career. Russell Sullivan, *Rocky Marciano: The Rock of His Times* (Urbana: University of Illinois Press, 2002), 14–16.

279 "baseball was a more virile pastime . . .": Longtime Tiger catcher Charley Schmidt, quoted in *Sporting News*, September 20, 1928, 3. Schmidt blamed the decline of baseball on the automobile: "As a result of riding to and from the park, of riding in the morning and in the evening, the ball players' legs do not get enough exercise. The consequence is that their playing on the field is retarded and their careers shortened. Such, at least, is Schmidt's observation. . . . 'The trouble with most of the ball players,' says Schmidt, 'is that they loaf too much and the heart can not stand the sudden switch in the amount of work it is called upon to do.'" And Schmidt was far from alone. Roger Bresnahan maintained in 1936 that "Modern baseball lacks strategy. . . . In the old days ball fans always were trying to out-guess and out-smart the opposition." *Sporting News*, May 9, 1936. And sportswriters with a limited knowledge of baseball history began to write as though early-twentieth-century catchers were the toughest generation. An obituary of Billy Sullivan, who began playing professional baseball in 1897, made these preposterous claims: "The man who invented catching—as the baseball players say—died today. . . . Before he came along, baseball catchers stood 20 feet behind home plate, out of danger from foul tips. Sullivan is credited with inventing the first chest protector and moving into the position catchers still use." Billy Sullivan Hall of Fame file: AP obituary, January 29, 1965. And a 1949 article about Chief Zimmer maintained, "It was Zimmer who changed catching from a snap job into the hardest working spot on the ball club." Lebovitz, "Zimmer, Oldest Catcher, Leafs Memory Book," 12.

279 "You watch . . .": Quoted in Falkner, *Nine Sides of the Diamond*, 323.

279 "The key to having soft hands . . .": Quoted in Rob Trucks, *The Catcher: Baseball Behind the Seams*, 88. Similarly, on page 87 of the same work, Bob Geren (yet another catcher who became a major league manager) is quoted as saying that a good catcher needs to have "a looseness in receiving the ball. Like a shortstop, just letting it come to them, with their body relaxed, relaxed and not tense in going and getting balls."

279 . . . flying him back to Boston and getting a police escort . . .: Bob Ryan, "Masked Man Rides to the Rescue," *Boston Globe*, May 2, 2006. Intriguingly, ESPN.com reported that the Yankees tried to acquire Mirabelli at the same time. The Yankees did not have a knuckleball pitcher; instead, in the tradition of the stockpiling of catchers that occurred in the 1870s, they apparently wanted to keep Mirabelli from rejoining the Red Sox.

280 "Base ball, as we used to play it . . .": William Clift, *The Tim Bunker Papers: Or, Yankee Farming* (New York: Orange Judd, 1868), 303–306. Clift was a Connecticut minister who was born in 1817 and died in 1890. Because of his tendency to put his own views in the farmer's mouth, this deservedly obscure book makes for rather tedious reading, yet it does provide considerable insight into why those who clung to the views of the Puritans revered the farmer and were alarmed by professional baseball.

280 Still stronger was the related concept that no respectable father would let his daughter marry a ballplayer: For example, minor league ballplayer Warren Beckwith had to elope with the granddaughter of Abraham Lincoln. Bill Lange, one of the best players of the 1890s, retired from baseball at the height of his career, reportedly so that he could marry into a socially prominent family. And, as Lawrence Ritter chronicled in *The Glory of Their Times*, 38–39, early-twentieth-century player Davy Jones gave up his high school sweetheart when forced to choose between her and baseball (though they met and married many years later, after both had been widowed). The father-in-law of Ed Williamson, one of the best players of the 1880s, explained that his daughter had married the ballplayer over their protests: "My wife thought that professional ball players were just not the class of people she would like to have her daughter thrown in with, and therefore she refused to allow Nettie to meet any of the men." *Boston Globe*, March 11, 1894.

280 "In the early days of baseball . . .": *Washington Post*, August 10, 1892, 10.

281 "a first-rate farmer . . .": Clift, *The Tim Bunker Papers*, 305–306.

281 "I believe in the division of labor . . .": Clift, *The Tim Bunker Papers*, 304.

282 His formation of "Boone and Crockett Clubs" to encourage "energy, resolution, manliness, self-reliance, and a capacity for self-help": Faragher, *Daniel Boone*, 325.

282 "It is a good thing . . .": Theodore Roosevelt, *The Strenuous Life*, 102.

282–283 "Roosevelt was sanguine in every sense of the word . . .": Edmund Morris, *Theodore Rex* (New York: Random House, 2001), 452.

283 "write another story in which the frontiersman . . .": Wertheim and Sorrentino, ed., *Correspondence of Stephen Crane*, 249, letter from Roosevelt to Crane, August 18, 1896.

AFTERWORD: THE MAN THE HALL OF FAME FORGOT

285–286 "The baseball cranks all sneer at me . . .": Unidentified clipping, written by Dale Lancaster, apparently from the *Aurora Beacon-News* in 1936.

286 "Placid, like a frog-pond . . .": Unspecified Boston paper, reprinted in the *National Police Gazette*, July 5, 1884.

287 "But I don't think . . .," "Imagine a batter . . .," "And imagine a catcher . . .," and "Both Mack and Jim White . . .": *Sporting News*, June 22, 1939.

288 "little chance . . . that White's name will be omitted . . .": "Boost Veteran Aurora Ball Player for Hall of Fame," *Aurora Beacon-News*, May 7, 1939, 26. The 1939 election was not the Hall of Fame's first class, as several elections had taken place before the Hall actually opened its doors.

Selected Bibliography

William P. Akin, "Bare Hands and Kid Gloves: The Best Fielders 1880–1899," *Baseball Research Journal* 10 (1981), 60–65.

Lee Allen, *The Hot Stove League: Raking the Embers of Baseball's Golden Age* (1955) (reprint, Kingston, N.Y.: Total Sports Illustrated, 2000).

David W. Anderson, *More Than Merkle* (Lincoln: University of Nebraska Press, 2000).

Marty Appel, *Slide, Kelly, Slide: The Wild Life and Times of Mike "King" Kelly, Baseball's First Superstar* (Lanham, Md.: Scarecrow, 1999).

W. W. Aulick, "One Hundred Notable Figures in Baseball: Mart King, Who Scorned All Precautionary Measures," *Auburn Citizen*, March 10, 1911.

"Backstops Are Deteriorating," *New York Telegram*, reprinted in *Duluth News Tribune*, November 14, 1909.

David Ball's biography of Kid Baldwin on the SABR BioProject (http://bioproj.sabr .org/).

Stan Baumgartner, "Signals," *Baseball Guide and Record Book 1947* (St. Louis: Sporting News, 1947).

Thomas Beer, *Stephen Crane: A Study in American Letters* (New York: Alfred A. Knopf, 1923).

"Behind the Bat with 'Nat' Hicks," *New York Times*, May 12, 1907, S4.

Phil Bergen, "Lovett of the Lowells," *National Pastime* 16 (1996), 63.

John Berryman, *Stephen Crane* (New York: William Sloane, 1950).

David Block, *Baseball Before We Knew It* (Lincoln: University of Nebraska Press, 2005).

"Boost Veteran Aurora Ball Player for Hall of Fame," *Aurora Beacon-News*, May 7, 1939, 26.

"A Born Billiard Player's Career," *Philadelphia Inquirer*, December 9, 1894, 24 (based on a sketch in the *Baltimore Sun*).

Joseph Campbell, *The Hero with a Thousand Faces* (Princeton: Princeton University Press, 1949).

"Catcher Is Brain Center of Successful Ball Team," *Albany Evening Journal*, December 18, 1911, 6.

"Catchers Make or Break Pitchers," *Aberdeen American*, April 29, 1911, 11.

"Catchers Now Pampered in Comparing of Old-Timers," *Auburn Citizen*, June 3, 1918, 2.

"Catcher's Part in Baseball: First Class Backstops Needed to Win Pennants," *New York Sun*, May 26, 1907, 33.

O. P. Caylor, "The Coming Catcher," *Cincinnati Enquirer*, reprinted in *Milwaukee Daily Sentinel*, August 19, 1878.

Henry Chadwick, *The American Game of Base Ball* (aka *The Game of Base Ball. How to Learn It, How to Play It, and How to Teach It. With Sketches of Noted Players*) (1868) (reprint: Columbia, S.C.: Camden House, 1983).

Henry Chadwick, *Beadle's Dime Base-Ball Player* (1860) (reprint: Morgantown, Pa.: Sullivan Press, 1996).

Henry Chadwick, "The Catchers" (two-part series), *New York Clipper*, December 30, 1876, and January 6, 1877.

"Charley Street Most Promising," *Washington Times*, December 29, 1908, 8.

James Charlton, ed., *The Baseball Chronology: The Complete History of Significant Events in the Game of Baseball* (New York: Macmillan, 1991).

Tommy Clark, "Good Catchers Sorely Needed in Major Leagues," *Washington Herald*, October 2, 1910, 8.

Byron E. Clarke, "Catchers of the '70s Were Stars in the Game," *Atlanta Constitution*, December 1, 1907, C2.

Ty Cobb, *Bustin' 'Em and Other Big League Stories* (1914) (reprint: William R. Cobb, ed., Marietta, Ga.: n.p., 2003).

Mickey Cochrane, *Baseball: The Fans' Game* (1939) (reprint: Cleveland: Society for American Baseball Research, 1992).

Sam Crane, "Buck Ewing," (Fifty Greatest series) *New York Journal*, January 20, 1912.

J. Hector St. John de Crevecoeur, *Letters from an American Farmer* (1782) (reprint, New York: E. P. Dutton, 1957).

William Curran, *Mitts: A Celebration of the Art of Fielding* (New York: William Morrow, 1985).

Michael Daisy, "When Commissioner Guiney Was Also DAC Baseball Great," *DAC News*, October 2007, 70-74.

Arthur Daley, "Catching Revolutionary," *New York Times*, June 24, 1946, 26.

Arthur Daley, "Knocking at the Door of the Hall of Fame," *New York Times*, August 31, 1943, 20.

David Dary, *Cowboy Culture: A Saga of Five Centuries* (Lawrence: University of Kansas Press, 1989).

"Developing Material for the Big Leagues, by Catcher Jack Warner," *New York Evening World*, February 15, 1904, 10.

Christopher Devine, *Harry Wright: The Father of Professional Base Ball* (Jefferson, N.C.: McFarland and Co., 2003).

Paul Dickson, *The Hidden Language of Baseball: How Signs and Sign-Stealing Have Influenced the Course of Our National Pastime* (New York: Walker and Co., 2003).

Paul Dickson, ed., *The New Dickson Baseball Dictionary* (New York: Harcourt Brace & Co., 1999).

"Don Juan of Shaven Head," *Los Angeles Times*, January 18, 1913, H1-H2.

"Dooin Tells of Catcher's Work," *Winchester* (Kentucky) *News*, October 17, 1908, 2.

John Doyle, "Catch the Curves," *Duluth News Tribune*, May 13, 1894, 5.

Paul Eaton, "When Ban Johnson Went to College," *Sporting News*, October 27, 1927.

Ralph Waldo Emerson, "Heroism," in *The Collected Works of Ralph Waldo Emerson*, vol. II, *Essays: First Series* (Cambridge: Harvard University Press, 1979), 143-156.

"Essays on Baseball: The Catcher," *Washington Herald*, May 23, 1909, 13.

Billy Evans, syndicated column, "Catcher Can Make or Break a Club; Brainy Backstop Is Invaluable to Team and Can Bring Results by Properly Directing Pitcher," *Philadelphia Inquirer*, January 21, 1917, 20.

John J. Evers and Hugh S. Fullerton, *Touching Second: The Science of Baseball* (1910) (reprint: Mattituck, N.Y.: Amereon House, n.d.).

David Falkner, *Nine Sides of the Diamond: Baseball's Great Glove Men on the Fine Art of Defense* (New York: Random House, 1990).

John Mack Faragher, *Daniel Boone: The Life and Legend of an American Pioneer* (New York: Holt, 1992).

Dick Farrington, "Bresnahan, Former Catching Star, Fighting Back at 60 from Crash of '29, That Turned His Wealth into Want," *Sporting News*, November 14, 1940, 3.

Dick Farrington, "O'Connor Looks Back at Lajoie's 'Eight Hits' After 22 Years as Exile from Organized Ball," *Sporting News*, February 23, 1933.

"First Pitcher to Curve Ball: Cummings Tells How He Made Discovery Which Revolutionized the Game" (syndicated), *Duluth News Tribune*, September 14, 1913, 3.

David L. Fleitz, *Cap Anson: The Grand Old Man of Baseball* (Jefferson, N.C.: McFarland and Co., 2005).

Russell Ford (as told to Don E. Basenfelder), "Russell Ford Tells Inside Story of the 'Emery' Ball After Guarding His Secret for Quarter of a Century," *Sporting News*, April 25, 1935, 5.

Mansfield J. French, "Stephen Crane, Ball Player," *Syracuse University Alumni News* 15 (January 1934), 3-4.

Hamlin Garland, "Stephen Crane as I Knew Him," *Yale Review* 3 (Spring 1914), 494-506.

Warren Goldstein, *Playing for Keeps: A History of Early Baseball* (Ithaca, N.Y.: Cornell University Press, 1989).

"Good Catchers a Necessity," *Chicago Tribune*, reprinted in *Duluth News Tribune*, December 13, 1904.

"Good Catchers Are Few and Far Between; Managers Have Pitchers to Spare, But Backstops Who Are onto All the Tricks of the Game Are Not to Be Had for Any Price," *Bellingham Herald*, April 18, 1908, 15.

Martin Green, *The Adventurous Male: Chapters in the History of the White Male Mind* (University Park: Penn State University Press, 1993).

Dan Gutman, *Banana Bats and Ding-Dong Balls: A Century of Unique Baseball Inventions* (New York: Macmillan, 1995).

Dan Gutman, *It Ain't Cheatin' If You Don't Get Caught: Scuffing, Corking, Spitting, Gunking, Razzing, and Other Fundamentals of Our National Pastime* (New York: Penguin Books, 1990).

John R. Husman, "Toledo's Own 'Duke of Tralee,'" *Toledo Magazine*, August 30-September 5, 1987, 4-7.

"Intended for Joke Was Original Mitt," *Fort Wayne Sentinel*, March 2, 1910, 8.

Frederick Ivor-Campbell, Robert L. Tiemann, and Mark Rucker, eds., *Baseball's First Stars* (Cleveland: Society for American Baseball Research, 1996).

Bill James, *The New Bill James Historical Baseball Abstract* (New York: Free Press, 2001).

Bill James and Rob Neyer, *The Neyer/James Guide to Pitchers* (New York: Fireside, 2004).

Hugh Jennings, *Rounding Third* (1925) unpublished manuscript.

Ban Johnson, as told to George Creel, "Slide, Kelly, Slide," *Saturday Evening Post*, April 12, 1930.

David Jones, ed., *Deadball Stars of the American League* (Washington, D.C.: Brassey's, 2006).

John F. Kasson, *Houdini, Tarzan and the Perfect Man: The White Male Body and the Challenge of Modernity in America* (New York: Hill and Wang, 2001).

Jack Kavanagh, *The Heights of Ridiculousness: The Feats of Baseball's Merrymakers* (South Bend: Diamond Communications, 1998).

Jack Kavanagh and Norman Macht, *Uncle Robbie* (Cleveland: Society for American Baseball Research, 1999).

Sid C. Keener, "From a 'Mite' into a Star," syndicated column, *Kansas City Star*, July 13, 1919.

Maclean Kennedy, "Charley Bennett, Former Detroit Catcher, Inventor of Chest Pad," *Detroit Free Press*, August 2, 1914.

Maclean Kennedy, "Greatest Backstop of Them All Was the Detroit Boy, Charley Bennett," *Detroit Free Press*, March 30, 1913, 20.

Kevin Kerrane, *Dollar Sign on the Muscle: The World of Baseball Scouting* (1984) (reprint, Lincoln: University of Nebraska Press, 1999).

Gene Kessler, "Deacon White, Oldest Living Player, at 92 Recalls Highlights of Historic Career That Started in 1868," *Sporting News*, June 22, 1939, 19.

"King Catchers," *St. Louis Post-Dispatch*, August 14, 1886, 12.

George B. Kirsch, *The Creation of American Team Sports: Baseball and Cricket, 1838-72* (Urbana: University of Illinois Press, 1991).

Malachi Kittridge, "The 'Heady' Catchers Win the Ball Games," *New Enterprise* (Madison, Florida), May 30, 1907, 6.

R. M. Larner, "A Careless Patentee," *Sporting Life*, April 26, 1890.

R. M. Larner, "Decker's Glove," *Sporting Life*, May 3, 1890.

T. J. Jackson Lears, *No Place of Grace: Antimodernism and the Transformation of American Culture, 1880-1920* (New York: Pantheon, 1981).

Hal Lebovitz, "Zimmer, Oldest Catcher, Leafs Memory Book," *Sporting News*, January 12, 1949, 12.

Peter Levine, *A. G. Spalding and the Rise of Baseball: The Promise of American Sport* (New York: Oxford University Press, 1985).

"Bob Lively," "Base Ball: How They Play the Game in New England," *Porter's Spirit of the Times*, December 27, 1856, 276-277.

Frank G. Loman, "The Man Behind the Athletics' Revival," *Sportlife*, September 1925, 23, 83-84.

James D'Wolf Lovett, *Old Boston Boys and the Games They Played* (Boston: Little, Brown & Co., 1908).

Lee Lowenfish, *Branch Rickey: Baseball's Ferocious Gentleman* (Lincoln: University of Nebraska Press, 2007).

Norman Macht, *Connie Mack and the Early Years of Baseball* (Lincoln: University of Nebraska Press, 2007).

Connie Mack, "How to Play Ball," multipart series, *Washington Post*, March 13, March 20, March 27, April 3, April 10, April 17, 1904.

Connie Mack, "Memories of When the Game Was Young," *Sporting Life* (monthly), June 1924.

Connie Mack, *My Sixty-Six Years in the Big Leagues* (Philadelphia: John C. Winston, 1950).

Christy Mathewson, *Pitching in a Pinch* (1912) (reprint: Mattituck, N.Y.: Amereon House, n.d.).

Tim McCarver with Danny Peary, *Tim McCarver's Baseball for Brain Surgeons and Other Fans* (New York: Villard, 1998).

John J. McGraw, *My Thirty Years in Baseball* (1923) (reprint: Lincoln: University of Nebraska Press, 1995).

"Modern Ball Hard for Defense," *Bellingham Sunday Herald*, February 27, 1910, 8.

Peter Morris, *Baseball Fever: Early Baseball in Michigan* (Ann Arbor: University of Michigan Press, 2003).

Peter Morris, *A Game of Inches: The Stories Behind the Innovations That Shaped Baseball*, vol. 1, *The Game on the Field* (Chicago: Ivan R. Dee, 2006).

Peter Morris, *A Game of Inches: The Stories Behind the Innovations That Shaped Baseball*, vol. 2, *The Game Behind the Scenes* (Chicago: Ivan R. Dee, 2006).

Peter Morris, *Level Playing Fields: How the Groundskeeping Murphy Brothers Shaped Baseball* (Lincoln: University of Nebraska Press, 2007).

Peter Morris, "Walter Walker: One of Baseball's Odd Lives," *National Pastime* 15 (1995), 97-99.

Ren Mulford, Jr., "Umpire Jennings: His Name Is Alfred Gordon, but He's Known as Alamazoo," *Idaho Daily Statesman*, January 6, 1892, 5.

Eugene C. Murdock, *Ban Johnson: Czar of Baseball* (Westport, Conn.: Greenwood Press, 1982).

Eugene Murdock, "Looking Back at 96," *Baseball Research Journal* 1976, 55-61.

Tim Murnane, "How the Stars Play Combinations," *Boston Globe*, March 10, 1889, 22.

Tim Murnane, "Lew Brown's Last Sleep," *Boston Globe*, January 19, 1889, 1.

Tim Murnane, "Work Behind the Bat," *Boston Globe*, October 25, 1891, 23.

Cait Murphy, *Crazy '08: How a Cast of Cranks, Rogues, Boneheads, and Magnates Created the Greatest Year in Baseball History* (New York: Smithsonian Books, 2007).

"Jim Nasium" [Edgar Wolfe], "Letters from an Old Sport to His Son at College," *Philadelphia Inquirer*, June 23, 1907, 4.

David Nemec, *The Great Encyclopedia of 19th Century Major League Baseball* (New York: Donald I. Fine, 1997).

Frank Newhouse, "Dangers of the Hero Behind the Bat," *San Francisco Call*, June 5, 1904, 14.

"New Method of Signaling Is Disagreeable for the Catcher," *Duluth News Tribune*, July 20, 1909, 7.

Steve O'Neill, "How to Play Baseball," *Charlotte Sunday Observer*, June 4, 1922, sec. 3, p. 1.

Gerard S. Petrone, *When Baseball Was Young* (San Diego: Musty Attic Archives, 1994).

David A. Pfeiffer and John Vernon, "Beyond the Box Score: Baseball Records in the National Archives," *Prologue: Quarterly of the National Archives and Records Administration*, Spring 2006, vol. 38, no. 1 (online version: http://www.archives.gov/publications/prologue/2006/spring/baseball.html?template=print).

"Pitchers Are Superstitious Lot: Many Star Slabmen Harbor Weird Imaginations About Certain Catchers," *Philadelphia Inquirer*, November 20, 1910, 4.

Murray Polner, *Branch Rickey* (New York: Signet, 1982).

Francis C. Richter, *Richter's History and Records of Base Ball* (1914) (reprint: Jefferson, N.C.: McFarland and Co., 2005).

Lawrence S. Ritter, *The Glory of Their Times* (1966) (reprint: New York: William Morrow, 1984).

Philip Ashton Rollins, *The Cowboy: An Unconventional History of Civilization on the Old-Time Cattle Range* (New York: Charles Scribner's Sons, 1922).

Theodore Roosevelt, *Ranch Life and the Hunting-Trail* (New York: Century Co., 1888).

Theodore Roosevelt, *The Strenuous Life* (New York: Century Co., 1900).

Howard W. Rosenberg, *Cap Anson 1: When Captaining a Team Meant Something: Leadership in Baseball's Early Years* (Arlington, Va.: Tile Books, 2003).

Howard W. Rosenberg, *Cap Anson 2: The Theatrical and Kingly Mike Kelly: U.S. Team Sport's First Media Sensation and Baseball's Original Casey at the Bat* (Arlington, Va.: Tile Books, 2004).

Howard W. Rosenberg, *Cap Anson 3: Muggsy John McGraw and the Tricksters: Baseball's Fun Age of Rule Bending* (Arlington, Va.: Tile Books, 2005).

Howard W. Rosenberg, *Cap Anson 4: Bigger Than Babe Ruth: Captain Anson of Chicago* (Arlington, Va.: Tile Books, 2006).

William J. Ryczek, *Blackguards and Red Stockings: A History of Baseball's National Association, 1871-1875* (Jefferson, N.C.: McFarland and Co., 1992).

William J. Ryczek, *When Johnny Came Sliding Home: The Post-Civil War Baseball Boom, 1865-1870* (Jefferson, N.C.: McFarland and Co., 1998).

I. E. Sanborn, "What's Put Our Cubs on Top? Bill Killefer! That's Answer," *Chicago Tribune*, July 7, 1918, A3.

Alan Schwarz, "Expert Ties Ex-Player's Suicide to Brain Damage," *New York Times*, January 18, 2007.

Alan Schwarz, "Lineman, Dead at 36, Exposes Brain Injuries," *New York Times*, June 15, 2007.

Alan Schwarz, "Study of Ex-N.F.L. Players Ties Concussion to Depression Risk," *New York Times*, May 31, 2007.

Alan Schwarz, "Wives United by Husbands' Post-N.F.L. Trauma," *New York Times*, March 14, 2007.

Charley Scully, "'Father of the Catching Glove' Admits Split Finger Fifty Years Ago, with Twin Bill Ahead, Was 'Mother,'" *Sporting News*, February 23, 1939.

Harold Seymour, *Baseball: The Early Years* (New York: Oxford University Press, 1960).

Tom Simon, ed., *Deadball Stars of the National League* (Washington, D.C.: Brassey's, 2004).

Richard Slotkin, *The Fatal Environment: The Myth of the Frontier in the Age of Industrialization, 1800-1890* (New York: Atheneum, 1985).

Richard Slotkin, *Gunfighter Nation: The Myth of the Frontier in Twentieth-Century America* (New York: Atheneum, 1992).

Richard Slotkin, *Regeneration Through Violence: The Mythology of the American Frontier, 1600-1860* (Middletown, Conn.: Wesleyan University Press, 1973).

Frank L. Smith, twenty-part history of baseball in Janesville, *Janesville Daily Gazette*, February 8-May 4, 1905.

Guy M. Smith (of Danville, Ill.), "He Could Catch Anything," Typescript in Jim McGuire file, National Baseball Hall of Fame and Museum.

Henry Nash Smith, *Virgin Land* (Cambridge: Harvard University Press, 1950).

Paul Sorrentino, ed., *Stephen Crane Remembered* (Tuscaloosa: University of Alabama Press, 2006).

Albert Goodwill Spalding, *America's National Game: Historic Facts Concerning the Beginning, Evolution, Development, and Popularity of Base Ball, with Personal Reminiscences of Its Vicissitudes, Its Victories, and Its Votaries* (1910) (reprint, Lincoln: University of Nebraska Press, 1992).

A. G. Spalding (as told to Tim Murnane), "Mike Kelley [sic] Refused $10,000 When He Was Broke," *Boston Globe*, December 24, 1905, SM4.

Alfred H. Spink, *The National Game* (1911) (reprint, Carbondale: Southern Illinois University Press, 2000).

R. W. Stallman, *Stephen Crane: A Biography* (New York: George Braziller, 1968).

Randy Starkman, "Hockey Concussions Take a Toll" and "Players Put Team Above Health" (two-part series), *Toronto Star*, December 23 and 24, 2007.

James L. Steele, "How the National Game Developed: Some Baseball Reminiscences," *Outing*, June 1904, 333-336.

"Stories of Early Base Ball Days Told by Charlie Bennett, King of the Olden Catchers," *Detroit News Tribune*, March 11, 1906.

Glenn Stout, "Blood Sport," *Inside Worcester*, Autumn 1993, 23-26.

"Striped Past of Alexander," *Los Angeles Times*, October 17, 1907, H9.

Dean Sullivan, ed., *Early Innings: A Documentary History of Baseball, 1825-1908* (Lincoln: University of Nebraska Press, 1995).

Cindy Thomson and Scott Brown, *Three Finger: The Mordecai Brown Story* (Lincoln: University of Nebraska Press, 2006).

Robert L. Tiemann and Mark Rucker, eds., *Nineteenth Century Stars* (Kansas City: Society for American Baseball Research, 1989).

"Training the Catcher," originally published in *St. Nicholas*, reprinted in *Brooklyn Eagle*, August 4, 1890.

John "Dasher" Troy, "Reminiscences of an Oldtimer," *Baseball Magazine*, April 1915, 78-80.

Rob Trucks, *The Catcher: Baseball Behind the Seams* (Cincinnati: Emmis Books, 2005).

"Try 'Don Juan,' Forgery Charge," *Los Angeles Times*, June 10, 1913, H7.

David Quentin Voigt, *American Baseball: From the Gentleman's Sport to the Commissioner's System* (1966) (reprint: University Park: Pennsylvania State University Press, 1983).

David Quentin Voigt, *The League That Failed* (Lanham, Md.: Scarecrow, 1998).

John Montgomery Ward, *Base-Ball: How to Become a Player* (1888) (reprint: Cleveland: Society for American Baseball Research, 1993).

Dixon Wecter, *The Hero in America: A Chronicle of Hero-Worship* (1941) (reprint, Ann Arbor: University of Michigan Press, 1963).

Stanley Wertheim, *A Stephen Crane Encyclopedia* (Westport, Conn.: Greenwood Press, 1997).

Stanley Wertheim and Paul Sorrentino, eds., *The Correspondence of Stephen Crane* (New York: Columbia University Press, 1988).

Stanley Wertheim and Paul Sorrentino, *The Crane Log: A Documentary Life of Stephen Crane, 1871-1900* (New York: G. K. Hall and Co., 1994).

"When Ball Players Wore Neither Gloves Nor Mask," *Miami Herald*, June 3, 1912, 5.

Edmund Wilson, *Patriotic Gore: Studies in the Literature of the Civil War* (New York: Oxford University Press, 1966).

Gordon S. Wood, *The Americanization of Benjamin Franklin* (New York: Penguin, 2004).

James Leon Wood, Sr. (as told to Frank G. Menke), "Baseball in By-Gone Days," syndicated series, *Indiana* (Pennsylvania) *Evening Gazette*, August 14, 1916; *Marion* (Ohio) *Star*, August 15, 1916; *Indiana* (Pennsylvania) *Evening Gazette*, August 17, 1916.

Tip Wright, "Rusie Was the Best," *Wilkes-Barre Times Leader*, March 7, 1910, 13.

David W. Zang, *Fleet Walker's Divided Heart: The Life of Baseball's First Black Major Leaguer* (Lincoln: University of Nebraska Press, 1995).

Larzer Ziff, *The American 1890s: Life and Times of a Lost Generation* (New York: Viking Press, 1968).

Player files at the National Baseball Hall of Fame and Museum for Doug Allison, Charley Bennett, Bill Bergen, Marty Bergen, Roger Bresnahan, Lew Brown, Doc Bushong, John Clapp, Bill Craver, Lou Criger, Harry Decker, "Buck" Ewing, Charley "Duke" Farrell, Nat Hicks, "Alamazoo" Jennings, Ban Johnson, Mike "King" Kelly, Jim "Deacon" McGuire, Ray Schalk, Billy Sullivan, Thomas Sullivan, Jim "Deacon" White, and "Chief" Zimmer.

Index

Baldwin, Charles "Lady," 81–82
Baldwin, Clarence "Kid," 186, 316, 328
Baldwin, Mark, 180
Balls and strikes, origins of, 37
Baltimore (Md.), 93, 103, 141, 146, 162,
    169, 183, 186, 218, 305, 307, 317, 328,
    356
Bancker, John, 186, 337
Bancroft, Frank, 134
Baraboo (Wis.), 98
Barbarossa, Frederick, 21
Barbed-wire fences, 126, 230
Barlow, Tommy, 71, 80, 167, 170,
    177–178, 180–181, 185, 334–335
Barnie, Billy, 52, 232, 358
Barr, Bob, 315, 339
Bartson, Charles, 341
"Baseball brains," 259–260, 262, 276
Baseballs, dimensions and liveliness of,
    28, 44–45, 60, 105, 117–119, 307, 350
Baseball Writers' Association of America,
    288
Batter's box as impediment to batters
    chasing sharply breaking pitches, 42,
    238, 306
Bay City (Mich.), 146
Beard, Daniel Carter, 283
Beckwith, Warren, 362
Beefsteak in gloves, 141
Beer, Thomas, 296
Behind men, 29, 37, 302–303. See also
    Pigtails
Bellan, Esteban, 318
Belyea, "Burpee," 130
Bench, Johnny, 278
Bender, Chief, 358
Bengough, Benny, 270
Bennett, Alice, 135
Bennett, Charley, 70–71, 73, 82, 101,
    111, 135, 144, 147, 191, 208–209, 211,
    221–222, 225–226, 245, 280, 289,
    327–329, 342–343
Bennett, J. E., 223
Benoit, Chris, 183
Berg, Moe, 278

Bergen, Bill, 264, 269, 359
Bergen, Marty, 187–188, 269, 288, 338
Bergh, John, 109
Bernstein, Kid, 329
Berra, Yogi, 94, 184, 278
Berthrong, Harry, 70
Bestick, 103
Beukeboom, Jeff, 335
Biggers, Willis, 78, 313
Binghamton (N.Y.), 71, 312, 332
"Bird cage" as term for mask, 123, 232
Black, Robert, 316
"Blackguarding," 299
Blacklist, 191–192, 194
Black Sox scandal, 275
Bliss, Frank, 62, 95–96, 318
Blocking the plate, 47, 217–218, 235, 251,
    253–256, 352
Blogg, Wesley, 174
Bloomer girls, 357
Bloomington (Ill.), 81, 112
Boerum, Folkert Rappelje, 40, 304
Bond, Tommy, 108–109, 111, 119, 128,
    160, 315
Bonin, Greg, 336
Boone, Bob, 279
Boone, Daniel, 16–22, 24, 81, 93, 95, 123,
    139, 181, 210, 261–262, 268, 282–283,
    299–301
Boston, 30, 32, 66, 84, 87–88, 94, 96,
    103, 108–109, 111, 118–119, 123–124,
    129–130, 132–133, 153, 159–160, 187,
    225, 246, 275, 279, 305–306, 311,
    314–315, 317–318, 322, 326, 332–333,
    344, 351, 357, 359–360, 362
Bowerman, Frank, 231, 246–247, 293,
    322, 358
Boxer's dementia. See Chronic traumatic
    encephalopathy (CTE) and
    Concussions
Boyle, Jack, 94, 143, 225, 292
Boy Scouts of America, 283
Bradley, Charles, 186–188, 338
Bradley, George, 66–68, 86, 106, 109,
    111, 116

Hindcatchers, 113. See also Behind men; Pigtails
Hines, Mike, 129
Hispanics as catchers, 97, 318, 357
Hit-and-run play, 162–163, 169, 258, 260, 354
Hoboken (N.J.), 175, 265, 305
Hockey-style mask, 278
Hofford, Joseph "Chick," 312
Hoge, Merril, 185
Holbert, Billy, 91–93, 96, 99–102, 104, 111, 266, 269, 311, 314, 317, 321, 337
Homer, 236
Hoover, Charley, 179–180, 185, 207, 335
Horner, Jack, 340
Hotaling, Pete, 123–124, 325
Hot Springs (Ark.), 263
Howard, Joe, 40, 305
Howley, Dan, 263
Hubbard, Al, 103–104, 146
Hubbell, Gersh, 310
Huggins, Miller, 275
Hulbert, William, 123
Humphries, John, 52, 315
Hunter, figure of, 16–18, 299–300
Hunter, Billy, 174, 334
Hurst, Tim, 215
Hutchison, Bill, 95–96, 164–165

Indianapolis, 85, 115, 190, 307
Injuries. See Chronic traumatic encephalopathy (CTE); Concussions; Hand injuries suffered by catchers
International Association, 118–119, 153, 308, 325
International League, 154, 194
Iodine and witch hazel, use on catchers' hands, 5
Irish as catchers, 41, 97, 175, 226, 268
Irwin, Arthur, 155
Irwin, Charles, 227–228, 288
Irwin, Vincent. See Nava, Sandy
Irwin, Will, 76–77
Ithaca (N.Y.), 71, 87, 312
Ives, Frank, 212–213

Jackson (Mich.), 345
Jacksonville (Ill.), 112, 180, 339
Janesville (Wis.), 60–63, 94, 112
Jennings, Alfred "Alamazoo," 101–102, 104, 111, 179, 227, 245, 315, 318, 349
Jennings, Hughey, 212
Jersey City (N.J.), 312
Jewell, Herbert, 40, 305
Jockstraps, 348
Johnson, 98, 174
Johnson, Byron Bancroft "Ban," 11–14, 25, 37, 46, 58, 70, 86, 122, 185, 190, 209
Johnson, Lyman, 30
Joliet (Ill.), 201
Jones, 103
Jones, Davy, 362
Jordan, "Gid," 52
Joyce, Colonel John P., 90, 323

Kaminski, Kevin, 335
Kansas City (Mo.), 95, 145, 190, 193
Keefe, Tim, 82, 147, 155
Keefe & Becannon, 155
Keenan, Jim, 85, 226
Keene (N.H.), 112
Kelly, Billy, 348
Kelly, Mike "King," 171, 179–180, 208–212, 211, 225, 274, 288, 291, 328, 343–344, 359–360
Kemmler, Rudolph, 80, 138, 314, 327
Kennedy, "Doc," 76, 164
Kennedy, Ted, 145
Keokuk (Iowa), 192, 202, 339
Kerins, John, 358
Kerr, Dickie, 288
Killefer, Billy, 246, 253, 266, 268, 270, 357
King, "Mart," 56–57, 59, 152
King Philip's War, 298
Kinsman (Ohio), 71
Kittridge, Malachi, 225–226, 238–240, 260, 269–270, 274–275, 293, 346, 351
Kleinow, Red, 240, 349
Kling, Johnny, 230, 256–257, 293

"Watching the bat instead of the ball,"
61, 73–74, 312
Waters, Andre, 182, 184, 335
Waters, Frank, 323
Watkins, William H., 358
Weak-hitting catchers, 44, 80, 92, 98,
177, 269–270, 314, 317
Weaver, Sam, 102–103, 111
Webster, Mike, 182, 185, 335
Wecter, Dixon, 21
Weight of catchers. See Size, ideal for a
catcher
Weiker, Leonard, 347
Welch, Mickey, 147, 344
Welch, Tub, 162–163, 172, 217
Weldon, Harry, 352
"West, Al," 103
Western League, 12
West Virginia University, 322
Weyhing, Gus, 151, 332
Wheaton, William R., 31
White, "Doc," 246
White, Elmer, 88, 316
White, Jim "Deacon," 50, 66, 67,
70–74, 76–77, 83–84, 88–89, 96,
108–111, 119, 136, 141, 153, 159, 207,
212, 214, 285–289, 311, 313, 315–317,
327, 332, 345
White, Will, 88, 111, 316–317
Whiting, Ed, 186, 337
Whitney, Jim, 129–130, 132–133, 214, 269,
345
Wild pitches. See Passed balls and wild
pitches, importance of preventing
Wilkes-Barre (Pa.), 56, 59
Williamson, Ed, 120, 343, 362
Williamson, Nettie, 362

Wilmington (Del.), 317
"Wind-pad," used to describe chest
protector, 139, 216, 232–234, 247
Wingo, Ivy, 274, 294
Winkelman, George, 212, 344
Winslow, William, 104
Witch hazel. See Iodine and witch hazel,
use on catchers' hands
Wolfe, Edgar. See "Nasium, Jim"
Wolters, Rynie, 83
Wood, George, 317
Woodbridge (Calif.), 323
Woodstock (Ontario), 133
Woodstown (N.J.), 320
Woodward, Rufus, 356
Woodward, Stanley, 356
Worcester (Mass.), 71
World Series, 272, 275–276
Wright, 104, 320
Wright, Al, 352
Wright, George, 74, 106, 124, 153, 317,
323
Wright, Harry, 44–45, 87–88, 91, 111,
113, 117, 119, 124, 130, 146–147, 286,
307–308, 316, 320, 323, 333
Wright, Hiram, 319

Yale University, 95, 103, 146, 215, 306, 345
Yates, Samuel, 301
York (Pa.), 355
Young, Cy, 273
Young, Nick, 92–93, 95, 317
Yuma (Ariz.), 342

Zettlein, George, 82, 110
Zimmer, "Chief," 141, 219–220, 226, 245,
293, 351, 361

A NOTE ON THE AUTHOR

Peter Morris has established himself as one of the foremost historians of early baseball in America. His *A Game of Inches: The Stories Behind the Innovations That Shaped Baseball* (2006) was the first book ever to win both the coveted Seymour Medal of the Society for American Baseball Research and the Casey Award from *Spitball* magazine as the best baseball book of the year. Mr. Morris has also written *But Didn't We Have Fun?*, an informal history of baseball's pioneer era; *Level Playing Fields*, about the early days of groundskeeping; and *Baseball Fever*, the story of early baseball in Michigan. A former national and international Scrabble champion, he lives in Haslett, Michigan. For more information, see his website, www.petermorrisbooks.com.